D1503637

Paternalism in Early Victorian England

David Roberts

Rutgers University Press
New Brunswick, New Jersey

Publication of this book was aided by the Research Committee
of Dartmouth College.

Library of Congress Cataloging in Publication Data

Roberts, David, 1923–
    Paternalism in early Victorian England.

    Bibliography: p.
    Includes index.
    1. Paternalism—England—History. I. Title.
HN385.R57   301.44′92′0942   79–14669
ISBN 0–8135–0868–1

To Helene

Contents

Acknowledgments

Many people have helped me in the writing of *Paternalism in Early Victorian England*. My brother, Clayton Roberts, of Ohio State University read an early draft of the manuscript, as did Perry Curtis of Brown University and Trygve Tholfsen of Columbia University. Their shrewd criticisms and helpful comments proved of great value in the writing of the final draft. David Spring of Johns Hopkins University and Anthony Brundage of California State Polytechnic University at Pomona read the chapters on the "Patriarchy of Sussex" and "Land and Its Duties" and offered useful suggestions. James Winter of the University of British Columbia read the manuscript with great attentiveness as did Shirley Kifer and Frank Fetter of Hanover, New Hampshire.

R. A. Lewis of the University of Wales at Bangor gave the manuscript a most thorough and conscientious reading. His generosity in time and industry was matched by his remarkable erudition about the smallest byways and most remote corners of Victorian England. E. P. Thompson was also kind enough to read the introduction and make helpful suggestions.

To all the above scholars I extend my warmest thanks.

Grateful acknowledgments should also go to the John Simon Guggenheim Foundation, the Social Science Research Council, and Dartmouth College for their generous fellowships and grants.

I would also like to thank the *Victorian Periodicals Review* for permission to use materials published in their journal.

And finally I would like to give special thanks to my wife, Helene, for the work she did on the manuscript and for the initial suggestion that the subject of paternalism was worth a book.

Introduction

In early Victorian England, no social outlook had deeper roots and wider appeal than that which twentieth-century historians call paternalism. It was an outlook held by landowners, captains of industry, clergymen, members of Parliament, justices of the peace, civil servants, newspaper editors, novelists, poets, and university dons. It was even held, as habits of deference, by agricultural laborers, operatives, and the worthy poor. It informed social attitudes at all levels of society and expressed itself in countless ways. It was an outlook as diffuse and varied as it was widespread and popular.

It had, at the time, no specific name. The early Victorians, to be sure, spoke of "patriarchal principles" or "a paternal government" but never of "paternalism." Their failure to do so is not significant. Medieval Englishmen never spoke of a "Medieval English Constitution," but numerous historians have attested to its reality. Early Victorian paternalism, like the Medieval English Constitution, did exist, though nameless in its day.

But it did not exist as a set of definite, logical, and clearly defined axioms. It could boast no laws or theories, as could political economy, nor did it even have the coherence of Jeremy Bentham's theory of utility or John Locke's theory of the social contract. It formed instead a set of varying attitudes and beliefs—attitudes and beliefs that could form different combinations in the minds of different people, often in a not too coherent form.

The social attitudes of men of affairs are seldom models of logical analysis. They are instead mixtures of many rational and nonrational elements: of self-interest and generosity, of a selfish attachment to institutions and a larger concern for the public welfare, of learning and ignorance, sensitivity and callousness. The results are social attitudes that are influential in the management of society but that are, because diffuse and protean, difficult to define. It is the main purpose of this study to describe those varying attitudes that formed the early Victorian's paternalist outlook and to analyze that outlook as it permeated different levels of society. Part one will deal with the intellectuals and their revival and amplification of old paternalist ideas, part two will describe these ideas at work in the day-to-day life of village and town, and part three will analyze their impact on politics and legislation.

Since, in this long tour, paternalists of every kind and persuasion will appear, it is necessary at the outset to define the main tenets of paternalism, to construct, as it were, a model of paternalism.

A Model of Paternalism

In any definition of the paternalist social outlook three aspects must be considered: paternalism's basic assumption about the framework of society; its doctrines concerning the duties of the wealthy, privileged, and powerful; and the many and various attitudes which, while not essential to the paternalist outlook, are often associated with it.

Almost all Victorian paternalists held four basic assumptions about society: it should be authoritarian, hierarchic, organic, and pluralistic.

That it should be authoritarian followed naturally from the very word paternal, which means fatherhood, and which is nearly synonymous with sovereignty. Fathers command and exact obedience. So do kings, judges, lords lieutenant, magistrates, bishops, archdeacons, squires, parsons, constables, and workhouse governors; their authority is of a paternal nature. That paternal authority, however, was not absolute in all spheres. The early Victorians were proud of their English liberties, of juries, open vestries, *habeas corpus,* toleration acts, and Parliaments. English paternalism, involving an authoritarianism that was tempered by common law and ancient liberties, was different from Austrian or Russian paternalism, and any definition of it must therefore be cut from a different cloth. But, that fact acknowledged, it could still be, in certain areas, severely, even cruelly, authoritarian. The typical paternalist believed in capital punishment, whipping, severe game laws, summary justice for delinquents, strict laws defining the duties of servants, and the imprisonment of seditious writers. He never doubted the sacred nature of paternal authority, whether exercised by magistrates at quarter sessions, by landlords on their estates, or by archdeacons presiding over ecclesiastical courts.

The paternalist also never doubted that God had created a hierarchical society and that such a hierarchical society was necessary and beneficial. The paternalist decried all leveling measures. Without inequality of property there would be no incentive for the poor to work nor the wherewithal for the wealthy to rule, develop the arts of government, and do charitable work. How could a landowner build cottages for the poor unless he was wealthy, how could a bishop guide his clergy and they their flocks unless they were superior in rank, degree, and wealth, and how could the governing classes attend Parliament and guide the nation's destiny unless they had wealth and privileges? Just as children are dependent on those above them in the hierarchy of the family, so are agricultural laborers, servants, tenant farmers, and curates dependent on those of higher rank. At the heart of a paternalist's hierarchical outlook is a strong sense of the value of dependency, a sense that could not exist without those who are dependent having an unquestioned respect for their betters.

Less obvious and less clear is the paternalist's third assumption, the assumption that society is organic. Yet it was an assumption that was tacitly accepted by most of them. Though they seldom used the term "organic," they did speak frequently of "the bonds of union" and of "old social bonds," and their dismay was quite universal in the 1840s that these old bonds were dissolving. Those who held a paternalist outlook believed in the body politic, one in which every part had an appointed and harmonious place. Whether a plowman or a bishop, each individual had his function, his place, his protectors, his duties, his reciprocal obligations, and his strong ties of dependency.

Though everyone had a function and an appointed place in an organic society, those functions and those places were by no means uniform or standard. That society was pluralistic was a belief that formed the fourth basic assumption of paternalism. Society consisted of many differing spheres, each with its own hierarchies, though each was part of a larger one. This pluralism distinguished English from Continental paternalism. On the Continent kings were the fathers and the governors of their subjects; in England the fatherly authority was more often the squire. On the Continent the intendants or the councilors were the eyes, hands, and feet of the body politic, the king its head. In Tudor times the same metaphor was applied to Henry VIII and his servants. But it was seldom applied to the Hanoverian kings or to Queen Victoria. After 1688 government in England become strongly local, a matter of municipal courts, quarter sessions, petty sessions, cathedral chapters, select vestries, ancient courts leet, and new improvement commissioners. It was also a matter of property. The next circle of authority for men of the governing class, beyond their immediate families and servants, was that which included their employees and tenants. It was a sphere that allowed government to be personal. To know and to be known by those one governed was central to English paternalism. Only personal intercourse with one's dependents led to the right management of the worthy and unworthy poor or of the idle poacher and the provident laborer. Nothing, of course, guaranteed such personal relations as did the rule of property. Property was the single most important source of authority over others, and it was the basis of political power. Since property was widely held, paternalism was widely exercised in many different spheres and forms. Society was thus not only authoritarian, hierarchic, and organic, but pluralistic. A belief in such a society was, then, the first ingredient of a paternalist outlook. The second ingredient was that in such a society everyone, whether rich or poor, had his appropriate duties.

The phrase, "property has its duties as well as its rights," became in the 1840s the hallmark of the paternalist. No other phrase said so much about paternalism's main aims and principal methods. It is a phrase that emphasizes "duties" rather than "rights." There is no doubt that paternalists believed in their own rights whether as titled nobility, holders of office, or landlords, but they based those rights on the usefulness of their station and rank and on the duties that they performed. They did not believe in equal rights for all or in rights based on natural law. Thomas Paine and Jean Jacques Rousseau were anathema to them since rights based on natural law became rights for all and thus led to equality, democracy, and rank individualism, in short, to all that was the antithesis of an authoritarian, hierarchic, and organic society. A belief in social duty and function, not in individual and inalienable rights, defines a good paternalist.

There were three principal sets of duties (among many) that the conscientious paternalist of superior rank felt he must perform: ruling, guiding, and helping. The duty to rule was primary and instinctive, flowing directly from wealth and power. To those beneath him a paternal lord owed protection, protection both from themselves and from others, and to insure such he needed to impose on them the laws of the realm and his own sovereign commands. It was his duty to rule his estate and his parish firmly and resolutely, even if it meant fining tipplers, locking up petty thieves, jailing poachers, transporting arsonists, and terminating the leases of slovenly farmers. It was his duty to suppress crime, riot, and disorder, to put to work the idle, to reprimand servants, to tell bailiffs how to manage the farms, and to see that vagrants were expelled from the parish.

It was also his duty to prevent such disturbances by guiding the lives of those dependent on him. He must exert a firm moral superintendence over the poor. Such superintendence was, of course, preeminently the duty of the clergy. The village parson preached morality to the poor on Sundays and visited them during the week to urge them to mend their ways. There was no idea of educating them above their station: an ability to read the catechism was sufficient, for from it and from attendance at church one could learn obedience, humility, sobriety, and right conduct. For those unable to learn such lessons there were the poor house and the jail, useful instruments of discipline. Guidance more than mere benevolence underlay the paternalist's sense of duty. Paternal authorities know what is good for those dependent on them just as a father knows what is good for his children. The moment the children, or those dependent on a landowner, claim that they know what is best for themselves, the paternal relation gives way to a relation between equals. A good paternalist is one who is both convinced that he knows what is good for his dependents and has the power to insist that his ideas be carried out.

The third set of duties that was incumbent on a model paternalist was that of helping the poor in their afflictions and sufferings. Soup should be dispensed during periods of severe want, coal should be sold cheaply in frost-ridden January, cottages should be built and let at moderate rates, and the poor law should be administered sternly and justly. Many writers on paternalism have defined the term too narrowly, limiting it largely to the performance of benevolent duties. Social critics sensitive to the sufferings of the poor have denounced the hardness and ruthlessness of the landowner and justice of the peace, thus making it seem that being benevolent is the core of paternalism. But benevolence was not really the core, it was rather only a part of a wider set of duties. For the paternalist the obligation to rule firmly and to guide and superintend were far more essential.

The wealthy were not the only ones with duties. In a system of paternalism obligations are mutual. The poor too had duties, those of conscientious service, promptness, politeness, and deference. The doctrine that everyone in a well-ordered society has definite duties is as necessary to any definition of paternalism as the belief in an authoritarian, hierarchical, organic, and pluralistic society. These four assumptions, joined with the doctrine of duties, form the core of the paternalist social outlook.

Around this core there clustered many different attitudes, no one of which was a necessary element of the paternalist outlook, but all of which contributed to make paternalism a rich, complex, and varied set of attitudes. One of these attitudes was that men of property and rank had managed society much better in times past. In those golden ages the lower orders were more deferential, the wealthy more benevolent, society more harmonious, and the body politic more truly balanced. In earlier ages the titled classes, not parvenus, ruled. Paternalism is conservative and backward looking, and it produces in every age the politics of nostalgia. Such a nostalgia forms the first of those attitudes that coalesced around the main core of paternalism.

The golden age of the past was usually one of rural simplicity, an age before manufacturers, overgrown financiers, and gigantic traders. Land, not money, ruled. Landowners had deep roots in their localities and thus firm bonds with those dependent on them. Land therefore preeminently qualified its owners for the performance of paternal duties. Money was rootless, mobile, free of obligations, knowing no duties. A deep hostility to the new forms of wealth, whether commercial, financial, or manufacturing, colored the outlook of most paternalists. It did not, however, color the outlook of all of them and was not an essential part of the paternalist social outlook. But like the politics of nostalgia, a hatred of the power of money was an attitude that had a strong affinity to the paternalist outlook.

So did a belief in the inevitability of poverty. Paternalists believed the Bible when it said the poor shall never cease out of the land; this belief formed a third attitude that frequently attached itself to paternalism. Few paternalists had any hope of remaking the world. They were not reformers. Evils could be mitigated, not ended. The cutting edge of destitution could be blunted by charity but not removed. Paternalists were skeptics not only about utopias but about major reforms. The ills of society could be lessened, not removed, and that largely by its members being better Christians, wiser landowners, more conscientious clergymen, and more industrious and sober workers, in short, by being better people. Thus a fourth attitude attaches itself to the core of paternalism— the belief that it was by the moral and spiritual regeneration of a nation's governing classes (and of those they governed) and not by copious legislation and a large bureaucratic government that a more Christian and stable society would be guaranteed.

A model paternalist could not help thinking in moral categories, whether it was about the duties of the landlords or the duties of the poor. There were just and unjust landlords just as there were the worthy and unworthy poor. That latter distinction permeated their thinking so deeply that it led to a fifth attitude attaching itself to paternalism, that morality should govern all relations, including economic ones. There should be a just price, a fair rent, and equitable wages, since such practices fitted in with a society where the doctrine of duty ruled more than the doctrine of rights of capital or rights of labor. A sense of a just economy also fit with the ideas of mercantilism, which taught that markets should be protected, that domestic trades should be defended from foreign goods, and that there should be a favorable balance of trade. These ideas fit well with the old ideas of a just price, a fair wage, and proper quotas, ideas with roots going back to medieval guilds.

But did all paternalists believe in the fair wage and the just price? Or even most of them? Probably not when they bought and sold land or made leases. Paternalism, when it deals with the just price, becomes diffuse and amorphous, more a matter of rhetoric than of practice. There was much rhetoric to paternalism, and it was not always consistent. Paternalists spoke much of the need for protection, for laws restricting foreign imports, for the regulation of the wages of stocking-frame workers, but they frequently yielded in practice to one of their favorite adages, "live and let live." It was an adage reflective of that laissez faire outlook that governed their actual practices, an adage not so strange to a governing class increasingly informed about the political economy of Adam Smith and not always hostile to Malthus and Ricardo.

Live and let live could even form a sixth of those attitudes that cluster around the core of paternalism. But it was an attitude that not all paternalists held. As one moves away from the central core of paternalism, it becomes more complex and ill defined. It is thus useful to keep in mind that at its center lie the four basic assumptions about the structure of society and the three principal sets of duties that superiors owe to their inferiors. A paternalist is thus one who believes that society can be best managed and social evils best mitigated by men of authority, property, and rank performing their respective duties toward those in their community who are bound to them by personal ties of dependency. To be a paternalist was to act toward dependents as a father does to his wife, his children, and his servants.

A model is an intellectual construct that is used to clarify forces or attitudes that in actuality exist in a confused, mixed, and muddy state. The strands of paternalism were, for example, almost always intermingled with strands from other social outlooks. For each person the proportions of paternalist and nonpaternalist strands differed. In William Sewell, a professor of moral philosophy at Oxford, the paternalist model found a nearly pure expression, while in Edwin Chadwick, the age's complete bureaucrat, a utilitarian belief in a laissez faire economy and in a centralized administration quite outweighed a small, but still dogged, streak of paternalism. Sewell and Chadwick lay at different ends of a spectrum that ran from the more to the less paternalist. Between them ranged most of the governing classes of England. Near Sewell, for example, came the seventh earl of Shaftesbury, the foremost of all in advocating a paternal government, and near Chadwick came the reforming Whig Lord Morpeth of Castle Howard, Yorkshire. Yet Shaftesbury was no pure paternalist, since his strong evangelicalism drove him to a broad, generalized, and diffuse philanthropy, one that was anathema to William Sewell. Neither was Lord Morpeth, though a stout advocate of political economy and Chadwick's coworker at the Board of Health, merely a utilitarian reformer, since at his Castle Howard estate he performed instinctively and fully the duties of a paternal lord.

In the middle of the spectrum were grouped people as different as Sir Robert Peel and Thomas Carlyle. Peel's social outlook, as squire of Drayton Manor, reflected paternalism's strongly localist and authoritarian strands, yet, as the disciple of Adam Smith and the repealer of the Corn Laws, he reflected that laissez faire whose immoderate individualism posed a threat to an organic and hierarchic paternal society. In Carlyle there existed a medley of insights, intuitions, aspirations, passions, dreams, and righteous indignation. In his turbulent breast a radical impulse to denounce authority for its sins warred against a conservative belief that only a paternal authority could hold society together. Myriad and complex, many-sided and variable, were the attitudes of those who, with differing degrees of fullness and ardor, espoused paternalist ideas. How then should one use the word "paternalist"?

There is no easy answer, no pat formula. Yet some rule, however rough, must be used. In parts one and two of the following study the label "paternalist" refers to those on the Sewell-to-Chadwick spectrum in whom the paternalist strands are more dominant than any other single set of social beliefs. In nine out of ten cases among the theorists, publicists, novelists, landlords, and clergymen that are examined, there are no great problems—the paternalist strands are large, many, and dominant. But there are marginal cases. With Thomas Chalmers and Thomas Arnold among the theorists, with Elizabeth Gaskell and Harriet Martineau among the novelists, and with most of the captains of industry, the paternalist assumptions, though most decisive, clear, and forceful, mix with rival social outlooks that are just as decisive, clear, and forceful.

In chapters ten and eleven the term is used more broadly in order to measure the full influence of paternalist ideas in Parliament and government. The term now includes the Morpeths, and even, on occasion, bureaucrats like Chadwick. No final and precise definition is possible of an outlook itself diffuse and of varied strands, particularly since they interweave in differing proportions with the strands of rival social attitudes. If these distinctions are kept in mind, the following examination of those who espoused paternalist attitudes should, in the end, lead to a clearer awareness of the pervasiveness, power, and complexity of this ancient and venerable outlook.

Social attitudes are powerfully influenced by a nation's institutions, institutions that are in turn a product of a nation's past. Such institutions as the justice of the peace, the landed estate, and the parish church had a profound influence on the evolution of paternalism, one that went back to medieval times. Paternalism was a venerable outlook, a matter of old ways performed time out of mind. Furthermore, to many of its most ardent protagonists its most perfect expression occurred in medieval times. With its institutional roots and its customary ways of thought running deep into the past and with its fullest realization supposedly occurring in feudal England, paternalism cannot be fully understood without at least a cursory glance at those centuries that shaped its theory and practice. This glance forms a necessary prelude to a discussion of Victorian paternalism.

Medieval Roots and Tudor Ideals

The governing classes of feudal England held many of the same assumptions, doctrines, and attitudes as did the early Victorian paternalists, though they expressed them in quite different forms. They believed in a body politic that was emphatically authoritarian, hierarchic, and organic, and they viewed society in terms of those degrees and ranks that ran from kings to villeins. Within those ranks each individual had his or her appointed tasks in furthering the common weal.

The feudal society, described as highly unified by later theorists, was in practice complex and pluralistic. Many knights and barons possessed the rights of private government because they held a fief from a lord, a lord to whom they owed definite duties. The lord in turn owed them protection and guardianship. It was a system, observes the great French historian Marc Bloch, that evolved in areas of Europe where the extended family was weak. The lord often acted as a surrogate father—the sons of his vassals were often pages at his court and, if their father died, his wards. Though there was a complex set of mutual obligations the controlling power was with the lord. Because this patriarchal, yet reciprocal, relationship was based on a system of landholding, there grew up the custom that land carried with it distinct and elaborate duties. It was a custom that would endure to the nineteenth century.

That landholding involved duties was reinforced by a second medieval institution, the church. The canon lawyers of that age argued that landlords had an obligation to give alms to the needy. They must do so because they "held" their property as a trust. Property, said the canon lawyers, was once common to all. Only the need to make it useful led to its being privately "held"; and though such a holding involved private returns it nevertheless remained a trust, a trust that required the rich to help the poor in times of need. The giving of alms, of course, also contributed to the earning of salvation. The custom of feudal vassalage and of Christian almsgiving combined in medieval England to help define the paternal functions of property.

Church property itself, according to canon law, was, even more than the property of laymen, part of the patrimony of the poor. It provided that wealth with which bishops and priests could feed the hungry, clothe

the naked, discipline the erring, and perform the sacred rites of the Catholic faith. If guiding, disciplining, superintending, and helping the poor forms a part of a definition of paternalism, then few in medieval England were more paternalist than the priests in their parishes. Brian Tierney even argues, in his *Medieval Poor Law,* that because of these and other churchmen, the poor were better cared for in the thirteenth century than at any other time until the twentieth century.[1]

Feudal relations and ecclesiastical works form but two of the four strands of medieval paternalism: the other two were the manor and the royal government—the feet and the head of the body politic.

Every villein had a lord to whom he owed services and from whom he received land and protection, but usually it was a lord he seldom saw. Knights and barons in the thirteenth century seldom met with villeins; stewards, not lords, usually presided over the manorial courts where villeins planned spring plowings and where cooperation and old customs blunted even the steward's directions. It was family, kin, and neighbor more than baron and steward that drew close the bonds of the village. The elders of these families were the village patriarchs, and it was the family that was the main guarantor of public order and the readiest source of mutual aid. Family feeling, extended by neighborliness and cemented by customs, rituals, and festivals, formed, along with the work of the village priest, that cohesive village society, which later Victorians romanticized as part of a lost paternal world.

The king, too, had a patriarchal role, though it was rather remote. He was the keeper of the peace and the protector of good and just laws. His judges were his servants, and they enforced the common law in every corner of the realm. Parliament was his high court and passed laws regulating everything from wages to the proper apparel of each rank in society. Yet for all its assiduousness in enforcing the law and for all its pretensions in regulating wages and dress, kingship played but a slight role in the social life of the average man. The king and his officials did little to enforce the laws governing wages and apparel, just as they seldom intervened with a paternal solicitude to aid the destitute and homeless. Such matters were the concerns of stewards, priests, and above all kinsmen and neighbors.

In the fourteenth and fifteenth centuries a great decline in population caused by the Black Death and the advent of a more commercial agriculture led to the breakup of villeinage and the weakening of the tightly knit village. Classical feudalism also yielded to bastard feudalism, the monarchy grew weak, and the church rich and lax. These developments and an expanding capitalism put great strain on the four institutions in which medieval paternalism had taken root. There seemed little of "common weal" or little of "unity" to the body politic at the beginning of the sixteenth century when social critics began to write of the ills that plagued England. In Thomas More's *Utopia* of 1516 one reads of rapacious landlords enclosing land for sheep grazing and high profits, of whole parishes depopulated, of engrossing merchants charging excessive prices, and of hoards of vagrants begging and committing crimes.[2] Medieval paternalism appeared to falter before the new economic forces.

Yet the Tudor social critics did not abandon the paternalism of their predecessors. On the contrary, they embraced it heartily and gave it a splendid literary expression. Their cousins in the King's Council and Parliament also translated it into an impressive array of royal proclamations and acts of Parliament.

Tudor social critics emphasized much more than their predecessors the paternal role of the gentry and nobility. The writings of the Tudor humanists and the legislation of the Tudor Parliaments thus led to three important developments: (1) the emergence of paternalism as part of the rhetoric and theory of the age, (2) the growth of the ideal of an educated, Christian, and virtuous gentry and nobility performing the duties of property, and (3) the establishment of a state paternalism not equaled until the twentieth century.

Arthur Ferguson in *The Articulate Citizen and the English Renaissance* has pointed out that few Englishmen wrote articulately about society until such Tudor humanists as Thomas More, Thomas Starkey, Robert Crowley, and Thomas Elyot.[3] While medieval men expressed their paternalism in village customs and canon law, the Tudor humanists and statesmen expressed it in brilliant dialogues and elaborate statutes adorned with idealistic preambles. In doing so, however, Tudor reformers did not abandon an essentially medieval world outlook. They believed in a Ptolemaic universe, divinely ordered and descending in a great chain of being from God and angels to man and beasts. Their cosmology corresponded to the medieval idea of a body politic. Both are hierarchical and ordered by law, and if the hierarchy is disturbed, there ensues chaos. "A public weal," wrote Sir Thomas Elyot in 1531 in *The Governor*, "is a body living compact of sundry estates and degrees of men." Chaos, he argues, would erupt if that order were disturbed by the introduction of equality.[4]

Thomas Starkey, a fellow Tudor humanist, was just as firmly hierarchical and organic in his assumptions about the body politic and even more sanguine about its harmonies. True civil life is "the living together in good order, one ever ready to do good to another." If such is pursued there will be established the "true, prosperous and perfect commonweal [where] every part . . . doth his office and duty required thereto with perfect love and amity to one another . . . as member and parts of one body."[5]

The Tudor intellectuals had a deep sense of an ordered universe whether it came from a medieval cosmology, Plato's *Republic,* or Aristotle's *Politics.* For Thomas Smith in *De Republica Anglorum* of 1583 it came from Aristotle. He found in the *Politics* the theory of the patriarchal origin of the state, a theory that saw the origin of the state arising from the extension of the family to larger units.[6] In an age that thought in such hierarchical, organic, harmonious, and patriarchal terms, the ideal of a paternal society was bound to grow strong. Tudor social theorists, in short, gave paternalism a coherent intellectual expression.

Paternalism also prospered because it fitted the new, wealthier, and better educated gentry's idea of itself. Thomas Elyot's book, *The Governor,* was expressly designed to teach the ruling classes those humanist values of virtue, learning, temperance, and honor, values that would make them "worthy to be governors of the public weal." Such worthy rulers came from those whom Elyot called "superior in conditions and property."[7] The Tudor humanists continued and expanded the medieval belief that property was a trust that carried with it definite duties. "All lordship of property," wrote the humanist Robert Crowley, "is held as a trust of God." Property owners, he added, are "but stewards and not lords over their possession."[8] Property, rank, title, privilege, learning, all these required of their possessors definite duties, whether as master to servant, landlord to tenant, or magistrate to citizen. It was the Tudor ideal to educate the propertied classes in the wisdom and virtue of Greece and Rome and in the holiness and charity of Christianity, and so to make them noble governors of men.

The third contribution of the Tudor age, and its greatest, was to implement its ideals by creating a truly paternal state. If paternalism's central doctrine is the duty to control the lives of those of lower rank within one's sphere, then the Tudor landowning justice of the peace (J.P.) was the greatest of paternalists, rivaled only by the Tudor judges and privy councilors who controlled the J.P.s. They were all inveterate meddlers and far more effective at it than their medieval predecessors. They wanted to regulate the prices of bread, beer, and wool, the games one played, the amount one drank, the nature of one's apprenticeship, and the clothes one wore. They arrested drunkards, fined those who did not attend church, and penalized the adulterous. They were also concerned for the subject's welfare. The Church was now Erastian, the monastic lands sold off, and the parish made a secular more than an ecclesiastical unit of government. A series of lengthy poor laws transformed the old alms-giving obligations into a legal rate on all property and placed poor-law administration under overseers and J.P.s. Nowhere is the state paternalism of the Tudor age expressed more clearly, both in its benevolent aim to relieve destitution and in its authoritarian discipline of the unruly, the riotous, and the vagrant than in these poor laws. It was the crowning achievement of a paternal state, an achievement that G. R. Elton in *England Under the Tudors* considers "far more effective . . . than anything the middle ages knew—something so effective that only the twentieth century has come to eclipse it."[9]

Just as most Tudor social critics agreed on the value and need of a truly paternal government, so they agreed on two other ideals, that society should be as hierarchic and ordered as the divinely created cosmos and that there should be an educated, Christian, and virtuous propertied class, conscientiously performing its duties. But not all of these critics shared these ideals fully. One of the most profound of them, Thomas More, expressed doubts about a society in which there were great inequalities and doubts about entrusting social duties to private property. In his *Utopia* of 1516 he condemned the institution of private property. He then sketched out a society in which property was held in common and there was economic equality.[10] Yet in its own fashion his ideal community was distinctly paternalist. The main governing unit in that community was the extended family. The patriarchs of the extended family ruled over wives, children, grandchildren, and servants, such a family forming one of the main economic and social units of society. Between these extended families and the few elders who ruled the state, there were no corporations or authorities. It was a combination of two kinds of paternalism, that of the family with its patriarch and that of the state with its elders. Such a government clearly excluded the paternalism of property, rank, and title, a form of paternalism that More believed would be vitiated by the avarice of man. More had seen too many enclosing landlords and engrossing merchants to believe that property would do its duties. A paternalist in his own fashion—a fashion that was to prove as irrelevant as that of Robert Owen's three centuries later—he was the first to perceive the greatest weakness of the paternalism of property, namely, the likelihood that private property would lead to oppression, not protection. It was a criticism that bothered few thinkers. It also bothered few articulate citizens of Stuart and Hanoverian England. Indeed, by the eighteenth century the paternalism of property held quite undivided sway, since Englishmen in the seventeenth century had destroyed the paternal state, diminished the role of the church, and undermined the intellectual framework of a hierarchic society.

Stuart Revolutions and Eighteenth-century Latitudinarianism

In 1598 the future King James I of England wrote in *The True Law of Free Monarchies* that a king was like a loving father who cherishes the welfare of his subjects and tempers his chastisement of them with pity.[11] It was good Tudor doctrine and one that James's son Charles carried out with vigor. Charles ordered his two most imperious servants, the earl of Strafford and Archbishop Laud, to employ his Council of the North and his Court of Star Chamber to check enclosures, administer a just and benevolent poor law, and establish religious conformity. Laud viewed the Star Chamber as his pulpit and used it to enforce not only the true religion but a just economic order. Everyone, he insisted, "must live in the body of the commonwealth and in the body of the church."[12] Laud was not the only Englishman with a passion for the paternal superintendence of the inferior orders; he had rivals among the Puritan clergy and gentry that he so detested. They too believed in an authoritarian and hierarchical world and in the stern moral superintendence of their dependents. They too protected, controlled, instructed, disciplined, coerced, and aided the poor. Probably at no other time in English history was there both in theory and practice and at all levels a more rigorous and comprehensive paternalism than in the decade of the 1630s.

A century later England was quite different. Paternalism, though by no means abandoned—particularly in practice—had retreated on all fronts. Three revolutions had weakened its hold on the minds of men: the constitutional victory of Parliament over Stuart absolutism, the intellectual triumph of the Newtonian world picture, and the economic ascendancy of capitalism.

Parliament's first victories over the Stuarts led to the dismantling of the paternalism of the king's government. In 1641 Parliament abolished Star Chamber, the Council of the North, and the Council of Wales, and hedged in as never before the king's power to govern through ordinances and his own servants. Lords lieutenant, justices of the peace, sheriffs, high constables, high bailiffs, and borough mayors were no longer called before Star Chamber and the Privy Council to answer for negligence or misdeeds. In the counties local government was sovereign, a fact that suited the tastes of a local power elite that remembered the persecutions of Laud's metropolitan visitations, the tyrannies of Cromwell's major generals, and James II's attack on the independence of boroughs. By 1688 the governing classes had developed an inveterate hostility to a strong central government. By 1714, after more than twenty-six years of war with France, they had also developed a hatred of expensive central government and high taxes. The guarantee the Hanoverian succession gave to parliamentary sovereignty was also a guarantee of the autonomy of local government. The attempts of the Stuart kings to unite the idea of a divine-right monarchy with the idea of a strong paternal government thus destroyed both. Charles's execution and James's flight ended the Tudor vision of a king at the head of a body politic directing all parts in the promotion of the common weal.

The scientific revolution also weakened the idea of paternalism. It destroyed the medieval-Tudor world picture. The triumphant cosmology of Kepler, Galileo, and Newton had little room in it for a hierarchic, organic, and miraculous chain of being that ran from God in his empyrean heights to the lowly insect. The universe was now impersonal, mechanical, mathematical, and uniformitarian. This scientific revolution probably had little impact on the practice of paternalism, on the day-to-day work of landowners, J.P.s, and clergymen. But it did on the intellectuals, for it helped provide the basis for those mechanical models of the political state that came from the pens of Thomas Hobbes and John Locke. The social contract was a bargain between the rulers and the ruled, and it was agreed to because of the power held by rational and calculating individuals. Such a theory was a considerable departure from Aristotle's theory of the patriarchal origins of the state or the argument of Robert Filmer in his *Patriarcha* that the king's absolute power derived from the absolute power of the father. John Locke devotes a chapter in his *Treatise on Government* to the refutation of Filmer's theory. The chapter, which is entitled "Paternalism," is not a plea for such a philosophy but a refutation of it.

The mechanical, individualist, contractual views of John Locke elicited from Tory writers in the reigns of Queen Anne and George I some vigorous replies, replies that led to a revival of the political ideals of paternalism. The political philosopher and statesman Viscount Bolingbroke, the poet Alexander Pope, and the satirist Jonathan Swift wrote once again in the vein of the Tudor humanists. Bolingbroke spoke of "the body politic," which he compared to "a patriarchal family, where the heads and all members are united by one common interest." Such a society, he said, would be distinguished by "authority, subordination, order and union."[13] Swift preached "On Mutual Subjection," praised subordination and hierarchy, and spoke of everyone having his appointed place and duties. Pope revived the idea of a chain of being and compared its hierarchy to that of the various degrees of men in society. These Tory writers saw in Locke's individualist and egalitarian ideas a reflection of a mechanistic way of thought that destroyed the personal world of deference, dependency, and obedience.

Even more distasteful to these writers because of its mechanistic, impersonal, and individualist mode of thought was the new way of thinking about the economy. It too rested on a belief in natural laws, laws that were so rational, harmonious, and self-regulating that individual self-interest rather than paternal concerns would promote the greatest good. Rights and self-interest, not duties and charity, would form the basis of society. Bernard de Mandeville in the *Fable of the Bees,* published in 1714, was the leading advocate of the new system of selfishness. In his essay he argued that the pursuit of self-interest produces the greatest amount of wealth and achievement and happiness in society, hence his terse subtitle, "Private Vices, Public Benefits." His essay was one of the first systematic expositions of laissez faire economics. Less systematic but more popular was Daniel Defoe's *Robinson Crusoe.* De Mandeville, Defoe, and many other eighteenth-century writers believed that the economy was governed by natural laws nearly as orderly and rational as those that govern the planets. By 1776 Adam Smith in his *Wealth of Nations* stated those laws in a logical and comprehensive form.

It is exceedingly difficult to measure the impact of intellectual change on social theories and practices. There is no doubt that the scientific revolution, the ideas of John Locke, and the new economic theories had an impact on the theoretical framework of paternalism, particularly in the realm of political theory. These ideas were simply not as congenial to an authoritarian, hierarchical, and personalized society as was the neo-Platonic and Christian world picture of the Tudor humanists. Probably only the new economic thought had much effect on the day-to-day practice of paternalism, and that effect was not too great since a squire's paternal disposition was rooted in his authoritarian temper, his hierarchic position, and the local institutions over which he presided. Such temperaments, positions, and institutions do not bend easily to new cosmologies or political theories. But they do bend to new economic forces. It was thus the third of the Stuart revolutions, the economic revolution, that had the greatest impact on the practice of paternalism.

It was the triumph of commerce and finance, not the Newtonian universe, that really distressed Bolingbroke and his circle. It was the malignant spread of trade and manufacture, the entry of parvenu families into landed society, the insidious influence of finance, the ubiquitousness of fundholders and speculators, and their alliance with Whig ministers, placemen, and pensioners, that worried Bolingbroke, Swift, and Pope.[14] Unchecked capitalism had upset that balanced and organic society in which the landed gentry and nobility in their Parliament, their quarter sessions, and on their estates promoted the public good. Great moneyed interests with no roots in local places or the past threatened to dissolve those bonds and customs that united the balanced commonwealth. The moneyed interests' most palpable manifestation was the supremacy of Robert Walpole's Whig party and its most distressing moment the financial disaster of the South Sea Bubble. Against the supremacy of the Whigs and money, Bolingbroke rallied the Tory squires, appealing to their nostalgia for that golden age when land held its rightful place. Bolingbroke and his friends expounded in their writings many of the ideals held by the Tudor humanists, but these ideals were no longer the ideals of a whole culture but rather those of a single, Tory, party.

The economic changes of the sixteenth and seventeenth centuries not only upset the balance and unity of the body politic at large, they weakened those institutions and customs that held the village together. The English social historian E. P. Thompson in "Patrician Society, Plebian Culture" of 1974 argues that in the eighteenth century the economic relations between landowner and laborer became increasingly a matter of a cash nexus, not of personal obligations—of market forces, not paternal concerns. Husbandman and yeoman and their small freeholdings yielded to the three-tiered system in which landowners leased large farms to tenant farmers who in turn employed, with little paternal concern, agricultural laborers. In the seventeenth century, population pressures, a growing sense of private property, a brisker individualism, and an increase of enclosures and land engrossing, had eroded many customary tenancies and seriously weakened the old cooperative village community. But though landowners abandoned close and personal economic relations with their workers, they still ruled the county as J.P.s and presided over annual feasts. They preserved what Thompson calls a "cultural hegemony." It was a more remote form of paternalism, one Thompson calls "as much theatre and gesture as effective responsibility."[15]

The result of these new commercial attitudes and the more remote paternalism of the squire was a latitudinarian attitude on the part of the governing classes toward those beneath them. It corresponded to the latitudinarianism of their eighteenth-century Anglican faith. The medieval Catholic religion had bound the villagers together through rituals, festivals, and alms. The Protestant Reformation destroyed many of those rituals and festivals but replaced them with a puritan discipline and faith. By the eighteenth century that discipline and faith were largely banished from rural areas, giving way to the lax rule of a secularized clergy and easygoing landlords. A latitudinarian religion thus fused with a latitudinarian society, one that was rational, prudent, and not deeply committed to any beliefs, not even to paternalism. Little wonder that E. P. Thompson in writing of eighteenth-century patrician society speaks of "the illusion of paternalism" and Harold Perkin in *The Origins of Modern English Society* writes of "abdication on the part of the Governors." Even contemporaries were disturbed. Edmund Burke wrote in 1756 that "pity, benevolence, friendship are almost unknown in high places" and that the "enormous luxury of the rich made them ignorant of how to help the poor."[16]

But had paternalism deteriorated that far? The answer depends upon what part of the complex system of paternal relations and writings one examines and how deeply. Paternalism certainly deteriorated in terms of the role of the central government. Sidney and Beatrice Webb in *English Local Government* found in the eighteenth century that the local "Rulers of the County" enjoyed "uncontrolled power." The result was that the thousands of local authorities that ran local affairs formed what the Webbs called an "administrative nihilism."[17] Ivy Pinchbeck and Margaret Hewitt in *Children in English Society* give a melancholy account of what that nihilism meant for the children who became apprentices. Without central supervision, local authorities grew negligent and indifferent to the apprentices' suffering.[18]

The new attitudes of the age also caused a deterioration in local government. Dorothy Marshall in *The English Poor in the Eighteenth Century* found that while the Elizabethans' main concern was "the prevention of poverty," the Hanoverians' was "to prevent a rise in the rates."[19] Men of property hated high taxes, and many also hated the burden of high office. Large areas in the eastern fenlands and northern moors had no J.P.s at all. Great landlords avoided that office. The lesser landlords who did work in local government often did so, according to the Webbs, with "ignorance and indifference," "melancholy incapacity," "cynical acquiescence to evil," "parsimony," "procrastination," "sullen torpor," and "scandalous maladministration."[20] These are familiar adjectives, some of which would fit fox-hunting parsons and capitalist landlords. There was in the early eighteenth century a calculating commercial spirit abroad, as there was a lax and easygoing indifference to paternal duties. It was an age in which the poet John Langhorne could, in 1774, write of

> The shuffling Farmer, faithful to no trust
> Ruthless as Rocks, insatiate as the Dust

and Oliver Goldsmith in 1769 could say

> But times are alter'd; trade's unfeeling train
> Usurp the land and dispossess the swain.[21]

The attitude of many in the governing classes, though by no means of all of them, was selfish, demanding, and parsimonious. They even pursued the idea of gaining a profit from the labor of paupers, and when that proved illusory they sought to save on rates by delivering the paupers to the harsh care of those contractors who took them for the lowest bid.[22] Even before Adam Smith they were bent on the creation of a laissez faire society.

Paternalism also deteriorated as a social ideal in the intellectual world. The eighteenth century produced little comparable to the social idealism of the Tudor humanists. Many in the eighteenth century, such as Pope, Swift, Goldsmith, and Langhorne, held paternalist assumptions and expressed them on occasion, but few besides Bolingbroke wrote at length about their importance or promise, and Bolingbroke's concerns were largely political. He wrote of authority, hierarchy, and the rightful place of land, but mainly because of the needs of a balanced body politic. His fears were of the overweening power of Whiggery and commerce. He did not write of the poor, he did not worry about enclosures, he did not concern himself with oppressed apprentices, and he spoke only in the most conventional terms of the duty of property. Nor were his ideas that pervasive in the age of Walpole. Thus for both the eighteenth-century intellectuals and for landowners, the paternalist outlook seems to have deteriorated considerably from the enthusiasm of Elyot, Starkey, and Crowley or the ambitions of Charles I, Wentworth, and Laud.

But this deterioration occurred more on the surface of eighteenth-century life and thought than at its center. Most intellectuals and most landowners of that age never questioned those basic assumptions about society that defined a paternalist. They all thought society should be authoritarian, hierarchic, organic, and pluralistic. Such assumptions were inextricably tied to the landed estates and magisterial bench of the titled nobility and wealthy gentry, to the parish livings and cathedral chapters of the Anglican Church, to the councils, courts, and guilds of the towns, and to the parish vestries with their overseers of the poor and village constables. Such institutions do not fade away before new ways of leasing land or the fashionable ideas of de Mandeville's *The Fable of the Bees.* Neither, in fact, did day-to-day practices change that much. That doctrine of duties that forms the other half of the paternalist outlook includes the three obligations to rule, to guide, and to help. The commercial spirit and the cash nexus of the eighteenth century may well have lessened the zeal of a landlord to help the destitute, but it did not lessen his desire to rule and guide those beneath him. Squire Western in Henry Fielding's novel *Tom Jones,* though not distinguished for benevolence, was not modest about exerting his authority. Squire Allworthy in the same novel was both distinguished for benevolence and firm in his authority. He performed all three sets of duties, ruling, guiding, and helping. Because the basic assumptions of paternalism did rest on institutions that had lasted many centuries, the continuities of that outlook are far greater than its changing patterns of rhetoric and theory, or even than its variations in practice, variations that the social historian has yet to measure accurately.

Even the changes in rhetoric and theory were modest. The social teachings of the Tudor humanists, with the possible exception of those of Thomas Starkey (whose main treatise was only published in the nineteenth century), form but a minor part of their considerations and are largely subordinate to their political theory. After the Wars of the Roses, law and order became the basic concern of Englishmen. Even the elaborate poor laws of Tudor statesmen were in large part inspired by the desire to keep down vagrancy and crime. From the late middle ages to the eighteenth century, the governing classes, predominantly landed, held the basic assumptions and performed the basic duties that define paternalism, but they did so in an unselfconscious and customary manner. The truth is that most of them did not think in terms of social problems and social theories. Except for Thomas More, Thomas Starkey, and a few others at the first of the sixteenth century, when economic and social changes were at a critical point, few Englishmen before the nineteenth century seriously sought out social remedies. It was only with the beginnings of the industrial and urban revolutions that Englishmen revived, amplified, and transformed paternalist ideas into a social theory and called for the more conscientious practice of paternalism as a social remedy for new and frightening problems. The revival, amplification, and transformation of those ideals as a social remedy is the subject of the following study.

Part One

The Intellectual
Revival

Chapter I

In Search of a Theory of Paternalism

In 1827 Kenelm Digby, an Anglo-Irish landowner turned amateur historian, published volume four of his romantic evocation of the beauties of feudalism, *The Broad Stone of Honour*. In 1847 Arthur Helps, private secretary to the Whig minister Lord Morpeth, published *Friends in Council,* an earnest discourse on the social duties of wealth. In the two decades between these two works some eighteen other English writers published more than thirty books that espoused paternalist social ideas. The same two decades also saw an endless outpouring of novels, pamphlets, and articles that championed the same principles. Never before and never after had so many writers espoused in so short a time paternalist ideas, and never before had the more thoughtful of them sought more seriously to place those ideas on a firm philosophical base.

The authors of these many works included quite a few writers of great reputation. They included, for example, the romantic poets Robert Southey, Samuel Taylor Coleridge, and William Wordsworth. In 1829 the poet laureate, Robert Southey, revived old Tudor ideals in *Sir Thomas More, or Colloquies on the Progress and Prospect of Society,* and in 1832 he republished those many pleas for a more paternal society that had graced the pages of the *Quarterly Review* and entitled them *Essays Moral and Political*. In 1830 the poet, critic, and philosopher Samuel Taylor Coleridge, in his book *On the Constitution of the Church and State,* placed paternalist theory on the metaphysical foundations of German idealism. In 1835, a year after his death, his nephew, H. N.

Coleridge, published some of his uncle's famous conversations at Highgate in a book entitled *Specimens of Table Talk* and in 1839 republished the poet's *Two Lay Sermons* of 1816, which had explored more deeply than ever before the philosophical and moral basis of a landed paternalism. William Wordsworth meanwhile published as a "Postscript" to his *Collected Poems* of 1835 his brief but incisive essay on the obligations of the higher classes toward the lower.

The search for a theory of paternalism was not limited to romantic poets, or to Tories and Anglicans: Presbyterian divines and Roman Catholic medievalists alike sought to find new answers to new problems by reviving and altering old attitudes. Scotland's most famous minister, the Reverend Thomas Chalmers, preached from the pulpit and the press on the social duties of the kirk and its property-owning elders. In 1826 he completed his three-volume work, *The Christian and Civic Economy of Large Towns,* a quite precise, logically argued, and elaborate blueprint of a paternalism that rested on church and property, though not on the state.

Far different in tone from the blueprint of this stern Calvinist were Kenelm Digby's eleven volumes, *Mores Catholici or Ages of Faith.* Published between 1831 and 1842, they glorify the medieval church as romantically as *The Broad Stone of Honour* had medieval chivalry. Digby was a historian and not a philosopher, and he does not, like Coleridge and Chalmers, treat in a theoretical way the social duties of property, church, and state. But, nevertheless, he exalts by his enthusiastic and vivid reconstruction of the medieval age those very institutions and attitudes that are so important to the paternalist position.

Far different from Kenelm Digby's romantic world of the past is Michael Thomas Sadler's mercantilist world of the present. Sadler, a Leeds merchant and Tory M.P., published *Ireland; Its Evils, and Their Remedies* in 1829 and his *Law of Population* in 1830. In these works he attempted to establish a new theory of political economy, one his biographer R. B. Seeley called "THE PATERNAL SYSTEM." It was a system whose leading characteristic was "to foster, to protect, cherish, encourage, promote." Michael Sadler's closest ally in this effort was his neighbor from Bradford and fellow agitator for the ten-hour day for factory workers, Richard Oastler. No systematic thinker, Oastler still had much to say in his forty-one pamphlets published between 1827 and 1841. In those pamphlets he showed how the old and trusted institutions of king, church, and land could be employed to solve the problems of factory, pauperism, and slums. Men as different as Oastler, Sadler,

Digby, and Chalmers thus joined the romantic poets Southey, Coleridge, and Wordsworth to form a pre-Victorian generation of intellectuals who sought to work out a theory of paternalism.

The early Victorian intellectuals that followed also had their ardent paternalists, anxious to develop a sound social philosophy for their trying times. They included men no less famous: Thomas Arnold, Thomas Carlyle, William Gladstone, and Benjamin Disraeli. In 1845, three years after Thomas Arnold's death, his close friend A. P. Stanley published *The Miscellaneous Works of Thomas Arnold,* a work that included Arnold's famous *Letters on Our Social Condition* of 1832 and his *Principles of Church Reform* of 1833. In these writings Arnold called for a reformed and enlarged church, which would join with earnest manufacturers and public-spirited landowners to ameliorate the sufferings of the poor. It was a call that Thomas Carlyle also made, though more stridently and with a greater emphasis on the state than on the church. In his *Chartism* of 1839 and *Past and Present* of 1843, Carlyle expressed his desire for a society in which authority at every level did far more governing, protecting, and guiding. Paternalists indeed came in many varieties ranging from the idiosyncratic Carlyle to that serious young Tory just down from Oxford, William Gladstone. In 1838 Gladstone alarmed his political patrons with his Coleridgean view of the Church's social role in *The State in Its Relations with the Church,* and in 1840 he further discomfited them by expressing his High Church sentiments in *Church Principles.* His future rival, Benjamin Disraeli, alarmed few and delighted many with his idealized portraits of paternalist landlords and model manufacturers in *Coningsby* in 1844 and *Sybil* in 1845.

Of lesser fame, but in terms of paternalist theory of greater importance, were the writings of R. B. Seeley, William Sewell, and Arthur Helps. Seeley, who was a London publisher and a strong evangelical, wrote *Memoir of the Life and Writings of M. T. Sadler* (1842), *The Perils of the Nation* (1843), and *Remedies Suggested for Some of the Evils which Constitute the Perils of the Nation* (1844), all three of which spelled out in detail Michael Sadler's PATERNAL SYSTEM. William Sewell, fellow and subrector of Exeter College and late professor of moral philosophy at Oxford University, published his ideal vision of a paternal world, *Christian Politics,* in 1844, the same year that Arthur Helps brought out *The Claims of Labour,* Seeley his *Remedies,* and Disraeli *Coningsby.* Measured by publications, the year 1844 was the high-water mark of the paternalist revival.

Seeley's *Remedies,* Sewell's *Christian Politics,* and Helps's *Claims* are

classic expressions of the paternalist outlook. Such was not the case with
F. D. Maurice's *The Kingdom of Christ* of 1843 or W. G. Ward's *The
Ideal of a Christian Church* of 1838. These works treat theological and
ecclesiastical matters and deal only secondarily with social theories. But
when they do discuss the church's role in relation to social problems
they are pronouncedly paternalist.

Dealing more directly with social questions are such exposés of social
distress as Lord Sidney Godolphin Osborne's *Agricultural Labourer* of
1844 and G. W. Perry's *The Peasantry of England* of 1846. Equally
direct were manuals for the practice of paternalism, such as the Reverend
John Sanford's 450-page *Parochialia* of 1845. Practical works, they offer
imaginative ideas and shrewd comments about how the wealthy can take
better care of their dependents. In many ways their practical proposals
and shrewd hints formed a firmer basis for a social theory of paternalism
than the Christian Socialist vision of John Minter Morgan or the medi-
evalist dreams of the architect Augustus Welby Pugin. Pugin in his
Contrasts of 1836 used his pictorial imagination, architect's pen, and
scholarly erudition to present a picture of that harmonious but lost world
of fifteenth-century ecclesiastical paternalism, while Morgan, in his
Religion and Crime of 1840, fused together Christian idealism, Owenite
ideas, and a firm conviction in the paternal role of the wealthy. Paternalism as a set of basic assumptions concerning the framework of society
and as a set of duties for various orders could be quite protean, serving
both as the backdrop to Pugin's medieval monasteries and as a frame for
Morgan's future temples of labor.

The names of Morgan and Pugin bring to twenty the authors who
between 1827 and 1847 published works espousing paternalist ideas.
There were, of course, others whose writings reflected these ideas. They
even find expression in those two celebrations of English manufactures,
Andrew Ure's *Philosophy of Manufactures,* published in 1835, and
W. C. Taylor's *Factories and the Factory System* of 1844. These many
works constituted that unprecedented efflorescence of paternalist ideas
that characterized social thought in the 1830s and 1840s.

Also part of that efflorescence was the republication and rereading of
the great classics. Far more Cambridge students in those years read
William Paley's *Moral and Political Philosophy* than Coleridge's *Two
Lay Sermons,* just as far more Englishmen read and reread Edmund
Burke's *Reflections on the Revolution in France* than William Sewell's
Christian Politics. It was indeed Burke's *Reflections,* first published in

1790, that started that wave of paternalist writings that crested between 1827 and 1847. Before 1790, to be sure, paternalist attitudes were widely held, but in a rather conventional, even tepid, way. After Burke these same conventional attitudes suddenly came to seem crucial, if society were not to dissolve into revolution. There is in the *Reflections* a far greater passion for a hierarchical and organic society in which the wealthy do their duties than in, for example, William Paley's *Moral and Political Philosophy* of 1785. Both authors assume a society based on private property, great inequalities, various ranks and orders, author-itarian landlords, a pastoral clergy, and an obedient laboring class, all with their respective duties. But in tone and feeling they are as different as was the latitudinarian eighteenth century from the romantic nine-teenth: Paley's arguments are cool, moderate, and utilitarian, Burke's passionate, eloquent, and based on moral absolutes.

William Paley, though very much of the eighteenth century, is not therefore unimportant to the history of paternalist ideas in the nine-teenth. The matchless expositor of his age's conventionalities, he based his belief in a paternal society on a mixture of biblical injunctions and utilitarian precepts, and it won him great popularity. Cambridge Uni-versity adopted his *Moral and Political Philosophy* as a text. In 1814 it was in its twenty-eighth edition and still inspired many a gentleman's platitude and many a clergyman's sermon. Believing that rights and duties were synonymous, he told the sons of the gentry that the best charity is to assist those "with whose behaviour and duties we ourselves are acquainted." Great proprietors should thus build cottages, erect manufactures, and cultivate wastes; the less wealthy gentry should serve conscientiously as magistrates, and the clergy should work among the poor and regulate their conduct.[1]

Burke's *Reflections,* though it is based on some assumptions common to Paley, was in many ways a reaction to Paley's urbane and comfortable world and its mechanistic rationalism. It was also a reaction to ideas far more radical than Paley would countenance. Just as the ideas of John Locke and the political challenges of the world of commerce and finance evoked from Viscount Bolingbroke a reaffirmation of the hierarchical and paternal society of a landed aristocracy, so did the ideas of English radicals and the violence of upstart French revolutionaries elicit from Burke a powerful statement of the same old ideas. The *Reflections on the Revolution in France,* though essentially a political rather than a social disquisition, still affirms with great eloquence a belief in a hierarchical, organic, and pluralistic society. Burke never doubts that the divison of society into rich and poor and the subordination of the latter form part of "the unalterable relations which Providence has ordained." For Burke "the rich are trustees for those who labour for them" and the guarantors of "those connections, natural and civil, that regulate and hold together the community of subordination." He is also particularly passionate against levelers who raise "servants against masters; tradesmen against their customers; artificers against their employers; tenants against their landlords; curates against their bishops; and children against their parents."[2] In expressing these hierarchical sentiments Burke said little that was original. What was new, however, was his placing such ideas on a more solid, philosophical base. He did this in three ways: first, by arguing that existing institutions were eminently useful since they reflected the pragmatic adjustments of past generations; second, by arguing that these same institutions reflected an enlarged morality, itself a part of a natural and divine law; and third, by arguing that society was so complex, intricate, and fragile that it must be held together by bonds of deference, affection, and habit. Society was organic and would, if subjected to the universal formulas of abstract reform, dissolve into chaos.

The brilliance of Burke's writing and argument coincided in the first two decades of the nineteenth century with a deep surge of English conservatism and patriotism, a conservatism and patriotism provoked by the French Revolution and the Napoleonic Wars. Since one of the main strands of conservatism was paternalism, that social outlook also enjoyed a revival. It was, for example, central in the writings of Samuel Taylor Coleridge, a writer who looked upon Burke as "the transcendental genius."

It is doubtful that any of the advocates of paternalism in the 1830s and 1840s would have disagreed with Coleridge's high estimate of Burke or Burke's high estimate of an organic and deferential society. Coleridge in 1816 urged the creation of a society in which "all classes are balanced and interdependent, as to constitute more or less a moral unity, an organic whole." In a similar vein Robert Southey in 1830 sung the merits of

> That appointed chain,
> Which when in cohesion it unites
> Order to order, rank to rank,
> In mutual benefit,
> So binding heart to heart.[3]

These are traditional sentiments, ones with which Oxford's William Sewell or London's Benjamin Disraeli would entirely agree. Only Thomas Chalmers and Thomas Arnold showed any tendencies to differ from these hierarchical and organic assumptions. There was in Chalmers's Scottish Calvinism an individualism that verged on the philosophy of self-help later developed by Samuel Smiles, and there was in Thomas Arnold's liberalism a belief that the government should help bring to an end society's grosser inequalities. But these tendencies toward individualism and collectivism never got out of hand. Chalmers never allowed his belief in self-reliance to weaken his belief in the need for a vigilant, superintending kirk, one that would "link and harmonize into one fine system, the various classes," and Thomas Arnold never allowed his alarm at exploitation to lead him to egalitarianism: "Equality," he wrote, was either "the dream of a mad man; or the passion of a fiend."[4] Even though the two Whigs Arnold and Chalmers differed from the two Tories Coleridge and Southey on Catholic Emancipation and the Reform Act of 1832, all four writers agreed that society should be authoritarian, hierarchic, organic, and pluralistic and that all in their various stations should do their duties. None of the above authors sought to alter the basic framework of society.

But they all had to make their paternalist assumptions more adaptable to what Thomas Carlyle called "the condition of England question," a phrase that became very popular in the 1840s and one that reflected the crucial fact that social, not political problems, had become paramount. The problems that Englishmen now faced differed from those confronting Bolingbroke—or even from those facing Burke. For Bolingbroke the main problem was the impact of social development on the body politic—the arrival of financiers in Parliament and men of commerce in the market for pocket boroughs. Even Burke was reacting to political ideas, to the democratic ideas of English radicals and French revolutionaries. But after the Reform Act of 1832 the political problems momentarily receded, while social problems became more acute. The articulate citizen now confronted widespread rural pauperism, overworked factory children, half-naked women in mines, mounting industrial accidents, underemployed and starving handloom weavers, crowded and disease-ridden slums, rising crime rates, an uneducated and ignorant populace, dismal overcrowded prisons, the cruel treatment of lunatics, homeless orphans, vagrancy, drunkenness, prostitution—the problems were endless. None of them of course was entirely new, but their accumulation was massive and forced the early and pre-Victorian paternalists to think through in a far more searching way than they ever had before the nature and function of those institutions that they hoped would form the basis of a viable and humane society. Englishmen could no longer speak perfunctorily of wealth doing its duty, of the clergy tending their flocks, or of a paternal government. They had instead to show persuasively that property by doing its duty could solve the problem of rural and urban pauperism, that the church could end the ignorance and immorality of an uneducated populace, and that a paternal government could protect its citizens from the harsh vicissitudes of an industrial society. Property above all had to show it could handle the urgent and multitudinous problems of industrial England, for property was everywhere the dominant institution of the realm. Property, not the government or the church, was England's sovereign institution, and on it thus fell the greatest role in the revival of paternalism.

The Sovereign Sphere of Property

Few phrases were cited more often in the Parliament and the press of the 1840s than the dictum "property has its duties as well as its rights." Private property was easily one of the most popular and entrenched institutions in the realm. The sons of the governing class read of its legality in William Blackstone's *Commentaries* and of its utility in John Locke's *Treatises on Government*. Its usefulness seemed evident to all. It stimulated industry, imposed order on the economy, provided the governing classes and the church with their incomes, and formed the basis of most charities. Property defined one's station in life and hence, according to Edmund Burke, one's duties. In carrying out those duties, Burke added, "the great must submit to the dominion of prudence and virtue" since if they do not, "none will submit to the dominion of the great." Such an understanding, he concluded, is "the feudal tenure."[5]

Coleridge shared with Burke a keen appreciation of property's feudal tenure. In 1816 in his *Statesman's Manual* he made it the centerpiece of his social philosophy. He was convinced that private property and not the state could best alleviate the destitution and suffering of the poor, and he was quite explicit in explaining to the owners of landed estates why they must care for their dependents. "The land is not yours," he exclaimed, "it was vested in your lineage in trust for the nation." It is also, he added, a Christian trust since "the law of God [has] connected indissolubly the cultivation of every rood of earth with the maintenance and watchful labour of men." For Coleridge land formed the soundest basis of a well-managed society because it made its proprietor a "free agent," and only a free agent could effect real reforms. "All reforms or innovations," he insists, "not won from a free agent, which does not leave the merit of having effected it sacred to the individual proprietor, it were folly to propose or worse than folly to attempt."[6]

That reform can emanate only from a free agent is a rather severe and narrow claim, one that would condemn as folly all reforms effected by a central government. Yet Coleridge insisted on it. Not only did property create the free agent needed for reform but it had two other salutary effects, it encouraged what Coleridge called and capitalized as HOME-BORN FEELINGS, and it also concentrated social benevolences and control on those smaller spheres of life in which there can be personal attachments, mutual knowledge, and parental discipline. "Let every man," Coleridge thus concludes, "measure his efforts by his power and his sphere of action."[7]

Coleridge was not departing from earlier or contemporary paternalist thinkers in insisting that one's first responsibilities are to those dependents whom one knows and that such knowledge arises from that mutual intercourse that occurs on landed estates. Edmund Burke was in 1795 convinced that the primary sphere of moral relations within the great contract is the small society, while Robert Southey three decades later said that the object of all Christians was "to promote the welfare and happiness of those who are in any way dependent upon him." In such a dependent relationship arise what Coleridge had called HOMEBORN FEELINGS. Thomas Arnold was so convinced of this central principle that he urged all men of property to organize their workers in small units in order to promote "mutual knowledge of each other."[8]

It would be difficult to exaggerate the early Victorian paternalists' attachment to those small spheres where property was sovereign. It was crucial to R. B. Seeley's exposition of Sadler's "PATERNAL SYSTEM," just as it was to William Sewell's grand design in his *Christian Politics:* in both systems all social control and benevolence occur between those who know each other and derive ultimately from the ownership of property.[9] Such a system fitted the English landlord's daily experiences as proprietor, magistrate, and neighbor and fitted also his jealous regard for his autonomy and his hatred of the central government. No institution in England was more ancient, powerful, wealthy, and venerated than the landed estate, and Coleridge was sociologically as well as psychologically perspicacious in making the sphere of the landed estate the core of his theory of paternalism.

The paternalists' great emphasis on the sovereign sphere of property led many of them to be severe critics of two of the more important movements of their age, the growth of philanthropy and the spread of manufactures.

Their hostility to philanthropy was a curious one. In many ways they shared the philanthropist's charitable compassion toward the distressed. Some even used the term "philanthropic" to describe the work of a lady bountiful. Yet deep down they had scorn for the larger works of philanthropy, particularly since such works ran counter to the idea of limiting one's benevolence to the smaller spheres of property. "I have never known a trader in philanthropy," wrote Coleridge, "who is not wrong in heart." "There is a vague and vagrant philanthropy," said Thomas Chalmers, "which loses much of its energy in its diffuseness."[10] The term "philanthropy" was, in early nineteenth-century England, often applied both to the efforts of evangelicals to convert blacks in Africa and infidels in London and to the visions of utopian philosophers such as William Godwin or Robert Owen. Both varieties were anathema to paternalists. The evangelicals were too full of cant and the utopians too full of dreams. Thomas Carlyle could not abide the former, and William Sewell distrusted the latter. "Most sick am I," exploded Carlyle in 1845, "of this sugary disastrous jargon of philanthropy." "Every attempt to embrace others in a spirit of indiscriminate promiscuous benevolence," wrote Sewell, "will only ruin the work." When paternalist writers as different in outlook as Coleridge and Chalmers in the 1820s or Carlyle and Sewell in the 1840s could yet agree in their hostility to philanthropy, there must have been some underlying reason. Arthur Helps in his *Claims of Labour* revealed in part that reason. "No sentimental philanthropy will do, nor even a warm and earnest philanthropy," he wrote, since the need is for "a sphere small enough for him to act."[11] For those who shared Burke's belief that small societies are the best basis for moral relations and Coleridge's exaltation of those HOMEBORN FEELINGS that arise from "private attachments and mutual knowledge," Bible societies in Bethnal Green, missionaries in Sierre Leone, and societies for the diffusion of useful knowledge in Manchester and Leeds were useless, wasteful, and dangerous.

There were, however, paternalists who were not hostile to philanthropy. Some like William Wilberforce, Hannah More, and the young

Lord Ashley combined very effectively both outlooks. The relationship of paternalism and philanthropy is complex. Some paternalists disliked, and very heartily, the practice of philanthropy since it extended benevolence and guidance far beyond the proper sphere of property, while other paternalists supported such extensions. These differences arose in part from differing theological positions: those with a High Church view of the sacredness of the works, ceremonies, and sacraments of the parish church saw the parish as the proper place for benevolence and guidance; the evangelicals on the other hand knew that salvation lay in the conversion and rebirth of the truly penitent whether they resided in Bethnal Green or in Sierre Leone, and so all preaching and all benevolences were good no matter how extended and diffuse. Philanthropy knew no bounds; its Bible societies and ragged schools could extend into the most sprawling of industrial towns. This diffuseness bothered the classical paternalist.

But then the classical paternalists of the pre-Victorian generation had difficulty admitting into their world any of those vast cities where ambitious manufacturers and disorderly workingmen destroyed all semblance of an organic society. "The greedy, grasping spirit of commercial and manufacturing ambition and avarice," wrote Southey as late as 1830, "is the root of all our evils." "The cause of our distress," said Coleridge in 1816 is "the overbalance of the commercial spirit in consequence of the absences or weakness of the counterweight." One of the best counterweights for Coleridge was landed property, for land was fixed and permanent, and its aims were the same as the state's, the good governance of men. Commercial property, on the other hand, had no more concerns than "the quickest profit and least cost." Since Coleridge estimated in 1816 that the commercial spirit had increased fiftyfold, he concluded that "it is not enough that the counterweight should be as great as in former periods . . . it should be greater."[12]

It was a sentiment Viscount Bolingbroke would have applauded and one that Sewell, Sadler, Oastler, and Seeley all shared. Seeley, to be sure, did admit in his *Perils of the Nation* that there were good manufacturers, but he said they were no more than one in fifty. The other forty-nine belonged to what William Sewell called "the inferior middle class." It was Sewell's opinion that that class was ruining the towns of England. Sewell wished the growth of manufactures either stopped (Southey's position) or severely regulated (Coleridge's).[13] But stopping the growth of manufacturing, or even regulating its growth, was no more realistic than Canute's holding back the tides.

Thomas Arnold, Thomas Carlyle, and Arthur Helps saw that the only realistic answer was to include manufacturers within that sovereign sphere of property that they believed could best grapple with England's social problems. There was indeed no reason captains of industry could not become model paternalists. As early as 1832, Arnold pronounced the chimneys of Sheffield to be as valuable to the well-being of the English as Lord Fitzwilliam's landed domains, for without them "England would be no better than Russia or Poland—we should be the mere serfs of a territorial aristocracy." Carlyle agreed. "With the supreme triumph of cash," he wrote in *Chartism,* "a changed time has entered; there must be a changed aristocracy." By 1850 Carlyle was extolling his captains of industry as an "aristocracy of fact, instead of the extinct imaginary one of title."[14] This "aristocracy of fact," according to Arthur Helps, should also include bankers and merchants and the owners of small workshops and retail stores. To educate them in the duties of paternalism Helps published in 1844 his *Claims of Labour.* In it he asked manufacturers and merchants to "eschew the grandeur and glitter of life," and to take care of "your dependents." "Do not," he said, "dwell more than you can help upon differences of nature between yourself and those with whom you live"; "don't be condescending"; "don't be careless in what you say"; "don't reduce your intercourse to mere cash payments"; "don't be too surprised at ingratitude"; and "do not be fond of the display of authority." To these many don'ts he added some do's: offer the workers "an intercourse which includes an interchange of thought" and behave toward them with "complete sincerity and earnestness" and with "a playfulness that will soften social distance." He ends by urging them to "take the rule of the father which is the type of all good government," and so give them well-ventilated mills, comfortable homes, playgrounds, lessons on "how to spend money," and "healthy and instructive amusements" such as zoological gardens and musical evenings.[15]

The early Victorian paternalist writers, with the exception of Oxford's Platonic dreamer William Sewell, had by 1840 accepted the captains of industry into their theories. They had to admit with Carlyle, "if there be no nobleness of them [manufacturers] there will never be an aristocracy more."[16] Most manufacturers had small firms in average-sized towns and so ruled over a sphere in which they could be free agents and develop HOMEBORN FEELINGS.

That is, some could develop HOMEBORN FEELINGS. Seeley had one in fifty doing so. It was not a bad estimate. But then did any more than one in fifty landowners have HOMEBORN FEELINGS? That question, even more than the relationship of paternalism to philanthropy or the place of commerce and manufacturing within a paternal society, posed the most painful dilemma for those who believed in the beneficent influence of private property.

Property, landed or manufacturing, simply was not performing its duties. It was an alarming fact, one that threatened the viability of a paternalism based on property. The paternalist writers themselves admitted these failures. Southey told of "landlords who rack rent their tenants and farmers who grind the labourers"; Michael Sadler allowed no romantic illusions to exclude from his writings references to engrossing farmers, landlord absenteeism, and the demolition of laborers' cottages; Thomas Arnold pointed out "the evils of the ultra aristocracy": the evils of rack renting, demolition of cottages, game laws, and absenteeism.[17] It was an old story, this complaint of rapacious landlords, older even than William Langland's *Piers Plowman* or Thomas More's *Utopia*.

Burke, Paley, and Coleridge even realized that these failures lay in the very nature of private property and its unequal distribution. "The whole business of the poor," noted Burke, "is to administer to the idleness, folly, and luxury of the rich." It was a remarkably candid admission but then so was the famous story of the pigeons in Paley's *Moral and Political Philosophy*. He compared the English economy of his day to a society of one hundred pigeons, ninety-nine of whom worked constantly collecting grain and eating only the chaff, in order to lay up the choice grains "for one, and that the weakest, perhaps the worst pigeon of the flock." Despite these caustic comments on the inequalities and injustices of eighteenth-century England, Burke and Paley benignly defended the utility of private property, as did Coleridge, though less benignly, for he too saw the injustices involved in the ownership of private property. "Property," he wrote, "is the bugbear—it stupifies the head and hardens the heart."[18]

The failure of property to perform its duties embarrassed those who had long looked to it for an answer to the most acute of social evils. Richard Oastler, for one, had long thought it the best answer, but after seeing landlord after landlord help enforce the harsh New Poor Law of 1834, he lamented "I had some hope in the aristocracy, now I have none."[19] Yet Oastler had nowhere to turn since he detested the central government more heartily than the power of land and had long despaired of the church. The result was that Oastler and many others who sought to construct a theory of paternalism could only persist year after year in pleading with property to do its duties. Another answer, of course, would be to turn to a paternal government, but most paternalists were deeply ambivalent about that complicated problem.

The Ambiguous Role of Government

The attitudes of early nineteenth-century paternalists toward the role that government should play in society were both complex and ambivalent. They were not quite certain, for one thing, what they meant by the term "government." To many of them it meant different things in different contexts. In terms of symbol and ceremonies, it meant Her Majesty and her court; in terms of high politics, Parliament and the cabinet; and, for governance, the administrative departments at Whitehall and the law courts off the Strand.

But these national institutions, however imposing, were remote to the average inhabitant of the countryside. For them government was the local J.P.s in their petty and quarter sessions, the mayors and aldermen in their boroughs, and the vestrymen, overseers, and constables in their parishes. Government thus formed in the minds of most paternalist thinkers a gigantic network that ran from the crown to the constable, or what Edmund Burke called a moral partnership of all those who were bound by "connections, natural and civil" into a "chain of subordination."

William Sewell in his *Christian Politics* spelled out in greater detail what Burke's moral partnership meant for paternalism. It would be a vast network of authorities. "The functions and offices of the state," wrote Sewell, "should be ramified and extended through all ranks to the very lowest . . . a juryman may develop the faculties required in a judge, even the little village school is a little world, the master acts there as a sovereign."[20] Such a world of many sovereigns acting at all levels was a "pluralistic" one, a fact that Sewell very self-consciously recognized by frequently using that term and using it in the most complimentary sense.

Sewell's "state ramified and extended through all ranks" and Burke's moral partnership made no clear distinction between public and private authorities—nor did most paternalist thinkers. Sewell called schoolmasters sovereign. Fathers were also sovereign over the family and landlords over the estate. Many of the latter were also J.P.s, though for the unhappy poacher brought before petty sessions (which were often held in the squire's country house) the distinction between the squire as landowner and the squire as magistrate meant little. Even philosophers like Coleridge and publicists like Seeley blurred the line that divided private from public authorities. Coleridge found "the democracy of England" not in Parliament but in "the corporations and the vestries, the joint stock companies, etc.," while Seeley argued vehemently that "it is the old English parish that we want, with its own parson, known and knowing every family, and its publicly chosen overseer."[21] For Coleridge a privately owned joint-stock company is part of the "democracy" of England, and for Seeley a parson is as much a part of parish government as an overseer. Schoolmasters, landowners, company directors, and parsons joined publicly appointed or elected overseers, constables, J.P.s, town councilors, and sheriffs to form a vast network of authorities each with its respective rights and duties. Each had its moral sphere, and according to Coleridge each reflected the "Idea" of the English state.

Some parts, however, were more valued than others, there being in particular a passion for local over national authorities. "It is the old English parish that we want," was Seeley's cry. Democracy is found in vestries and corporations, exclaimed Coleridge. No paternalist writer until Carlyle differed from this dogma. "If there is an excellence in the English constitution," said Richard Oastler, "it is that it leaves the inhabitants of every locality to manage its affairs."[22] It would be difficult to exaggerate the importance of locality and local government in paternalist thought: they were central to its most basic assumptions. Some, to be sure, like Arthur Helps, spoke "of the happy admixture of central and local authority," and some, like Southey, looked often to Parliament for protective legislation. Southey proposed many schemes calling for parliamentary action, while Sadler and Oastler bowed to no one in their zeal for an act that would impose the ten-hour day on textile factories.[23] But in doing so they were not calling for a larger central bureaucracy. Sadler and Oastler, for example, were adamantly opposed to the establishment of factory inspectors. They were convinced that if there were a ten-hour law on the books, local forces would see that it was enforced. "A happy admixture of central and local" meant a central government that helped, not hampered, local government, that gave more powers to local authorities, not more commissioners to the central government. Helps in his *Claims of Labour* called on Parliament to pass regulations on the dwellings of the poor and the state of the streets, but he wanted the owners of property and local authorities to execute these regulations.[24] Southey and Arnold also wished for acts of Parliament pure and simple, ones that empowered, not checked, local authorities. Southey was the most prolific of all in dreaming up schemes for a paternal government, but he explicitly spoke of their execution being delegated to local authorities: landowners, not the government, would thus employ paupers for the cultivation of waste lands, and the parson and not a government inspector would manage the local school. The actual administration of Thomas Arnold's bold plan for "a wise and active legislation" that would employ the jobless on public works fell to either the parish's leading ratepayers or to county authorities.[25] There would be no Benthamite commissioners. Not all paternalist writers were zealous advocates of legislation by Parliament, but those who did urge such legislation frequently did so in order to enlarge the powers of local government, the church, and private property. It is a distinction that should be kept in mind when discussing the paternalists' use of the term "government." They had a decided preference for local over central government, and within their concept of local government a decided preference for private over public authorities. They saw in landowners, parsons, schoolmasters, and company directors the most truly paternal of authorities. The ownership of property was still the basic fact of social and political life, and not only was its sphere the most inviolable of all, but it was the ownership of property that qualified one to be a J.P., an M.P. or a town councilor. Yet as basic as property was, it formed but one part of that complex network of institutions that formed Burke's moral partnership or reflected Coleridge's "Idea" of the state. Ecclesiastical, legal, family, and titled privileges fused with property in parish, county, and town to form those undifferentiated and restricted localities that were the central objects of a paternalist's affections. In such a world it was not always clear what paternalists meant when they demanded a more paternal government.

It was also not clear to what extent they wished the government to intervene in social and economic affairs. If the intervention of government meant the intrusion of a centralized bureaucracy, all paternalist writers except Thomas Carlyle were generally opposed. Many of them, to be sure, supported legislation strengthening local government. But even in this area there was considerable jealousy of government intervention, particularly since such intervention did violence to three rather strongly held assumptions: a belief in self-regulating and harmonious economic and social laws, an insistence that the lower classes be self-reliant, and a high regard for the voluntary principle in the world of charities.

That paternalists believed in self-regulating laws may surprise some. A reading of Edmund Burke's *Thoughts on Scarcity,* however, should end that astonishment. He in no way hides his laissez faire economics. "Labour," he bluntly asserts, "is a commodity"; "the monopoly of capital . . . a great benefit"; and the pursuit of profit by "middlemen and jobbers, factors, speculators" a salutary practice. He defends the growth of large farms and is confident that "if the farmer is excessively avaricious, so much the better," since there is an "identity of interest . . . [that is] self-evident, due to the benign and wise Disposer of all things, who obliges all men . . . in pursuing their own self-interest to connect the general good with their own individual success." He called the laws of commerce the laws of Nature and of God, and though he acknowledges that government can "prevent much evil; it can do very little positive good." In general the less the government does the better. Burke wanted his statesman to remain in "the superior sphere" of high policy and not to descend "from a province to a parish and a parish to a private house."[26]

Coleridge probably winced in reading Burke's praise of avaricious farmers and profit-seeking jobbers, but he still shared Burke's belief in the laws of commerce. He was decidedly opposed to any government interference with landowners. He told the gentry in his *Lay Sermons* that their estates were "secured indeed from all human interference by every principle of law." The state should not regulate land. It should not even regulate commerce, but only manufactures. Coleridge wished to leave commerce to "the maxims of trade [which include] the unqualified right to do what I like with my own."[27]

Not every paternalist thinker agreed with Coleridge's praise of "maxims of trade" or Burke's laissez faire economics. Southey never felt at home with political economy, and William Sewell disdained it. But Southey and Sewell never questioned the sanctity of private property or the existence of harmonious social laws. They condemned political economy mainly because it preached the selfish principle and promoted the spirit of competition and individualism. Sewell and Southey believed in private property and self-regulating laws based on property as strongly as did Burke and Coleridge, but in their minds these self-regulating laws arose not from the pursuit of profit but from those paternal duties incumbent on the ownership of land. They believed in an identity of interests, but one based on property doing its duties. They too wanted government to leave property alone; and though they denounced the avaricious spirit of capitalism, their own belief that property had its duties as well as its rights led them to oppose government intervention as strongly as any believer in the laissez faire principles of political economy.[28] This general hostility to government allowed paternalist theorists to choose to incorporate or not to incorporate the axioms of political economy within their systems. Edmund Burke chose to, and with such fervor that Adam Smith called him his disciple. Thomas Chalmers also adopted laissez faire principles, winning a reputation both as a preacher of paternal doctrines and as a writer on political economy. Most paternalist writers, of course, had difficulty fusing laissez faire economics with a paternalist outlook because political economy ultimately led to a society whose unfettered individualism would destroy society's deferential bonds. But their antagonism to political economy's excessive individualism did not mean that they did not possess a moderate individualism of their own—one that formed the second reason they were jealous of government intervention.

The advocates of paternalism believed that the poor should be self-reliant, should stand on their own two feet, and should not be dependent on government. Thomas Chalmers was the most austere in holding this belief, as well as the most sanguine about its possibilities. He believed that the schoolmaster, the preacher, and the elders could so train up the poor in industry and frugality that neither church nor state would need to grant relief to the poor.[29] Chalmers was of course somewhat untypical. A Presbyterian minister and a resident of Scotland, which had little public relief, he reflected that country's strong Calvinist tradition of individual self-reliance.

But even Southey and Coleridge in discussing the poor shared some of Chalmer's sternness and his belief in the need for self-reliance. Coleridge in 1816 denounced the payment of relief to the able-bodied because it encouraged imprudence, and Southey in 1829 said he would give "the worthless poor no more relief than that which would prevent them from famishing." He added that poverty would disappear "if the poor were taught their duties . . . and became provident."[30] It was not an attitude conducive to the growth of a broad and generous welfare state.

Neither was the paternalist's high estimate of the voluntary principle in the field of charities conducive to the growth of such a state. If welfare had to be given to the distressed, it should be done through coal and blanket clubs, soup kitchens, almshouses, dispensaries, hospitals, and orphanages; and if the lower orders had to be educated, it should be in church schools whether Sunday or day; and if the lower orders needed reforming there were penitential homes, the Society for the Reformation of Manners, and the discharged prisoners' aid societies. The world of charities was vast, and it was a private world based on property, one in which, according to Burke, the government had no place. "In the province of charity," he wrote, "the magistrate has nothing at all to do: his interference is a violation of the property he is to protect."[31] Burke's successors agreed in considering inviolable the rights and prerogatives of private charities, particularly if the charities were in any way related to the church. Any government interference with their schools and colleges aroused furious opposition.

That many charities were corrupt and spent the income of the charities on banquets for the trustees rather than on the poor bothered them little, since real reform could not be legislated but had to come from the spiritual regeneration of the individual, from people becoming better. "I have no faith in Act of Parliament Reform," exclaimed Coleridge, "let us become better people." His faith in better people acting voluntarily to redress grievances was indeed so great that he looked to the earnest Christian boycotting slave products, rather than state intervention, as the best means of ending the slave trade. His friend William Wordsworth thought that the ending of slavery in the colonies should come from the voluntary actions of the individual slave owners and not from an Act of Parliament.[32]

That becoming better people and not reorganizing or remaking society would best reduce social evils was a widespread expectation among paternalist writers and one that fitted in with their anxiety to defend the status quo and with their love of local government. In Richard Oastler these dispositions and beliefs combined to produce a prolonged outcry against the evil of centralization. After watching the central government's poor-law commissioners force paupers into dismal workhouses, he decided, according to Cecil Driver, his biographer, that "the fundamental issue was spiritual, not organizational, and that until by some means the hearts of men could be changed these evils would continue." Southey and Sadler in the 1830s expressed very similar sentiments, as did Helps, Sewell, and Carlyle in the 1840s.[33] They wanted men of station and property to undergo a change of heart more than they wanted additional government bureaus. The paternalists in the early nineteenth century did not seek out new programs or schemes as much as they sought out a new moral resolve, a greater effort at benevolence. They agreed with Burke that "the only sure reform [is] the ceasing to do ill."[34]

By disposition religious and conservative, the paternalists looked to a

spiritual regeneration within existing arrangements for their social philosophy and not to changes in those existing institutions that they so
venerated. A hostility to innovation in a country with a weak central
government thus became a defense of an existing laissez faire philosophy.
Coleridge in 1816 concluded that the main aims of government had
largely been "realized to a degree unexampled in any other old and long
peopled government." He saw no great reason to expand those aims,
aims he once stated should be restricted to the "withholding or retard-
ing of all extrinsic and artificial aids to an injurious system." Michael
Sadler was also skeptical about change and about a larger government.
He not only said that the intervention of government was in itself an
evil but quoted Francis Bacon that "all innovation is with injury." One
of the best of adages, he said, was "live and let live."[35] The view that
innovation was with injury and that one should live and let live were
popular sentiments among paternalists, ones that expressed their liking
for the well-established, customary, and unregulated society they inherited
from the eighteenth century and ones that prized highly property, locality, "the maxims of trade," and voluntary charities.

Though paternalist writers were opposed to the growth of a bureaucratic and meddling government, they were in no way shy about calling
for an authoritarian one, a fact not without tensions and ambivalences.
All but Chalmers, Arnold, and Helps were for a government that would
suppress seditious writings, close down libelous presses, punish criminals
severely, repress disorderly meetings, and penalize dissent. Edmund
Burke, who wished the government to control thought because opinions
combining with passions "have much influence on actions," was a fervent
supporter of William Pitt's repressive legislation of 1795. Burke's successors Coleridge, Southey, and Sewell shared this authoritarian disposition. Southey loved feudalism because "there was a system of superintendence everywhere." He was eager to transport dangerous libelers to
Australia, superintend more closely public houses, and "punish vaga-
bonds and idle persons and curb the seditious press." Coleridge argued
that the state in theory could repress heresy and in practice ought to
suppress lotteries, close theaters on Sundays, and exclude dissenters from
Oxford and Cambridge and Catholics from Parliament.[36] William Sewell,
also an opponent of Catholic Emancipation, was also an enemy of heresy
and sedition. In his *Christian Politics* he called for "one external authority to harmonize all acts." The paternalists loved monarchy and could
not resist wishing it stronger. Coleridge rejoiced at the resurgence in

Europe of a "disgust with representative government" and its turn toward "a pure monarchy . . . in which . . . the reason of the people shall become apparent in the will of the King." Disraeli in his novels saw in a resurgent monarchy the true protector of the people, and Thomas Carlyle in 1850 called for "a King made in the image of God, who could a little achieve for the people." In *Past and Present,* published in 1843, Carlyle had declared that the end of government was "to guide men in the ways wherein they should go."[37]

There was more romantic rhetoric in these statements than realistic intent, yet their underlying authoritarian tendencies were anything but rhetorical when it came to laws against seditious writings, the defense of capital punishment, or support for coercion acts in Ireland. What was wanted was not a government of more departments but of more statutory powers enabling local authorities to suppress dangerous agitators.

The distinction between an authoritarian government and a meddling government—a distinction unconsciously assumed more than self-consciously defined—increased only further the complexity and ambivalence of the paternalists' views of the proper role of government. None of the paternalist writers was systematic in his analysis of the proper functions of government. Their many deeply held beliefs about property, maxims of trade, and voluntarism and their tendency to look to a spiritual regeneration within the status quo, led them to oppose the growth of a more active government. But they also, on other occasions, had reasons—authoritarian, humanitarian, and self-interested—to call loudly for a more active government, for one that protected children from rapacious manufacturers, farmers from cheap foreign grain, and merchant shippers from foreign competition. As early as 1818, Coleridge in *The Grounds of Sir Robert Peel's Bill (for the Regulation of Factories) Vindicated* urged the government to end child labor in the factories, while in 1830 Robert Southey called for "a patriarchal, that is to say a parental government," one that would facilitate enclosures, reform settlement laws, abolish urban interments, finance emigration, promote colonization, regulate factories, revive guilds, and help establish sisters of charity. Arnold and Helps had their schemes too, and they too spoke out on occasion for a stronger government. The paternalist writers were not always modest in their terminology. Just as Southey called for a "parental government," so Michael Sadler called for a "Protective State" and William Wordsworth for one that stood "in *loco parentis* to the poor." Sadler was a stout supporter of mercantilist legislation while Wordsworth wanted the legislature to make "effectual provision that no one shall be in danger of perishing."[38] Paternalist thought did have a strand to it that promoted government intervention. But it was a strand that was intertwined with a decided preference for local and private authorities. Sadler and Wordsworth, like Arnold, Helps, and Southey called for legislation, not government departments, and they looked for the execution of laws to the persons of station and rank in local spheres, whether owners of estates, managers of charities, or parish and county officials. It is the intertwining in their thought of these various strands that makes the paternalist writers so ambivalent about demanding the intervention of an effective administrative state.[39]

There was in fact only one paternalist writer among the twenty listed above who really wanted a powerful government, Thomas Carlyle, and then mainly in 1850 when he wrote *The Latter-Day Pamphlets*. In that work Carlyle saw the state as the "key stone of a most real organization of labour," one that would organize all paupers into industrial regiments, force captains of industry to cooperate with it, and organize the clergy and teachers into "sacred corporations."[40]

Carlyle was a Scotsman who was thirty-nine years old by the time he settled in London. He was by then steeped in French and German ideas. He had fewer roots in English life than Sewell, Helps, or Seeley and fewer loyalties to parish, magistracy, and church. Furthermore, he had been touched by Saint Simonian ideas on the planned and efficient organization of labor—even organization by the state. These facts, in addition to his violently impatient temperament and his worship of might, led him to call for captains of industry and sovereign bodies to organize the idle into regiments of industrial soldiers. But his call had little effect. Not only was he too vague and bombastic in calling for "Industrial Colonels, Workmasters, Life-Commanders, equitable as Rhadamanthus and inflexible as he," but he ridiculed most legislative remedies by calling them mere "Morison's Pills." He was inept on specifics. In 1839 he ended his *Chartism* by calling for two remedies, education and emigration, remedies that the press called mere commonplaces. "He is as ignorant of remedies," said the *Sun*, "as the Duke of Buckingham and Mrs. Bradshaw."[41]

The same was true of Southey and his prolific schemes. There was more fancifulness than effective planning in his guilds and sisters of charities. His friend Henry Taylor of the Privy Council Office told him he would make no statesman as he was blind to difficulties, and the ebullient Southey agreed, adding that he saw England's social evils in moral and religious terms, not in economic or administrative ones.[42]

But it was more than merely thinking in moral and religious terms that prevented Southey from translating his schemes into legislative realities: there was also the fact that he, like the other paternalist writers, saw government as a vast network of private and public authorities within which vested interests held sway, and to Southey, deservedly held sway. "Vested rights," he wrote, "are the key stone of the social edifice."[43] Such a belief, when combined with temperaments that were averse to viewing society in technical, abstract, and statistical terms kept paternalist theorists from ever rivaling utilitarians and economists as the architects of an administrative state. The paternalist writers were not statists, and they did not look to the state for panaceas. Much more promising to them as a panacea was that institution they considered the most sacred of all, the Church of England.

The Paternal Mission of the Church

Deeply religious persons in early Victorian England had an affinity with the paternalist outlook. The very image of God our father in heaven is a paternal one. To preach, instruct, warn, exhort, correct, and guide were the deeply felt duties of those who carried out Jesus' command to go forth and preach the gospel—and many of these duties are also paternal ones. It is thus not surprising that of the twenty paternalist writers all but one were men of earnest Christian faith—the one exception being again Thomas Carlyle. Carlyle, of course, would be incensed to have his intense yea-saying faith in Providence, History, Morality, Truth, and Fact not considered religious, but to his more orthodox contemporaries he was dangerously pantheistic. Indeed there is a striking similarity in the fact that just as his pantheism pressed hard on his Calvinism, so in the *Latter-Day Pamphlets* did a strong statism press against a more pluralistic and traditional paternalism. There was too much of the radical in Carlyle for him to remain comfortable with old orthodoxies, Christian or paternalist; but for those who had faith in the saving grace of Christ and his father, the Christian church had a truly paternal role to play.

English paternalists had other particularly strong reasons for looking to the Church of England: it was an old and venerable institution with roots in a glorious past; it was also, in their own time, wealthy, well established, and active; and finally it, of all institutions, held out the promise of transforming men and so society.

That it had a glorious past, particularly in medieval and Tudor times, may raise the eyebrows of skeptical twentieth-century historians but not

of those many early Victorians of diverse outlooks who joined William
Cobbett, Richard Oastler, Benjamin Disraeli, and Augustus Welby Pugin
in believing that before the Reformation and the dissolution of the
monasteries there was a church that actively cared for the poor, preached
social responsibilities to the rich, and educated all in holiness, piety, and
righteousness. The Reformation, according to these writers, destroyed
that world. Monasteries no longer opened their gates to hungry travelers,
friars no longer tended the sick and destitute, cathedral schools ceased
to educate the sons of gentlemen and grocers alike, the chapels and
chantries of towns no longer gave the people spiritual solace, and, worst
of all, the state wrested the care of the poor from the more humane
ministrations of the parish priest. The organic community of medieval
times was destroyed, and in its place arose the crass, competitive, secular,
mammon-worshipping world of commercial and industrial England. The
contrast overwhelmed Pugin and inspired him to publish in 1836 his
Contrasts, with its famous illustrations contrasting a medieval and a modern town. The medieval town was a sea of spires crowning ecclesiastical
buildings that helped people, the contemporary town a crowded scene
full of socialist halls, lunatic asylums, jails, gas works, workhouses, and
factory chimneys.[44] Robert Southey had the same vision as Pugin of the
happy united ecclesiastical society of medieval times. Both in his *Book
of the Church* and in his *Thomas More* he looks back with great nostalgia to those abbeys that dispensed alms, schools that educated, nuns
who nursed the ill, and parish clergymen who visited and prayed for the
poor and instructed feudal barons in their Christian duties.

But however romantic was Southey's vision of a lost world it could
not compare to the rhapsodic nostalgia of Kenelm Digby in *Broad Stone*
and *Mores Catholici.* Digby's mind was lost in reveries of the past. What
a wonderful age it seemed to him: "No lawyers, no rich manufacturers
. . . no speculators," but instead venerable curates caring for their flocks
and abbeys, monasteries, chapels, chantries, hospitals, all with men of
piety praying for and succoring the poor, and a poor not overly educated
but meek, dependent, obedient.[45] Though later ages have rightly
doubted these romantic visions, many early Victorians did not. They
loved Southey's and Digby's evocations of the past mission of the Church,
just as they delighted in William Cobbett's *Protestant Reformation* with
its glowing picture of monasteries that "helped all that were in need
of relief, advice and protection," that "promoted rectitude in morals";
and of hospitals, over fifty for every county, that "were always open to
the poor, to the aged, the orphans, the widows, and the strangers"; and

whose generosity was emulated in turn by the opulent classes.[46] Many early Victorians thus believed that the pre-Reformation Church did far more for its votaries than did the secular, latitudinarian Church of their day. And just as they paid Pugin to revive the Gothic style, so they looked to the Church of England to help refashion society according to the ideals of the past.

The materials for that refashioning existed in the wealth and power of the Church of England. With 11,342 benefices, 2 archbishoprics, 24 bishoprics, 26 chancellorships, 28 deans, 61 archdeacons, 574 prebendaries and canons, 330 minor cathedral offices, and a total income of more than nine million pounds, the Church of England formed a present reality almost as promising as the visions of its past glory. William Wordsworth in his "Postscript" stated that the Church could meet the challenge of those new ugly manufacturing towns that Pugin found so forbidding. What the new towns lacked, said Wordsworth, was the feudal influence of landed proprietors; they therefore needed the presence of the Church. They needed, he said, "ministers . . . of irreproachable manners and morals, [men] thoroughly acquainted with the structure of society." As solutions went it was not without merit: the Church of England was one of the wealthiest institutions, and its 11,948 clergymen formed a personnel more than half the size of England's entire central bureaucracy.[47] The nonconformist churches and the Roman Catholics also had their chapels and churches, their endowments and contributors, and their ministers and priests. England was, furthermore, still a believing nation.

Promising also was the fact that, according to Coleridge, the Church of England and parts of nonconformity reflected a powerful spiritual force more vital than its material resources, namely, the "Idea" of a truly "National Church." That Church, which Coleridge said represented "Nationality," would, because of its own extensive property, be independent of civil government, though still a part of the larger "Idea of the State." It would, wrote Coleridge, "comprehend the learned of all denominations, the sages and professors of the law, jurisprudence, medicine, and psychology, of music, of military, and civil architecture, of their physical sciences."[48] This body, which Coleridge called the clerisy, would do all that Southey's abbeys, schools, universities, sisters of charity, and parsons would do and more. The clerisy would, above all, whether in parish schools, universities, or academies, educate and civilize the people.

Coleridge delighted in expressing his social theories in the language of German idealism, in discerning those essential "Ideas" that defined historical institutions. Others found such Platonic reasoning less necessary. Men as pragmatic as Thomas Chalmers and Thomas Arnold saw in a more active church the same promise of social improvement as did Coleridge, but they expressed it in plainer language. Chalmers wanted the local church to be the town's chief paternal authority, with the ministers, elders, deacons, and schoolteachers its fatherly guardians. The elders were to visit the poor and by prayers and Bible reading spread the gospel. Nothing, said Chalmers, would be so reformatory and so productive of sobriety, industry, and self-reliance. The deacons would visit the indigent, not so much to grant relief as to find them jobs or to discover those of their kin who could help them. Only the smitten of God—the blind, the halt, the diseased—would receive relief from the kirk and that only from a fund voluntarily given in the spirit of Christian charity. There would be no state relief at all for the poor. Chalmers's paternalism rested solidly on the church.[49]

The idea of reviving and expanding the order of deacons was a most attractive one for those who looked to the church as the foundation of a more paternalist society. Thomas Arnold urged that the Church of England include laymen in its order of deacons and have them visit the sick, manage charitable subscriptions, and share with the minister his many clerical duties. Arnold, whose *Principles of Church Reform* was published in 1833 and republished in 1845, also wished to subdivide all large dioceses and multiply the number of bishops so that there would be one for every large town. He also wished to apply the incomes of prebends and rich benefices to new urban churches, enforce residence on the absentee clergy, and discipline corrupt and sporting parsons. The clergy and deacons of this reformed "Diaconates," like Chalmers's ministers, elders, and deacons, and like Coleridge's learned men, would instruct the lower orders in habits of industry and virtue and their superiors in their Christian responsibilities.[50] Few paternalists would disagree with Arnold's vision in terms of its goals, but many of them, particularly if High Church, found his means scandalous. Imagine redistributing the wealth of the Anglican Church! And imagine laymen performing services reserved to the ordained priest!

The Reverend William Sewell, who had as exalted a view of a clerisy as Arnold, and who also called for the multiplication of bishops and a larger clergy, wanted more parliamentary grants, not the redistribution of the Church's wealth, and he was totally opposed to laymen doing priestly functions. For this last reason he also disapproved of R. B. Seeley's desire for laymen to become district visitors. Seeley, who felt that the clergy were "the natural guardians and advisors of the poor" and could "achieve what no mere legislation can ever attempt," wanted district visitors to help the clergy care for the destitute and the ill. High Churchmen could not abide the intrusion of the unordained into pastoral work, even though the spiritual famine and temporal destitution of large cities cried out for their use. High Churchmen like Sewell were indeed unbelievably sanguine in their expectations of what the ordained clergy could do alone. Sewell even asked Parliament to transfer the poor laws from the state to the church, since only the clergy could discriminate between the worthy and the unworthy poor.[51]

William Sewell's belief that the clergy could better care for the poor than the state and that the Church of England could refashion society along Christian principles reflects a quite extraordinary faith in the transforming powers of that Church, and it was a faith evangelicals shared. Whether High Church or Low, whether he presided over the magical sacrament of the mass or inspired the rebirth of the soul through faith in Christ, it was the man of God, not the man of property or public office, who had the miraculous powers of remaking men. And since it was a cardinal proposition of paternalism that spiritual regeneration, not the passage of more legislation, would reform society, it followed that the men of God held the true means of building a better world.

It was also an age increasingly persuaded of the powers of education. Paternalists in the past had doubts about educating the poor, but by the 1830s, with the rise of radicalism, crime, large cities, and the efforts of the National Society and the British and Foreign School Society, the education of the lower orders had became inevitable. If inevitable, however, it must be the Church that controlled it.

Belief in the redeeming powers of the Church was great and extensive, coloring even the outlook of the Christian Socialists. For F. D. Maurice, in his *Kingdom of Christ,* the church would be the architect of a new society, one in which cooperation, not competition, would be the rule, and for his fellow Christian Socialists, John Minter Morgan and J. M. Ludlow, the key institution for that socialization would be the parish. The parish and not the state would create a cooperative society, and the paternalism of both squire and parson, not the common ownership of property, would be their means. The Christian Socialists of the 1840s were far more Christian than socialist in outlook, and far more paternalist than democratic. Ludlow's remedy for distress was for men of wealth to cooperate with the clergy and to use the parish's vestry as a means of creating temples of labor for the employment of the jobless. John Minter Morgan, in his *Religion and Crime,* published in 1840, wanted the same elite to use the parish for the formation of village institutes, which would include labor exchanges, reading rooms, and friendly and temperance societies, and which would distribute soup and coal to the necessitous poor. The "intelligent and wealthy" would supervise these institutes and would exclude from them the unworthy poor, the illiterate, drunkards, and gamblers. Ludlow's temples of labor and Morgan's village institutes were secular as well as religious, and some would doubt that they fulfilled Coleridge's vision of a clerisy. But the center for these temples and institutes was the parish, that ancient ecclesiastical unit of the church, and in the writings of F. D. Maurice, the leader of the Christian Socialists, it is clear that the church, not the state, not even property in common, would be the means of transforming England from a competitive and individualistic society to a cooperative and organic one.[52]

In an age as intensely religious as was early Victorian England, paternalists of all persuasions saw the church as one of the central means of forming in the future a better society. This hope for a future regeneration through religion combined with a nostalgic view of the church's medieval past and with an awareness of its practical immediate strength to make the paternalism of the church a very central part of those larger theories of paternalism that were developed by early nineteenth-century intellectuals.

Great and earnest as were the promises held out by a resurgent church, they were promises doomed to collide with two irrepressible forces: dissent and the state. Nearly one-half of those attending a church service in the 1840s did not go to an Anglican service but to services conducted by the Methodists, Congregationalists, Baptists, Presbyterians, Quakers, Unitarians, Swedenborgians, and Roman Catholics.[53] In Scotland they divided their attendance between the established and the reformed church. How could one establish a clerisy from such disparate faiths? That question had to be answered before the paternalism of the church could be effective.

For some, like Coleridge, Arnold, and Maurice, the answer was a more comprehensive church, one that included more than Anglicans; for the less liberal the answer was a church exclusively Anglican. The High

Church William Sewell supported such an exclusiveness, as did his foe on the evangelical front, R. B. Seeley. Both, for example, wanted the Church of England to assume sole control of education, Sewell because he could not endure cooperating with "a desecrated, creedless, church-less state" and thought it perilous to have common intercourse with those in "a state of heathenism, heresy and schism," Seeley because he looked forward to the time when "we have gained the victory over the dis-senters."[54] Such a prospect was an impossibility. Sewell and Seeley were indulging in fantasies, fantasies that their fellow Anglicans W. G. Ward and Arthur Helps avoided by saying nothing at all about the matter. Coleridge, Arnold, and Maurice were not so timid. Coleridge in *On the Constitution of the Church and State* would have his clerisy include the learned of all Protestant denominations and Arnold all Christians except Quakers, Unitarians, and Roman Catholics. Arnold's list of those to be excluded makes him appear less tolerant than Coleridge, but Coleridge's tolerance in *Church and State* proved rather academic and did not fit his outbursts in *Table Talk*, where he could exclude dissenters from univer-sities and Catholics from Parliament and where he spoke disparagingly of sectaries and of the toleration of heresies. Coleridge could not square the circle of his vision of an active clerisy and a truly national church with the realities of secularism and sectarianism. Thomas Arnold in try-ing to resolve this dilemma was specific, with the result that he irritated all parties. The dilemma was, in fact, unresolvable unless men either agreed on theological truths or on their unimportance.[55]

F. D. Maurice, professor of English literature and modern history at King's College, London, had the boldness to attempt to bring about the former. He tried to persuade all faiths to agree on certain basic truths about the meaning of baptism, eucharist, and the creeds, these truths being, he thought, equally revealed to all by man's conscience and man's mystical intuitions. On these essential truths he would build a universal church, a church whose extended activities would end that egotism and competitiveness that was tearing England apart.[56] The theological basis for such a church was less rationalist and less secular than the ideas of Thomas Arnold, but it was unorthodox enough on the doctrine of eternal damnation to lose Maurice his professorship. The abuse poured on Arnold and Maurice showed that the idea of combining Anglican and non-Anglican Christians into one active clerisy was in the 1840s a will-o'-the-wisp. No one seeking to construct a viable theory of paternalism could solve the problem of the role of dissent in an expanded clerisy.

Neither did any of these writers solve the problem of the relationship of church and state.

Had the Church of England been wealthier or had its resolve to apply its wealth more equitably been greater, there would have been less dependence on the state. For the Congregational and Baptist voluntarists the answer was simple: the state should have nothing to do with religion. It was the solution of Thomas Chalmers who called for the entire separation of church and state. The other extreme was also voiced by a Scotsman, Thomas Carlyle, who wanted his "New Downing Street" to organize the clergy into "sacred corporations." Chalmers would reduce the state to the role of mere policeman and judge and expand the church's role in education and poor relief. His voluntarism had a theocratic edge to it, the church managing what the state usually did. A church resting solely on the contributions of its congregation and its own property would be paramount in civic affairs. Carlyle would do the reverse. Though he insisted that all societies needed an "Aristocracy and Priesthood, a Governing Class and a Teaching Class," his disdain of the Church of England in the 1840s was too intense to accord the priesthood much of a role. Despite talk of eternal verities and fulminations against skepticism, Carlyle was a secularist, and his paternalist heroes were captains of industry and sanitary inspectors, not clergymen.[57] Between the extremes of Chalmers's voluntarism and Carlyle's statism other theorists of paternalism sought their respective solutions.

For Coleridge the church was separate from the civil government, but both were part of the idea of the state. It was an interesting synthesis of two ideas, a dialectical resolution of two powerful forces. But it did not work even for Coleridge himself because he preferred the church to the state. He wanted the church to rest securely on its extensive property, and he, somewhat like Chalmers, wanted it to control many secular affairs. His clerisy and not a government department would incorporate the work of lawyers, professors, and men of science. He preferred the church, not the state, to manage society since the church, not the state, was a "democracy." It was a democracy, he added, because it treated men as individuals while the state treated men as classes.[58] "Democracy" did not mean majority rule for Coleridge but personal participation in local spheres; hence the church joins parishes, corporations, and joint-stock companies in constituting those local and restricted spheres in which democracy would exist. It is a peculiar definition but one that underlines once again how paternalist theory valued so very much a pluralistic world of local spheres. Since private property gave these spheres autonomy and the central government threatened them, the classical paternalist thinkers remained jealous of any state control of the church. Thinkers theologically as different as Sewell, Maurice, and Seeley thus united in wanting the Church of England to be a national, established, and favored Church, but one that would be in no way controlled by the state. William Sewell, after watching Parliament grow neutral toward the Church of England, decided that the state had become "powerful only for evil," and he therefore no longer sought its aid. But he was still jealous for the Church's own prerogatives, its church rates, its tithes, its fees, its property. He hoped upon these prerogatives to establish a monopoly over education and the relief of the poor. "The voluntary principle," Sewell finally proclaimed, "has always been recognized and maintained by the Catholic Church."[59]

F. D. Maurice, far more liberal than Sewell, still was jealous of the state. He was most distressed when his colleague at King's College, the Reverend John Allen, became, in 1839, an education inspector, distressed because, as he wrote Allen, the Church, not the state, had the right to supervise schools. Seeley felt equally jealous, as did his friends Sadler and Oastler, a jealousy coming not only from their inordinate loyalty to the Church of England, but strengthened by a fierce dislike of a state that enforced the New Poor Law.[60]

Only two, besides Carlyle, of those who sought to construct a paternalist society, really looked to the state: Thomas Arnold and J. M. Ludlow. Arnold wished the church to fuse with the state; the two were, he said, really identical, the ends of both being the truly Christian commonwealth. Since Arnold considered that "religious society is only the civil society fully enlightened," he concluded that "the State in its highest perfection is the Church."[61] Arnold's fusion of church and state was for Sewell, Seeley, and Maurice a chilling sentiment, as Erastian as Carlyle's New Downing Street. It was also as blasphemous to many as J. M. Ludlow's novel solution to the ancient problem of church and state: Ludlow proposed that Parliament grant money to all faiths and allow each to create its own clerisy. There would thus be competition among the sects to do the most Christian work in the creation of a paternal society. To the devout Anglican, whether High Church or evangelical, Ludlow, Arnold, and Carlyle were secularists and liberals, not true believers in Christianity. To true Christians it would be blasphemy to give money to a creed that taught falsehood; Parliament should give

grants to their faith alone or to none. But it was obvious that after 1832
the reformed Parliament would give to all faiths or to none. Parliament
in fact could only create a secular paternalism, a fact that led John Henry
Newman to withdraw from serious thought on the social question. In
1877 he wrote a letter explaining why. For fifty years, he said, "there has
been a formidable movement . . . towards assigning in the national life
political or civil motives for social and personal duties and thereby
withdrawing matters of conduct from the jurisdiction of religion." He
gave as examples of such withdrawals the advent of the New Poor Law,
civil marriages, and school boards. He said that such measures "tend to
the destruction of religion."[62] Newman, like his fellow Tractarians,
shared the basic assumptions of paternalism, most particularly its emphasis on the church's role in training up and succoring the poor. But he did
not write about it. An exceptionally keen and sensitive thinker, he saw
the hopeless dilemma of applying Coleridge's idea of a clerisy to a society
filled with religious divisiveness in a nation that was becoming increasingly secular. The promise of the church to remake man and society was
just as brittle as the hope of property doing its duties, and the paternalists' view of the proper role of the church was as complex and ambivalent as their view of the state. The paternalist outlook had many noble
ideals and many concrete strengths, but it also had many weaknesses.
Why then did it win the support of some of the most profound thinkers
of early nineteenth-century England and elicit in that period more books
and pamphlets on its behalf than at any other time in English history?

Reasons for the Revival: Social, Intellectual, and Institutional

The above analysis of the attempt of early nineteenth-century writers to
construct a theory of paternalism in terms of the duties of property and
the paternal role of government and church imputes to their writings
more system and coherence than belongs to them. Only William Sewell
in his *Christian Politics* constructed a unified and consistent social philosophy. It is a strange work, neglected in its time and neglected still. It
is an ingenious work, Gothic in its pronounced love of a pluralistic
society yet like a well-built Gothic cathedral possessing a unity. Sewell
fuses together the major and minor axioms of paternalism into a lovely
whole, but as a result his edifice seems idealized and unreal, almost a
caricature. It was probably unwise to put together the not always con-

cordant parts of the paternalist outlook: better and more convincing was the preaching and extolling of its particular parts within the context of particular issues. This is a fact that most writers of a paternalist persuasion, whether Coleridge in his *Lay Sermons* or Arnold in his *Letters on Social Conditions* or Helps in *The Claims of Labour,* realized. These writers were in great part proselytizers of specific solutions and wisely resisted the construction of a comprehensive system.

Not all, however, were proselytizers; some were dreamers. Digby in *Broad Stone* and *Mores Catholici,* Southey in *Thomas More,* and Pugin in *Contrasts* were not looking so much for solutions as directing the attention of their readers to the beauties—social, religious, and architectural—of the past. But though these proselytizers and dreamers did not seek, in Sewell's self-conscious and systematic manner, to build a logical social theory, they did reflect those assumptions and attitudes that constituted the paternalist outlook. Certainly none of them contradicted or denounced any of those assumptions, even if they did not put them together. Their collective writings thus strengthened all those axioms that William Sewell fitted together so harmoniously in *Christian Politics.*

It was a social outlook that for all its weaknesses enjoyed enormous popularity. It did so because it reflected three sets of historical forces that converged in early nineteenth-century England. The first of these forces was the economic and social changes that resulted from a population explosion, the advent of capitalist farming, an industrial revolution, and urbanization. The second force was the intellectual developments associated with historical studies, romantic literature, and evangelical religion. The third was a strong conservative attachment to old and tried institutions.

The economic and social changes of early nineteenth-century England were momentous and led directly to the revival and invigoration of paternalist ideas. They forced the governing classes to think seriously about social problems. The manufacturing depression of 1816 and Sir Robert Peel's bill on child labor in factories in 1818 led Coleridge to publish in the field of social thought. The French wars were over; social discontent and depressions now dominated men's minds. In 1817 Southey told a friend that "the steam and spinning engines" had caused unprecedented and dangerous changes, ones producing "vice, poverty, wretchedness, disaffection, political insecurity." That danger was still great in 1832 when Thomas Arnold asked, "Has the world ever seen a population as dangerous . . . as the manufacturing population of Great

Britain, crowded together in their most formidable masses?"[63] The very titles of paternalist writings show them to be a response to social upheavals: Carlyle called his first social tract *Chartism,* and R. B. Seeley entitled his two expositions of the paternal system *The Perils of the Nation* and *Remedies Suggested for Some of the Evils which Constitute the Perils of the Nation.*

Among the perils that haunted these thinkers, that of the breakdown of a hierarchical and unified society loomed large. Coleridge laments, in a letter to a friend, that society no longer "resembles a chain that ascends in a continuity of links," Southey sees in the decline of the small farmer "the loss of a link in the social chain," Helps is uneasy over the rise of "a disconnected society," and Arnold finds the workers' neighborhood nothing but "a mixed multitude of persons . . . with nothing to bind them."[64] This sense of the disruption of a hitherto harmonious and deferential society colors the response of these writers to an increasingly urban England and accounts in part for their turn backward to the paternalist world of the past. They feared greatly the consequences of its dissolution.

They also feared violent disorders. The Chartists had revolted in 1839 and rioted again in 1842. These were years of acute depression. They were also years in which government commissions brought to a climax their revelations of those abuses that resulted from profound economic changes in town and country. These abuses did not follow from the industrial revolution alone. Children had long been exploited on farms, in cottage industry, and in small shops. Nor was the standard of life in the 1830s and 1840s lower than in the eighteenth century. What had happened was a concentration of abuses in towns, a new standard of expectations on the part of workers, and on the part of the governing classes a growing awareness of social problems and a belief that they could be remedied. The severe depression that persisted from 1839 through 1842 focused and accentuated all of these changes. It is then no accident that the six years between 1839 and 1845 saw the publication of the quite explicitly paternalist pleas of Carlyle, Seeley, Helps, Sewell, Disraeli, Morgan, Osborne, Sanford, and Perry, and the republication of Coleridge's *Lay Sermons,* Arnold's social tracts, and Southey's *Book of the Church*—some seventeeen works in all. Two decades later, in the prosperous fifties and sixties, such pleas gave way to the ideal of a laissez faire society, as expounded by Samuel Smiles, Herbert Spencer, the *Economist,* and the Charitable Organization Society. The revival of paternalist ideas was, however short-lived, clearly a response to social and economic changes.

Economic and social changes do not alone explain the revival and amplification of paternalist ideas. These same changes drove others to champion other solutions, whether it was to create more philanthropic societies, more government departments, a more laissez faire society, or more Owenite communities. Intellectual developments also influence a person's perception of social problems and their solutions. In some cases, as with Kenelm Digby and William Sewell, these developments seem far more important than the social perils of the moment. Such perils seldom invaded Digby's quiet chambers at Trinity College, Cambridge, or Sewell's study at Exeter College, Oxford, or their lofty works of history and philosophy.

Digby indeed seemed the embodiment of those three intellectual developments that favored paternalist writings: a growing interest in history and past times, a romantic turn to feeling and passion in literature, and the growth of religious seriousness. All three developments formed part of the nineteenth century's reaction to the mechanistic philosophies, arid rationalism, and skeptical deism of the eighteenth century, and all three are crucial to Digby's writings.

The influence on Digby's works of Sir Walter Scott and of the blossoming of medieval studies was great. He admitted that his boyhood reading of Scott led to his *Broad Stone of Honour*. Many others also delighted in Scott's re-creations of past ages. Coleridge said that he read Scott's Waverley novels two or three times.[65] Scott's novels were probably more widely read than the works of any other author by the young men who, by the 1840s, were the rulers of England. Scott did not preach any specific paternalist doctrines in his novels nor did he romanticize the past as glowingly as Digby. But as an admirer of Burke he valued highly those institutions that are the backdrop of his enthralling tales— particularly those of property and authority. His celebration of the stability and excellence of ancient institutions and ways, rather than any sermons on the duties of property, furthered the growth of paternalist attitudes.

His exciting tales and graphic descriptions of past times also led to a ready escape from the ugly realities of industrial England. Scott, of course, was not alone in this new interest in the past; it was quite the rage. In 1839 hundreds of gentlemen and ladies attended the medieval tournament at Eglinton, Scotland, while from 1806 to 1836 John Lingard, Francis Palgrave, and Sharon Turner wrote about the remote world of Anglo-Saxon England. Alfred the Great, St. Augustine and Bede, the monks of Jarrow and Rievaulx, the begging friars, and feudal barons all became the new heroes, and all reflected a society that seemed beautiful in its hierarchical and authoritarian unity.

The paternalist societies of medieval times also seemed to produce men of greater sensibility and feeling than the eighteenth century with its Robert Walpoles and Bernard de Mandevilles and its Popes and Chesterfields. For men who preferred the warmer and more personal responses of Wordsworth to the calculations of men always prudent, the intimate personal relations involved in paternalism had a great appeal. They certainly did for Digby. He was distinguished above all, according to his friend Julius Hare, by "a compassion of the heart."[66] Many an early Victorian found just that in Wordsworth's sympathy toward suffering in "The Ruined Cottage" and "Female Vagrant." "The compassion of the heart" was, however, no preserve of Tory poets. It informed Robert Burns's humanity, Shelley's idealism, and Keats's sensibility and was part of a pervasive shift in values that, as a reaction to eighteenth-century restraint and rationalism, heightened in many the resolve to relieve suffering by becoming, as Coleridge put it, a better person. When faced with the alternatives of the laissez faire principles of Ricardo, the arid *Constitutional Code* of Bentham, or the Calvinist strictures of the evangelical philanthropists, the injunction to be a better person within spheres where intimacy could occur seemed the best solution to the alarming ills of society.

Digby, and many like him—Coleridge, Southey, Wordsworth, Sewell—also reacted to the deism of the eighteenth century and turned to a more devout and earnest faith. It was an age of serious religion, whether in the form of William Wilberforce's earnest evangelicalism or John Henry Newman's Anglo-Catholic revival. At Oxford in the 1830s that revival made the deepest impression on the youth of England, just as at Cambridge Charles Simeon and the evangelicals inspired many of its undergraduates. No other intellectual development had a greater impact on the revival of paternalism than the new seriousness with which early Victorians took their religious faith: it inspired countless model squires and model parsons as it did most of the authors of paternalist writings. This new seriousness led to a demand that ecclesiastical institutions play a much larger role in society and to a belief that the answer to social problems lay with the moral efforts of the individual. "There is no other means whereby nations can be reformed," wrote Southey, "than by that which alone individuals can be regenerated."[67]

The turn to religious seriousness, like the historical interest in the past and the romantic movement in poetry, was in part a reaction to the ideas of the eighteenth century. Intellectual movements, being dialectical, occur in part as responses to earlier ideas that no longer satisfy and to rival ideas that seem abhorrent. The ideas of political economy had such an effect: they drove some to expound more vigorously than ever before the tenets of paternalism. Southey was certainly inspired to extol the organic, deferential, and paternal society because it provided an antidote to the crass individualism of Malthus and Ricardo. The Coleridge of *Table Talk* ("political economy is humbug") felt the same way, as did Thomas Carlyle. William Cobbett, half paternalist, half radical, railed against the political economists, as did Seeley, Oastler, and Sadler. For Sadler, hatred of political economy was an obsession. Seeley said that Sadler formulated the PATERNAL SYSTEM as part of his "endless war against the system of the political economists."[68]

Intellectual developments work in many ways, both as reactions to older and rival systems and as reflections of ideas deeply woven into existing institutions. Paternalist ideas in the 1830s and 1840s did both, winning them the support not only of the romantic, historically minded, and deeply religious among intellectuals but of those thousands of ordinary persons who were attached to the local parish's management of the poor or the bishop's superintendence of his diocese. Two books published in the late 1960s demonstrate how the *viz inertia* of institutional life gave a persisting power to paternalist ideas: J. R. Poynter's *Society and Pauperism, English Ideas on Poor Relief* and R. A. Soloway's *Prelates and People, Ecclesiastical Social Thought in England.* Poynter deals with more than twenty writers on the poor law who published between 1795 and 1835 and Soloway with the writings of those archbishops and bishops who ran the Church of England from 1783 to 1852. Both found many strong paternalists among the writers they studied. Though some of the poor-law writers were advocates of the new political economy, Malthus among them, few doubted that the gentry, clergy, and farmers should control, superintend, and care for those beneath them. The Reverend Edmund Poulter had no doubts in 1795 that the landlord and farmer had fatherly roles to play. He urged them, as magistrates and overseers, to judge both a family's earning power and its proper level of expenditure and then grant only as much relief as needed—and not a penny more. "It is more useful," he wrote "to teach them to spend less, save a little, than to give them more." The poor-law pamphleteers of the early nineteenth century thought instinctively in terms of controlling the lives of those beneath them: J. N. Brewer in 1807 demanded "a strict moral regimen in which a contention in moral decency and parental care, would replace the village cudgelling match," while Thomas Bernard in 1799 urged "the GUARDIANS AND PROTECTORS OF THE POOR" not only to give those who cannot work relief but to find jobs for the jobless and give children regular employment at home or in schools of industry.[69]

All of these injunctions would fit well with the social outlook of the Anglican bishops. The eighteenth-century bishops passed on to their nineteenth-century successors a hierarchical and paternal vision of society. Bishop Horsley, in 1786, assumed that God and nature had created ranks and economic inequality. "Thus every man's ability," he told the clergy, "of being serviceable to the public, is limited by his habits and genius to a certain sphere."[70] It is an opinion not unlike Coleridge's insistence on HOMEBORN FEELINGS, and one amplified in the nineteenth century by many bishops who emphasized the parish as that "certain sphere" most central to the "habits and genius" of the clergyman. The growth of evangelicalism led both clergy and laymen to superintend their parishes with a conscientiousness not seen since Puritan days—and the challenge being laid down by the evangelicals, High Church clergymen redoubled their zeal for parish work. From Turvey in Bedfordshire, where the Reverend Legh Richmond in the beginning of the century created a model parish with cottage lectures, Sunday schools, savings banks, and friendly societies (which could have no banquets, could not meet at the public house, and had to hear Richmond on "Mutual Support, Unity and Patience") to the spiritually destitute East End of London, where Bishop Blomfield in 1836 planned to create fifty new churches each with its school, visiting society, and charities, the idea that the clergy should be the main instruments of social reform and control had become an inextricable part of the Church of England.

The publications of the Reverend Legh Richmond and Bishop Blomfield along with endless sermons by clergymen of all persuasions had also made these ideas commonplace.[71] Thus when Coleridge, Southey, Arnold, Sewell, and Seeley gave the church a large place in their paternal schemes, they were not so much pioneers in creative thinking as realists in their perception of what institutions counted as important in early nineteenth-century England. As disciples of Burke and admirers of the status quo, these men could hardly find a better instrument for meeting the challenges of England's alarming economic and social changes than those most venerable of institutions, the church and the parish, particularly since they also fitted in with the intellectuals' predilections for medieval ways, intimate personal relations, and religious piety.

The convergence of these social, intellectual, and institutional forces explains why for all their weaknesses paternalist ideas enjoyed such popularity. One other factor also helped, the absence of a clear and convincing solution to existing social problems. There was a vacuum in the 1830s and 1840s of proven and viable social theories. The hope that a laissez faire society would solve every problem suffered from the severe depression of the early forties and from the sheer mass of social abuse; that philanthropy could redress these widespread evils was doubtful; and very few Englishmen were ready for a welfare state. What then was to be done? Why not revive and invigorate paternalist ideas, give them a sounder philosophical basis, plead more ardently for the performance of those duties incumbent on rank and wealth, and urge that people be better within their own spheres? Such was the answer of many intellectuals. But to be effective such ideas had to be both applied to concrete problems and made popular. Such was the job facing the editors and contributors of those quarterlies and monthlies that were read in the 1840s far more frequently than the abstruse metaphysics of Coleridge or the elaborate idealizations of William Sewell.

Chapter II

Paternalism Made Popular

The English electorate in the summer of 1841 was in a Tory mood. A decade of innovations had exhausted the popularity of the Whigs. Chartism had been suppressed. Europe lay quiet. The Reform Act had not ruined England. Church reform allayed the louder cries of dissent. And Sir Robert Peel's Tory government had a majority of seventy-six in the House of Commons.

Yet not all was well in England. Particularly disturbing were those vexing social problems that Thomas Carlyle called the condition of England question. What should be done about ignorance, drunkenness, and mounting crime? Must crowded, diseased slums be allowed to fester? What of child labor, harsh poor laws, pauperism, unemployment, and accidents in factories, mines, and railways? The problems seemed as endless as they were urgent. The social condition of England constituted, indeed, one of the greatest problems facing the Tories in 1841. It was a problem whose ultimate solution rested with the social conscience of the Tory party.

The term "social conscience," like the label Tory, is seemingly neat and precise, but the neatness of both terms is deceptive. There were many Tory social consciences, not one social conscience. They varied from problem to problem and from Tory to Tory. Yet diffuse and varying as they were, they still rested on a set of shared assumptions, assumptions that no historian can neglect in describing England's response to the challenges of an industrial society.

The problem remains, then, how best to describe and analyze these shared assumptions. A reading of parliamentary debates can help, but in their concentration on practical problems—on workhouses, sewers, and mining ventilation—they reveal little of the larger intellectual developments at work. A reading of Edmund Burke, Samuel Taylor Coleridge, Robert Southey, and William Wordsworth will throw light on these larger intellectual developments, but not on workhouses, sewers, and mines. Furthermore, in the summer of 1841, Coleridge's *Lay Sermons* of 1817 and his *Church and State* of 1830, would be no more likely to grace the reading tables of Tory country houses, town houses, and clubs than would Southey's *Colloquies with Sir Thomas More* of 1829. What did grace these tables, and were much read, much passed around, and much talked about, would be the oracular voices of Toryism, the *Quarterly Review,* or *Blackwood's Magazine* and *Fraser's Magazine.* *Blackwood's Magazine* was a journal whose mocking satires and Scottish railleries led it to rival, in the 1830s, the *Quarterly's* solid circulation of 10,000—only to be rivaled in turn in the 1840s by *Fraser's Magazine,* a journal also mocking and satirical.[1] These three important periodicals dealt with workhouses, sewers, and mines as well as with Burke, Coleridge, and Southey. Their many articles indeed bridge the gap between abstract intellectual developments and concrete social problems. They thus permit, as few sources do, a broad look at both the underlying assumptions of the Tory social conscience and its efforts to grapple with the thornier social problems of early Victorian England.

They do this particularly well because they were all Tory. Tory also were the *English Review,* the *Oxford and Cambridge Review,* the *British Critic,* the *Christian Remembrancer,* and the *Dublin Magazine.* Three major and five minor periodicals thus brought to the libraries and salons of the governing classes the basic social outlook of the Tory party—an outlook that found expression in more than three hundred articles written by those nameless authors whose anonymity has long plagued historians of Victorian England.

Because of Walter and Esther Houghton's invaluable *Wellesley Index to Victorian Periodicals* and their files at Wellesley, the names of sixty-nine of these reviewers are now known. The biographical information that these names have unlocked has proved rich and rewarding. It, along with the articles themselves, permits a close analysis of the nature of the social attitudes of these popularizers of paternalism, particularly as they responded to three powerful forces: the intellectual developments of the age, the pressures of concrete social problems, and the subtle influence on them of their class background and social surroundings.

The intellectual developments of the age were, for most of the sixty-nine reviewers, embodied in the names of five great writers, Edmund Burke, Sir Walter Scott, Samuel Taylor Coleridge, William Wordsworth, and Robert Southey. Of these five Burke was the most quoted, especially by the Reverend George Croly, a biographer of Burke, and by John Wilson Croker, Tory M.P. and long the *Quarterly's* political editor. For Croly, who in the 1840s wrote eight articles on social matters for *Blackwood's,* Burke was "the noblest philosopher" of the age, and for Croker, who had an article in nearly every issue of the *Quarterly,* Burke was "the greatest authority who ever wrote on political ethics."[2]

For Croly and Croker, both sixty in 1840, Burke was part of the excitement of their youth. For most of the other sixty-seven reviewers, whose average age in 1840 was thirty-four, not sixty, the excitement of their youth was Coleridge and Wordsworth, and of their boyhood, Sir Walter Scott. The contributors to *Blackwood's* held Scott in particular reverence: the lawyer William Aytoun wrote of a boyhood reading Scott on the hearthrug; Edinburgh's professor of belles-lettres, J. D. Blackie, fondly remembered "leisure hours pouring over Walter Scott's matchless stories," while the novelist Samuel Warren pronounced Scott "the great genius," "the colossus."[3]

Scott was also a close friend of John Wilson Croker and in the 1820s wrote articles himself for the *Quarterly.* In 1825 Scott's son-in-law John Lockhart became the *Quarterly's* editor, a position he held until 1853.

While Scott entranced Aytoun, Blackie, and Warren in their boyhood, he did not excite them intellectually as much as Coleridge and Words-worth. Blackie, who remembered Scott's matchless tales, found Coleridge in 1831 "the greatest" figure in the intellectual world of London. A year later Blackie had "a fit of Wordsworthian fervour," an experience also shared by his *Blackwood's* colleague, the barrister W. H. Smith. Smith, who contributed many articles on social issues, called Wordsworth's rescue of him from Byron "a sort of moral conversion." The essayist Thomas De Quincey, much older than Blackie or Smith, wrote that the *Lyrical Ballads* of Coleridge and Wordsworth was "the greatest event in the unfolding of my mind . . . an absolute revelation of untrodden worlds."[4] John Wilson, the guiding genius of *Blackwood's,* had a similar revelation upon reading the *Lyrical Ballads,* and like De Quincey became a close friend of the two poets. Wordsworth had an unusually strong impact on the contributors of *Blackwood's*: J. F. Murray called him "the great ornament of our age," while Charles Neaves toasted him at many an Edinburgh banquet.[5]

Fewer of the *Blackwood's* writers toasted Robert Southey, but he did not go unrecognized. Archibald Alison, who wrote fifteen articles on social problems for *Blackwood's* in the 1840s, met Southey in the Highlands, and they talked until midnight. "He made an impression," said Alison, "which will never be effaced." The *Blackwood's* authors were fervent admirers of the Lake Poets: it is thus not surprising that in 1832 Coleridge had expressed "his perfect identity of sentiments, principle and faith with *Blackwood's Magazine*."[6]

The contributors to the *Quarterly* also admired the Lake Poets. Its editor John Lockhart knew and admired them all. "He bent low," said his biographer, "at the shrine of Wordsworth." He also called Southey "a wonderful political writer" and had him contribute many articles in the 1820s, articles that impressed on that periodical a tradition of paternalist thought that was continued in the 1840s by another friend of Southey's, the young Lord Ashley. Lockhart also sought articles from H. N. Coleridge, editor of many of Samuel Coleridge's works, from the Reverend Henry Milman, who venerated Southey, and from Southey's close friend Henry Taylor, who in the December 1842 *Quarterly* called Wordsworth, Coleridge, Southey, and Scott the "four greatest literary geniuses in their generation."[7]

With Lockhart at the *Quarterly,* and like Lockhart a Balliol man, was Dean Lake, a proselytizer at Oxford of the ideas of Wordsworth and Coleridge. He remembered "vainly endeavouring to imbue . . . [W. G. Ward] with Coleridge and Wordsworth." The effort was not in vain. Ward later wrote the very Coleridgean *Ideal of the Christian Church.* He also contributed articles to the *British Critic,* whose first two editors were John Henry Newman and Thomas Mozley. On the demise of the *British Critic* in 1843, Thomas Mozley's brother James started the *Christian Remembrancer,* with contributions by R. C. Church. Church spoke reverently in its pages "of our own Coleridge." Ward, Church, and the two Mozleys were part of that Tractarian movement whose "philosophical basis" was, according to John Henry Newman, Coleridgean.[8]

Coleridge was indeed a powerful, almost sovereign, force in the 1830s. John Kemble regarded him as a greater sage than John Locke, and Henry Reeve called him a "great luminary." The historian Kemble and the journalist Reeve were contributors to the *British and Foreign*

Review, not a Tory journal, but decidedly paternalist.[9] Coleridge's influence, as great at Cambridge as at Oxford, is also evident in the *Oxford
and Cambridge Review,* the journal of those ardent members of Young
England who came down from Cambridge in the 1830s.

The contributors and editors of *Fraser's Magazine* also admired Cole-
ridge. Its assistant editor in the 1830s, J. A. Heraud, was called "the
conscientious follower of Coleridge." Its editor until 1842, the eccentric
Irish journalist William Maginn, was a friend of Coleridge. He said
Coleridge had "acted strongly upon the mind of the day." Under
Maginn's editorship *Fraser's* denounced the utilitarians for wishing to
replace "Scott, Coleridge, Wordsworth, and Southey with Bentham,
McCulloch, Mill, and Ricardo."[10]

Sir Walter Scott and the Lake Poets had a powerful impact on the
Tory reviewers of the 1840s. It was an impact more aesthetic than political, a fact that J. D. Blackie shrewdly observed. Said Blackie of his
colleagues at *Blackwood's,* "they were men who professed to be Tories,
perhaps less on political than on romantic grounds."[11] It is an observa-
tion that helps explain why the poet Wordsworth, who wrote little on
political and social issues, had such a striking effect. W. H. Smith, who
in the 1840s contributed ten important social essays to *Blackwood's,* confessed that Wordsworth had saved him from Byron's "protest against
the whole cruel order of things." He did so by teaching him "the spirit
of obedience and reverence" and communicating to him "the impulse to
accept the order of the universe . . . to faithfully discharge the near
and known duty."[12] Wordsworth's deep sense of the rightness of nature
and God's ways, of the value of simple personal truths and simple and
personal acts of goodness, assured many readers that all was not Benthamite calculus, political economy, and Whig complacency. For that,
said William Sewell, the *Quarterly's* most prolific advocate of paternalism, the nation owed him a greater gratitude than it did Coleridge, for
Wordsworth had made the first "step to the restoration of a [better]
philosophy, [one] in a safe direction."[13]

The high praise that the Tory reviewers of the 1840s gave to Burke
and the romantic poets does not necessarily prove any direct influence of
one writer upon another, though it also does not preclude it. No one can
know whether Archibald Alison's outburst in *Blackwood's* against the
political economists owed anything to his midnight talk with Robert
Southey or to his reading of Southey's writings any more than one can
know whether John Wilson's praise of Southey as a "genius, rich and

rare," proves that Southey inspired him to make *Blackwood's* an ardent advocate of paternalism.[14] But what these examples do show is a strong, a very strong, affinity between the intellectual outlook and social ideas of Burke and the romantic poets and the intellectual outlook of the Tory reviewers.

That such an affinity existed is also evident in the fact that these reviewers agreed with Burke and the romantics on certain fundamental propositions about the organization of a paternalist society: namely that it should be hierarchic, authoritarian, and organic, and that it should be based on land, church, and locality.

That society should be hierarchic and authoritarian few Tory reviewers doubted, since only through inequality and obedience would there be permanence and order—the basis of what W. H. Smith told *Blackwood's* readers was "the unalterable nature of our social pyramid." Smith feared equality. So did Southey's friend Henry Taylor. "There is nothing so ungenial and unfruitful," Taylor wrote in the *Quarterly*, "as social equality." He expressed this view in an article defending Wordsworth's sonnets in praise of capital punishment. He rejoiced that the great poet "nowhere advocates equality of station." Inequality was also important because it led to subordination, a quality *Fraser's* called "indispensable where the social structure consists of grades." Tory periodicals were unabashed in demanding obedience, patience, submission, and dutifulness. "The great body of mankind," pronounced Archibald Alison in *Blackwood's*, "stand just as much in need of the direction of others as children in school."[15]

The Tory reviewers also wanted an organic society, a society they associated with feudalism. Their enthusiasm for feudalism was astonishing. The *Oxford and Cambridge Review* judged feudalism "the most perfect form of society since Jewish theocracy." *Fraser's* found in the landlordship of the duke of Richmond an admirable example of "modern feudal relations"; and three of *Blackwood's* contributors championed it, one of them the Reverend Longueville Jones declaring it to be "the highest form of civilisation." These reviewers admired feudalism since, according to Alison, it "conferred power and influence at home on those only who were interested in the welfare of the people."[16] Since only those who knew their neighbors personally could have a true bond of sympathy with them, society should consist of unified, small, and organic communities. In the 1840s capitalism, urbanization, centralization, utilitarianism, political economy, Chartism, and socialism all threatened such an organic society by treating its members as a mere collection of atoms. Against this view the Tory reviewers protested. "Society is not a heap of sand," wrote William Sewell in the *Quarterly*, but "a union of many in one." "A body is not the sum of particles," said *Fraser's*, but "the idea of plurality in unity." "Without a social hierarchy," *Fraser's* continued, "organized and organizing, without authority to uphold the same, without submission thereto, no complete organism can exist."

William Sewell, in the *Quarterly*, defined these "organic bodies." They were to consist of landlords "exercising faithfully, earnestly and affectionately the duties of little monarchs," and at the center of every village, "an ecclesiastical establishment." Together they would bring the "feudal system" in which "the master of the soil should stand as much as possible in a fatherly way to his tenants."[17]

Such an organic community had to be based on land. Land alone, said Croker in the *Quarterly*, provided the foundation of government. W. H. Smith in *Blackwood's* called land "an absolute necessity," and his colleague De Quincey proclaimed primogeniture and the church "the basis of our civil constitution."[18] Squire and parson would rule those corporate communities that formed the indispensable units of society. It was a partnership that was a reality in countless rural parishes. One of those parishes was Cholderton in Wiltshire, and its parson was the Reverend Thomas Mozley. In 1840 he wrote in the *British Critic* that property has its duties as well as its rights. But he doubted if property other than land would do its duties. He called factories "houses of bondage" and the steam engine "a new and enormous calamity," one destructive of "the moral units of society." He much regretted that "tall chimneys have supplanted . . . heaven directed spires." The *Quarterly's* William Sewell had a solution for Mozley's worries: "raze, if you like, to the ground half of an overgrown metropolis."[19]

The mercantile spirit and its uglier manifestations, the factory and the overgrown city, haunted most of the Tory reviewers. But since most of them had no desire to raze half of an overgrown metropolis, they looked, as Wordsworth had in his "Postscript" to his *Collected Poems* of 1835, to the holy mission of the Church of England. None of the Tory periodicals had anything but enthusiasm for the social mission of the church, long a pillar of feudal society. The *English Review*, the *British Critic*, and the *Christian Remembrancer*, all edited by Anglican clergymen, demanded an enlarged and active clergy.[20] They not only wanted more bishops, priests, and cathedral institutions, but collegiate institutions, hospitals, houses of mercy, female penitentiaries, sisters of charity, and monasteries. *Blackwood's* was also for "following out the Church scheme fearlessly." For the Tory reviewers the Church of England, divinely ordained and apostolic, had a place in it for a diaconate which, under a bishop's superintendence, could manage schools and almshouses and guarantee an effective use of the offertory. The *English Review* in 1844 proclaimed that the offertory was the safest remedy for many of the evils of pauperism, and it urged bishops "to visibly lift up the cross and pastoral staff in the streets of our crowded towns." It also wanted monasteries to train up Christian warriors. Invoking the days of Wilfred and Ethelred it said, "The 19th century must, after all, come back to the seventh, or sixth, nay even the first." The *Oxford and Cambridge Review*'s medieval dreams centered on monasteries, religious holidays, and sisters of charity, the favorites of Young England, while the *Quarterly* championed female penitentiaries for fallen women.[21]

All of these schemes involved the Church of England and many of them called for state support, but none included nonconformists. By the late 1840s many paternalists realized that state aid to schemes exclusively Anglican was impossible; they thus espoused the voluntary principle. Their refusal to include nonconformity and their pleas for the use of the offertory suggest how deeply their social outlook reflected their theology. Poverty did not disturb them as much as heresy. The main evils were skepticism and secularism, not child labor and bad sanitation. "Latitudinarianism in its various shapes," said the *Oxford and Cambridge*, "is the one most dangerous adversary . . . to national amelioration."[22]

Another dangerous adversary was the growth of a centralized state. These Tory periodicals hated the odious principle of centralization. Yet the same periodicals often called for a patriarchal government—*Fraser's* in 1843 calling it the "best of all forms of government" and the *Oxford and Cambridge* praising it as the opposite of the laissez faire principle. Their hatred of a centralized state and their praise of a patriarchal government seem contradictory. But they are not if one understands what was meant by a patriarchal government.

Fraser's, in praising such a government, presented a model of it for the colony of New Zealand. In that model the power to govern went largely to the great landlords, secondarily to the church, and only thirdly to the legislative council. Nothing at all was said of a central bureaucracy. It was a model that fitted the *Oxford and Cambridge* definition of patriarchal government as "supervision, care, and kindness, carried out in all relations of society."[23] Like Burke and Coleridge, the Tory reviewers saw government as a partnership of all who were part of the social hierarchy. "Every man," said the *English Review,* "should culti- vate the region which Providence has assigned him." "Let each man take care of his own part," said the *Quarterly,* "and the whole will take care of itself."[24] The romantic extreme of that dream found expression in the Reverend Longueville Jones's pleas in *Blackwood's* and in William Sewell's plea in the *Quarterly* for noblemen to lead voluntary regiments of armed men.

The noblemen would be from the locality, and their rule would be personal. In describing the Tory social conscience of the 1840s, it would be hard to exaggerate the importance of the local community and of personal relations. It was only in the parish and county, only with the rule of landlord and parson, that a hierarchical, authoritarian, and organic society could be preserved. Such a rule lay at the heart of Tory paternal- ism. It was for this reason that Tory reviewers disliked philanthropy and political economy. It was a dislike they shared with Burke, Coleridge, Wordsworth, and Southey.

A philanthropy that meant a personal benevolence in a small com- munity they did not dislike, but a philanthropy that was extended, dif- use, and general won from them only the most pejorative of adjectives. They wrote of "platform philanthropy," "claptrap philanthropy," "the pernicious cant of universal philanthropy," "pseudo-humanity and phil- anthropy," "the cant of humanity," "weak and short sighted benevo- lence," and, pointing explicitly to the evangelicals, "the unctuous silki- ness of Exeter Hall." "Philanthropy," said *Blackwood's,* "does not work, she talks." The author was S. R. Phillips, also editor of the very Tory weekly *John Bull,* and he went on to denounce Charles Dickens, whose works he associated with "the exertions of modern philan- thropy."[25] Dickens's egalitarian humanitarianism also annoyed other Tory journals. The *English Review* chastised him for holding "our aris- tocratic institutions responsible for our partial social destitution," and the *Oxford and Cambridge* for "espousing feelings of brotherhood but forgetting the religion on which it is based." The *British and Foreign Review* complained of "too much kindness of heart," and W. H. Smith of *Blackwood's* of his "overstrained sentimentalism and flashy philan- thropy."[26] Such flashy philanthropy, extended, diffuse, and general, un- dermined those fixed and known duties of men of rank and station, which can exist only in small localities.

The personal relationships that bound together small localities were also endangered by political economy with its hard and impersonal cash nexus. *Blackwood's* disliked the dogmatism and coldness of the economists, as did the *Oxford and Cambridge* and *English Review*. But they did so more because of their romantic and aesthetic sensibilities than on economic grounds. How unromantic to talk of the iron law of wages and the arithmetical increase of food and the geometrical progression of population, and how unspiritual to talk of a calculus of pain and pleasure.

But as unaesthetic as was the language of political economy, the Tory reviewers were not hostile to its principles. Alison, *Blackwood's*'s leading social theorist, avowed that in his youth "I took with . . . ardour to the study of political economy." Thomas De Quincey, author of *The Logic of Political Economy*, wrote much in *Blackwood's* in praise of the truths of David Ricardo. Croker, a disciple of Burke, shared Burke's enthusiasm for Adam Smith.[27] Croker spoke often in the *Quarterly* for laissez faire principles. He hated, he wrote, that "pruriency for legislation" that arose from "false and dangerous estimates of . . . the legitimate power and duties of government." The *Christian Remembrancer* agreed. In an article praising John Stuart Mill's *Political Economy* it concluded, "As direct remedies all legislative enactments must be powerless."[28] The Tories disliked political economy's open selfishness and crassness, but because of their attachment to private property, they supported, in practice, laissez faire principles. It was a support that they felt in no way contradicted their vision of a hierarchic, authoritarian, and organic society, a society resting on the paternal duties of land, church, and the local magistracy.

The vision of such a society was very old and very widespread. It did not originate with Burke and the romantics. But it did receive from those writers a brilliant and forceful expression. Burke argued eloquently that such a society reflected the wisdom of history. Coleridge gave it metaphysical dress and expounded at great length on the public duties of the church. Wordsworth made it an appealing part of his religion of nature. In Scott's novels it formed a splendid backdrop to his exciting stories of past ages. In Southey's *Colloquies* it received the support of Thomas More's wisest words and the medieval church's most generous sentiments. In the works of these geniuses an old and venerable vision became fresh again, inspiring in its ideals and compelling in its criticism of the crassness of utilitarianism and political economy. But was it a viable vision? Could it meet the test of reality? Could it solve the problems of pauperism, child labor, ignorance, and crime and meet the challenges of Ireland and unhealthy towns?

With more than a tenth of the English on poor relief, pauperism in 1840 was certainly the most widespread of these problems. It was a problem that many felt the Whigs had only aggravated by the New Poor Law of 1834. That law led to the infamous workhouse test, a policy that denied relief to all able-bodied paupers unless they entered these hateful houses. The Tory response to pauperism was stern. De Quincey told *Blackwood's*'s readers that pauperism is "radicated in the nature of man, which is wicked." Even *Fraser's*, always more compassionate, attributed destitution to an individual's failings more than to the vicissitudes of trade.[29] Some Tory reviewers found man so sinful that they considered poverty itself healthy. "Nothing but the deepest and bitterest poverty," wrote the Reverend Thomas Mozley in the *British Critic*, "will subdue the uneducated classes." "If there were more comfort and ease," he added, "what still worse bondage of sin and punishment." Pauperism being "radicated in man," there was little that laws could do. Mozley thus concluded his article, "We are not taxing the legislature, or any rank or order or profession with heartless wrong. There is no one to blame."[30] *Fraser's* in 1845 agreed. "Agriculture," they wrote, "neither requires nor is benefitted by over-anxious interference," a sentiment Coleridge expressed in his *Lay Sermons* when he insisted that land be "secured indeed from all human interference by every principle of law, and policy." It was a sentiment that led George Croly in *Blackwood's* to pronounce the very idea of a poor law "a direct contradiction to the principle that man should be a provident animal."[31]

With such assumptions about poverty, yet hostile to all Whig measures, it is not surprising that the Tory reviewers were ambivalent about the New Poor Law. They were by no means its consistent enemies. The *Quarterly* even had one of the assistant commissioners, Sir Francis Bond Head, defend it, workhouse test and all. *Blackwood's* also had a poor-law official write about it, a William Collis. Collis was more critical, voicing the Tory squires' great objection to a law that weakened local government, particularly by denying it the power to discriminate between the worthy and unworthy poor.[32] The centralization brought about by the law was what most alarmed the Tories. *Fraser's* denounced the law as "new fangled." But newfangled it wasn't by the 1840s, a fact that explains why the *Quarterly* and *Blackwood's* defended it. "The principle of conservatism," said Charles Neaves in *Blackwood's*, "is *viz inertia.*" It was a principle fundamental to the Tory social conscience. It explains, for example, why *Blackwood's* defended the English Poor Law in 1846 but opposed a similar law for Scotland in 1847. By 1846 the English law was already part of English institutions. Scotland, on the other hand, had in 1847 a system in which relief was given through the church. *Blackwood's* urged, in both instances, no change.[33]

Viz inertia also influenced their view of child labor. None of the Tory reviews pioneered in that field. They were supporters, of course, of existing laws, and they praised Lord Ashley's bill for excluding women and children from mines, but beyond that they did not go. They defended the rightness of child labor where it did exist. Mozley in the *British Critic* called the employment of children in agriculture a necessity; *Fraser's* argued that seamstresses deserved freedom from government regulations as much as an artist at his easel; the *English Review* warned of "precipitous legislation" and advised trust in the private employer; and the *Quarterly's* George Taylor, a Durham farmer, branded as enthusiasts those who criticized employers who overworked seamstresses and millinners. Taylor added that these girls were not underpaid.[34]

Among the Tory reviewers, however, there was one who really cared, the young Lord Ashley. In an article in the *Quarterly* he described the plight of infants working fourteen and fifteen hours a day in hosier and pin-making shops, at iron works and forges, in silk and lace mills. He ended by reminding Parliament of its duty to protect the weak. It was a vague request made with far less enthusiasm than the plea that followed: "Above all open your Treasury, erect churches, send forth missionaries of religion, reverse the conduct of mankind."[35] It was the dream of many a Tory paternalist that the wicked would repent and, as Coleridge put it, become "better people." Once this had occurred churchmen and employers together, locally and voluntarily, would protect infant labor.

The same local and voluntary efforts could also help educate the lower classes—though so widespread was their ignorance that it also needed the aid of Parliament and the Church, Parliament to give the Church money, the Church to guarantee that instruction was truly religious. Almost all of the Tory reviews favored such a scheme. But what of the half of England who were not Anglican? Dr. Hook of Leeds proposed to solve that problem by creating rate-supported schools and allowing them to give separate religious instruction in the faith of one's choice. Of Tory reviewers only the Reverend Henry Milman of the *Quarterly* supported Hook's plan. *Fraser's* thought it impractical and expensive; the *Oxford and Cambridge* called it "preposterous"; and the *English Review* said it would produce infidels.[36] *Blackwood's* was silent about it, though in 1840 Archibald Alison had opposed grants to other than Church schools, and in 1849 the Reverend Longueville Jones defended the Church's scheme and warned of "the hydra-head of dissent."[37]

Although Milman liked Hook's plan, evidently his editors, Lockhart and Croker, had doubts about it. Two years later they published an article hostile to publicly financed and publicly managed schools; the author was the ex-premier of France, François Guizot. "We depreciate all interference," Guizot wrote, "that is not necessary." He opposed all general systems of public education and argued that education belonged to "the private and voluntary . . . to religious zeal." Guizot's religious voluntaryism, far more than Milman's plea for a comprehensive and public system, defined the Tory social conscience's view of education.[38]

A zeal for voluntarism also informed the paternalist's view of Ireland. "No direct legislation," said *Blackwood's* in 1844, "can affect the social condition of Ireland." John Croker concurred. In the very midst of the famine, he used the *Quarterly* to condemn public works, to denounce the granting of wastelands to the poor, and to urge the reduction of the existing poor rates. In place of such public measures he urged trust in the "active benevolence at work in Ireland."[39] The Tory reviewers had a most sanguine belief in the Irish gentry and clergy. *Fraser's* said they were "universally kind, forbearing, and considerate." *Fraser's* thus looked to their "paternal authority and superintendence" and not to Parliament, for the mitigation of Ireland's sufferings. *Fraser's* wanted the landlords and clergy to teach the Irish "obedience to the laws" and impose on them "social and moral discipline." The *Quarterly* echoed these sentiments. "The Irishman needs," it said, "someone to look up to, to love, to devote himself to." All this fitted perfectly with *Oxford and Cambridge's* view that Ireland's salvation lay in "each in his own sphere . . . doing deeds of individual justice and mercy."[40]

Profound voluntarists as they were, the Tory reviewers nevertheless did not oppose all aid from Parliament. John Croker did not object to parliamentary loans to landowners or to subsidies to railways—nor did *Blackwood's*. Croker called both part of the protective system.[41] That system—like the Corn Law which formed its capstone—was an indirect one, one that did not protect the poor directly because such a policy would undermine the efforts of men of property and rank. It was far better that men of property employ the poor on railways than that the poor possess half an acre of wastelands.

The Tory reviewers had a great fondness for railways. That railways charged excessive rates, made huge profits, had many accidents, and put third-class passengers in open carriages run at a slow pace, bothered them little. When Gladstone presented a bill to end these abuses, he found *Fraser's, Blackwood's,* and the *Quarterly* resolute in opposition. *Fraser's* called the covering of third-class trains an example of "pseudo-humanity" and government planning of new lines "Whiggish-radical centralisation." Croker considered the improvement of third-class trains "unjust, uncalled for" and insisted that they would "unsettle the habits of the poor." Improvements, he said, would come from "spontaneous developments," a view not at variance with those of Sir Francis Bond Head, who asked *Quarterly* readers to trust to the self-interest of the companies for the lessening of accidents. *Blackwood's* also opposed any government control from London.[42] No Tory journal demanded an increase in government regulation, though all, following *viz inertia,* supported existing laws. It was a respect for property, and not a disposition to anarchy, that led the Tories to oppose new laws. If new laws coerced criminals and checked mounting crime, they had no objection.

Indeed the very increase of crime, according to the Tories, came from too much leniency. "Justice" announced *Blackwood's* in 1844, "leans too much to the side of mercy." Alison, who believed that the age's greatest chimera was that education lessened crime, wrote in *Blackwood's* that crime had increased in those categories where capital punishment had been abolished.[43] Capital punishment was a favorite penalty with Tory reviewers. The *Oxford and Cambridge* liked it because it embodied the principle of retribution.[44] Tory reviewers also liked harsh prisons. "Every inmate," said W. H. Smith of *Blackwood's,* "should feel an irresistible domination . . . and submission." *Fraser's* found the "no punishment mania" alarming and demanded that adultery, if by women, be made a crime, and that beggars be whipped, that flogging be kept in the navy, and that fagging be preserved at schools. Fagging it regarded as part of a "paternal system."[45] Crime, like poverty, arose from wickedness and could only be controlled, not ended.

Though crime could be blamed on sinful man, cholera could not. It arose from water polluted by the bad drainage of filthy slums. The first response of the Tory to disease-ridden slums was to do nothing—*viz inertia* again. In 1840 Dr. Ferguson, in the *Quarterly,* declared that laws on public health were already "sufficiently stringent and sufficiently comprehensive." The squires, the clergy, and the rich, he said, could handle these matters. Then came Edwin Chadwick's 1842 report on England's sanitary horrors. The *Quarterly's* Sir Francis Bond Head promptly called for legislation.[46] So did Robert Sowler in *Blackwood's*, but reluctantly. In an article on Manchester he praised the model houses and neighborhood that Lord Francis Egerton had built for his workers and urged all employers to be as paternal so that there would be no need for an act of Parliament. "The legislature may do something," he said, "but much more must be delegated to private exertion." The same reluctance, hesitation, and timidity—the hallmarks of the paternalists' social conscience when facing the need for government interference— marked Lord Ashley's article on London's common lodging houses. Despite a vivid description of these dreary houses and their dreary neighborhoods, he called for no legislation. Instead he issued a plea to "all ranks and professions, to every holder of property, to consider these evils."[47] His point of view involved a trust in property that Dr. W. A. Guy of *Fraser's* did not share. Dr. Guy, when he saw the sanitary horrors of London, called for a strong Board of Health.[48]

In the late 1840s *Fraser's's* view of government became more inter-ventionist than the *Quarterly's*, and less paternalist. The Tory periodicals each had unique personalities. The *Quarterly* was proud, aristocratic, staid, and pontifical, and its articles were tough minded, thorough, con-servative, and stern. *Blackwood's*, being often the work of lawyers with literary ambitions, was polemical, satirical, combative, and clever, con-stantly pouring epithets on Whigs, utilitarians, economists, and philan-thropists. *Fraser's*, the product of London, was bumptious, gay, com-passionate, idealistic, and in its articles sensitive to suffering but vague about remedies. The *Oxford and Cambridge* was romantic and medieval. The *English Review, British Critic,* and *Christian Remembrancer* were all obsessed with the decade's greatest debate and saw social problems from the center of an embattled and divided Church of England.

In the pages of the Tory periodicals—whatever their individual per-sonalities—there evolved a growing tension between two powerful forces, the intellectual ideals of the romantics and the hard reality of social conditions. Adding to that tension was a third force, the social background of each reviewer, his class, his rural environment, his edu-cation, his occupation, his institutional loyalties, and his social milieu.

The class background of the Tory reviewers certainly did not favor radical solutions to social problems. All but two of the sixty-nine reviewers came from the upper classes. Three were the sons of peers and eight the sons of landed gentry; seventeen had fathers who were prosperous businessmen; the fathers of nine held good livings in the Church of England; five fathers were physicians, one to George III; five more were barristers and three officers in the army. Of the sixty-nine reviewers, forty-nine attended a university, three others attended military college, two attended the Inns of Court (where they met some of the forty-nine who had been at universities), and one had a medical education.

Almost all were either raised or went to school in the countryside. In their schools as in their families they experienced authoritarian and patriarchal ways and in the country saw squires and parsons at work. In some cases the squire or parson was their father. "It was a favorite walk of all of us," reminisced Alison, "to accompany our father to visit the cottages of the poor—the impression produced by these visits was never afterward effaced."[49]

Even those raised in England's older towns had happy memories. The Reverend John Armstrong of the *Quarterly* was raised in Bishop Wearmouth. Later he wrote of towns that "had rows of ancient alms-houses, built before the hurrying tide of commerce." Oxford and Cambridge universities were also built before the "hurrying tide of commerce,"[50] a felicitous fact for thirty-two Tory reviewers attending these centers of modest learning and much pleasure. Lockhart found Balliol a great contrast to his home town of Glasgow. His biographer says he had for Balliol "a warm relish." Later, back in Glasgow, he was "never so solitary," confessing, "I feel no sympathy with mercantile souls."[51]

After university, for many it was the law. At *Blackwood's* Alison, Aytoun, Blackie, Smith, Warren, and Phillmore were lawyers and at the *Quarterly*, Croker, Croly, Lockhart, and Moir. In the social and intellectual matrix from which arose the paternalist social conscience, the study and practice of law was no small ingredient. One's occupation is seldom unimportant. Favored with prosperous parents and privileged education, twenty-three of the sixty-nine reviewers became Anglican clergymen, eighteen lawyers, seven landed gentry, seven civil servants, four physicians, two journalists, one a headmaster, one an artist, one a Scottish parson, and one a Unitarian minister. All were successful, and that success bound them closer to the establishment.

William Aytoun, for example, was a lawyer for a railway firm, his colleague at *Blackwood's*, C. D. Brady, owned land in Ireland, and Mortimer O'Sullivan of the *Quarterly* was a rector in the Church of Ireland. Aytoun wrote two articles on railways, both against increased government interference; Brady and O'Sullivan wrote articles on Ireland that also declaimed against government interference, in this case against interference with Irish landlords and clergymen.[52] It is unlikely that Aytoun expected larger legal fees if the government did not interfere or that Brady and O'Sullivan expected larger rents and tithes from less government meddling in Irish affairs. But as successful lawyers, landowners, and clergymen they were a part of those institutions they sincerely felt should manage social matters. They also dined in the society of lawyers, landowners, and clergymen. It was the social milieu and shared assumptions that counted.

This is certainly true of the clergymen who wrote on education. The *Quarterly, Blackwood's,* and *Fraser's* all asked Anglican clergymen to write on that subject. The editors of the *Christian Remembrancer, English Review,* and *British Critic* were also clergymen. These men were part of an institution that played a dominant role in the shaping of the Tory social conscience.

Property, whether in land or in railways, was also dominant in shaping that conscience. John Croker and the *Quarterly* were property's stoutest defenders. In discussing railways Croker called for "a scrupulous respect for existing interests," and in warning against the repeal of the Corn Law he argued that this law, by maintaining the income of land, contributed to the greater good of society.[53] The Tory paternalist believed that property and the church, acting in local spheres, could best provide for the poor, deal with criminals, and clean towns. For them property and the church involved duties as well as rights, benevolence as well as self-interest. "Vested interests," Southey had said, "are the key stone of the social edifice."

The social milieu of the Tory reviewers was also important. Many of them liked high society. Lockhart's diary is full of the names of peers with whom he dined. At the *Quarterly* he insisted "that articles must be by men of the world," men aware "of the tone of thought and feeling in the highest and best society." Archibald Alison also had a passion for society, one that is seldom absent in his *Autobiography:* quite ecstatic are his accounts of dinner with the archbishop of Canterbury and the duke of Richmond. Richmond he met at the famous medieval tournament of 1839 given by the earl of Eglinton. Eglinton was also a friend of William Aytoun of *Blackwood's.* Of old gentry stock, Aytoun abhorred "rudeness and all that was disorderly in social intercourse."[54]

Besides the social milieu there were political connections and considerations. A good editor knew his friends and his readership. "We must look," wrote Lockhart at the *Quarterly,* "for an audience to the clergy and country gentry." Croker was superb for both. He told Lockhart that "as to the Irish Church I have already embarked the *Quarterly* in an unhesitating support of that—the outwork of the Church of England."[55] John Blackwood, London editor of *Blackwood's,* was just as sensitive to England's ruling classes. "I am dubious of publishing it," he said of an article by Gladstone on the Corn Law, for it "will be apt to offend the Duke of Buckingham and that party." John Blackwood's correspondence shows a clear commitment to the agricultural interests: "Mr. Stafford O'Brien called from the Protection Society"; "Sir Edward Bulwer was here today and wants to do a small octavo volume advocating the Corn Laws." One after another the ardent protectionists dropped in at the London office of *Blackwood's,* so often indeed that Lockhart predicted it would become "a chapel of ease" for the Tory Carlton Club.[56]

By class, rural upbringing, education, institutional affiliation, and social, literary, and political friendships, most of the sixty-nine reviewers were tied to that paternalist ideology that they also found attractive for intellectual reasons. But there was one element in social England that influenced their outlook in a way antithetical to paternalism: the city.

The city was a fearsome phenomenon. "In our crowded cities," exclaimed the Reverend Robert Lamb in *Fraser's,* "the human mass is increasing in a ratio that is fearful." "Hamlets are grown into cities," lamented Lord Ashley in the *Quarterly,* "without calling forth mutual sympathies, of master and servant, landlord and tenant, employer and employed." "The vast preponderance of crime is to be found in manufacturing towns," confessed Archibald Alison in *Blackwood's,* "and there too destitution, sensuality, and profligacy . . . advance with unheard of rapidity," since in such centers "the restraints of character, relationships and vicinity are in great measure lost in the crowd." In the breakdown of rural and agricultural connections, Alison noted a year later, the poor "become dissatisfied with the station . . . which Providence has assigned them." Factories had destroyed parental care while the absence of superiors as neighbors left the poor—whom he likened to children—without guidance. For Alison, who learned his social philosophy from his father's visits to the rural poor, to confront, as sheriff of Lanarkshire, a wider urban area of 350,000 souls, 5,000 of them "utterly destitute," was traumatic. It led him to tell *Blackwood's's* readers that "individual benevolence and local exertions" were altogether inadequate for manufacturing communities.[57]

Published accounts of urban evils even penetrated the quiet world of the countryside. Thomas Mozley, after reading Dr. Cooke Taylor's *Notes of a Tour in the Manufacturing Towns of Lancashire*, confessed, "my old illusions of a paternal system had been tested by the facts, and had now vanished away."[58]

To plunge into the slums of a large English city could be a transforming experience. A reviewer for *Fraser's*, who called himself "an ordinary of Newgate," wrote that "the transition from a peaceful country village to the metropolis was sudden and striking."[59] Once very orthodox, he learned as chaplain of Newgate of a world he had never imagined. It was a world whose ugliness the eight paternalist journals never attempted to hide, even though they often highlighted its more picturesque features. *Blackwood's* ran a series of eight articles on London life by an Irish novelist, John Murray. His novel *The Viceroy*, published in 1841, was filled with paternalist idealism. His pictures of London, though picturesque, entertaining, and droll, were still candid about the great gap dividing an indifferent rich from a destitute poor. The *Quarterly's* articles by Lord Ashley on London's poor also painted honestly the plight of the suffering of London. So too did *Fraser's*, where William Thackeray described the horror of public executions and Dr. W. A. Guy the filth of diseased slums. These periodicals made no effort to obscure facts that government reports, popular novels, popular journals, and the experiences of life had made commonplace. The principal problem was what should be done.

Not many of the sixty-nine reviewers felt much confidence in giving an answer. Lord Ashley at least had the boldness to try. "We have an established Church," he wrote in 1846 in the *Quarterly*, "abundant in able and pious men [and] . . . the efficacious virtues of the voluntary principle. We have a generous aristocracy and plethoric capitalists and a government pledge to social improvements. Who will come forward? Why not all?"[60] The eclectic Ashley would have the paternalists of church and property join philanthropy and a reforming government to mitigate London's squalor. As an ardent supporter of model lodging houses, ragged schools, bath- and washhouses, and evangelical Bible societies, he favored philanthropy above all. Ashley's article sounded a chord of response in Dr. Guy of *Fraser's* in 1844 in a long article entitled "Great Cities." The city provides, *Fraser's* said, "a territory" where the philanthropist "may expatiate, where in all of his pains and all of his sacrifices he is sure of repayment, the electric properties of benevolence and sympathy . . . are drawn out of the rapid contact of masses."[61]

Great cities not only encouraged philanthropy, they also encouraged individualism and a reforming central government, two other rival outlooks to paternalism. John Murray observed in *Blackwood's* that it is "a moral certainty that in London industry, good conduct and perseverance can lift a man from nothing into the proud position of being his own master."[62] Murray's claim is no doubt exaggerated: not every man in London could become "his own master." But what is important is that one could do so far more easily in London than in rural England.

That in London a man could become "his own master" subverted the principles of dependency and deference. Such a fact was therefore, however much the paternalists valued self-reliance, an antipaternalist fact. The growth of the central government with a welfare bureaucracy was another antipaternalist fact. The urban world, whether Manchester or London, created both the problems and the collectivist mentality that encouraged the growth of the central government. *Fraser's* was, for example, the most deeply influenced by the London environment and because of that experience became the most collectivist. It grew impatient of those smaller, more intermediate spheres of government so dear to paternalists. Dr. Guy had lived long in London. His articles in *Fraser's* were severe on the local parishes and their vicars, on property, and on local government. They had all failed to support sanitary reform and improvement. He ended his discussion of that failure by saying, "We would rather trust to the central government than to the local authorities."

In Edinburgh, Dr. William Alison, brother of Archibald, was undergoing as an urban doctor experiences similar to those of Dr. Guy, and from his experiences came articles in the late forties in *Blackwood's* that were similar to Guy's articles in *Fraser's*. He was skeptical about property doing its duties, dubious of local benevolence, and ready to call for more government intervention. He demanded a public poor law. He also, as Robert Sowler of Manchester had done, urged Parliament to act to remove sanitary evils. Manchester's Sowler, Edinburgh's Alison, and London's Guy embody in their experiences the corrosive effect of urbanization on paternalism.

They also exemplified new intellectual developments: the growth of science, particularly medicine, the enthusiasm for statistics, the investigative role of popular journalism, and the search for the laws governing society. Science, statistics, investigative journalism, sociology—these are a far cry from Wordsworth's and Coleridge's poetic and philosophical revolt against the rationalism of the eighteenth century. New problems, new generations, new environments, and new ways of thought were leading to ideas that, even in the Tory periodicals, began to rival the paternalist social outlook. Paternalism seemed divorced from reality. It thus found refuge in the more imaginary world of the novel.

Chapter III

Paternalism and Rebellion in the Early Victorian Novel

The early Victorians had an omnivorous appetite for novels. With nearly two-thirds of them literate, with increased prosperity and cheaper book making, and with no cinemas, no television, and no automobiles, the novel reigned supreme as a source of excitement, of adventure, and even of enlightenment. It carried the readers away from grim row houses to dreams of elegant country homes where dashing baronets won the hands of rich heiresses. It also plunged them into the satanic mills of Manchester and the littered alleys of Whitechapel. It ranged up and down the gamut of society, reflecting at all levels the social concerns and attitudes of its many diverse peoples.

Among the diverse social attitudes that these novels reflect, none was more pervasive and more traditional than paternalism. It was a social outlook that had older and deeper roots than its three closest rivals among social outlooks: the economists' vision of a laissez faire society, the evangelicals' hope of an expanding philanthropy, and the utilitarians' belief in a reforming government. Paternalism, in striking contrast to laissez faire individualism, emphasized those mutual bonds and deferential patterns that defined England's organic and hierarchical society. It also, in contrast to the diffuse and impersonal work of philanthropic organizations, emphasized the smaller sphere of the landed estate, the parish, and the mill and the known authority of the squire, parson, and millowner. And finally, it had no belief, as did the utilitarians, in reforming laws and governmental departments, but emphasized the duties of property and the role of the church.

Early Victorian paternalism varied as widely in its expressions as did the novels that reflected it. There were indeed many different kinds of novels in the 1840s. Within that diversity, however, one can discern four kinds of novels that contain insights into the working of paternalism: romances of the fashionable world, stories of the lower classes, tales of religious and moral edification, and dramas of London life.

The romances of the fashionable world, for example, reveal much about the widespread popularity of paternalism and its ties with almost all of the old and venerable institutions that defined English life. Evidence of such popularity and ties is particularly to be found in the works of the two most prolific novelists of the 1840s, Catherine Gore and G. P. R. James. Mrs. Gore wrote twenty-four novels in that decade and James twenty-eight. They both wrote what some call silver-fork novels and others call novels of the upper ten thousand. Their heroes and heroines were of the nobility and gentry, their settings, country houses and vicarages, and their plots full of passionate loves and fierce quarrels. They in no way preached social reform, and in no way did they disturb the social conscience of the early Victorians. They were as much novels of escape and dreams as were the Hollywood movies of the 1930s. But they nevertheless disclose much about paternalism, itself increasingly an escape and a dream. It is not so much in the plots that Gore and James reflect paternalist attitudes, as in the settings, the social customs, and the stock characters.

These were novels of castles and parks, villages and inns, proud earls and wicked squires, stern magistrates and selfless curates, and the worthy and unworthy poor. It was also a world of disobedient sons and daughters, a fact around which not a few of the plots revolve. It is a world in which everyone knew or should have known his or her place. Evard Morrison, in James's romance *Charles Tyrrell*, knew, for example, his place. He had been intimate at school with Charles Tyrrell, the heir to a baronetcy and a great estate. That intimacy tempted Morrison to attach himself to this future baronet. But remembering his father's sage advice, he told himself, "There were two paths for me to follow: either to seek associations above myself—to take my chance of rising . . . to society of a high grade; or to content myself with the middle class." He chooses the latter and lives happily ever after.

But such was not the fate of Jervis Cleve, the protagonist of Gore's *Peers and Parvenus*. Only the son of an agricultural laborer, he rises through the patronage of a lord and his own intelligence to win a degree from Cambridge. At that time his friend advises him, "Be a village curate, rather than a courtly chaplain; be a country school master, rather than a bear leader to a lord." Full of hubris, Jervis refuses the advice, becomes a bear leader to a lord, and boldly seeks the hand of an earl's daughter. The offer of marriage is refused, his even more parvenu brother is caught in crime, and Jervis's career ends in ruin. He had reached too high. Deference, a sense of place, obedience, whether of son to father, wife to husband, or tenant to squire, are as much a part of the texture of these novels as castles, parks, vicarages, and peasant cottages are part of its scenery. It was part of what Andrew Stalbrooke in G. P. R. James's *The Gentleman of the Old School* called "all the imperceptible shades and grades of life and station that [run] from the cottage to the palace, from the castle to the hovel."[1]

Andrew Stalbrooke, the owner of Stalbrooke Castle, is irreproachable as the guardian and benefactor of the village poor, whether as magistrate, landlord, or friend. The silver-fork romances not only reflected the patriarchal settings of rural life and the texture of its deferential ways, they also made its patriarchal duties explicit by the use of certain stock characters, the benevolent squire, the kindly parson, the lady bountiful. The novels of the upper ten thousand abound with such models. Gore, in *Men of Capital* creates the good squire in Mr. Mordaunt and the bad squire in Mr. Cromer. Mordaunt improves the laborers' cottages, gives them garden allotments, builds schools, abolishes game preserves, and pays the apothecary to care for the poor. Squire Cromer, in contrast, does nothing for the village.

The clergy also loom large in the silver-fork romances. J. F. Murray, in his *The Viceroy*, draws the portrait of the Reverend Edward Harvey, a compassionate parson who visits and consoles the poor and sees that they are well housed and fed, since he knows that "the improvement in their temporal condition must precede all spiritual regeneration."[2] Murray is not a noted novelist. An Irish journalist and writer for *Blackwood's*, he is one of those many authors now long forgotten, who turned out hundreds of silver-fork romances, many of them featuring model paternalists. These endless romances, like the Hollywood movies of the very rich, had no specific social message, but they did present a picture of society that, in structure, in texture, and in characters conditioned many to accept as natural that paternalist status quo which, however imperfectly, governed rural England. It is this unobtrusive conditioning, with its strong emphasis on deference and obedience, that made these novels more than a mere reflection of the pervasiveness of paternalist ideas; it also made them reinforcements of that dominant social outlook.

In the 1840s the silver-fork romances faced a rival in a new species of fiction, the novels of the lower classes. One of the first to write such was Mrs. Trollope, with her exposure of factory conditions in *Michael Armstrong, The Factory Boy,* published in 1840, and her exposé of the cruelties of the New Poor Law in *Jessie Phillips* of 1844. She was followed by Benjamin Disraeli. The silver-fork romancer who wrote *Coningsby* in 1844 discovered in 1845, in *Sybil,* that there was not one nation but two and that the second was full of the poor and the wretched. William Sewell's *Hawkstone* of 1845, Mrs. Gaskell's *Mary Barton* of 1848, and Charles Kingsley's *Yeast* of 1848 and *Alton Locke* of 1850 also did their best to make the miseries of the poor as vivid to Englishmen as the dreamland of the upper ten thousand. An industrial revolution, a population explosion, and rapid urbanization had all combined to produce an avalanche of social abuse, an avalanche of abuse the details of which were made widely known by countless parliamentary investigations, each with its resulting series of huge folio volumes. With varying degrees of verisimilitude, compassion, bathos, and melodrama the novelists transformed these reports of oppression and exploitation into pity-evoking tales. They also, and with varying degrees of conviction and tentativeness, saw the solution to this exploitation and oppression in a revived and active paternalism.

The two most ardent advocates of the paternalist solution were Benjamin Disraeli and William Sewell. Both were, apart from their novel writing, active in the revival of paternalist ideas: Disraeli in Parliament, William Sewell in the *Quarterly Review.* In order to propagate these ideas both made their novels of the lower classes also social tracts. They preached in these novels the full and classic theory of paternalism. Their heroes lamented that society had become so atomistic, looked back to a golden age when a Catholic Church and a feudal barony protected the poor, wished for an organic society based on mutual bonds, pleaded for a strong monarchy and church, and yearned for a hierarchy in which all of rank and property did their duties to their dependents and the dependents in turn were loyal and trusting.

There are, however, differences between Sewell's and Disraeli's social tracts; Sewell's *Hawkstone* is narrow and intolerant, Disraeli's *Sybil* broad and comprehensive. Sewell denounces all that is anathema to his High Church, Tory prejudices: evangelicals, dissenters, Chartists, Roman

Catholics, teetotalers, freethinkers, athenaeums, workhouses, economists, women philanthropists, and manufacturers. "I wish," says his hero Ernest Villiers, "it were the old times again when landlords and tenants and labourers all hung together; and we had none of these ugly factories." To fulfill this wish Villiers, lord of the manor of Hawkstone, rids that town of evangelicals, dissenters, Chartists, teetotalers, women philanthropists, and its ugly factory—a considerable accomplishment, since when he arrived the town was infested with them. He builds in their place a library, a school, a cathedral, a monastery. In the monastery young Oxford men pray twice a day, and in the school they teach the peasants, whom they call children, "not to rise above a higher sphere than that in which nature has placed them."[3]

Disraeli dreamed his paternalist dreams in a more generous spirit. He too has monasteries, Anglo-Catholic churches, and alms-giving landlords, but with a shrewd air of modernity he includes, as Sewell never would have, Carlyle's captains of industry as model paternalists, and he is nowhere intolerant of any particular religion. Disraeli dresses up his paternalism in a motley garb, a colorful and attractive mix of medievalism and modernism, of conventionalities and idiosyncracies, all informed by a compassionate feeling. It was a grand though not very realistic vision, but a vision that, however unrealistic, presents a moving plea for a revived paternalism that is quite unrivaled by any other novelist of the 1840s.

Coningsby and *Sybil* are not, however, unrivaled as accurate pictures of the condition of the working classes. Mrs. Gaskell's *Mary Barton* and Mrs. Trollope's *Jessie Phillips* both provide a fuller, better balanced, and more intimate picture of urban and rural laborers. Mrs. Trollope, like Disraeli, had a weakness for melodrama, and it seriously flaws her *Michael Armstrong, The Factory Boy;* but in *Jessie Phillips* she controls more successfully her desire to exaggerate the wretchedness of the poor. *Jessie Phillips* is seldom read these days, but it offers one of the fullest accounts in fiction of the harsh impact of the New Poor Law, particularly of the cruelty of that bastardy clause which, by totally excusing the putative father from supporting his illegitimate child, placed that burden entirely on the unwed mother and the parish. *Oliver Twist* presents a more dramatic workhouse scene, but it is much briefer and is far more of a caricature than is the picture of the workhouse in Mrs. Trollope's *Jessie Phillips*. Mrs. Trollope is almost as realistic about the miseries of rural life as Mrs. Gaskell is about the urban life of Manchester.

Neither of these authors had effective solutions for these social evils, and so both fell back on the tradition of paternalism. To say that they had no solutions is in no way to disparage the worth of their novels. It is not the function of novels to offer solutions, and those that do often weaken their aesthetic impact. But though disquisitions about remedies add little aesthetically, few novelists can plunge the reader into work-houses and industrial strikes without mentioning a better scheme of things. For Mrs. Trollope that better scheme was a paternalist one, a position Mrs. Gaskell also came to, but more reluctantly. In *Jessie Phillips* Mrs. Trollope writes nostalgically that "there used to be many, and there still are some, villages in England where the resident gentry have familiar personal acquaintances with every poor family in the parish." The story of *Jessie Phillips* is the story of the breakdown of such acquaintances. The son of a rich landlord makes Jessie, the daughter of a poor widow, pregnant. Because of the bastardy clause he is not held responsible, and Jessie must go to the workhouse. Ill when birth approaches, she wanders away from the workhouse, has the child in a shed, wanders on further and faints. The landlord's evil son finds the child in the shed, kills it, and lets the blame and an indictment of infanticide fall on Jessie. It is a lurid melodrama but ends happily as a truly kind clergy-man and a benevolent squire prove her innocent. The same salvation comes to *Michael Armstrong* in the form of a lady bountiful, a Mary Brotherton. Mary's answer to the evils of the factory is, "Let each in his own little circle raise his voice against these horrors . . . AND THESE HORRORS WILL BE REMEDIED," a plea made more explicitly paternalist when her friend Mr. Bell points across the valley to a model factory "where the voice of misery is never heard for there the love of gold is chained and held captive by religion and humanity."[4]

The paternal solicitude of millowners and landowners is still the key to all remedies. Mrs. Gaskell can go no further in *Mary Barton*. Though it is the most truthful and most moving account of factory operatives written in the 1840s, it ends with only a brief plea to the millowners to be more benevolently paternalist. Mrs. Gaskell could not, given her generation and class, accept Chartism, trade unionism, or Owenite socialism. She also had the wisdom to know that so widespread was unemployment because of the depressions of the 1840s that preaching laissez faire economics and self-help morality provided no answer. So at the end of the book she creates a penitent millowner. She has Mr. Carson, whose arrogant son was murdered by Mary's father, visit a workingman's home and confess "that a perfect understanding and complete confidence and love might exist between master and men, that the truth might be recognized that the interests of one were the interests of all," and that the workers should be "bound to their employers by their ties of respect and affection, not by mere money." Seven years later in *North and South* Mrs. Gaskell has moved no further in search of a remedy for industrial strife. In *Mary Barton* a millowner becomes penitent because his son is shot, in *North and South* another stern millowner, Mr. Thornton, becomes kinder because he falls in love with Margaret Hale, a handsome and strong-willed woman from the south of England where paternalism is woven into rural life. Margaret makes him a paternalist manufacturer.[5] But how effective in removing widespread exploitation are remedies that require the murder of a millowner's son or a love affair with a strong-minded woman in order to turn hardhearted millowners into softer-hearted ones?

So ubiquitous indeed were hardhearted millowners and oppressive landowners in the 1840s that not every novelist found in paternalism the happiest solution. Charles Kingsley, for one, was of an undecided mind. His *Alton Locke,* a novel about the wretched life of tailors and the seductiveness of Chartist ideas, includes an admiring portrait of Lord and Lady Ellerton. The lord is a model paternalist who lowers rents, gives up his hounds, improves cottages, grants allotments, and opens his picture gallery to the people, while the good Lady Ellerton pleads with the workers to abandon Chartism and "give up their will to God's will," and to cooperate with the priesthood about whose work in medieval times she is rapturous. Kingsley was not above looking to lords and priests to reform social abuse. In *Yeast,* a novel about the agricultural poor, he has the shrewd gamekeeper, Tregarva, tell the hero, Lancelot, "Everyone sees these evils except just the men who can cure them, the squires and the clergy." Kingsley, though tempted to find the remedy in squires and parsons and Lord and Lady Ellertons, still has doubts about them. The same shrewd gamekeeper, Tregarva, denounces Lord Vieuxbois, the kindly and patronizing landlord who by giving too much poor relief corrupts the poor. "He's making his people slaves and humbugs," says Tregarva, adding, "He fats prize labourers, sir, just as Lord Minchampstead fats prize oxen and pigs." Lord Minchampstead was an improving landlord who by giving too little poor relief, drove the poor into the workhouse. Neither lord pleased Tregarva or, one would assume, Kingsley. Neither did Tractarian and evangelical clergymen please Kingsley; he satirizes them savagely and in doing so knocks out one of the solid props of paternalism, the paternalism of the church, just as his strictures on the lords Vieuxbois and Minchampstead knock out the other prop that holds up paternalism, the paternalism of property. All that is left is the paternalism of the state, but he will have none of that. His hero, Alton Locke, condemns "a bureaucracy of despotic commissioners," and his admirable Lady Ellerton wants a "state founded on better things than Acts of Parliament." In distrusting the state Kingsley was at one with Disraeli and Sewell. Sewell's hero, Ernest Villiers, "smiled in melancholy scorn at the name of acts of Parliament," while the wise Sidonia in *Coningsby* says, "Rely upon it that England should think more of community and less of government." The paternalists among the novelists of the 1840s were decidedly not for a state paternalism, but were for what Lord Egremont in Disraeli's *Sybil* called "far greater exertions in our own spheres." But just such exertions by Tractarian clergy and labor-fattening lords won Kingsley's distrust. He could thus only conclude in *Yeast*: "What a chaos of noble materials here—all confused it is true—polarized, jarring, chaotic—but only waiting for the one inspiring Spirit to organize and unite and consecrate this chaos into the noblest polity . . . ever realized." For some readers such a passage, with all its Carlylean echoes, will only elicit that response which Lancelot gave to Tregarva's denunciations of Vieuxbois and Minchampstead, "I don't see my way out."[6]

Though Kingsley may have had trouble seeing his way out, the authors of the numerous tales of religious and moral edification did not. They were true believers in paternalism. Two of them, Charlotte Elizabeth and Elizabeth Sewell, were convinced that it was their mission to preach paternalism to the young and so wrote simple and engaging tales that inculcated its exquisite virtues. Elizabeth Sewell, sister of William Sewell, wrote *Amy Herbert,* a story about Mrs. Herbert and her daughter and their visit to the country house of a peer. Amy is initiated into its paternalist ways by accompanying the lady of the house in a visit to the poor and by giving alms to the poor. To Amy's naive question why some are so very wealthy and some so very poor, she is told that "it is the will of God." She is also taught in the course of the story that "vulgarity is to wish to be thought of higher rank than you are" and that "visits to sick persons . . . make us more contented and grateful than all the sermons that were ever preached." The world of *Amy Herbert* is the same refined, elegant, and polite world of the silver-fork romances, though in place of the worldliness of Gore and James there are pious homilies on deference and obedience. The same pious homilies are in Charlotte Elizabeth's *Helen Fleetwood,* though the scene is not that of the upper ten thousand but of Disraeli's second nation.

Helen Fleetwood is the story of a widow driven from her rural cottage by a capitalist farmer. She ends up in a mill town, living on the earnings of her daughter who works long hours in a factory where the overseer beats her. The beatings arouse the anger of the widow's son who comes close to rebellion. His rebellion, however, is stayed by the wise mother who tells him not only that "we are all sinners," but that he must not begrudge the millowner his wealth since "it was due to his enterprise and perseverance." We must, she says, "take the laws as we find them for our duty is to submit." The son, subdued, gains a fine job under a model landlord who is a paragon of paternal virtues and a splendid foil for the hardhearted millowner.[7]

If the readers of Elizabeth Sewell and Charlotte Elizabeth had not, by adulthood, learned deference and obedience, they could be further edified by the novels of High Church clergymen. Such works as the Reverend Robert Armitage's *Ernest Singleton,* the Reverend Francis Paget's *The Pageant,* or the Reverend William Gresley's *Clement Walton* brought to full ripeness paternalism's righteous morality. All three of these novels are remarkably specific and didactic about the duties of property and the role of the clergy. In fact so specific and didactic are they that they resemble colloquies and dialogues more than novels. Their ideas were also interchangeable since they are all reflections of that paternalistic orthodoxy that had its center in Oxford and its prophet in William Sewell. Sewell was professor of moral philosophy at Oxford and author of the age's definitive statement on paternalism, *Christian Politics.* Sewell, not Newman or Pusey, affixed paternalism firmly to the Oxford movement. The novels of the reverends Paget, Armitage, and Gresley simply spelled out this orthodoxy in desultory and sententious tales. The accent in these novels is strongly Christian and strongly for the increased role of the clergy, for what Armitage called a "shepherd clergy," a clergy made up of priests who would visit the poor, console the dying, discipline the erring, and educate the ignorant, all working under bishops who were not too proud to visit "the low abodes of misery." There would even be sisters of charity to care for the ill. This shepherd clergy would be a partial realization of Coleridge's idea of a clerisy, a body of religious and learned men educating and caring for the poor. Armitage called Coleridge "our favourite."

The three Tractarians, Armitage, Paget, and Gresley, also urged landowners to view private property as a trust, to realize that the wealthy are
stewards of God, that they must "see that cottages are clean and fit." But
though the three priests wanted landlords to build clean cottages, their
main plea was for the preaching of the true religion, for in it lay the
answer to social problems. "The dangers and miseries of a popular out-
break will be annihilated," said Armitage, "in the same ratio that ungod-
liness is removed. All that the people desire, is simply to be cared for."[8]

It may have consoled the reverends Armitage, Paget, and Gresley to
believe that the people simply desired to be cared for, but it was an
illusory belief. It is very unlikely that *Ernest Singleton*, *The Pageant*,
and *Clement Walton* were read by one hundreth of the people who
every month in 1839 waited breathlessly for the next installment of
Nicholas Nickleby.

The novels of Charles Dickens are neither silver-fork romances nor
religious tracts, and while they do deal with the lower classes and can
on occasion be considered novels of the lower classes, they were much
more than that. Furthermore, they did not conclude with even an
Elizabeth Gaskell's tentative or a Charles Kingsley's confused paternalism. Dickens's novels had an added dimension to them that led them
away from paternalism and toward humanitarianism, and away from
deference and toward rebellion. That dimension was the world of London, a world even more profoundly antipaternalistic than the towns of
Lancashire and Yorkshire. It was London that also produced the sprightly
and impish satires of Douglas Jerrold and the lively mockeries of
Theodore Hook.

That Dickens should be considered a humanitarian rather than a
paternalist might be disputed and disputed even by readers of *Nicholas
Nickleby*. In that novel the Cheeryble brothers, city merchants, rescue the
down-and-out Nicholas, employ him at a fair wage, and see that he, his
mother, and his sister live in a nice house. "We cannot allow those who
serve us well" says the benevolent Charles Cheeryble, "to labour under
any privation or discomfort that it is in our power to remove." Dickens
scarcely ever penned such a purely paternalist sentence, unless it was in
A Christmas Carol or in *Hard Times*. In the former, Scrooge's conversion makes him "a second father" to Tiny Tim, and a second father of
great generosity, while in *Hard Times* Stephen Blackpool complains that
the factory owners are "not drawn nigh to folk wi'kindness and patience
and cheery ways" but "ratin 'em as so much Power, and reg'latin 'em as

if they was figures."[9] That Dickens, a many-sided reflector of English life and a man who liked every kind of benevolence, would on occasion rejoice that property owners like the Cheerybles or Scrooge should do their duties should not be surprising, but it should not lead one to see in him the orthodox outlook of the paternalist; he was instinctively much too antagonistic to authority, particularly cruel, proud, and arbitrary authority, to preach the doctrines of deference and obedience, just as he was much too immersed in the vast, democratic ocean of London life to find social salvation in the local spheres of the known and the personal. Dickens's benevolence could not tolerate these bounds. Even the Cheeryble brothers could not fit within the local spheres of the paternalists. For one thing, they were not of superior rank. Dickens makes them humble: "Thousands," he says, "wouldn't invite them to dinner" because "they eat with their knives and never went to school." Furthermore, their benevolence is not limited to their dependents; they were active in support of subscriptions for almshouses, charities, hospitals. The same was true of Scrooge. He became a humanitarian, not a paternalist. The ghost who scares him into goodness replies to his protest that his concerns are only with business with the exclamation; "Business . . . mankind was my business. The common welfare my business. Charity, mercy, forbearance and benevolence, were all my business." The business of Dickens's benefactors was just that, common and extended, humanitarian and philanthropic, rather than paternalist, and its greatest and most lovable practitioner was Mr. Pickwick, a man of no castle or hall, of no title or rank, of no vicarage or rectorship, but Mr. Pickwick, "former occupation unknown," of Goswell Street, where his front room looked onto "human nature in all its phases"; Mr. Pickwick who, indifferent to the paternalists' distinction of worthy and unworthy poor, befriends the ungrateful Mr. Jingle in a debtors' prison; Mr. Pickwick, restless and mobile, who, knowing no local sphere, moves from Ipswich to Bath to Dorking.[10] Out of the motley, egalitarian, active, multitudinous world of London, there could not arise an outlook in which benevolence was confined to the worthy poor or fell within the sphere of good squires and a shepherding clergy.

But besides the fact that the universality of Dickens's metropolitan humanitarianism fitted ill with the constricted sphere of rural paternalism, his rebelliousness fitted ill with deference to authority. *Nicholas Nickleby,* though it offers the somewhat paternalist Cheeryble brothers, also offers rebellion. Nicholas rebels against schoolmaster Squeers, rebels against his uncle, and rebels against Snipe's father, a rebellion that elicits a most satirical reference to "parental instinct." Nicholas's sister also rebels against her uncle and then, with pungency and spirit, against the first two aristocrats Dickens chose to portray in his novels, the sybaritic Lord Verisopht and the ruthless Sir Mulberry Hawk, the latter receiving from the rebellious Nicholas quite a beating. Whether it was Verisopht, Hawk, or Squeers, or in *Oliver Twist* the workhouse master Bumble and the magistrate Fang, all are mercilessly caricatured, and all, in their spheres, are authority figures of a paternalist society. Even the sacred authority of a husband and a father are treated as objects of rebellion. In *Hard Times* Louisa rebels against both her husband, Mr. Bounderby, and her father, Mr. Gradgrind.

Dicken's flair for caricaturing men of authority finally hit the doctrines of paternalism at dead center in *The Chimes.* In that Christmas tale, the baronet Sir Joseph Bowley announces, "I am your perpetual parent, . . . I will treat you paternally." As "the Poor man's Friend and Father," Sir Joseph says he will "endeavour to educate his mind by inculcating on all occasions the one great moral lesson . . . entire Dependence on my-self." Sir Joseph tells the poor men he loved them very much, which love he expressed by playing skittles with his tenants, a comforting act since "everyone said that now, when a baronet and a son of a baronet played skittles, the country was coming around."[11]

Only the most obtuse of early Victorians could miss this broad satire on Disraeli's Young England and on all rural, maypole-dancing, cricket-and-skittles-playing paternalism. Dickens, a product of London, found such paternalism a pale and tepid answer to the vast, infinite suffering of a sprawling metropolis.

Dickens's good friend and fellow Londoner, Douglas Jerrold, took no more buoyant a view of such a paternalism. In *St. Giles and St. James* he mocks it through deft caricatures of pompous parsons, ignorant magistrates, and the spoiled sons of the gentry. Ebenezer Snipeton is one such magistrate. He denounces the poor as "obdurate and hopeless" and un-justly sends the novel's hero, St. Giles, to prison. Another ignorant magistrate, Justice Wattles, is feted by his tenants even though he has just judged as innocent of a local murder the spoiled son of the local squire. The son of the squire had in fact committed the murder. In the same Kentish town there is a pompous parson, Dr. Gilead, who recalls the glorious days of the pharaoh, tells his parishioners of "the social ne-cesssity of the many trusting the few," and exhorts them "to put away conceit and faith in their own weak judgment and to be obedient to their betters [who are] appointed to guide and protect them."[12] In his caricatures of Snipeton, Wattles, and Gilead, Jerrold is as distinctly irreverent of authority as Dickens in his caricatures of Bowley, Verisopht, and Squeers. The skeptical, urbane, and mocking London intellect penetrated the rhetoric of paternalism far more thoroughly than the serious, earnest, individualist intellect of Lancashire, Yorkshire, and Norfolk, the three counties that produced Charlotte Brontë, Elizabeth Gaskell, and Harriet Martineau. Few wrote more fervently on behalf of a staunch North Country independence, yet none of them escape its earnestness and seriousness enough to allow a satire of paternalism.

Rebellion there is, or at least defiant independence, in Charlotte Brontë's *Shirley* and Harriet Martineau's *Deerbrook*. In *Shirley* the heroine rebels against her uncle as Nicholas Nickleby had against his. As soon as Shirley is of age she tells her uncle, "Having ceased to be your ward, I have no guardian." She then rejects her uncle's choice of a husband, a man whose estates and rank fitted hers, and chooses instead to marry a lowly and eccentric tutor. Dr. Hope of *Deerbrook* is equally individualistic in withstanding the libelous charges of the villagers and the intrigues of the lord of the manor, Sir William Hunter. But the staunch independence and self-reliant ethos of Brontë and Martineau, like that of Mrs. Gaskell, lead to no rebellion against paternalist ideas. Dr. Hope and his wife are conscientious in their visits to the ill and plead as piously as does Mrs. Trollope in *Jessie Phillips* for "the honest genuine acquaintances among the poor." The novel also ends happily with a festivity at the local lord's manor hall, over which Sir William and Lady Hunter preside with paternal graciousness. Charlotte Bonté is just as respectful to such authority. Shirley, a landowner in her own right, and one who speaks of "all the cares and duties of property," is a model paternalist. A lady bountiful who visits schools and the poor, she organizes her clergymen to give clothing where it is needed and food where most appreciated. Charlotte Brontë considered it the duty of the upper classes to relieve social distress. In *Shirley* she has a pauper shout out that people are starving. She then has the pauper say, "Them that governs mun find a way to help us; they mun mak' fresh orderations."

Where the West Riding's Charlotte Brontë and Norwich's Harriet Martineau present rectors who dispense clothing, doctors who visit the poor, and paupers who demand of the governing classes "fresh orderations," Theodore Hook gives the reader humorous pictures of the Reverend Slobberton Mawks, who "fancied he could domineer over the poor," of Justice Minton, who with "not a bit of evidence" sends "the idle dog" to the treadmill for sheep stealing, and of Mrs. Minton who "trumpets piety and charity" to the poor.[13] These caricatures occur in Theodore Hook's hilarious *Peregrine Bunce,* and in mockery and comedy they resemble Dickens and Jerrold. Hook, in fact, was the High Church and high Tory editor of *John Bull* and in that journal espoused the ideas of paternalism. Mrs. Gaskell and Harriet Martineau, on the other hand, were Unitarians and radicals; yet Hook's portrait of ladies bountiful and paternal magistrates is infinitely more irreverent toward paternal authority than the portraits drawn by the two Unitarian radicals.

This paradox points to two truths about paternalism; first that it was not the preserve of any class or party, and second that it ill suited life in a sprawling metropolis. Theodore Hook, like Dickens, was totally and completely a Londoner, and he was, like Dickens and Jerrold, part of London's bohemian world of actors and journalists, a world that produced cockney comedy, not Lancashire seriousness, and it was just such an ebullient, bubbling, parodying wit that lured even the good Tory Hook to mock magistrates and ridicule parsons. Paternalism rests on locality, the limited sphere, the known authority, and deference, social characteristics not only indubitably true of rural parishes, but also largely true of industrial towns. Mrs. Gaskell's Manchester, Harriet Martineau's Norwich, and Charlotte Brontë's Keighley, were still local, circumscribed towns with known authorities. Not so London. Charles Dickens in *Dombey and Son* describes its awesome capacity to devour people. Standing on the Great Northern Road, Harriet Carker meditates on the fate of those pouring in. "Swallowed up in one phase or other of its immensity, towards which they seem impelled by a desperate fascination, they never returned. Food for the hospitals, the churchyards, the prisons, the river, fever, madness, vice and death—they passed on to the monster, roaring in the distance and were lost."[14]

The monster that was London contained social problems far too serious for paternalism, just as it produced those middling, mobile classes far too independent for paternalism's condescending ways. Paternalism had to bow to London's immensity.

Paternalism was in fact slipping in the esteem of many throughout England. The early Victorian novels, particularly the silver-fork romances and the tales of moral edification, certainly reflected its widespread popularity and show how intertwined it was with existing institutions, just as the novels of Sewell, Disraeli, and Gaskell reflect the revival of paternalism as a social remedy, a revival that was a response to the industrial revolution's avalanche of abuse. But the early Victorian novels show more than its popularity and its revival, they also show a great uneasiness with its authoritarian ways. For Dickens, Hook, and Jerrold that unease burst forth in caricature and satire; in Kingsley, Brontë, Gaskell, and Martineau it shows itself in a more circumscribed form, in criticisms of clergymen, in defiance of guardians, in pictures of proud doctors fighting a whole village. Paternalism was a hierarchical outlook that imposed deferential patterns on private and public spheres, on husband and wife, and on magistrate and subject. The early Victorian novelists knew no real solution to public problems of poverty and industrial exploitation, and so they fell back on paternalism; but in the private sphere, where novelists are at their best, they were growing restive at its pomposities, condescensions, and authoritarianism. It thus happened that the early Victorian novelists not only reflected and reinforced many of the assumptions of paternalism but the keener and more sensitive practitioners sensed very acutely its deficiencies. The same early Victorian novels that reflected a revived paternalism contained also the seed of rebellion that would mean its decline.

The intellectual revival of paternalist ideas that occurred in the first half of the nineteenth century, and of which the novels of the 1840s were a part, was for many early Victorians an intellectual event of importance. It helped many to make sense of the alarming and fearful present by underscoring the dependability and security of past ways. These old ways, they were told, provided the materials for an effective social theory. It was an assurance that helps in part to explain the astonishing revival of paternalist ideas.

The growth of paternalism was, however, more than a revival. It took on a life of its own, creating new forms of old elements. It was as much an efflorescence of social theories as a revival, its Coleridges and Southeys, Arnolds and Carlyles, forming new syntheses from past truths and fresh insights. These new syntheses were far more explicit, self-conscious, comprehensive, and keenly argued in social and economic terms than were the writings of their Tudor, Stuart, and eighteenth-century precursors. The ingredients—a belief in an authoritarian, hierarchical, and deferential society, in the Christian stewardship of wealth, and in man's sinfulness and poverty's inevitability—were old, but in bringing these beliefs together and applying them more fully and cogently to specific social problems, the paternalists were developing new and more elaborate theories.

In sheer pages of print, in numbers of books, articles, and sermons, it was an impressive intellectual event. Paternalist ideas became enormously popular. Yet they were not efficient in solving those new problems that stimulated their revival and efflorescence. They offered few effective solutions to the plight of the overworked milliner or the evil of the undrained street. How then to explain their pervasive acceptance?

One answer is that paternalism was practical in satisfying the intellectual and psychological needs of those educated and ruling classes that were confused and a little frightened by startling social, economic, and intellectual changes. The paternalist intellectuals offered these classes a vision of society that both preserved traditional norms and promised to resolve growing tensions. Robert Southey's *Thomas More* and Benjamin Disraeli's *Sybil* turned men's minds to medieval guilds and monasteries and the possibility of their revival, while G. H. Francis in *Fraser's Magazine* turned their minds to model dukes in every county and William Sewell in the *Quarterly Review* to ecclesiastical centers in every village. These guilds and monasteries, model dukes and ecclesiastical centers, could never lessen a milliner's long hours (or those of the agricultural laborer) nor could they drain a street, but the stories about them did create a mental world of such harmony and stability that one need not think of poor milliners and field laborers and undrained streets. It was also particularly comforting when accompanied by a call to religious seriousness and improved morality.

Ideas in history perform many different functions and often run in parallel but separate channels. Paternalism, though it reflected widely held attitudes and common institutions, could live and grow in different worlds. Its function at a magistrate's bench differed from its function at soirees in Belgravia. Some mutual interchange, of course, there was. Country magistrates read Sewell in the *Quarterly* on Carlyle, and the intellectuals read in the press of magistrates sentencing poachers. They even talked often on common topics and debated the same political issues, but, as is apparent in their style and tone, their aims were different. William Sewell's style and tone was lofty, detached, and unruffled, producing a vision comforting to those yearning for stability; Thomas Carlyle's style was angry, denunciatory, exhorting, a delight to those who were indignant over the ruder features of the new civilization; and Thomas Arnold's style was earnest, solemn, and grave, an assurance to those who were anxious to believe that sheer morality would solve economic problems. Others, such as Seeley, Disraeli, Helps, and Alison, created other visions—evangelical, nostalgic, homely, and stern—that helped many of the educated among the upper classes to meet those intellectual and moral quandaries begot by rapid economic change, social tensions, and the decline of religion. In fulfilling these needs the intellectual revival of paternalism was indeed functional and practical.

Far different in tone and style from the Sewells, Carlyles, and Arnolds were the speeches of the duke of Richmond, the earl of Chichester, and Serjeant D'Oyly. Given at agricultural association meetings, diocesan gatherings, and quarter sessions, they were plain, unpretentious, unselfconscious, and confident. They represented the idea of paternalism at work in a different world, moving in separate channels. In the activities of these local leaders of rural life, as in the activities of model millowners and parish priests, one observes paternalism at work at the very grass roots of society.

Part Two

Paternalism at the Grass Roots

Chapter IV

The Patriarchy of Sussex

The social attitudes of a country are only in part a result of the writings of its intellectuals. They also reflect its economic and social interests. How property is owned and how classes and institutions are organized is quite as important in defining a social outlook as the intellectual advances of seminal thinkers. Though the development of pure mathematics or theology might largely reflect intellectually autonomous developments, the growth of social attitudes is without doubt intimately involved in a nation's economic structure. The interests, prejudices, and ideals of land-owners were as significant as the writings of romantic poets or philo-sophical idealists in forming the early Victorian social conscience. Indeed since landowners were more numerous and wealthy, had greater political power and a higher social status, they probably were more significant. In many ways it is thus more fruitful to read the speeches of wealthy land-owners than the rhapsodic dreams of Young England. If a social philoso-phy is to prove viable, it must work at the grass roots. It must not only inspire the fashionable ideas of London drawing rooms and clubs, but define the attitudes and practices of landlords, magistrates, and clergymen in such rural counties as Sussex.

In 1835 Thomas Horsfield published *The History, Antiquities, and Topography of the County of Sussex.* In that study he listed, parish by parish, some 470 owners of Sussex's 1,140,000 acres. Of the 470, 25 were noblemen (including 2 dukes and 13 earls), 19 were baronets, 9 knights, and 17 Anglican clergymen, and 21 had military titles ranging from captains and majors to admirals and generals. Those called esquire numbered 138 and those listed as "Gentleman" 19, while 111 were called "Mr.," and 97 were listed by their names alone. About 13 of the nobility and 4 of the gentry had estates ranging from 5,000 to 28,000 acres, the remaining ranging from 100 to 5,000 but mostly between 500 and 1,000. There were the grandees, and there were the gentry, the earl of Egremont with 28,000 acres in 14 parishes and the average squire with 500 to 1,000 acres in 2 or 3 parishes. To these 470 landowners Horsfield adds the names of 230 clergymen who enjoyed one or more livings in Sussex, the average income of which was around £300. Thirty-seven of those livings were in the patronage of Sussex laymen, 6 belonging to the duke of Norfolk, 3 to the duke of Richmond, 5 to W. S. Poyntz (who also owned 8,000 acres in 12 parishes), and 15 to the earl of Egremont. These grandees, gentry, and clergy, some 700 individuals, dominated the political and social institutions of Sussex.[1]

Two sons and one brother of the duke of Richmond, the son of the earl of Egremont, the son of the earl De La Warr and the son of the duke of Norfolk sat in the House of Commons for Sussex. With them in the Commons sat baronets and gentry, men such as Sir Charles Burrell, Bart., of an old Sussex family and W. S. Poyntz of the 8,000 acres. Almost all of the M.P.s from Sussex were Sussex men, the only outsider in the 1847 delegation being Spencer Walpole, who had felicitously married the daughter of the earl of Egremont. The Sussex Bench, appointees of the lord lieutenant, the duke of Richmond, was equally aristocratic. The earl of Chichester, owner of around sixty-five hundred acres in nine different parishes, chaired the East Sussex Quarter Sessions, the earl of Surrey, son of the duke of Norfolk, the Arundel magistrates, while on the West Sussex Bench sat the dukes of Richmond and Norfolk and the earl of Egremont, whose 12,000, 20,000 and 28,000 acres respectively constituted much of the western part of Sussex. Sitting with them were other lords and gentlemen of Sussex. The political hierarchy reflected rather precisely the economic structure.

The social hierarchy and the social ideas of Sussex reflected nearly as precisely that economic structure. One has only to read in the *Sussex Agricultural Express* of the many dinners of the Sussex agricultural associations to observe the Sussex social hierarchy in action. The *Sussex Agricultural Express* never failed to report these festive occasions. On June 15, 1844, for example, it gave a full account of a dinner of the Petworth Agricultural Society at the Swan Inn. At the head table sat the chairman of the meeting and the lord lieutenant of the county, His Grace the duke of Richmond. He was flanked by the bishop of Chichester and Archdeacon Manning and the leading esquires of western Sussex. At the front tables sat fourteen clergymen, more esquires, and ninety gentlemen. The laborers were "at the other end of the room." On December 14, 1844, it was the duke of Norfolk's turn to chair an association dinner, this time that of the Steyning Fat Stock Show, and he was in turn flanked by the duke of Richmond, the earl of March (Richmond's son), Lord Edward Howard (Norfolk's son), Sir Charles Burrell, Bart., Sir H. D. Goring, Bart., Sir James Duke, Bart., and Major Sandringham. The largest and most prestigious of the association meetings was the West Sussex Agricultural Association's annual meeting at Goodwood, the duke of Richmond's estate. In 1846 the duke of Richmond presided at a head table that included the earl of Chichester, the bishop of Chichester, and a distinguished visitor, East Somerset's M.P., Mr. Miles. The workers were again at the other end of the hall. It had long been the custom for the laborers to eat separately and join the rest only to receive their prizes, but the duke of Richmond broke that custom at Goodwood and had them dine with the gentlemen, though he included only the prize winners and seated them at the back of the hall.

The Sussex patriarchs could be infinitely condescending. In 1845 when apprised of dire food shortages, Richmond's neighbor, the duke of Norfolk, recommended the poor take a bit of curry powder. "A pinch of this powder," he said, "mixed with warm water . . . warms the stomach incredibly . . . and a man without food can go to bed comfortably on it."[2]

These many dinners were part of the cattle shows, plowing matches, stock and root contests, and annual meetings of local agricultural societies. At these dinners, whether at Goodwood or the Swan Inn or Arundel's Norfolk Arms, one found a microcosm of that hierarchical and patriarchical society that dominated Sussex. It was a patriarchy based on the ownership of land.

The social attitudes expressed in the speeches and toasts that enlivened these assemblies reflected the needs, interests, and functions of the county's ruling elite. They spoke, and they spoke enthusiastically, of the friendly intercourse and neighborliness these convivial gatherings represented, and of the social harmony and unity of all classes. The landlords, the clergy, the farmers, and the laborers, said the duke of Richmond, sat together in friendship since "their interests were closely and intimately connected." He called his awareness of these intimate connections "an old fashioned feeling" that was "instilled into him in early youth." The plain-spoken, crusty duke was quite frank about the material advantage of such connections, reminding the landlords of "the advantage . . . of honest, industrious and meritorious men working properties." Such an indubitable advantage made it in the landowner's interest to treat the laborer well and to tie closer the mutual connections by granting them quarter-acre allotments. Richmond called this granting of an allotment the granting to the laborers of "a stake in the hedge," and he did just this for 1,500 of the laborers on his estates. Such good treatment meant good laborers and good crops.

The landowners of Sussex believed in an economic harmony of interests quite as much as did the political economists, though they expressed it in moral, not market, terms. Archdeacon Henry Manning, a favorite at these meetings, told the duke of Richmond that he, Manning, "abhorred the political economist's expression labor market," a term that implied men "could be cast together into some great sea . . . where all moral relations, all the duties . . . all the affections and charities of life . . . are cast aside." At the same banquet the archdeacon told the laborers at the other end of the hall of the social pyramid, which God had ordained, in which the multitude should be poor and the few rich. He did add that God had imposed on the rich certain duties.[3] The identity of interest in rural Sussex was not merely that of everyone's stake in the hedge, but of the reciprocal duties that belonged to landlord, clergy, farmer, and laborer.

The august lords who toasted the clergy, farmers, and laborers at these dinners spoke much of duties. The duke of Norfolk pleaded with landlords to improve the cottages of the poor; the earl of Chichester urged landlords to relieve the distress of all who had won certificates of good conduct; the earl of March said "it was the duty of landlords to employ every good laborer"; Lord Edward Howard praised allotments as adding to the comforts of the poor; and the duke of Richmond had only praise for all the lords who "reside on their estates and encourage rural sports." Every class, except the laborers, told the other classes of their duties—two farmers, Mr. Oliver and Mr. Broughton, even having the temerity to suggest that landlords lower their rents and employ agents who knew more about agriculture than rack renting. The clergy, of course, were greatly experienced in exhorting the upper classes to their duties. They urged the wealthy to support the village school and parish church, build good cottages, and visit the poor.[4]

In their mutual toasts to each other, landowner, clergyman, and farmer did not forget those responsibilities that a Christian stewardship imposed on the wealthy. But though they did not forget to talk of such reponsibilities, neither did they dwell overly much on them. Most of their admonitions were aimed at the laborers. The agricultural associations had two aims, improvements in the practice of agriculture and improvements in the conduct of the workers. There were prizes for two kinds of behavior, for the raising of fat cattle or huge turnips, and for good conduct. The Sussex landlords believed that nothing would promote the well-being of the laborers more effectively than their own good conduct. "The truest way to improve the laboring poor," said Archdeacon Manning, "is to induce them to improve themselves." It was the duty of the laborers, added the marquess of Cambden, "to rely on their own resources for support and not to depend on other relief." They should "not spend their money in drinking, but in clothing their family" and should "stay their lifetime with one lord." To encourage such good conduct, prizes were given for neat cottages, for raising large families without going on parish relief, and for long service with one lord. With these money prizes came certificates of good conduct to hang on the cottage wall and many sermons on the iniquity of indolence, wasteful extravagance, improvidence, and beer shops.

The Sussex landowners took a very stern view of the poor. They were condescending, moralistic, insensitive, and smug. The unselfconscious and self-assured duke of Richmond told one banquet audience that he had never heard a tenant address an angry word to him. The Sussex landowners expected the poor to be grateful and dutiful, particularly patient in distress, and particularly affectionate to their lords. The poor, said the earl of Chichester, should "in times of difficulty be moral, thrifty, and prudent . . . [for] it was for this end that these trials were inflicted upon us, to make us thoughtful of our conduct in this world and to make us think of our still more important duties to God." The duke of Richmond was just as demanding. He promised to discharge all men of bad character and would have no one on his estate who spent money in a beer shop. If a laborer did err but promised to reform he could stay, though at a reduced wage. For the duke "the man who labours for affection is worth a hundred who work for hire." He wanted his workers loyal, moral, and obedient; at Petworth in 1842 he entreated them "to fear God, honour the Queen, and obey the laws." In return Richmond, and, it was hoped, the gentry of Sussex, would provide steady employment, allotments, prizes for huge turnips, schools for the children, the neighborliness of summer cricket, and after forty years of never having gone on parish relief, a certificate of good conduct and dinner at the back of the hall with the duke.[5]

The vision of a harmonious, friendly, unified community under the loving care of a lord was an idealized one. It was the projection of the landlord's image of himself as a model employer. But it was a vision by no means limited to landlords and their agricultural banquets. It is also found—though with modifications—in the charges and sermons of Sussex's bishop, archdeacons, and prebends. They too projected an idealized image of their social role.

The bishop, archdeacon, and prebend of Chichester, along with the archdeacon of Lewes, had an exalted and ambitious view of the role of the Church of England. They felt themselves to be part of a religious revival. Looking back at the eighteenth-century Church in Sussex, they saw only torpidity and latitudinarianism, but looking forward in the 1840s, they saw a renewed spiritual life and an expanded social role. They were determined not only to revive the two most traditional functions of the clergyman, the performance of the services of the Church and the visitation of his flock, but to expand the Church's role to include the education of the poor and the moral superintendence and discipline of all parishioners.[6] The two archdeacons, Henry Manning of Chichester and Julius Hare of Lewes, certainly included these four functions in their conception of a clergyman's duties. In their charges to the clergy they called for improved church services, more frequent visits to the poor, the ill, and the dying, and the stricter admonition of sinners. In their visits the clergy were to give spiritual counsel and to guard their parishioners from serious error. There must also be, for Puseyites such as Manning, two solemn and impressive services every Sunday and a religious service each day. For the Broad Church clergy, like Hare, there must be long, serious, earnest, and learned sermons. But these were traditional goals. What Manning and Hare urged that was new was the creation of an extended educational system—supported by property, guided by the Church, and devoted to the reformation of the poor. It was a goal that had the enthusiastic concurrence of their bishop, Ashurst Turner Gilbert. Peel had chosen Gilbert in 1842 as the new bishop of Chichester. As bishop, Gilbert directed much of his energy within the Chichester Diocesan Association to the establishment of two training schools from which, it was hoped, would come excellent Christian teachers for every parish school in Sussex. In his *Pastoral Letter* of 1843 he confessed that the Church had not in the past educated the poor, and because of this failure crime and infidelity had gone unchecked. In a moment of exuberance he assured his audience that education would take eighty out of every one hundred criminals off the court calendars. He admitted ignorance was not the only cause of crime, there was also poverty, but he added that education would also end poverty. Education would, he promised, make the poor better laborers, better servants, more peaceful subjects, more prudent—in short, firmer links in what Gilbert called "the mysterious chain of mutual dependency in which human beings are bound to each other."[7] Manning and Hare echoed Gilbert's enthusiasm for Christian instruction of the poor, but they were more severe than their bishop on the failure of landlords to support parish schools. Gilbert, to be sure, had said, "It was an awful responsibility to be entrusted with wealth," but when he found in 1842 that only twenty-two laymen in the diocese of Chichester gave but £114 to support its training schools, he could still exude happiness over the subscriptions of "that small but shining band."

The High Church Manning, far more skeptical of diffuse philanthropy than the Low Church Gilbert, frankly avowed his disapproval of such subscription begging. Like the sacraments or the giving of alms, any offerings for the support of Christian instruction should be a fixed and certain duty, one performed within a definite sphere and toward one's own dependents. Land, said Manning, not charity, was responsible for education. "The Lords of the manor and Lords of the soil" should erect and endow schools, "while the clergy might then by their service render it available." "It was," he added, "the principle of the feudal system."

Julius Hare, a product of Cambridge and an admirer of Coleridge, though far removed from Manning's High Church ideas, agreed on this paternal principle. In his "1841 Charge" to the clergy he called on the farmers to "provide that the children of their labourers shall be carefully brought up and instructed" and that "our landlords must be taught that their possessions are not given to them of God to be squandered in reckless self-indulgence but . . . as benefactors and guardians of all the poor on their estates." Hare's charges, like those of his bishop, were filled with pleas to landlords to support and to the clergy to manage village schools. They also call for the revival of ecclesiastical discipline over the erring sinner. The problem of bastardy aroused Hare's righteous anger, and he urged the clergy and the laity to punish this sin. Manning shared the same indignation about unpunished sin and insisted too on a

strict ecclesiastical and social punishment. These two doughty archdeacons wanted the Sussex clergy to reprimand the rich for their extrav-
agances, the farmers for their avariciousness, and the poor for their dis-
obedience. Manning would even revive the practice of imposing fines
on the erring as a form of spiritual penance.

The clergy of Sussex were not humble about their role in the Sussex
patriarchy. The prebendary of Chichester, James Garbett, in a sermon
The Church's Power, claimed that the clergy were the possessors of
"sacred mysteries . . . the mediators and sacrificers" to God for man.
It was thus their right and duty "to rebuke transgressors in high places";
"to minister to men's souls as diseased by sin"; "to clothe . . . the
naked, visit the deserted, feed the hungry." Since the misery of the poor
"defies civil and legislative enactment," only the Church, he argued, "can
secure to them . . . their own." "Comparatively speaking," he concluded, "we have little to do with the rich . . . our business is with the
lowly and the poor." Garbett even employed the term "clerisy" in his
appeal for a paternalism of the Church.[8]

These were noble ideas. They not only won much support from the
clergy of Sussex but also from those laymen who constituted "that small
shining band" and who were active in the Chichester Diocesan Association. Chief among these laymen and chairmen of many of its meetings
was the earl of Chichester. At these meetings the good earl spoke as
eloquently for Christian education as he did at the quarter sessions for
strict obedience to the law and at the East Sussex Agricultural Association
for benevolence to the poor. His patriarchical domain in East Sussex was
extensive. As a much desired chairman, he presided over the annual
meetings of the Agricultural and Labourers' Friend Society, the Chichester Diocesan Association, the Lewes Deanery Committee of the Society
for the Propagation of Christian Knowledge (S.P.C.K.), the Church
Missionary Society, the board of the County Hospital, the East Sussex
Agricultural Association, and the Brighton Savings Bank. He was also
the "acting manager and auditor of the accounts" of that savings bank,
just as he was an examiner at Brighton's training school for mistresses.
As chairman of the East Sussex Quarter Sessions he not only presided at
the trial of criminals but helped administer the Horsham Gaol, the Lewes
House of Correction, and the local constabulary.[9] Then there were his
own 6,500 acres in nine parishes and the schools, churches, and beer
houses thereon. With such a myriad of patriarchal powers and roles it
would be difficult for the farmers and laborers to know whether they

were in the presence of the paternalism of land, the paternalism of the Church, or the paternalism of the state. The distinction would never have occurred to them, or even to the wise and learned earl. Sussex was an organic society. Its paternalistic institutions and ideas were integrated. The Church owned much land, and archdeacons and bishops dined to the left and right of dukes at agricultural association meetings; landowners supported the Church with tithes, church rates, and subscriptions, and earls chaired diocesan meetings; and both landowners and clergymen sat on the East Sussex Quarter Sessions as magistrates. The chairman of that bench was the earl of Chichester, and in his charges to the court, just as in the ecclesiastical charges of bishops and archdeacons and the agricultural speeches of dukes and earls, he expressed the social aspirations of the ruling elite of Sussex.

The earl of Chichester, as chairman of the East Sussex Quarter Sessions worried much about the rising rate of crime in the early 1840s and about the means of reducing it. He accepted as useful greater education and an improved police but looked beyond them to "the individual efforts of good men." He thus pleaded with "the most respectable persons in different stations of life" to do their utmost in their "private capacities . . . to promote religion and virtue, [and] discourage all kinds of immorality." He would have them check the beginnings of crime by putting down beer houses and promoting habits of sobriety, all within "the immediate sphere of their influence." Crime would not increase if this were done, Chichester concluded, as it "would be quite impossible because quite contrary to the moral economy that God had established."

The earl of Chichester, like the bishop of Chichester, and indeed like the duke of Richmond, saw social problems in strict moral terms. They all believed in "the moral economy of God." They saw the world in terms of the wickedly disposed and the well conducted. Their very perception of society, their deepest ingrained categories of thought, were intensely moral. It thus was possible for the earl of Chichester to sentence Charles Thomas, aged eleven, to seven years' transportation for stealing two pair of clogs valued at two shillings and William Gain, aged twenty-seven, to only eight months for stealing a lamb worth fifteen shillings. Thomas was, said Chichester, "a wicked, bad lad" and Gain "of excellent character." The habit of perceiving social problems in moral categories not only led to that nearly ubiquitous distinction between the worthy and the unworthy poor, but also to hopeful expectations that the erring poor could be persuaded to emulate the virtuous lives of their superiors. Deeply ingrained in paternalist thought was the belief in the great efficacy of moral example. "By the good conduct and example of those who were in responsible station in life," said the earl of Chichester, "bad men may be brought to a better sense of their moral and religious duties." The duke of Richmond had expressed the same sentiments in extolling the value of hanging certificates of good conduct on cottage walls. The winning of a certificate would be an example for other laborers to emulate.[10] The setting of such moral examples, particularly by superior persons, formed part of that larger moral reformation of the lower classes that the Sussex landed classes hoped would bring a better order to their not so harmonious society.

If good example failed to excite the emulation of virtue, there was always the rod of authority. The discipline of the erring by authority was central to Sussex paternalism. The earl of Chichester was no more ready to tolerate errant behavior than Archdeacon Manning or the duke of Richmond. His sentences at quarter sessions were severe, his treatment of vagrants strict, and his ideas on idle paupers harsh; for vagrants it was the jail, not the workhouse, for criminals solitary and bread and water, and if repeatedly fractious, corporal punishment, and for the idle paupers who drank, a month in jail. What Manning felt about unwed mothers and Richmond about denizens of beer shops, Chichester felt about criminals, vagrants, and idle paupers: they were wicked and needed discipline. "It was the paramount duty of parents and masters," he told the quarter session, "to watch over and endeavour to control all the evil propensities of their servants."[11]

In the earl of Chichester's charges to quarter sessions, in the ecclesiastical charges of the bishop and the two archdeacons to their clergy, and in the speeches of earls and dukes to the agricultural associations, the elite of Sussex presented their social philosophy and social goals, their vision of the good society, their idealized image of a truly paternalist community. But was this world more than mere rhetoric and fancy? Were the gentry, the clergy, and the farmers beneath them carrying out their injunctions?

A further examination of the columns of the *Sussex Agricultural Express* suggests that the gentry and their ladies and the clergy were indeed attempting to carry out these injunctions. From 1840 to 1846 the *Express* reported more than three hundred occasions when the wealthy helped the poor. These occasions were of every kind, as heterogeneous as the givers and the festive days. At Storrington "the poor children of the parish were bountifully regaled with old English fare, roast beef and plum pudding"; "at Battle a fine Ox was butchered for the poor by a gentleman of the place"; "on Christmas eve the Hon. R. Curzon, of Parham House regaled the whole of the work people on his estate with . . . boiled beef, plum pudding, and good old ale, as is the usual custom"; "the Reverend J. Gould, acting on the old proverb 'all work and no play makes Jack a dull boy' has kindly set apart a most commodious field . . . for cricket"; and from the rector of Rotterfield to forty pupils, the annual gift of a shirt, flannel petticoat, and common prayer books. At Arundel in preparation for the arrival of Prince Albert, the duke and duchess of Norfolk gave the pupils of the local school "hats, bonnets, and frocks," and at Brighton's Union School upon Queen Victoria's marriage, "each scholar received an orange, a white ribbon and a small book." On December 5, 1840, the *Express* reports that the duchess and duchess dowager of Richmond "with condescending kindness" made "many errands of mercy to the dwellings of the poor," and in February of 1841 that "the private benevolence of Lady Domville has supplied coal and soup to many."[12]

The most common of these benevolences was the distribution of coal, soup, bread, or beef. Sometimes it was soup alone, sometimes bread alone, or if not bread, flour; at other times it was bread and coal, or soup and coal, or coal and clothing; the permutations were many, but the elements the same: the food, fuel, and clothing so needed by the poor. These benevolences were highly functional, being direct responses to the dire needs of the poor. It was not accidental that nearly 90 percent of the dispensations of food, fuel, and clothing occurred in December and January. They answered both the material needs of the poor and the ceremonial desires of the rich. Many of them were listed as "seasonal benevolences." "Monday being St. Thomas's Day," says the *Express* on December 26, 1840, "gifts were distributed as usual to the poor of Wadhurst." And on New Year's Day the earl of Arundel and Surrey gave 600 loaves of bread and 200 gallons of beer to "the necessitous poor." Such gifts, part of the rituals of the Christmas season, also met the urgent needs of the winter months, a season of layoffs, snow, and frost. Since the Poor Law Commissioners discouraged outdoor relief to the able-bodied and since to place families of six or seven in the workhouse for three or four weeks was both cruel and expensive, the gentry and clergy expanded old yuletide rituals to solve modern problems of welfare. The yuletide rituals themselves may well have long ago grown up for these very reasons. St. Thomas's day was also known as "dole" day. Seasonal charities were very useful, a fact that the *Agricultural Express* admitted in March of 1846 when it noted that "the mildness of the present winter and increase of employment" had lessened the privations of the poor and thus "the various local charities . . . have also been in less active operation . . . and the soup charity is much less in request." The winter of 1840-41, the worst in fifty years, saw the reverse, and local charities had never been more active. The *Express* shrewdly noted in December of that year, "Small aids, timely bestowed will frequently save a parish from heavy expense." It also, with equal shrewdness, noticed that such help "carries to the heart the most delightful sensations."[13] Being charitable was not so unpleasant. The *Express* noted in the same issue that the dispensers of one charity "spent the night in the Dorset Arms in the most agreeable manner, highly delighted . . . having promoted the comfort . . . of the poor." Being charitable thus was both useful and delightful; nor was it all that expensive. The fuel, food, and clothing were not given to the poor for nothing. They usually had to pay a fee of one or two pennies to prevent them from being corrupted by a totally free dole and to teach them habits of frugality. Besides the penny or two the poor also owed the rich gratitude. The Sussex landowners taught their poor to express that gratitude with all the zeal of fathers teaching their children to be thankful. Gratitude played a psychological role in promoting that deferential posture so indispensable to the working of agriculture and the ordering of village society.

There is some doubt, of course, that the poor whom the *Sussex Agricultural Express* recorded as forever grateful were in fact grateful. The speeches of landowners and the charges of clergy and the accounts in the *Express* of soup charities and butchered oxen and beef and plum-pudding rituals all formed a part of the rhetoric and ceremonialism of the upper classes. They do not necessarily prove that the paternalism of the Sussex elite substantially helped the poor. All was not as harmonious as the duke of Richmond and Lady Domville rhapsodically claimed. There were deep fissures in the idealized paternalist world of Sussex. They even revealed themselves in the *Sussex Agricultural Express.* An editorial in August of 1845 stated rather bluntly, "Our rural population is sorely demoralized and miserably degraded and its component parts are alarmingly unhinged." The owner and editor of the *Express* was W. E. Baxter, an extensive farmer and son of the famous Lewes publisher, John Baxter.

His own outlook, as reflected in the *Express*'s editorials, was impeccably paternalist. Fifty years ago, he lamented, "the squire resided on his estate, farmers kept unmarried workers in their homes and there were truly reciprocal duties arising from affections; now there is less residence, low wages, and instead of the resident squire giving workers good cottages, good wages, a cow and a garden, a few prizes at agricultural association dinners." But these prizes "do not produce upon the labourer's mind the cordial feelings which a kind master's kindly bestowed gift awakens." "Nothing," he keenly added, "is more galling . . . than the elaborate condescension of a superior in rank," and nothing is "more meaningless than digging up a retired rustic for a prize at a dinner."[14]

Baxter's editorials raise the question that nags all social historians: to what extent was a set of social ideals actually carried out? Did the rhetoric of agricultural association dinners and the ceremonial rituals of seasonal benevolences mean a truly paternal solicitude for the poor?

The answer to that question must be a mixed one. It both did and did not mean such solicitude. Take for example the four greatest of the Sussex grandees, the two dukes, Richmond and Norfolk, and the two earls, Chichester and Egremont: the record of their activities shows both solicitude and indifference. Richmond, for one, was energetic and attentive toward the poor. His private papers show his concern: he inspects the Westhampnett workhouse, talks at length with the medical officer, goes over the accounts of a "penny club" and of the girls school at Boxgrove; grants some allotments, examines a local school, subscribes to the local infirmary, reviews the report on the Petworth House of Correction, and once a year visits those Westhampnett pauper lunatics who had been sent to private houses in London. The duke of Norfolk was less active. Known as the "pig fattening" duke, he was nevertheless assiduous in agricultural improvement. He was also quite constant in his residence at Arundel, gave to charities and hospitals, supported Arundel schools, and insisted on doing what most farmers did not do, employing laborers in the winter.[15] The earl of Egremont and the earl of Chichester both won greater reputations as paternalists than did the duke of Norfolk. A fellow parishioner, after telling the Poor Law Commissioners of Egremont's employment of 150 men during the winter and of his helping more than one thousand to emigrate, concluded by praising his remarkably generous public spirit, a spirit that led him to lower cottage rents at Petworth from £5 4s a year to £2. Egremont was of the Wyndham family, and he and his brother Colonel Wyndham were often mentioned in the *Agricultural*

Express for their munificence. But it was as nothing when compared to the most ardent paternalist of them all, the earl of Chichester. The Sussex historian, Thomas Horsfield, was quite ecstatic about "that excellent nobleman" and his "indefatigable attention to the comforts and improvement of the poor on his various estates." "Let our nobles," he added, "generally tread in his steps." Chichester had turned over much of the parish of Felmer to allotments for the poor. He was also indefatigable in chairing meetings for good causes.[16] Like the duke of Richmond he gave copiously of his energy and time to translate paternalist ideas into practice. No reading of the earl's long memorandum of 1834 to the Poor Law Commissioners or his innumerable charges to the quarter sessions can leave any doubt of his earnest concern for the poor. The same holds true of any survey of the duke of Richmond's outpouring of time and energy. But even with these patriarchs the picture is mixed.

The same duke of Richmond who annually visited pauper lunatics of Westhampnett Union also paid hard-working laborers ten or eleven shillings a week and erring ones less, and that at a time when many considered twelve shillings the barest subsistence wage. There was, furthermore, no compelling economic pressure for such a wage. The assistant poor-law commissioner for Sussex reported in 1835 that while in the western part, a part dominated by Richmond, Norfolk, and Egremont, the average wage was 9s 8d, in the eastern part the wage was 12s. The duke of Richmond could be both generous and severe. On his son's coming of age he entertained 700 of the country nobility, gentry, and farmers and gave a grand ball to all his tenants. But in the same year as the grand ball he allowed his own parish's school to remain uncompleted for want of money. By 1849, a decade later, none of the schools in the ten parishes where the duke had land could qualify for a Committee of Council grant, though sixty-one other Sussex schools could. It might be that the duke was so generous to his schools that these schools needed no government grants, but the reports of school inspector John Allen on Sussex schools raise doubts about this possibility, doubts furthered by the duke's tightness toward subscriptions. Allen found in 1846 that rural schools in his district (which included Sussex) suffered from both a scarcity of qualified teachers and a want of adequate funds. The duke, who had left Goodwood's school uncompleted in 1839 from want of adequate funds, in the same year refused to help form an institution to supply coal to the poor at cost.

The duke of Norfolk could be equally tightfisted. A memorandum to the Poor Law Commission in 1838 shows him, as the lord of several hundreds, demanding in his own court leet a six-shilling to fifteen-shilling payment from all tithingmen. Since these payments had long come out of the poor rates, their collection had hurt no one visibly. But after the Poor Law Commission outlawed the payment of them from poor-law rates, the duke's insistence on their collection from the tithingmen hit the pockets of "mere labourers." The duke of Norfolk also refused to make any improvements on the rundown Horsham House of Correction though as lord of the manor, its upkeep was his responsibility.[17] Both these complaints against Norfolk lie hidden in the duke of Richmond's private papers, along with complaints about other landowners, about Sir Charles Burrell's refusal to give to charities and about Colonel Wyndham driving cottagers out of some of his parishes. The earl himself, sole owner of Petworth, presided over a workhouse school judged by the government inspector as "extremely limited and defective."

The avoidance of poor rates by destroying, or refusing to repair and build, cottages was a scandalous practice that one would not expect of Colonel Wyndham, a nobleman so highly praised by the *Sussex Agricultural Express*. But then much lay hidden in the world of earls and dukes and other landowners. A pamphlet on housing and a government report on settlement in Sussex showed both intense crowding in loathsome slums in Chichester and a want of cottages in the outlying rural areas of West Sussex, a disturbing fact since so much of West Sussex, north of Chichester, belonged to Norfolk, Richmond, and Egremont. The Egremont family at Petworth House owned nearly twenty-six thousand acres. "Every soul for miles around," said the assistant poor-law commissioner, "is more or less under the influence of the autocrat at Petworth House."[18] Autocrats they were. On the return in the 1847 election of Richmond's son, the earl of March, a letter to the *Sussex Agricultural Express* announced that none dared oppose him and that "they were living under the Duke of Richmond, Lord Egremont and two or three more of them." The autocratic vein in paternalism can be seen not only in Richmond's dismissing workers who drank in beer houses and Colonel Wyndham's ridding his parish of the poor, but also in the decisions of these noblemen as magistrates.

An analysis of either the earl of Chichester's East Sussex Quarter Sessions or Serjeant D'Oyly's West Sussex Quarter Sessions, on which the dukes of Richmond and Norfolk and the earl of Egremont sat (along with the earl of Winterton and Richmond's son Lord Lennox), shows a considerable severity. The harshest sentences, seven to fifteen years' transportation, went for the theft of sheep and cattle and repeated poaching. Even when the value of a stolen ewe was less than the value of a stolen watch, it received much heavier punishment, no doubt a reflection of the dominance of landowners over jewelers on the Sussex bench. But even those fortunate to escape seven years of transportation still received from the earl of Chichester—that "excellent nobleman"—sentences of six months to a year at the treadwheel, with the first week of every month in solitary. If the sentence was less than six weeks, the prisoner was to have a diet of bread and gruel alone. For some, the more refractory, there was private whipping. For stealing sixpence worth of faggots one laborer received fourteen days' solitary. The paternalists might indeed be solicitous of the poor, but they were both severe on the erring and tightfisted guardians of the public purse. They spent on food for prisoners in the Petworth Town Gaol £6 9s 1d per prisoner per year, a sum the prison inspector said was insufficient. Dietaries, however, could be even more meager. At the Lewes House of Correction, which was under the earl of Chichester's East Sussex Quarter Session, the yearly food bill for each prisoner came to only £5 12s 8d. The earl of Chichester, though conscientious about the poor, would never coddle them. In 1834 he told the Poor Law Commission that he "was thoroughly convinced of the general impolicy of all legal provision for indigence."[19]

If the solicitude of the earls and dukes for the poor was a mixed one, so was the concern shown them by the gentry and clergy. The record varies. One can read in the *Express* of the more than three hundred reports of seasonal benevolences, soup kitchens, coal distribution, and clothing clubs and find in these reports the names of some fifty to sixty public-spirited gentlemen, generous ladies, and altruistic clergymen. But as Horsfield's study shows, there were nearly seven hundred gentlemen, ladies, and clergymen in Sussex's 315 parishes. Since it was the *Sussex Agricultural Express*'s announced policy to print all notices of benevolence, one wonders about the six hundred and forty or so not mentioned from 1840 to 1847. Some, of course, may have been benevolent but too modest to inform the *Express,* but there cannot have been many such. Many were no doubt apathetic. It is quite clear, for example, that many were apathetic about education and housing.

Two of the foremost duties of a good squire and caring parson were the housing and the education of the poor. Most did not supply these at an adequate level. Two government reports are quite unsettling on this

score: Captain Robinson's report in 1850 on housing and the Reverend
John Allen's report in 1845 on Sussex schools. Captain Robinson said of
Sussex and Kent, "there is a great deficiency [of housing] in rural districts," a judgment that agrees with the remarks of a landlord near
Chichester who told Captain Perry that farm laborers lived "in wretched
. . . hovels." The reason for the "great deficiency" and "wretched
hovels," said Captain Robinson is that "cottage property is generally
disliked by large proprietors." "Sometimes," he added, "cottages are
considered unsightly and are pulled down . . . [while] in parishes in
the hands of one person often they are either destroyed or suffered to
fall down for want of repair." Furthermore, "not only are they suffered
to fall down from want of repair, but their number is diminished by
destruction and the resident poor are thus got rid of." The poor "thus
got rid of" poured into the larger towns, into overcrowded sections of
Chichester, Horsham, Lewes, Brighton, and Hastings, areas quite removed from those neighborly intimate connections that the duke of
Richmond had found such a charming old-fashioned idea. Captain
Robinson did, however, praise the Sussex landowners as leaders in the
granting of allotments.[20]

It was a mixed picture, as varied as the report on Sussex schools made
by two of Her Majesty's inspectors of schools, the Reverend John Allen
and the Reverend William Brookfield. From these reports a historian
could paint both a glowing and a dismal picture of education in Sussex,
either by celebrating the names of those sacrificing clergymen and generous gentry who built schools, provided books, examined the pupils,
and paid for able teachers or by exposing those parishes without schools
or with defective ones. Both pictures could be based on John Allen's
reports of 1845 and 1846. Allen, a positive thinker, wished to emphasize
achievements, but also an honest observer, he could not hide inad-
equacies. His own generalizations note "want of adequate funds" and
"scarcity of qualified teachers," facts that are not surprising as most
teachers were paid less than 13s 3d a week. This appeared to Allen "a
sadly low estimate of the claims and position of a teacher of the poor."
It was an estimate about three shillings a week above the standard wages
of the agricultural laborer. By 1850, largely because of aid and stimula-
tion from the central government, Sussex schools were improved: sixty-
one qualified for grants, nearly a third of these being in the six towns of
Chichester, Hastings, Brighton, Lewes, Battle, and Westbourne. The
reports on these schools list the annual subscriptions to thirty-one of

them. The mean of these subscriptions came to only forty pounds a year. The poor themselves, through the school pence, gave roughly twenty pounds a year. A subscription of forty pounds for thirty-one of the sixty-one best schools in Sussex is a meager amount, especially when it is remembered that the average parish possessed property that, according to the Poor Law assessment, rented at over £5,000 a year and that the average incumbent of a parish received, according to the Ecclesiastical Commission, around £300 a year. No wonder that at these schools, the best among the 315 parishes of Sussex, only 30 percent could read words longer than four letters. Rural Sussex did little to educate its young. "The children of the poor are taken away to labour at such an early age," said the Reverend Richard Burnett, chaplain of Lewes, in 1840, "as almost precludes the possibility of acquiring . . . more than the art of reading and writing"; "the lower orders . . . are not in an instructed state," said the vicar of Cuckfield in 1843; "there are many persons," said the Reverend C. M. Klavert of Petworth, "who object to the education of the working classes," as it makes them "dissatisfied with their station."[21] Both Sussex's limited effort at education and its failure to build adequate housing suggest that a truly paternalist concern to instruct and house the poor was felt by only a small minority.

Part of the difficulty of translating paternalist ideas into practice came from the often overlooked importance of the tenant farmer. The patriarchs of Sussex were not omnipotent or omnipresent. Archdeacon Hare was right to plead with the farmers to see that children went to school, since it was the farmer, not the landlord, who employed them at an early age. Of what use was a school supported by the landlord and the parson if, because of the farmer, children never attended, or if they did, left at age ten? The tenant farmers who leased most of the arable land of Sussex are too often neglected by the social historian. Their social outlook was also crucial. They applauded, at agricultural association banquets, the paternalist rhetoric of earls and archdeacons about social unity and the identity of interests of all classes and even, on occasion, spoke such sentiments. But their actual performance was not always so altruistic.

Many of them, for example, paid very low wages and laid off their workers at the first sign of frost. Some even hired child labor at from twopence to sixpence a day, in preference to adults, and others cheated the workers in their piecework contracts. These are serious charges, but there is evidence for them. Julius Hare, a sober and intelligent observer, noted that boys go to the fields at ten, nine, and eight years of age, and at "6d, or 4d, nay for 2d." Timothy Shelley, a prosperous squire said it was widely known that "when flour had risen twenty-five percent farmers doled out only some five percent more as wages." In the Poor Law Commission's papers on Sussex Union management and in the columns of the *Express* it is clear that wages in Sussex varied from nine to twelve shillings a week, better than Wiltshire's seven to eleven, worse than Yorkshire's and Northumberland's average of thirteen.[22] The farmers were a hard and flinty lot. A memorandum to the duke of Richmond tells of West Sussex farmers cheating the laborers on contracts for piecework, while a government report in 1843 on women and children in agriculture tells of East Sussex farmers around Battle paying workers in scrip drawn on local stores whose prices were 25 percent higher than normal, stores in which the farmers sometimes had interests. The acquisitiveness of the Sussex farmer does not present a happy picture. "Farm houses" in Sussex, said G. W. Perry, "are everywhere improved, but a large portion of farm labourers live in wretched, cheerless hovels. Rents have risen in an extraordinary manner."

This acquisitiveness does not represent the entire story. The farmers were not free from the pressures of landlords who raised their rents along with the rise in the price of grain. Landlords also owned the cottages whose rents had risen extraordinarily. Furthermore, the farmers also did their paternalist chores. They too did unpaid work as overseers or guardians of the poor and spent long hours judging cases and helping distribute relief. They worked alongside the squire and clergyman in performing these tasks. It is to their credit, as can be seen in the records of the Sussex poor-law unions, that these farmers blunted some of the cruel edges of the New Poor Law: they urged that the old and infirm be allowed to leave the workhouse for a few hours at midday; they asked that two or three children of large hard-pressed families be taken into the workhouse so the rest of the family could remain in their cottage; they insisted, despite the orders of the Poor Law Commission, on roast beef and plum pudding on Christmas day; and they were generous with medical relief and helped families in need to emigrate. Above all, they continued to give more relief outside rather than inside the workhouse. In the mid-1840s they spent four times as much on outdoor relief as they did on those inside the workhouse. This is not to say that the farmers were always generous to the poor or that the welfare of the poor was their main concern. Where their own poor rates and assessments were concerned they could squabble and obstruct, and they hated to waste one more penny on the poor than was required for their barest needs and a rare Christmas dinner. They failed to hire chaplains for many of their workhouses, allowed most of their workhouse schools to remain defective, and hired and supported harsh and incompetent workhouse governors, one of whom seduced the women inmates and another of whom stole milk and cream from the inmates' spare diets. To the old and infirm of whose moral character they had doubts, they could be as severe as the duke of Richmond was on habitués of beer houses. They were at times quarrelsome and petty. At Cuckfield the chairman complained of "turbulent and designing members." He called them "blackguards" and the "more unprincipled and jobbing portion of the community" against whom the "respectable Guardians" need protection. The "blackguards" were often the farmers, "the respectable Guardians" the landowners.[23] Paternalism at the grass roots in Sussex was organic: the different levels of the social pyramid—the nobility, gentry, clergy, farmers, and laborers —did work together. But to say that it was organic is not to say that their interests were identical. Often they were not, nor did all work in harmony. It was a symbiotic relationship and one not free of the cash nexus, of rent rises and wage cuts and political partisanship. Yet even the haggling and bickering were part of a known, customary, and local community, a distinctly deferential and hierarchic society and one that both helped and failed to help the poor.

This symbiotic relationship is nowhere clearer than in the meetings of the guardians of the poor. Jealousies, hostilities, factionalism, callousness, and insensitivity were all present, but despite the squabbles and factions, these guardians and ratepayers and relieving officers did far more for the poor than all the more charming seasonal benevolences, soup kitchens, clothing clubs, and agricultural prizes. However harsh were some of the orders of the Poor Law Commission and however negligent and severe were some relieving officers and workhouse governors, through this law the landlords and farmers of Sussex did pay out for the care of the poor roughly 10 percent of the assessed value of their property. The heart of paternalism is an insistence that property has its duties. In no way, then, were the farmers, squires, and nobility of Sussex more paternalistic than in the thousands of man-hours and thousands of pounds that they expended on the upkeep of the poor. In 1847 they spent £144,881 in poor rates, the largest part of which went to those outside the workhouse. However harsh the New Poor Law appeared, it was through that law that the wealthy took the most paternal care of the poor.[24]

The wealthy of Sussex did not pour forth this bounty on the poor simply because their dukes and earls spoke of the duties of property and their bishops and archdeacons preached Christian stewardship. They did it because it was required by acts of Parliament. Their most significant effort was part of the paternalism of the state, and not just part of the local, intimate paternalism of the quarter sessions and parish vestry that was so organically tied to the paternalism of property, but part of the impersonal, legal, centralized, distant paternalism of London.

The attitude of the Sussex patriarchs to that centralized state paternalism was exceedingly ambivalent. By and large they did not like it. "Centralisation is a French nostrum," said the *Sussex Agricultural Express*, "which the Whigs imported into England, we like it not." "It deals with men as if they were machines," it added, "rather than moral agents." The duke of Richmond quite agreed and worked hard to prevent the centralizing police and lunacy acts of 1839 and 1845 from applying to Sussex. He had great pride in the capabilities of the Sussex magistracy and the town constable to handle its poachers and felons, and he himself would vouch for the private house in London to which the Westhampnett Union sent its pauper lunatics. A similar pride was expressed by Serjeant D'Oyly who wrote an angry letter to Richmond complaining that Queen's Bench would no longer allow the West Sussex Quarter Session to impose "the punishment of hard labour in convictions for bad assault." He found this act "a slur on the magistrates."[25] Even farmers resented London's meddling inspectors. They heeded and duly administered the New Poor Law, but they warred with its assistant commissioners, asking for instance that married couples be allowed to live together and opposing plans for district schools. The reports of the inspector of poor-law schools of 1849 on the dismal state of schools in Sussex, like the report of the lunacy commissioners in 1850 on Sussex's refusal to build a county asylum, show a deep hatred of centralization, particularly when the central directives might increase local rates. The Sussex landowners and farmers hated higher rates as passionately as they took pride in Sussex's local autonomy.[26]

Yet it would be a mistake to see this localist strain as entirely at odds with the paternalism of a centralized state. The Sussex landowners in particular were not truculent localists like the northern, urban radicals, and this for two reasons: first, they were protectionists on the Corn Law, and second, they truly believed in a deferential and authoritarian society.

That they were unyielding protectionists springs directly from the soil, social beliefs again reflecting economic interests. "East Sussex is the strongest area in England against free trade," exclaimed the *Express*. It was a strong claim, one that West Sussex might contest with its distinguished duke of Richmond as president of the British Agricultural Protection Society. Most of Sussex, except parts of Lewes and Brighton and a few other boroughs, was protectionist. The duke of Richmond was thoroughly protectionist, even mercantilist. He would not only protect all branches of agriculture but wool traders, silk weavers, and factory workers. He was for the ten-hour day for factory operatives and condemned "the mad theorists from Manchester." But his protectionism and that of other Sussex grandees had its limits. It did not mean the central government should protect agricultural laborers or interfere with landed property. On this point the Sussex landowner saw eye to eye with political philosophers like Burke and Coleridge, only the landowners expressed their views in homely phrases like "live and let live."[27] The *Express* called that phrase "a homely but very truthful saying" and linked it with their argument for the Corn Law. For Parliament to repeal the Corn Law was, in their eyes, for Parliament to interfere. "Live and let live" was the rural form of laissez faire, only with a twist, in that it meant above all leave the status quo untouched, leave the dominant interests of that status quo unhampered. For Sussex landowners and farmers this meant leave landed property alone, leave quarter sessions alone, leave overseers, archdeacons, and constables alone, above all protect the price of corn by leaving the existing Corn Law alone. That the philosophy of "live and let live" should include governmental interference to support the price of corn was, of course, logically inconsistent —but then social philosophies need not be logically consistent as long as they are functionally integrated with local interests, which they were in rural Sussex.

The protectionist aspect of Sussex landowners, qualified as it was by a strong localism and a "live and let live" outlook, does not alone explain their willing cooperation with assistant poor-law commissioners and school inspectors. They also had a deeply ingrained deferential regard for authority, even that of assistant commissioners and inspectors. In 1834 the poor-law reformer Edwin Chadwick told Lord John Russell that the duke of Richmond was "by no means cordial" to the New Poor Law and was, indeed, "a defender of the mischievous labour rate plan." But in 1838 the assistant commissioner to Sussex wrote that the duke was his great ally in coercing obstreperous farmers into working with the new law. The same assistant commissioner obtained the willing cooperation of Norfolk and Egremont.[28] Not one large landowner in all Sussex opposed the New Poor Law, and though farmers grumbled over its arbitrariness and the clergy wrote letters of humanitarian protest about its cruelties, they usually followed their lords and cooperated. In rural societies like Sussex, localism is deeply ingrained, but so is obedience to authority; hence such a culture can never develop that rebellious, self-conscious, truculent localism that the assistant poor-law commissioners met at Huddersfield, Bradford, and Rochdale.

In Sussex the paternalism of property was both jealous of and yielding to the paternalism of the central state. The county landholders were, after all, dutiful subjects of Her Majesty and devout believers in monarchy. That fact is best exemplified in that conscientious public servant, the earl of Chichester. Unlike the duke of Richmond he was in favor of establishing a county lunatic asylum and a county constabulary, both to be inspected by London. He also urged that Parliament interfere to help the poor emigrate, and he welcomed the Committee of Council on Education minutes of 1846 which granted money to teachers and to pupil teachers. So did the hard-pressed clergy. They felt directly the poverty of their schools and so recognized the value of the Committee's grants. "In many cases," observed the school inspector John Allen, "the deficiency between income and expenditure of a school falls upon the curate."[29] The two archdeacons in their charges had expressed some high ideals for the role of the clergy. Not a few of them endeavored to fulfill those ideals. In their letters to the Poor Law Commission pleading for more generous relief, in their organizing of emigration committees, in their visits with criminals and the poor, and in their promotion of schools many of the clergy of Sussex qualified for Coleridge's clerisy. But for all their generosity their efforts fell short. The average of subscriptions was still forty pounds for the thirty-one best schools of 315 parishes. Real aid to education, like real aid to the poor, came when the paternalism of the central state was combined with the paternalism of property and the church. John Allen's report of schools in Sussex in 1844 tells of scanty funds and untrained teachers, the Reverend William Brookfield's report of 1850 tells of able teachers, improved buildings, and much larger government grants.

The paternalism of the dukes, earls, bishops, squires, farmers, and parsons of Sussex, admirable in its ideals of the duties of property and the mission of the Church, never met the age-old needs of the rural poor as fully as its defenders claimed or hoped. It also could not cope with

new problems. It was a static outlook devised for a stable society, an
outlook that held that the poor will always be with us, and docile at that.
But in the 1840s not even Sussex was stable. Its rate of pauperism,
around 12 percent of its inhabitants, was much larger than those in
manufacturing areas. The rapid rise in population brought widespread
unemployment and poverty. In a poignant memorandum an assistant
poor-law commissioner tells how after all of the earl of Egremont's zeal
to help 1,000 of the poor to emigrate, Petworth was as full of unem-
ployed paupers as before. Many of the earl of Chichester's sanguine
hopes that education would diminish crime and poverty also broke apart
on the new realities. The coming of the railways, the rise of fashionable
watering places, and the growth of fishing and smuggling produced alien
and disturbing social elements, elements whose higher wages and earnings set higher standards of expectation. It was not so much that the
paternalism of Sussex was insincere or hypocritical, but that there was a
gulf between its rhetoric and its practice and a larger gulf between its
practice and the formidable problems it faced. It lacked any dynamic,
imaginative, or innovative approach that could solve those problems
with an effectiveness that an age of progress, education, and greater
wealth expected. As William Baxter had said in the *Express*, it would
no longer do to bring some rustic before an agricultural association and
give him a prize.

Chapter V

Land and Its Duties

The grass-roots paternalism of Sussex was not untypical of the rest of rural England. There were, to be sure, regional differences. Norfolk, around Castle Acres, with its commercial farming and use of "gang" laborers, seemed almost destitute of the softer tones of paternalism; Cumberland landowners adopted the somewhat feudal practice called "bondages" in which every cottager bound a daughter to the master for a year's service; in Yorkshire the landlords disliked granting allotments, while in Kent they granted them profusely. But despite these regional idiosyncrasies the various areas all believed that landed property had definite responsibilities as well as privileges. There were few rural areas in which clerical charges, speeches to agricultural societies, and news-paper editorials did not express the same paternalist ideas as Archdeacon Manning, the duke of Richmond, and the *Sussex Agricultural Express.* Also rare were the areas without seasonal benevolences of beef and ale at Christmas, and of coal deliveries and soup kitchens to tide one over January. Throughout England, also, rural magistrates delivered stern lectures and stiff sentences to delinquents. Lord Stanley, addressing the Liverpool Agricultural Association voiced the familiar promise of such associations, the "bringing together all the classes of the community." The Reverend C. A. Hulbert's speech to the earl of Dartmouth's ten-antry in Yorkshire included the familiar dictum, "property has its duties as well as its privileges." The *Western Luminary's* picture of the dean of Exeter, the earl of Devon, Lord Courtenay, and Sir Thomas Acland all praising allotments for laborers at the St. Thomas Labourers' Society of Exeter is reminiscent of Sussex meetings, as is the *Shrewsbury Chronicle*'s description of the duke of Sotherton, the bishop of Lichfield, and Robert Slaney presiding over a meeting of the Church Extension Society. In the *Farmer's Magazine* of 1844 there were full reports of many meetings held at the East Riding, Stamford, Stewpone, Draycott, and Burton-on-Thames in which the same social vision is expressed, the vision of an active clergy and a conscientious landlord class improving the condition of the laboring poor. There were also the same reports on seasonal charities and soup kitchens and quarter sessions justice. The *Stamford Mercury*'s description of Christmas dinner at the workhouses and the opening of the infant schools could have come from the *Sussex Agricultural Express,* as could the *Western Times'*s publication of the charge made by Exeter's recorder, a charge quite as sanguine in its expectation that education would reduce crime as those of the earl of Chichester and quite as severe too in the punishments meted out.[1] Poor-law and education reports also made it clear that the farmers and gentry of Shropshire and Suffolk fought over outdoor relief and expenditures on education with the same mixture of generosity, niggardliness, severity, and moral censoriousness as the farmers and gentry of Sussex. Throughout rural England the governing classes believed that the answer to most social problems lay with the condescending solicitude of the grandees, the neighborly kindness of the gentry, the admonitory and consoling attention of the clergy, the strict discipline of magistrates, the teaching of the schoolmaster or mistress, and the careful dispensations of the poor-law guardians. It was a highly personal, quite unsystematic, and extremely variable social system, often more a matter of ideals than realities. It was also a very old system, though not one rigid with age. Indeed in the 1840s it was undergoing a revival, a revival marked by three definite changes from the narrow and more formal paternalism of the eighteenth-century village. The first of these changes was the multiplication of the duties expected of landowners, the second was the fervor and fullness with which these ideals were preached, and the third was the attempt to attach these paternal relations to a set of durable institutions.

That the duties of landowners had multiplied is clear when one compares the paternalist manuals of the 1840s—those of Godolphin Osborne, G. W. Perry, or John Sanford—with John Mordant's *The Complete Steward* of 1761 or Thomas Gisborne's *An Enquiry into the*

Duties in Men of the Higher and Middle Classes, published in 1794. John Mordant in 1761 asks his "Complete Steward" to "promote the ease and comfortable subsistence of [his] tenants and dependents" by keeping vagrants out of the parish, preventing the richer tenants from seizing common land from the poor, and attending the vestry to see that justice is done to the poor. At the vestry he must see that only those unable to work or with huge families receive relief without some hard labor. He should also reside on his estate some of the year and mix with the tenants "in affable behaviour."

It is not a very long or formidable inventory of duties, but Thomas Gisborne's list in 1794 goes little further. In a ten-page section on the duties of a landlord he includes choosing and encouraging industrious tenants, charging fair rents, improving drainage, offering long leases, and supplying "constant and growing employment and thus preventing the vices and disorders which derive their origin from idleness." He would also have landlords encourage "the settlement of families and the increase of population" by "augmenting the quantity and reducing the price of provision." He ends by urging them not to be "unmindful of the welfare of the infirm and disabled nor the children of the lowest classes."

By 1838 the duties of land had increased considerably. In that year Lord Sidney Godolphin Osborne published *Hints to the Charitable* in which he outlined the duties of land in a village economy. Osborne would not only have the landlord do his poor-law chores and attend to improved agriculture and charge fair rents, but he should help form, support, and supervise penny clothing funds, benefit clubs to insure against illness, savings banks, loan funds, the wife's friendly society, and the endowment of the children's society. The landlord should also build and maintain good cottages and good schools—infant, day, and Sunday. G. W. Perry in his writings added the duty of establishing industrial schools and the granting of allotments.[2]

Few landlords in the 1840s measured up to all of these duties, but most took part, on occasion, in the second change marking the revival of paternalism at the grass roots: the increased fervor and rhetoric with which these ideas were extolled. If they did not speak at the various societies, they often attended and applauded. The increasing activity of the agricultural associations in the 1840s reflects an anxiety on the part of landowners to reassert their basic social philosophy as an answer to a growing criticism of their special privileges and failings. The *North-*

ampton Mercury traced this increased activity to the political disputes over the Corn Law. There was indeed a decidedly defensive tone to much of the paternalist revival, defensive not only against anti–Corn Law agitators but against rioters and incendiaries. The Select Committee on Allotments of 1843 frankly attributed the rage for allotments in the 1830s to the agricultural riots of 1830–1831.[3] If the rhetoric in pamphlets, rural newspapers, sermons, and agricultural-association speeches rose to a new intensity in the 1830s and 1840s, it was in part because the agriculturalists felt themselves on trial.

The rage for allotments was of course more than mere rhetoric. It marked the third change in rural paternalism, the attempt to attach paternal relations more firmly to a set of fixed and definite institutions. In the pamphlets of Osborne, Perry, Ingestre, and Sanford, in the columns of the *Labourer's Friend Magazine* and the *Farmer's Magazine,* and in countless rural papers came a series of articles and manuals outlining a working paternalism. These pamphlets, articles, and manuals contained endless schemes for transforming the older, more circumscribed, variable, and personalized paternalism into a more systematic and institutionalized paternalism, one that, because of the participation of the agricultural laborer, would lead to greater self-reliance and independence, though one that was never to go beyond the limits of deference. Hence it was important that the landlord establish clothing and coal clubs, savings banks, and loan funds into which the laborer would invest a penny or two a week. They should also form clubs where women could save their pennies to cover future costs of bearing children and friendly societies where they could save in case of future sickness or burials. It is, said Osborne, "a foolish and weak species of benevolence which would rather give a shilling unconditionally than upon a plan which induces good habits."[4] It was important to have a plan, one whose object was to encourage industry, frugality, and providence. Industrial schools gave such encouragement, as did loan funds and above all, the leasing of a quarter of an acre for spade husbandry—the famous allotment.

The plea to landlords to lease allotments to laborers represents the most vigorous expression during the 1840s of the new paternalism. The plea was quite ubiquitous, and though the response was not quite so ubiquitous, the granting of allotments was popular. Three thousand laborers possessed them in Kent. The allotment was the best mode of institutionalizing paternalism: it gave the laborer the added food to tide him over the January frost; it kept him working in the evenings and away from the beer shop; it earned him the extra pennies for the clothing club; it awakened his interest in agricultural improvements; it gave him, as the duke of Richmond shrewdly observed, a stake in the hedge.

The effort throughout rural England to revive, expand, and institutionalize at the village level an efficient, active, and beneficent paternalism, one based on the duties of the landed classes, was a generous and noble one. But was it actually realized throughout the rest of rural England any more extensively then in Sussex? The answer to that question is difficult to give. F. M. L. Thompson, the leading authority on nineteenth-century English landed estates, only ventures the judicious statement: "Paternalism had always been a patchy affair, those who lived in 'open' parishes without squires had never known much benevolence, and those who had looked up to a country gentleman had probably received less succour and protection than those living without the orbit of a magnate."[5]

That the magnates were solicitous, on many occasions, is true. The great dukes of the realm in the 1840s, the dukes of Bedford, Northumberland, Newcastle, Rutland, Grafton, Devonshire, and Argyll all won praise for their benevolences. Bedford built and let at uneconomic rates 288 model cottages on his Devonshire and 374 on his Bedfordshire estates. The third duke of Northumberland, before his death in 1847, rented good cottages at low rates and provided allotments. The fourth duke remodeled the school and added to it industrial and agricultural schools. The duke of Newcastle granted 2,000 allotments in Nottingham, 500 more than the duke of Richmond in Sussex. Devonshire proved to be one of the most enlightened landlords in Ireland.[6] Grafton won praise for the great attention he gave to the poor and for his very moderate rents, Rutland for an unaffected friendliness, and Argyll for efforts to save his people from famine. Said a contemporary of Rutland, "It seems to have been at all times the pride and happiness of the Duke to reside in the county . . . in daily intercourse with the middle and humbler classes, interesting himself in their condition, their wants, and their circumstances, and identifying himself with all their concerns."

The seventh duke of Argyll enjoyed no such luxury as Rutland's walks with prosperous tenants; instead he was confronted with the poverty of 5,000 Highlanders. His son's memoirs record that when the seventh duke's father died in 1839, the new duke "lost no time in establishing personal intercourse with numerous tenantry." He visited them all and expended his capital in agricultural improvements and in replacing the old thatched hovels with "slated and commodious houses." During the potato famine the son and father borrowed £10,000 from the government to sustain their people. They seldom evicted tenants, and they frequently helped those who wished to emigrate.[7]

Many earls, like the great dukes, fulfilled faithfully the paternal duties of land. The earls Fitzwilliam, Leicester, Dartmouth, Carlisle, Devon, Rosebery, Aberdeen, and after 1851, Shaftesbury, were all active in their various ways, Fitzwilliam championing better medical relief, Leicester renting good cottages at a loss, Dartmouth distributing prizes for spade husbandry, Carlisle building a reform school, Devon working for a county lunatic system. Rosebery and the seventh earl of Shaftesbury won the praise of Edinburgh's *Witness,* the former for building cottages with two comfortable apartments, the latter for remedying his father's neglect of their Dorset estates. Shaftesbury records in this way his first visit as earl to these estates: "Aug. 22, the debts are endless . . . every sixpence I expend . . . is borrowed . . . Aug. 25, Car [his sister] has offered to build me four cottages. . . . Heartily do I give God thanks. Sept. 6, shocking state of cottages. Sept. 13, No school of any kind at Pentridge . . . I determine under God to build one."[8] Shaftesbury also ended the truck system and fraudulent piecework contracts that had grown up under his father's neglect. The Victorian magnate, whether an evangelical like Shaftesbury and Dartmouth or a rationalist like Carlisle, was often more conscientious about the duties of land than his Regency father. But not all Regency peers were as negligent as the fathers of the seventh earl of Shaftesbury and the seventh earl of Argyll. The earl of Aberdeen had since 1804 improved his Scottish estates. They were in a wretched state in the year that he inherited them, and he thought of permanent absenteeism, but rejected it. Instead, says his biographer, "he drained, he planted, he built. New schools rose in every parish, new buildings on every farm."[9]

For dukes and earls such a patriarchal largesse is built into the very size of the property and grandeur of the title. When the earl of Aberdeen's eldest son came of age, there were nearly a thousand of his tenants and people to dinner, and for the duke of Richmond's son, 700 were entertained. To receive such deference at twenty-one and to look forward to inheriting tens of thousands of acres, to being a lord lieutenant, or chairman of quarter sessions, to controlling a dozen livings, to sitting in the Lords, demanded a paternalist outlook, however perfunctory the performance.

The patriarchal paternalism, however, need not always be benevolent.

Authority, power, command, and surveillance—these are attributes far more essential to patriarchal paternalism than benevolence, compassion, sympathy, and generosity, virtues that are more its embellishments. The House of Lords, after all, also included the second duke of Sutherland and the marquess of Londonderry.

The second duke of Sutherland in 1854 spoke at a meeting of the male inhabitants of the parishes of Clyne, Rogart, and Golspie. He pleaded with them to join the army and resist the czar. He offered each a bounty of six pounds. After an embarrassing silence an old man rose and announced that the county felt that if the czar himself ruled Sutherland, "we could not expect worse treatment . . . than we have experienced in the hands of your family for the last fifty years." The experience of the last fifty years had been tragic: more than 10,000 evicted from their homes, houses destroyed, towns pulled down, and families separated. To work, marry, or worship one needed the sanction of the duke or his stewards. Where once 10,000 lived and farmed, there were some forty huge sheep farms.[10]

The hauteur and arrogance of a marquess could be as great as a duke's. The marquess of Londonderry published a letter expressive of such qualities in the July 13, 1843, issue of the *York Herald*. It was addressed to those striking in his collieries. After telling them that they were "stupid," "insane," and "beaten," he added, "I found you . . . indifferent to my really paternal advice and kindly feelings." He then announced the eviction of more striking tenants in order to make room for more strikebreakers from his Irish estates. "The civil and military," he said, will protect these Irishmen. "I must do so," he ended, in order to defend "the majesty of the law and the rights of property" and to do "my duty to my family and station."

Lord Londonderry, a landlord and colliery owner of great wealth, was both ruthless in evicting tenants and solicitous about his people. The paternalism of even one magnate can be mixed. The high Tory Londonderry never worked women in his mines as had the radical earl of Durham, in whose estate management the historian David Spring can find little of benevolence. Spring also found little of benevolence in the duke of Buckingham's estate management though much of it in the duke of Bedford's. Paternalism is, as Thompson said, a patchy affair. The radical M.P. Sharman Crawford called Londonderry one of the best landlords in Ireland and the mining inspector Hugh Seymour Tremenheere praised Londonderry as "very liberal and effectual for education." But Tremenheere found education at the earl of Durham's collieries deficient. Even the second duke of Sutherland wished to do good. "Not being a hunter or sportsman," he wrote in 1848, "I know of no occupation more . . . agreeable to myself than going about among them [the poor] . . . sometimes rebuking . . . or commending. This is the position of duty."[11] But he adds that he can do little on a property large enough for half a dozen proprietors.

The exalted nature of a duke or earl and the magnitude of their properties brought to patriarchal paternalism a loftiness, hauteur, remoteness, and impersonality that was almost unavoidable. For a more personal and intimate paternalism of land, one must turn to those model country gentlemen, those exemplary squires, who showed a loving care for that most viable of paternalist units, the small estate in which all the tenants and laborers and their wives and children look up to the squire as the father of the parish.

Three such estates in the 1840s were Ketteringham in Norfolk, Barton in Suffolk, and Terling in Essex, ruled over, respectively, by Sir John Boileau, Sir Henry Bunbury, and the Honorable J. J. Strutt. All three men were agricultural improvers keenly aware that only a productive and efficient agriculture could sustain the well-being of their multiplying parishioners. Sir John Boileau, a member of the Royal Society, loved science and loved to experiment with crop rotation and better drainage; Sir Henry Bunbury, when he first took over Barton inspected every inch of the parish, examined its various soils, and after making himself acquainted with every tenant and laborer, regrouped his farms for greater efficiency; and J. J. Strutt called his tenants together to give them, as he put it, "a harangue on capital, labour, and manure." All three believed that fair rents and wages and winter employment were desirable and economically profitable.[12]

They also all believed in those three village institutions so crucial to a laborer's welfare: the comfortable cottage, the half-acre allotment, and the parish school. Bunbury built new cottages for twenty-eight families, enlarged many more, and erected a few for retired servants; Boileau not only built cottages for his laborers and houses for his tenant farmers, but "taught them how to keep them neat and clean"; and Strutt improved or rebuilt all the houses in his village. Both Strutt and Boileau also built new schools. All three were zealous about allotments. Bunbury in 1854 published an article on them for the *Journal of the Royal Agricultural Society*. His rules were to make none larger than half an acre, to charge a nominal rent, to pay the poor rate himself, and to place them near the laborers' cottages. He found that thirty-eight acres divided among ninety-eight renters produced yearly harvests worth from £3 10s to £5 per allotment, a yield so attractive that only one laborer in twenty-eight years let his rent fall in arrears. Food worth £3 10s to £5 was highly valued by those living on subsistence wages, but it was not the material but the moral good that pleased Bunbury; in twenty-eight years only one laborer lost his allotment because of a crime, a fact that, set against a Suffolk filled with rick burning, justified Bunbury's view, shared by Strutt, that allotments diminished crime. Strutt was a magistrate, as were Boileau and Bunbury, both of whom were also high sheriffs. All three were sovereign in their parishes. Boileau delighted in calling himself "the father of the parish" and announced in his prayers at church that he wished to be "the father of the fatherless, the husband to the widow, a peace maker and a teacher of the poor." Boileau prepared his footman for confirmation, held daily prayers with his family and servants, exhorted those who failed to attend sacraments, and would have no dissenters as tenants. When servants sinned they were censured at family prayer. Boys who stole were whipped. Men who struck for higher wages were confronted first with the military, then with arguments from political economy that magistrates and guardians could not afford to raise wages, and two days later with a rise in wages that Boileau engineered. Bunbury, like Boileau, was well educated, the possessor of a fine library, a Whig and an Anglican, a believer in political economy, a giver of balls, and a sportsman who kept game. He too ran his parish with firmness. So did J. J. Strutt, but on evangelical lines that were anathema to Boileau and Bunbury. Strutt denounced balls, parties, and hunting and dedicated himself to parish work. "I have all the parish," he wrote in 1831, "on my hands." He called the owners and occupiers together and persuaded them to resolve to "do our utmost to improve the religious, moral and temporal state of the poor by endeavouring to make them attend the worship of God; by punishing theft, drunkenness and idleness, and by giving fair and adequate wages."[13]

In the model parish paternalism of Boileau, Bunbury, and Strutt, agricultural improvement, the institutions of allotment, the improvement of cottages, the school, and the moral sovereignty of the squire loom large. To these elements the squires added a warm intimacy. It was not beneath Boileau's dignity to sit with the sick among his parishioners and to pray with them, nor was he so selfish as to cut off the wages of the winter jobless and refuse to feast the poor every January on roast beef, plum pudding, and ale. Nor was Strutt of Terling insensitive to the poor when, as overseer, he vowed "to allow the aged tea and sugar and salt butter," just as his wife was not too proud to help the poor organize a ladies' lying-in fund. Bunbury showed his warmth toward the laborers by defending them publicly in the matter of incendiarism in Suffolk. In the *Bury Post* of July 14, 1844, he wrote that much of the blame for these fires came from "inadequate wages . . . [and] frequent dismissals of the labourers from employment if it is too wet or too dry." He told the readers of the *Post* that he had found "plenty of good feeling" from that "simple minded, well meaning and so grateful" class. He ended with one of the pithiest of paternalistic sermons: "Let land and cottages to labour at reasonable rates; pay them wages in fair proportion to the work they do; discharge them not because there was a day of rain or a day of frost; talk to them, talk with them, come to know them, advise them, and encourage them. You will have no more fires."[14]

There were in England nearly two hundred and fifty thousand landowners. Few of these were dukes or earls, and not many were model squires. Bunbury's exhortation had no great effect. "It is a saddening thing," said the historian of Suffolk, John Glyde, in 1852, "that Sir Henry's practical letter . . . has not stimulated the Suffolk landowners generally to give the allotment system fair trial." Glyde's survey of Suffolk's 423 landowners and 42,400 agricultural laborers shows that "model" squires were the exception. He found that because of a great redundancy of labor, Suffolk landowners were paying 7s 6d while Lancashire landowners were paying 15 shillings. He also found allotments were not general since farmers objected to them. He found overcrowding in dismal cottages, which caused a great amount of immorality. There were also ill feelings between master and servants because "during the slack season many are cast upon the parish."[15] Sir Henry Bunbury, the exemplary squire, was as exceptional in Suffolk as the earl of Shaftesbury was in Dorset. One can form a charming portrait of rural paternalism by citing from Shaftesbury's diary his resolve to build cottages, but it does not enhance the portrait to cite from that same diary accounts of wretched cottages and of "those petty proprietors [who] exact five fold rent for a thing five fold inferior in condition. It is always so with these small landowners." Glyde's survey of Suffolk and Shaftesbury's cryptic "it is always so" support a picture of exploitation that was more fully developed in the 1843 report on women and children in agriculture submitted to the Poor Law Commissioners, and in the 1847 report of the Select Committee on Settlement and Removal. One of the worst abuses these two reports exposed was the widespread existence of inferior housing. Witness upon witness, clergymen, doctors, poor-law guardians, barristers, land agents, and farmers, described the over-crowded, run-down, leaky, filthy cottages, with their one main room damp and close and their one bedroom serving a family of six or seven with sometimes an extra roomer. The promiscuity that ensued shocked the Victorians more than any other fact of rural life. "In nine villages out of ten the cottage is still nothing but a slightly improved hovel," exclaimed Lord Sidney Godolphin Osborne, a judgment that also fits the testimony of witnesses from Devon to Northumberland and for most rural counties between. Nor did these improved hovels come cheap, it being not uncommon to charge four or five pounds a year.[16]

Many landlords did not even build cottages, and others tore them down. Those living in cottages in a "close" parish, one owned by one or two landowners, gained a settlement in that parish, and if ill, old, or job-less, gained relief from that parish's poor rates, rates the landlord had to pay. Fewer cottages meant fewer poor with settlements and so lower rates. Demolishing cottages or just not building them was an evasion of the responsibilities of property, the very antithesis of paternalism, yet nineteen witnesses before the Select Committee on Settlement spoke of the practice as widely done. No witness denied the general extent of this practice. Their estimates form a melancholy judgment of the landlords of close parishes: "It has been done very much indeed"; "a great many parishes where cottages have been reduced very much"; "a great tendency to pull down their cottages"; "in many smaller parishes there are often no cottages"; "it has been acted on extensively"; "in other places in one of the eastern counties—the cottages are very fast diminishing"; "in close parishes proprietors often pull down cottages"; in three parishes of a Warwickshire union "all were pulled down"; in Suffolk "where parishes are under one proprietor they get rid of the poor people." These judg-ments were not made by Chartists or anti-poor-law agitators but by as-sistant poor-law commissioners, magistrates, poor-law guardians, and clergymen; and to these indictments of the owners of close parishes they added "even in open parishes . . . cottages are shocking," and "in many parts of England there is a great destitution . . . of cottages." The accepted reason for avoiding building cottages was to avoid higher rates. But in Dorset that tireless apostle of paternalism, Lord Sidney

Godolphin Osborne said the motives went beyond concern with rates, that in fact for many landowners "that population is looked on more or less . . . as a nuisance." He added that the evil of not building cottages existed in Dorset "to a very great extent." Many of the rural poor in the 1840s were forced to live in market or manufacturing towns and to walk three, four, or more miles to work. In these towns there were few neighborly bonds that tied all classes together. The landlords were remote and the farmers unfriendly. That there is a "tie between farmer and labour," said a magistrate in 1847, "is a delusion." The copious testimony in the reports of the special assistant commissioners investigating women and children in agriculture and the reports of the 1847 Committee on Settlement make it clear that in housing, the model squire and the cottage-building earl were rare and the indifferent landowner common. It was a judgment that two paternalist journals corroborated. "Nor are landlords and farmers," said the *Times*, "apt to care much for cottages." "The great majority of the owners of land," said the *Oxford and Cambridge Review*, "have regarded cottages as a nuisance and have deliberately done all that lay in their power to diminish their number."[17]

It was not only on the matter of housing that the average landowner expressed a greater interest in the cash nexus than in the duties of landed property. He expressed it also in the wages he paid, in the rents he charged, and in the leases he demanded. The wages, of course, were partly determined by the farmers, and the farmers, said James Sparshott, "are got very hardhearted." Sparshott, a thatcher born in 1747, was testifying in 1837 to the Select Committee on the Poor Laws. He spoke of a golden age when malt was half a crown a bushel and "every poor person could have a barrel of beer." Now, he added, they drink water, house rents are very high and wages very low. Wages were indeed low, but how low depended upon where you lived. In 1843 they ranged from seven to nine shillings a week in Wiltshire, Dorset, Devon, and Somerset to nine to eleven shillings in Sussex and Kent and twelve to fourteen in Yorkshire and Northumberland. Three witnesses from Dorset, a clergyman, a doctor, and a farmer, confessed that it was a mystery to them how the poor lived on such wages. It was indeed a mystery since one witness testified that six shillings was the minimum needed to buy food alone, not to mention rent, coal, candles, and clothing, for a family with two children. The mystery was solved in part by sending their boys to the fields and their daughters to do service. Boys went to farm work, according to an assistant poor-law commissioner "as early as 7 in some few instances, but generally at 9 or 10." The hours were eight to four in the winter, six to six the rest of the year. The farmers, like the manufacturers, found child labor cheaper. They paid children at the very start 1s 6d week and by age eighteen paid them 3s 6d. Farmers and landowners in Wilts and Devon paid seven to nine shillings a week to adults instead of the twelve to fourteen customary in Yorkshire because the labor market allowed it.[18]

The land market also allowed the landowner to demand high rents and short leases from the farmer. Two select committees, one in 1847 on the game laws and another in 1848 on agricultural customs, offered revealing glimpses into the struggle of lessors and lessees of farms. Farmers in both hearings insisted that so great was the demand for farms by men with skill and capital that the landowners had the upper hand. Ten or twenty farmers with capital, said one land agent, will show up if I advertise a farm for rent. Landlords were not shy in exploiting this advantage, not only charging high rents, but offering nothing in compensation for improvements of the property. In some cases, where improvements were considerable, landlords even evicted the improver in order to rent the property at a higher price. A tenant in town had a right to compensation when he left a building that he had improved; a tenant in the countryside making the same kind of improvement received nothing. Asked why this disparity existed, a barrister responded curtly, "The tenants in towns have more power than the tenants in the country; it appears that the tenants in the country were a good deal more under the power of the landlord."

The landlords used that power to good effect in preserving their monopoly over the shooting of game. It was rare that tenants won the right to shoot game, most leases reserving that privilege for the landowner. The result was, for fields near those covers where hares and game birds were preserved, considerable crop damage, damage ranging from two to six pounds per acre. In one district game destroyed one-fourth of the crop. The landlords, said most witnesses, rarely paid full compensation for the damage.[19] "Farmers are got very hardhearted," said the ninety-year-old Sparshott. The farmers could reply in turn that the landowners had got very hardhearted.

Some hardhearted landowners even sought high profits from that quintessential paternalist act, the granting of an allotment to the laborers. "My fear is," said Sir George Strickland, M.P. from Yorkshire, "that this allotment system is an excuse for getting rack rents, very high rents."

Landlords, of course, almost always rented and seldom gave allotments. The custom was to charge the same rent that they would to a farmer. It was said that not to charge for allotments would undermine the worker's self-reliance. The same belief led to charges for clothing clubs and for coal and soup dispensed in the winter. It taught the poor the elementary economic lessons that the cash nexus ruled agriculture more than did benevolences. That such a nexus did rule agriculture was again made clear when two staunch paternalist squires and M.P.s, Joseph Henley of Oxfordshire and Charles Newdegate of Warwickshire, told farmers appearing before the Select Committee on Agricultural Customs that compensation for improvements should be a matter of private contracts and under no circumstances of government legislation. The landowners of England, when it came to rents, cottages, leases, wages, and allotments believed in the profit motive, hard bargaining, and market forces. "Live and let live" was one of their cherished mottoes, but it was live and let live in a society in which the powerful reaped the rewards. "Gentlemen and landowners talk much of identity of interest and harmony of land-lords and tenants," said W. H. Little to the Abergavenny Farm Club in 1845, "but however beautiful this may sound in theory . . . it is not under existing circumstances true in fact."[20]

The reports that tenant farmers gave to the select committees on agri-cultural customs and on the game laws and the picture that W. H. Little presented to the Abergavenny Farm Club tell but one side of the story. There was another side, one quite obvious to those many landlords of the 1840s who received a smaller return from their rents than if they had invested the same amount of capital in government consols or in rail-roads and textiles. Agriculture, except the most scientific and advanced, and that on good soil, was not the source of great profits, a fact that may well explain why many landlords haggled over leases. But even the extent and bitterness of such haggling is often exaggerated. In countless cases, even where leases were yearly, there existed a continuing trust and friendship between landlord and tenant. The drawing up of a bal-ance sheet between avaricious and generous landlords is a matter for the economic historians. It is sufficient for this study simply to register the mixed judgments given of the landlord's treatment of his tenants and to register also that in most cases his rents were large enough for him to discharge his social duties to those parishioners who were dependent upon him.

The record of his discharge of these duties is not creditable. Many were rather niggardly, for example, toward the village school. The reports of the education inspectors speak of the Norfolk landed classes as doing "little to aid education," of "the apathy of the country gentry in Bedford, Cambridge, and Huntingdon, towards education," and of "very poor agricultural schools in the West." These reports also speak of landed proprietors in the west who felt schooling made the poor too ambitious, and of counties in the north where the worst teachers "were in small and ill paid village schools," where throughout the district there was but one teacher per 111 listed pupils, and where only one in three teachers was "duly prepared" for his or her job. The inspectors ascribed this condition to "the indifference of the many." The same indifference, joined to a demand for child labor, explains why in 1852 in the southwest three-fourths of all pupils were ten and younger. After ten it was the fields, and if one tired of the long hours and low wages and took to poaching, there was prison.[21]

Poaching was the swiftest road to serious crime. It was an enormous temptation to adventuresome youths who loved to roam the countryside, to poverty-stricken youths who at twelve or thirteen were paid to steal pheasant eggs, or to young men of twenty who heard in the beer shops that those farmers whose crops were damaged by hares viewed a poacher as a hero. In Buckinghamshire in 1843 nearly one in four of those committed to prison were sent there for game offenses. Most commitments were made at hearings before one or two magistrates. These magistrates, almost always landowners, were not too knowledgeable about the law. S. M. Phillipps, undersecretary of state at the Home Office, told the Select Committee on Game Laws that of 1,849 committals from May 1844 to March 1845, "a great many have been illegal," and there was "a very great deal of irregularity and injustice." It was his opinion, and the opinion of other witnesses, that landowning magistrates enforced game laws far more harshly than they did other laws protecting property.[22] The game laws alienated the farmer because they allowed hunters to destroy part of the crop and because they caused young poachers to be tried in a manner calculated to encourage disrespect for the law. Game laws were hardly likely to cement those bonds between the classes that the duke of Richmond celebrated as being part of "the old-fashioned way."

Once in prison the young poacher was a ward of the state. It was the landowner's duty as magistrate to act *in loco parentis* for prisoners as well as for the insane. It was one of their few paternalist duties that had a formal legal basis. All the magistrates sitting in quarter sessions had the legal power to raise and spend the county's money on prisons and asylums, and those who were visiting justices to a prison or asylum had the power to supervise them. They also had an obligation to do so, but it cannot be said that they always performed that duty with generosity. The Lunacy Act of 1845 required all counties to build asylums. By 1850 only sixteen had done so; twenty-three had not. The Commissioners in Lunacy had long urged that the insane be removed from the back rooms of workhouses and be sent to licensed houses, yet in 1847, 9,000 of the 23,000 of unsound mind in England were in workhouses. The 1847 report of the commissioners noted that poor-law guardians, fearful of having to support lunatics in asylums, simply adopted a strict and narrow definition of that term and called those who were mentally ill, mentally well.[23]

The main reason there were no asylums in twenty-three counties and that 9,000 insane were in workhouses was a fear of increased county and poor-law rates. The prison inspectors found the same fear motivated the landowner who as magistrate acted *in loco parentis*. In 1849 Captain Williams, one of the inspectors, found the Southampton jail "discreditable," and yet the magistrates refused to build a new one as it would be too expensive. In Durham the magistrates found a schoolmaster too expensive an item for the county house of correction, and at Radford in the Honour of Peverell they had a debtors' prison of which the inspector said, "I have seldom witnessed a scene of more real and abject misery." On a tour of prisons in Wales and the southwest, Capatin Perry found instance after instance of inertia and failure to improve—and this as late as 1854. Not all prisons were dilapidated. Most had been improved in the late 1830s and the 1840s, improved particularly by adopting the Home Office's favorite discipline, separate confinement, a discipline in which prisoners could see and talk only with guards, chaplains, or schoolteachers, and that not too frequently. Discipline when *in loco parentis* was severe. Frederick Hill in 1849 reported that in northern prisons flogging was frequent. Captain Perry found treadwheels far too common. At Wells the newly built prison had cells that were only nine feet by four feet six inches, and there was no airing yard. To have the landed class as magistrates *in loco parentis* could be grim. To a country boy raised in an overcrowded cottage, consigned briefly to an overcrowded school under an untrained master, sent to work at 1s 6d a week at age ten, and then involved as one of "the great many" whom S. M. Phillipps said were illegally committed for poaching—to such a boy life was hard indeed, particularly if sent to the Spalding Lockup, a "dismal, filthy black hole . . . with no ventilation, no light, no drainage and no convenience."[24] For such a boy paternalism was not the glittering dream it was for Coleridge and Southey, but a cruel reality.

The above picture of the landed classes performing their paternal duties is partial. It has singled out failings and severities. The same parliamentary reports that tell of high rents, squalid housing, inadequate schools, and dismal prisons, also tell of the multiplication of clothing and medical clubs and of more and better schools. Benevolence, sympathy, and conscientiousness interleave themselves with callousness, covetousness, and negligence to form the "patchy" pattern of paternalism at the grass roots. The same report on Dorset that tells of the spread of clothing clubs also notes that many women had but one dress, and thus when it became wet from rain or perspiration they were forced, on coming home from work, to retire to bed until the dress had dried out. The report also told of many men who could not attend church for want of a suit.[25] These are the counties of seven-to-nine-shilling wages, and they were the counties with clothing clubs. The very destitution of the laborer led men like Osborne and Perry to plead with property owners to form coal and clothing clubs and to set up soup kitchens. It was not Captain Swing riots and corn-law agitations alone that spurred on the revival of paternalism; the actual poverty and destitution in parts of rural England, particularly when publicized, promoted it. When laborers became richer, as they did in cotton factories, they no longer needed coal and clothing clubs.

Among the parliamentary reports that describe paternalism in the countryside, the most important are those of the Poor Law Commission. They tell for rural England as a whole roughly the same story that they told of Sussex, namely that landowners willingly cooperated in establishing and administering the Poor Law Amendment Act of 1834. The peers, except for Lord Stanhope and one or two others, were not hostile. No fewer than fifty-one peers and twenty baronets were, in 1838, chairmen of boards of guardians, a group that included the duke of Richmond and the earls Fitzwilliam and Devon.[26] The memoranda of the assistant commissioners speak of their cooperation: "Lord Dartmouth, in whose house I am living, has given great and valuable support"; "Lord Spencer introduced me to many gentlemen"; "The Duke of Grafton enters fully into our objects"; "Lord Howe declares himself a convert . . . and is of great help"; "During the disturbances, Lord Ebrington accompanied me." To have the county's leading magnates at one's side was reassuring. But they did more than entertain, introduce, and accompany assistant commissioners, they also performed administrative chores. The duke of Bedford and Lord Southampton had workhouses built, and Lord Ebrington helped form medical clubs.[27] Nothing could equal the help of a peer. How delighted must the commissioners have been to receive the report that the duke of Rutland "is zealous for our cause."

Below the peers were the gentry, and they too cooperated. "The magistrates and gentry," said one assistant, "have cooperated." "All my chairmen except at Bridgeport," boasted another, "are Members of the House." The assistant was fortunate since in 1838 only twenty of the chairmen of boards of guardians were M.P.s. More impressive was the number of clergymen who presided over the board of guardians: ninety-one of them were elected chairmen in 1838. The elite of the countryside saw in the New Poor Law an efficient means for land to do its duty. Peers, baronets, M.P.s, and clergymen presided over nearly one-third of the 584 boards of guardians in England and Wales.[28]

It also saw in that law a way to hold onto and consolidate its power in a deferential society. Anthony Brundage in an article on "The Landed Interest and the New Poor Law" argues persuasively that the law "incorporated the many hierarchically structured 'deference communities' " and so "*enhanced* the aggregate influence of those local magnates whose influences were principally exercised within these communities."[29] Many of the fifty-one peers, seventy-one clergymen, and twenty baronets who in 1843 joined the untitled gentry to chair boards of guardians worked with assistant poor-law commissioners primarily in order to be sure that their parishes within the county formed or helped form the boundaries of the new unions, which would leave them in a truly patriarchal position—such, Brundage shows, was the duke of Grafton's role in the Pottersbury Union in Northampton and the role of other magnates in other counties. Through such influences the greater landowners of England made sure that the administration of the New Poor Law came under the control of the rural elite.

That elite performed its duty in harness with farmers and shopkeepers and in ways that varied from the refusal to award outdoor relief and to prescribe ample diets in workhouses to an insistence that workhouse diets be sufficient and outdoor relief be given to the infirm and the elderly. They would enforce harsh discipline and yet grant medical relief generously. It is a story too large for this study, but it deserves mention in order to add balance to the one-sided picture of their failings.

But if it fills out the picture of land doing its duties, it does so in a way that does not allow an unambiguous final assessment of the paternalism of land. It is ambiguous because the impetus for better medical care and better treatment of the insane came far more from national laws and central bureaucrats than from local landlords. In the same way, the impetus to build parish schools came from government grants and government inspectors. The landed classes deserve approbation for their role in that partnership of central government and local authorities that resulted in improved poor-law administration, better schools, new prisons, and more asylums, but it is unlikely that the landed classes, if left solely to themselves, would have been as dynamic or efficient.

The landed class was ambivalent toward the central government. Their general attitude varied from the deepest hostility to a grudging approval. Even the attitude of a single landlord could vary, favoring the central government's role in the poor laws and education but opposing its interference in lunacy or police. Landlords were also ambivalent in that, though they seldom urged new centralizing measures and usually opposed such laws in Parliament, they did, magistrates and law-abiding Englishmen that they were, cooperate in their enforcement.

Acting on their own they failed even to extend very widely the highly praised system of allotments. Efforts to increase allotments, a prime symbol of the new paternalism, foundered on landlord apathy. The Select Committee on Allotments admitted in 1843 that the very reason for their holding hearings was to explore whether parliamentary legislation might not help promote the distribution of allotments. They believed legislation necessary because "this method of benefiting the poor has, from various circumstances, not been sufficiently adopted by the proprietors of land." Indeed as the hearings themselves show, many of the allotment schemes had their origin in the work of the Labourers' Friend Society, a society more representative of London and the northern towns than of rural areas. That society reflected philanthropic impulses more than the paternalism of the known and limited sphere. The lament of that society was that so few landlords would lease them land for allotments.[30] The rage for allotments was abating, and the Select Committee looked to government legislation as a means of encouraging its spread. But Parliament turned down the idea. The Tory paternalists who sat on the committee, M.P.s like Lord John Manners and W. B. Ferrand, wanted no paternalism of the central government interfering with those local areas where responsibility for social administration traditionally fell to the paternal role of land. They wanted, in respect to allotments, no partnership with the central government even though such a partnership had done its duties well in the fields of the poor law, prisons, lunacy, and education. Where it acted on its own, in housing, game preservation, wages, rents, allotments, and hours of labor, its record was not distinguished. The paternalism of landed property, in which Coleridge and Southey had such hopes, had not proven itself an effective answer to the pauperism and wretchedness of the rural poor.

Chapter VI

The Shepherds and
Their Flocks

Many of the some thirteen thousand five hundred clergy of the Church of England viewed themselves as shepherds enjoined by God to protect both the eternal and the temporal welfare of their flocks. The archbishop of Canterbury had in 1844 explicitly informed them that "the objects of the Church are two fold, corresponding with the injunction of our Lord to preach the gospel and . . . to feed His flock." Other bishops expanded that charge to clothing the naked and visiting the sick, thus carrying out the words of Christ in the Book of Matthew, "For I am hungered, and ye gave me meat . . . naked and ye clothed me; I was sick and ye visited me." Christ also praised those who gave drink to the thirsty, took in strangers, and visited prisoners. Verses 35 and 36 of Matthew 25 formed for the shepherds of the flock a noble and oft-repeated command. There were even clergymen who carried the injunction to visit and succor the poor further. The leader of the Tractarians, the Reverend Edward Bouverie Pusey, proclaimed that "we need a clergy to penetrate our mines, to emigrate with our emigrants, to shift with our shifting populations, to grapple with our manufacturing system," and the bishop of London asked his clergy to inspect the sanitary conditions of the poor men's dwellings, to teach them cleanliness, and to see that, if the dwellings were too miserable, the proper officers improve them. These injunctions to feed the hungry and visit the poor were of a heroic and exacting order. J. B. Sumner, bishop of Chester, asked his clergy to visit 3,000 families in the year in addition to the sick and aged. The bishop of Oxford, Samuel Wilberforce, told his clergy in 1848 that "as instructors and guides of thought and opinion . . . they should closely watch all measures which tend to promote the general welfare, and above all the morals of the people." The bishop felt that these increased duties were one of the "most favourable symptoms of our time." These duties included protecting women from panderers, limiting the hours for the selling of liquor, preserving the sanctity of the Lord's day, ending brutal sports, stopping "grievous abuses in charitable trusts," and improving prison discipline.[1]

The clergy did not expect these visitations and these measures to cure the problems of poverty, disease, or crime. No such hubris informed their expectations. These visits were for consoling the afflicted, ameliorating the destitute, admonishing the erring, and saving the lost. Shepherds tend flocks; they do not remake society. The clergy of England were just as persuaded of the inevitability of poverty as they were of the requirement to feed the hungry and clothe the naked. The same bishop of Chester who urged his clergy to feed the hungry and clothe the naked also announced that the "poor shall never cease throughout the land." Deuteronomy 11:15 thus joins Matthew 25:35,36 as one of the more important scriptural bases of the social conscience of the Church of England. Feed, clothe, visit the poor, but never expect these visits to end poverty, sickness, or suffering. Sinful man must bear his lot. Visitations were to console the poor in their inevitable suffering. Suffering to most churchmen, high or low, was providential. Both the Irish famine of 1846 and the cholera epidemic of 1848–1849 were widely considered as God's punishment on sinful man. "Famine a Rod of God: Its Provoking Cause —Its Merciful Design" was the title of a sermon delivered in 1847 by Liverpool's very popular incumbent of St. Jude's Church, the Reverend Hugh Mac Neile. "The immediate and merciful object of such punishments," said Mac Neile, "is to call the inhabitants of the suffering to repentance."

This conclusion hardly formed a call to action for the remedying of evil and the reform of society other than to be more penitent and devout. But then the bishops and clergy did not wish to remake society. To a remarkable extent the charges delivered by the bishops and the sermons preached by the clergy apologized for and defended the existing society. They not only said poverty was inevitable, they said that so was great wealth existing alongside poverty. Only a few, like the Reverend W. F. Hook, vicar of Leeds, worried about the injustice of gross inequalities.

He wrote Archdeacon Samuel Wilberforce in 1843 that "bishops [should] give up their huge incomes and become as poor as Ambrose or Augustine." "You see," he added, "I am almost a Radical." Wilberforce did not agree with the heterodoxies of this "almost a Radical" dean. "There always has been poverty; always want," he said, just as "God has ordained differences of rank."[2]

Three assumptions allowed the clergy of the Church of England to reconcile an acceptance of great inequalities in rank and wealth with a plea for Christians to show compassion to the poor: first, the belief that God himself ordained a hierarchical, unequal, and yet harmonious world; second, the belief that wealth and rank carried with them the duty of Christian stewardship and hence were useful and necessary; and third, the belief in the need of superior ranks for controlling and reforming the frail, the ignorant, and the sinful.

The first of these assumptions led the clergy to denounce all demands for equality or independence. "Independence and perfect equality," said the Reverend William Gresley, the prebend of Lichfield, "are not good for man. It is far better there should be rich and poor, master and servants . . . in order to call forth . . . our self-denial, charity, humility." Such distinctions were divinely ordained. "Poverty is his infliction," said the Reverend Samuel Green of London's Christian Instruction Society, and "wealth is his gift. The gradations of society are his appointment." His fellow Anglican the Reverend Arthur Martineau in a series of sermons on duty that abounded in quotations from Coleridge and Wordsworth, claimed that "order is God's first law, and therefore each has his appointed station and each should keep it." All, he added, are part of "a framework of society that runs from parent and child, husband and wife, to ruler and ruled."[3]

Christian charity also poured forth more generously when it was part of the Christian stewardship made possible by great wealth. That wealth carried such duties was often expressed by the bishops. The rich, said the bishop of Salisbury, face great dangers in the future world since "they have the deep responsibility of God's Stewardship." The bishop of Llandaff "has ever inculcated," said his biographer, "the maxim that property has its duties as well as its rights." Few clergymen differed from their bishops about the importance of inculcating the maxim in their affluent parishioners. The myriad of social ills of early Victorian England were quite beyond the actual visitations of 13,500 shepherds. They also required the Christian stewardship of the wealthy laymen and laywomen. The wealthy Christian must also visit the poor, be kind to his or her servants, fair to his or her employees, and concerned for the sick. It was the duty of Christians, said the Reverend Thomas Dale to the wealthy worshippers of St. Pancras, "to feed the hungry, to clothe the naked, to provide a refuge for the widow, an asylum for the fatherless: to be the eyes to the blind and feet to the lame, and to give solace to the sorrowing and defence to the oppressed."[4] Just as the clergyman's life as a model shepherd should inspire the emulation of the rich, so the exemplary life of the rich should inspire those beneath them. It was through the combined Christian efforts of these two groups, through the conscientious and loving use of those talents that God had entrusted to them, that the early Victorians would mitigate those afflictions that were Adam's curse.

The poor, too, had their duties, the duties of being sober and industrious, contented and obedient. Subordination was ordained by God. "The book of Providence," said the Reverend Francis Close, perpetual curate of Cheltenham, "is one grand scheme of subordination." The clergy even told the poor they were better off than the rich. "I know but one advantage which the rich have above the poor," said the Reverend Alexander Watson, "though I know of many which the poor have above the rich." He conceded that he was speaking of spiritual, not material, things and that the one advantage of the rich over the poor in winning salvation was that they had the wealth with which to be charitable. The poor need only be meek and humble in order to inherit the kingdom of God.

Most clergymen thought that society was quite nicely put together. Many had as sanguine a view of its harmonies as did those political economists some of them disliked. The bishop of Chester declared that Providence had decreed that all evils have "a corresponding remedy." Their deep belief in an all-wise Providence led to a belief in a harmonious identity of interest. All was mutually beneficial. Excessive riches do not hurt the poor, said Reverend Gresley, because "no man, however rich, can appropriate to himself much more than his just proportion of the necessaries of life and so deprive the poor." His proof of this axiom was that "no man can consume the good of fifty." The poor were, said London's most popular preacher, the Reverend Henry Melvill, an absolute boon to the rich, for without them "it would be hard to make progress in genuine piety." "Selfishness," he told his flock, "is one of the most common of the tendencies of our nature," and therefore having "amongst us objects which continually appeal to our compassion . . . is wonderfully adapted to . . . counteracting that tendency." This evangelical clergyman found an echo in the sentiments of the High Churchman, the Reverend Francis Paget, rector of Elford. "If we provide for the sick and needy," said Paget, "we shall ourselves be delivered in the day of our trouble."[5]

For most clergymen the world was harmonious but only up to a point. There were always sinners who needed reproving. The third assumption underlying their acceptance of the hierarchical world of inequalities was their acute sense of the need for authority. Such authority demanded men of rank and station. "Submit yourself to every ordinance of man for the Lord's sake," was an unquestioned part of their social outlook. The Reverend T. R. Bentley reminded his flock that "all power is of God and the magistrates 'beareth not the sword in vain.' " With the growth of large towns and so of infidelity, crime, drunkenness, and Chartism, the age itself demanded increased firmness. "Obedience," cried out the Reverend Francis Close, "must be obtained, whether by reason, or affection, or moral suasion or the rod."[6]

The clergy was indeed not shy of the rod. They defended the flogging of juvenile criminals, the birching of delinquents, heavy fines on drunkards, and harsh workhouses for the indolent. "The workhouse," said the Reverend Henry Milman, the dean of St. Paul's, "should be a place of hardship, of coarse fare, of degradation." It might seem presumptuous of the shepherds of the flock to speak of birching in jails and degradation in workhouses, but the clergymen of the Church of England had a larger view of their role in society than that of being mere shepherds. They saw themselves and their parish as central to the workings of the paternalist society. Some spoke of the Church as "the lynch-pin" holding society together, some of its being "the great social machine," and others of the Christian ministry as the "natural link between high and low, the rich and the poor." "The Church," said the Reverend W. J. Conybeare to his audience at the Chapel Royal at Whitehall in 1842, was "a catholic society, divinely instituted for social ends."[7] Many clergymen were active as magistrates, others as chairmen or vice-chairmen of boards of guardians. Some farmed, and many were visitors to prisons and lunatic asylums and helped manage charities and hospitals. They were acting in what Samuel Wilberforce in his 1848 charge called "your several spheres."

In those spheres they could be very firm. The chairman of the board of guardians who presided over the Andover workhouse scandal was the

Reverend Christopher Dodson. Despite the revelations of the Select Committee of cruelties at Andover workhouse, he defended its drunken and dishonest governor and its most meager diet. Not all clergymen, however, defended the New Poor Law. Not a few of them led in the attack on it. The Reverend C. Fawcett Watts of Bath reported its horrors in letters to the *Times,* the Reverend Thomas Sockett of Petworth in Sussex appeared before the 1837 Select Committee on the Poor Law to recount its injustices, and the Reverend W. V. Jackson in *A Sermon on the New Poor Law* in 1838 scared his parishioners with the story of a man who would rather murder his children than send them to a workhouse. They often exposed abuses: the Reverend J. Fendell, rector of Bucknell, revealed the flogging in a Lincoln workhouse, and Reverend Stephen Buller of Droxford exposed that union's poor diet. A few dreamed of a far better system than that built around severe legal tests. The remedy lies not in laws, said the Reverend Robert C. Waterston in his *Address on Pauperism,* but in the principles of the gospel.[8] The clergy produced some sharp critics of the New Poor Law, but all were eclipsed by the fulminations of Parson Bull of Byerley. The township of Byerley was near Bradford, and the high Tory Reverend G. S. Bull was its curate. He was a true and tireless shepherd of his flock. He built a school, organized temperance lectures, encouraged sick clubs and benefit societies, visited the poor, campaigned with Richard Oastler for the Ten Hour Act, and finally joined Oastler in his long, loud, and sustained attack on the New Poor Law. Bull believed "the poor had a right to a share in God's bounty; that this was scriptural and bound up with the right of land."

Bull's declamatory addresses and writings about workhouse horrors were not notably accurate. His fiery indignation and his distortions must have embarrassed many of his fellow clergymen—certainly the ninety-one who chaired boards of guardians in 1838. One of them, the Reverend J. H. Underwood of Ledbury boasted that his board anticipated the more stringent rules of the commissioners by a year and a half.[9] The attitude of the clergy to the New Poor Law ranged widely between Bull's fiery denunciations and Underwood's cold anticipation, with a majority, probably quite a large majority, supporting it. Like the landowners with whom so many of them worked (and by whom some were appointed), they did not see the poor-law union and its workhouse as being at variance with either the authoritarianism or the benevolence of their paternalist thought. Those clergymen, like the Reverend Lord Sidney

Godolphin Osborne, who urged property owners to pay the poor fairer wages, build them better cottages and schools, and see to their improved condition, also supported the New Poor Law. Most thought the workhouses and poor-law unions were a means toward that improvement: they therefore cooperated with the law. But they did not accept all its severities. In the 1840s, boards of guardians from rural Sussex to urban Lancashire very much blunted the rigid use of the workhouse test, and in that blunting many a clergyman, whether as chaplain to the workhouse or as guardian, had a part. It was his duty, after all, to see that the poorer members of his flock were not ill used.

Most clergymen, though aware of the occasional need of the rod of discipline—workhouse or jail—preferred what the Reverend Francis Close called "reason or affection or moral suasion." As guardians of the parish's morals they preferred to use the school, not the prison. They were as fully persuaded of the truth of Jeremiah—"Train up a child in the way he should go, and when he is old he will not depart from it"—as they were of the injunction to feed the hungry and clothe the naked. "To train up a child" was, indeed, of greater importance as it concerned the soul. John Keble in the parish of Hursley in the 1840s considered few duties more important than catechizing the young in the schoolroom, while the Reverend Robert Armitage of the Easthope Rectory in the diocese of Hereford pronounced the schoolmaster second in usefulness only to the clergyman. To Charles James Blomfield, the bishop of London, schools and churches were both part of the Christian mission. "Where a church is built," he told his clergy, "schools . . . are sure to follow." "It is," he added grandiloquently, to "this combined provision for the spiritual and moral wants of the people that the country must look, under God, for the cure of its most dangerous disease." The bishop of London was an enthusiast for Christian education, and this led him to tell his clergy that more schools would mean fewer prisons, an optimistic view that not all of the clergy held, certainly not the Reverend T. J. Hussey, rector of Hayes in Kent. Hussey had doubts about education, particularly that overeducation, which "prematurely develops the intellect until, too weak for its giddy height, it totters on the verge of insanity." Between the optimism of Blomfield and the pessimism of Hussey, the clergy voiced differing expectations of schooling. By and large most of them worked for it, though only if it were solidly religious, which meant for them the catechism, the services, and the doctrines of the Church of England. Most of them also wished education limited to reading and writing and the inculcation of correct personal morals and correct social attitudes. The bishop of Salisbury in 1845 told his clergy it was useless to ask for the schooling of the poor to extend beyond nine or ten years of age, since the pressure of poverty demanded their employment.[10] But still a basic education in school until ten was needed and beyond that a continued inculcation of proper attitudes in attendance at church. The clergy knew man was sinful and that sinfulness in the form of indolence, drunkenness, and extravagance led to much of his distress. Because of this fact the clergy felt that if the parson, the schoolteacher, and their employers trained the poor properly, disciplined them firmly, and admonished them with both rigor and kindness, it would mitigate much unnecessary suffering.

The above account of the clergymen's conceptions of their duties as shepherds to their flock is based on a reading of many episcopal charges, sermons, and memoirs of the clergy of the Church of England. Not every bishop or clergyman agreed on every point. But though clergymen varied on their emphases and nuances, they did share, whether Tractarians, evangelicals, or Broad Church, many basic ideals about the role of a shepherd as a visitor, consoler, educator, and discipliner of his flock. It was a set of ideals particularly suited for rural areas where the parish was small enough for the clergyman to know all in his flock and where dissent was weak enough not to disturb the needed homogeneity. It was in parishes such as Chilbolton in Hampshire, Witney in Oxford, and Durweston in Dorset that the parochial ideal found a concrete and effective reality. In Chilbolton the Reverend Richard Durnford, Sr. chastised the farmers for treating the poor harshly, gave the poor allotments from his own glebe lands, set up a school at his own expense, and stored up faggots to sell to the poor at a cheap rate in the winter. His wife also helped. "Day by day she used to visit the poor at their houses and she knew them as if they were part of her family. She provided daily good soup for the most destitute, wine, medicine, and other necessaries for the sick and weak." At Witney the Reverend Charles Jerram divided his parish into areas of sixteen contiguous dwellings "for all of which he found visitors who kindly undertook to discharge this labour of love." He also built two good schoolrooms, an infant school, gave half-year examinations himself, visited the old and the ill, and ended pugilistic fights. The most active of all was the Reverend Lord Sidney Godolphin Osborne of Durweston, Dorset, with his coal fund, wife's friendly society, penny clothing fund, benefit club, savings bank, allotments, blankets sold cheaply, and visits to the laborers' cottages.[11] In these three parishes and in many more throughout England, the parochial idea alleviated in practice, if it did not remove altogether, the poverty and destitution of the agricultural laborer.

The Church of England consisted of cathedral towns as well as parishes. There arose in those towns, as a supplement to the parochial idea, the cathedral idea. It evolved particularly at Salisbury under its bishop, Edward Denison, its canon residentiary (and future bishop), Walter Hamilton, and Sidney Herbert of nearby Wilton House. Denison told his clergy in his charges that "the service of ordination expressly entrusts its ministers with the guardianship of the poor," and that the Church was "the teacher of her children." He boasted of his Diocesan Board of Education and its training schools for schoolmasters in Winchester and for schoolmistresses in Salisbury. He saw in diocesan institutions a means of molding and controlling society. He even urged that the ecclesiastical courts become much more active for they had "a powerful influence."

His canon, the Reverend Walter Hamilton, agreed completely. Hamilton, as the secretary of the Diocesan Board of Education was convinced "cathedrals . . . ought to be centers of religious education." A devout priest, who wore his cassock every day of the week, he helped his bishop establish in the cathedral close a training school for schoolmistresses. He also helped establish a penitentiary for girls who had fallen. After 1854 he became famous as bishop of Salisbury. He became the "bishop of the poor." Every year at Epiphany he gave at his palace a dinner of roast beef and plum pudding for one hundred of the needy of Salisbury. All of these activities pleased Sidney Herbert, M.P. But Herbert had even greater dreams. In 1849 he published *Proposals for the Better Application of Cathedral Institutions* in which he outlined a bold scheme. In addition to the existing Diocesan Board of Education and training schools, he would establish a Diocesan Pastoral College to educate men for the clergy and an affiliated college to educate the laity, and there would be an inspector of schools, a secretary for the Diocesan Church Building Society, and an inspector of diocesan societies and charities. "We want," he proclaimed, "an army of missionaries to combat ignorance and infidelity."[12] It was a grand vision, one that both reflected the reality of the bishops' increasing role in the Church and concealed the fact that neither diocesan zeal nor diocesan revenue was sufficient to give reality to the vision. G. F. A. Best, in *Temporal Pillars: Queen Anne's Bounty, the Ecclesiastical Commissioners, and the Church of England,* speaks of the bishops' "rise to new importance," particularly as "organizers and primary patrons of diocesan education and church building societies." They began, Best says, really to govern the Church. In 1838 and 1839, in response to governmental schemes of education, twenty-four diocesan and subdiocesan boards of education were established. These boards and the training schools for schoolmasters and mistresses caused great excitement and raised great expectations. By pouring out hundreds of teachers, they would truly make the Church the educator of the people. But though they reflected the new power of the bishops, they did not reflect any new sources of revenue or zeal. The bishop of Salisbury in his 1845 charge admitted that the Diocesan Board of Education had run out of money. This lack of money was a brutal fact of life, a fact that the secretary of the Committee of Council on Education, James Kay-Shuttleworth, had known for some time. In 1843 he wrote a blunt note to Lord John Russell about these diocesan plans: "Neither the clergy nor the laity were equal to the design. They did not care sufficiently for the people or they did not see how such a system of education would exalt the pretensions and increase the power of the Church. They have not made the necessary sacrifices and they have failed."[13]

The cathedral idea, like the parochial idea, had its limits. Both were better fitted for rural than urban areas. But there were those like the Reverend Francis Close, the Reverend Walter Farquhar Hook, and Bishop Blomfield who were convinced it could meet urban problems. For the Reverend Francis Close it was perhaps not too bold a claim, since Cheltenham was a prosperous watering place of only 30,000 souls. For the Reverend W. F. Hook it was bold indeed, since his parish of Leeds was a mill town numbering 152,054, most of whom resided in his large parish, a parish seven miles in diameter. Some 88,741 of them lived in the township proper, a township with only 13,000 seats in its ten churches, of which only 5,500 were free seats, the remainder being reserved for the owners of pews. Eight churches had no residence for a minister. The whole town had only twenty-five clergymen for its 152,054 souls, or one minister for every 6,000. Since Leeds abounded in dissenters and dissenting chapels, Hook's problems, though quite formidable, were nowhere near as awesome as those that faced the bishop of London. London's northeastern and eastern districts averaged one church per 19,000 inhabitants and one clergyman for every 14,000. For Bethnal Green there was only one church for every 35,000 and only one national school for 70,000.[14] To claim that the Church of England could feed the hungry, clothe the naked, and train up the child in the way he should go, amid the squalor of Bethnal Green, the crowded tenements of Leeds, or even among the 4,000 poor congested in Cheltenham's St. Paul's district, was a magnanimous and courageous claim, but one that was audacious and illusory. The effort of these three churchmen, and many like them in other towns, to carry out these illusions forms one of the more dramatic events in the revival of the traditions of paternalism in early Victorian England. It was an event that was fortunately accompanied, in some instances, by an energy and a conscientiousness that was partly commensurate with its audacity.

When the Reverend Francis Close became perpetual curate of Cheltenham in 1825 he found only two churches for 18,000 souls, and very few attended any school at all, but by 1841 there were six churches for 36,000, and by 1847 the *Cheltenham Chronicle* reported that 17,000 pupils attended various Church of England schools in the Cheltenham area. There were also many active Church-supported benevolent institutions ranging from orphanages to Magdalen houses. The Reverend W. F. Hook was equally active. He rebuilt Leeds's dilapidated parish church at a cost of £28,000, built ten new churches, seventeen parsonage houses for seventeen ministers, created, with the help of an act of Parliament, the passage of which he engineered, seventeen new parishes, all endowed, and established twenty-one schoolrooms accommodating 7,500. There were now sixty clergymen instead of twenty-five. The bishop of London, as masterful an administrator as Close and Hook, could boast of employing in Bethnal Green eleven additional clergymen having under their immediate direction fifteen schoolmasters or mistresses, one hundred Sunday school teachers, eight scriptural readers, 101 district visitors, all engaged "in making known the truths and duties of our holy religion to that vast and long neglected mass of human beings; and in administering to their temporal wants."[15]

In his efforts to civilize and Christianize East London, Bishop Blomfield was helped by some very dedicated clergy. In Whitechapel he appointed an evangelical as rector in 1837, the Reverend William Champneys. Between that year and 1860, according to George Kitson Clark in his *Churchmen and The Condition of England 1832–1885*, Champneys built three churches and founded schools for boys and girls, including a special ragged one for those too badly clothed for the parish school. Champneys formed a shoeblack brigade to employ vagrant boys and local associations to promote the health and comfort of the workers and provided the coal whippers with a hiring office so that they would no longer be paid their wages in pubs. In addition, the evangelical laity provided soup kitchens, refuges, and scripture reading. In Whitechapel, as at Leeds and Cheltenham, there evolved an expanded, active, shepherding clergy, a clergy often reinforced by Christian laymen, one similar to that clerisy of which Coleridge dreamed. But the aging Coleridge, who was still alive when Blomfield initiated his scheme, was not happy with all its features. He deprecated Blomfield's use of district visiting societies even though Blomfield insisted that all visitors work directly under a clergyman. Coleridge said such societies were but "a Scotch eldership in disguise."[16]

Coleridge would have been even less happy with the Reverend Francis Close's vast array of philanthropic societies. Close was an ardent evangelical, Hook High Church, and their respective efforts reflected their theologies as well as their differing urban circumstances. For Hook the Church and its ordained churchmen had always to be at the center of all efforts, whether administering sacraments or consoling the sick, while for Close (and less so for Blomfield) any pious and devout Christian layman could help the priest in his visits.

Hook's great effort in Leeds was thus aimed at creating more parishes and more clergymen. The idea of a parish church of the divinely ordained possessed him, not the idea of an evangelical society of the reborn. He envisioned the parish as a family of the baptized, one with a single church in which all received the sacraments from their ordained pastor, a pastor who catechized the young, supervised the school, visited the sick, and administered holy rites. It was the small population of a rural parish that allowed the parochial idea to work in the countryside. Hook's idea was to apply it to towns by breaking down one large parish into seventeen small ones. To do this he gave up £400 of his £1,200 income and gave up all his original power over the churches of Leeds. He still, however, was the charismatic leader and inspirer of the Leeds clergymen, instilling in them exacting ideas of their role as shepherds. "We lived together to save money," wrote one of Hook's young clergymen, "so that we could have more to spend on the poor. We rose at six [to pray]. . . . At half past seven [came] . . . the early morning service. . . . At nine the day schools had to be opened with prayer and religious instruction . . . to the older scholars. From school the transition was natural to the districts, where the anxiously expected visits were made . . . [followed by] a service, marriages . . . baptism and burials. . . . It was usually ten o'clock [at night] before we had wearily reached home."[17]

The Reverend Francis Close and his clergy worked just as tirelessly, only in other, more evangelical ways. While Hook and his ordained disciples were inveterate visitors to the poor, Close and his disciples were inveterate organizers of societies. "Perhaps there is no town of equal size," bragged the *Cheltenham Chronicle*, "possessing a greater number of benevolent institutions than Cheltenham." There were indeed many such institutions and hardly a one not chaired by Close. Not only did he chair the usual missionary societies and the S.P.C.K. and the Church Pastoral Society, he also chaired the annual meetings of those societies that supported the Dispensary and General Hospital, the Orphanage, the Magdalen Hospital, and the Old School of Industry. Educational meetings were his favorites: he was in the chair at the meetings that promoted infant schools, the National Society schools for the poor, the Proprietory School, Cheltenham College, and the Ladies College. He was known as the pope of Cheltenham. Handsome, admired by the ladies, imperious, he was idolized by the fashionable and feared by the lowly. The young radical journalist George Jacob Holyoake went to prison because Close would have none of his blasphemy. The dour editor of the *Cheltenham Journal*, who never laughed at any one else's jokes, laughed at Close's. High Churchmen trembled at his evangelical polemics. His social outlook combined a traditional paternalism with an evangelical philanthropy. He could dispense coal and bread to the poor and present prizes to school children with the best of the Sussex clergy, but he could also promote early closing movements, enforce sabbatarianism, close down theatres, and abolish horse racing with the best of the evangelicals. He was more than a shepherd to his flock, he was their complete patriarch.[18]

Few High Churchmen shared the pope of Cheltenham's zeal for philanthropic societies. Such societies removed moral duties too far from the Church, its rituals, and its sacraments. "If all Christians were like the early ones," said the High Church Reverend William Gresley, Close's mortal enemy in theological disputes, there would be "no need of those numerous private associations which now exist." "That a work should be left to voluntary associations, which is so obviously the province of the Church collectively," said the Reverend John Sanford, vicar of Dunchurch in Worcestershire, "must be regarded as a painful anomaly." "The Church," said the Reverend Francis Paget, "ought to be one great club, or benefit society [with] baptism . . . its seal of admission."

The Church alone would be the source of alms. The Reverend T. J.

Hussey, in a sermon entitled *The Christian Obligation to the Poor of a Sacramental Character,* denounced "the delusive complacencies of a selfish and vainglorious philanthropy." Only by reviving the offertory as part of the divine service, said Reverend Paget, can one escape "hypocrisy and ostentation and get in the habit of thinking more of the responsibilities which wealth involves."[19] As part of their efforts to make the church "one great club, or benefit society," it was necessary that pew rents be abolished. How else could the parish church comprehend the poor in a true benefit society? It is this fact that explains why such High Churchmen as the bishop of Exeter campaigned so tirelessly for the rights of the poor to free sittings yet did so little to alleviate their destitution and squalor outside the Church. His social outlook, like that of most High Churchmen, was Church centered.

The need to include all who took the sacraments in a great benefit society was the theme in 1850 of a week-long ceremony consecrating the Reverend William J. E. Bennett's Church of St. Barnabas at Pimlico in Knightsbridge. The flower of the High Church attended and preached: Keble, Pusey, Manning, Sewell, Gresley, Paget, and Henry Wilberforce. The new church was for rich and poor alike. It had no pew rents. And accompanying it were a school for boys and girls and a college for the residence of four clergymen. The church, school, and college were the Reverend William Bennett's answer to the evils of the city. Appointed perpetual curate of St. Paul's in Knightsbridge in 1843, Bennett was shocked by the contrast of great luxury and abject poverty. The pew rents of St. Paul's, which averaged fifteen pounds a year, excluded the poor from any hope of communion or baptism. In their degraded dwellings in Pimlico or around Hanover Square they were in Bennett's eyes "uncared for by the clergy . . . their families unbaptized, themselves in ignorance, and habitual sin their sole rule of life." He studied all the parliamentary reports on the subject and wrote in 1846 *Crime and Education,* a work in which the great contrast of wealth and poverty continued to haunt him. He told his readers that excessive wealth violated the law of nature and would lead to revolution. There is "a grievous disease," he said, among us. The cure of that disease he announced, was religion, and the cure would be achieved by building a church, a school, and a college. "How better to manifest our love for the poor than by . . . living with them in their very streets as an ecclesiastical body." On June 11, 1850, his dream was realized as the bishop of London consecrated the Church of St. Barnabas, its school, and its college for those four clergymen who would see that the poor were cared for, their families baptized, ignorance ended, and sin no longer the sole rule of life. There were also to be sisters of charity to help the clergymen build a parish in which all would form part of a holy catholic church. Paget, speaking at the consecration, was hopeful that such efforts would "end the spiritual and material destitution in the largest metropolis in England."[20]

Paget's and Bennett's hopes were extravagant. Wealthy Belgravia might help the poor of Pimlico, but despite Bishop Blomfield's and William Champneys's efforts, the East End still saw poverty and ignorance. In the year after they celebrated the opening of St. Barnabas, the London Diocesan Board of Education could raise only £360 to help its 353 schools. There is no doubting the sincerity and altruism of the Tractarians at St. Barnabas, but there is reason to doubt their sense of the magnitude of the problem. They had worthy aims and performed worthy acts, but their outlook, like that of almost all within the Church of England, suffered from some severe limitations.

Among these limitations five were increasingly obvious: (1) an inadequate and inadequately distributed revenue, (2) too few really effective shepherds, (3) too narrow a concern for the salvation of souls, (4) a disinclination to disturb the status quo, and (5) a jealous regard for the Church's privileged position.

Its resources, though inadequate to attain all its aims, were by no means modest. The radical John Wade in his *Extraordinary Black Book* of 1831 places the total revenue of the Anglican clergy at £9,459,565. This includes revenue from tithes, lands, fees of all sorts, Easter offerings, lectureships, chaplaincies, and chapels. In addition, the government had in 1818 and 1824 voted one and a half million pounds for church building. Many voluntary societies, like the Church Pastoral Society, the Church Building Society, and the National Society, also raised thousands of pounds. The Church of England also had the income of Queen Anne's Bounty to help its poorer livings. In the 1840s it also received 82 percent of the government grants for education, grants that by 1849 totaled £529,000. But for all that, it was not enough, except for one item, that of church building. By 1850 the Church could not even fill the existing churches. This is in part because not all, or even most, of the working classes wished to attend. In London and the manufacturing towns of the north, only one in ten of the working classes went to church. What was really in short supply were adequate incomes for those parish livings that Hook brought to Leeds, Champneys to Whitechapel, and Bennett to St. Barnabas. The Church's endowment was not large enough for the multiplication of such parish work. It was also not fairly distributed or administered. The bishop of Durham received £19,000 a year, the bishop of Llandaff only £900. There was the same inequality among the parish priests: the income of a few rose to over a thousand pounds a year, while 860 of them received less than fifty pounds. The Ecclesiastical Commission, established in 1835, sought to reform the worst of these inequalities by applying surplus cathedral incomes and incomes of suspended and useless canons to poor livings, but this resulted in only £30,000 more per year to the thousands of necessitous clergy. Meanwhile seven bishops, those of Lincoln, Exeter, Bristol, Worcester, Ripon, Oxford, and Durham, spent considerably more to rebuild, build anew, or lease new palaces, most of them some miles from the cathedral close. The Ecclesiastical Commission gave £4,800 to Samuel Wilberforce to acquire Cuddesdon outside of Oxford and £15,000 to the bishop of Ripon for a residence. The bishop of Exeter rebuilt his palace one hundred yards away from the old one at great cost.[21]

A church that pours money into new palaces for the bishops while many parish priests are miserably paid and many districts quite unattended, both wastes scanty resources and sets a poor model for charity. Nor could the Church of England claim to be the teacher of all the people, despite the efforts of the National Society and Diocesan Boards. Their efforts to create a Church system to educate all the people did not, even with 82 percent of the parliamentary grants, keep up with the growth of population. The reports of the education inspectors contain two refrains: praise of the zeal of the clergy for education and lament at the want of funds. The reports of the late 1840s and early 1850s speak of a clergy who are "of expert assistance," of "utmost frankness, reasonableness and courteous accommodation," and are "enthusiastic for education." They were "zealous and cooperative," "unquestionably . . . the great promoters of elementary education," and very "sacrificial." Many of their sacrifices resulted from the want of funds. The same reports that praise the clergy also note that the "financial burden weighs heavily on the clergy" and that there is "great deficiency of money" and "a want of adequate and constant funds." In 1852 William Kennedy said of his district, "The want of funds is constantly growing worse and worse," and in 1853 John Norris reported of his district, "The existing provisions are wholly insufficient to meet the needs of the population."

The poorest districts had the greatest need of education, but because financing was largely local, they had the greatest want of funds. Furthermore, since these schools were below standard they were ineligible for government grants. The Church of England's National Society should have supplied these funds, but even by 1845 one of the early education inspectors, the Reverend F. C. Cook, had observed that "their funds . . . are in a depressed state." The clergy simply did not have the resources to be the teachers of their flocks.[22]

Neither did they have the resources to feed the hungry and clothe the naked. Except for occasional seasonal benevolences at Christmas, temporary (and again occasional) distribution of cheap soup, blankets, and coal, and sporadic efforts during the worst of trade depressions to help the poor in towns, the clergy accepted the fact that the feeding and clothing of the destitute belonged to the poor-law boards. The wants of the poor were so vast as to make the Church's assumption of the duty to feed and clothe the hungry entirely rhetorical.

Money was not the only resource lacking. The clergy also lacked the Closes, Hooks, and Champneys to carry out these many social duties. Among the 13,500 clergymen few came close to their standards. Many of them were not unlike the Amos Bartons, Maynard Gilfils, and "old Mr. Crewe" portrayed by George Eliot in her *Scenes of Clerical Life* and the Septimus Hardings and Theophilus Grantlys portrayed in Anthony Trollope's *The Warden*. The evangelical Amos Barton was "plebeian, dim and ineffectual" and "palpably and unmistakenly commonplace"; Maynard Gilfils, of a more latitudinarian school, was "an excellent old gentleman, who smoked very long pipes and preached very short sermons," and who hunted and dined with the local squires and preached occasionally in his spurs; while old Mr. Crewe "delivered inaudible sermons on Sunday," and the rest of the week "scraped together a large fortune out of his school and curacy." Trollope's Harding was a benign precentor at a cathedral and a warden of a charity for twelve elderly gentlemen, the £800 income of which mostly went to the warden, and Trollope's Grantly was an industrious archdeacon but as hard and ambitious for preferment as the sleekest bishop and absolutely opposed to any reform in the use of the £800, or in the use of any other income or revenue of the Church of England. These portraits, though they caricature faults, are not hostile ones. George Eliot finds Barton, Gilfils, and Crewe lovable, and her portraits excel in showing how intimately, warmly, and admirably these parsons become part of village and town life. But such clergymen were not effective reformers of social evils, nor, indeed, did they ever entertain such an idea. Neither did such an idea occur to Harding, warden of Hiram's Hospital, although he was a most lovable man. Grantly was certainly no reformer, though he "performed with a rigid constancy, his duties."[23] His main passion, as it was for many clergymen, was for advancement. George Eliot and Trollope can be criticized for neglecting the Godolphins, Champneys, and Dunfords, but an account that omitted the Bartons, Gilfils, Crewes, Hardings, and Grantlys would also be one-sided. There were indeed a great variety of clergymen, ranging from fox-hunting sybarites and absentee pluralists to passionate evangelicals and devout High Churchmen. Edward Bickersteth, rector of Watton, Hertfordshire, was an example of the passionate evangelical. The redoubtable Bickersteth, besides publishing sixteen volumes of theology, wrote innumerable pamphlets and lectured throughout England for the Protestant Association. When in Watton, he made his four o'clock visits to the schools or the sick poor and gave cottage lectures in which he warned against novels, dancing, and vain and idle songs. The Reverend Robert Isaac Wilberforce was as devout a High Churchman as Bickersteth was an evangelical. In his 1843 *Charge to the Clergy* he urged that they demand a meeting of the Convocation of the clergy in order to devise a system of subordinate deacons and more active churchwardens, all to be used in parish work. Above all he urged clergymen to see that all were baptized, since baptism and not holy orders brought one into the holy Church.[24]

George Eliot in her characterization of the Reverend Mr. Tryan in *Scenes of Clerical Life,* depicts a clergyman who is truly active for the poor. In this portrait she shows how evangelicalism could reinvigorate the paternalist ideal of the clergy as active shepherds of their flocks. The rise of evangelicalism, along with the challenge of a revived dissent, discredited the fox-hunting parsons and lessened their numbers. These two challenges in turn helped evoke the equally serious Tractarian movement, which further filled England's parishes with more active shepherds. But despite these revivals, the model shepherd, like the model captain of industry and the model landlord, was in the minority. The lack of such active reforming shepherds, joined to limited revenues, meant that the idea of solving or relieving England's main social grievances through the paternal role of the Church was as doomed to failure as trust in captains of industry and paternalist landlords. It was a fact that the Church of England clergymen would never admit, so involved were they in their main mission, which was the salvation of souls.

The average parson was far more interested in theological issues than in social matters, in the proper path to salvation rather than the proper way to reform society. Among some fifty charges and 350 sermons used as the basis of this analysis, only about one in four charges and one in twenty sermons spoke of social problems, and then they were seldom the central topic. The clergy's concerns were with salvation, whether by experiencing a rebirth in Christ or by the holy grace of sacraments. Not a few sermons were on a moral theme, but in personal and not social terms. Most sermons were theological, particularly after the Tractarians launched in the 1840s a prolonged, time-consuming, and narrowing debate on the nature of apostolic authority, the value of rituals and sacraments, and the virtue of baptismal regeneration. This deep concern for salvation not only marked their sermons, it defined to a great degree the efforts of these clergymen in visiting the dwellings of the poor. They went into these homes far more to bring the poor into the fold of the Church than to improve their dwellings or enhance their meager diets. The High Church was not alone in this preoccupation. "The sole end at which the Low Church leaders aimed," wrote the Reverend W. H. B. Proby in the *Annals of the Low-Church Party in England*, "was the conversion (or conversion and edification) of individual souls."[25]

The concern for saving souls combined with the fear of disturbing existing social arrangements precluded effective solutions to the problems of destitution, bad housing, long hours of overwork, oppression of child labor, inequality of wealth, and misery. The Reverend Francis Close, for example, in 1842, a year of deep depression, preached only one sermon for the poor. It netted from five churches £595. The sum seems large, but for five churches it compares poorly with the cost of the twenty private balls and numerous public entertainments given in January of 1842 in Cheltenham's handsome assembly rooms. Yet Reverend Close was so overcome by this generosity that he asked, "What will the poor man say now, can he again be induced to rail against the Church of England?" That £595 could bring much benefit to the 4,000 of St. Paul's district who were depressed in 1842 is doubtful, but then Close, who was unstinting in his labor for hospitals, schools, and church sittings never considered it possible for the Church to elevate the 4,000 poor of St. Paul's from a condition he felt was inevitable. Neither, according to the Reverend Richard Dawes of King's Somborne, Hampshire, did most of the clergy. Dawes was another model shepherd. He invested his own money and energy to build one of the best schools in England, one that went beyond reading, writing, and the catechism to geometry, algebra, and agricultural chemistry. He was a shrewd and severe observer of his fellow clergymen. It was his judgment that most of them were suspicious of a really useful secular education and that most were quite willing to settle for mere "charity schools that would keep the labouring classes . . . entirely apart from the classes immediately above them."[26]

The clergy of England had little inclination to support any radical changes that would help the poor. Some, as J. T. Ward in his *The Factory Movement* has shown, did support the Ten Hour Bill for factory operatives. The "almost Radical" Hook chaired a meeting for that bill, a meeting in which he announced that in any struggle between the middle and working classes he would side with the workers. But neither he nor those of his fellow clergymen who supported the Ten Hour Bill desired to change a system based on the dominance of property and privilege, particularly if the change endangered their own property and privileges. Least of all did the bishops wish such change. "The bishops," complained Lord Ashley in 1844, "are timid, time serving, and great worshippers of wealth and power. I can scarcely remember an instance in which a clergyman has been found to maintain the cause of the labourers in the face of the pew holders."[27]

It was a jealousy of their own exclusive privileges and rights, the fifth limitation in their outlook, that loomed so large in the educational controversy of the 1840s. Few social duties ranked higher in the minds of the clergy than the education of their parishioners, yet they could neither fulfill that duty adequately nor abide the state doing so. It was quite evident to Hook in Leeds that, however magnificent were the Church's efforts, the poor of Leeds multiplied faster than did the Church's schools. He had the candor to publish in 1846 a plan for local rate-supported schools, the students of which must also attend religious instruction under a clergyman of their own denomination two afternoons a week. It was a wise compromise and a workable solution. Tractarians and evangelicals denounced it. Reverend Close condemned it in a pamphlet, claiming that such rate-supported schools would exhaust the rates in the same manner as did the old poor laws.[28] Bishop Blomfield also opposed any such incursion into the Church's field. Aware that 82 percent of government grants went to Church schools, Close and Blomfield were all for such grants, the more the better, but never if they led in any way to rate-supported schools whose religious instruction was not exclusively Anglican. Their attitude to the state was ambivalent and expedient. They were for it when it helped the Church, against it if it hurt them or helped dissent. They were for local rate-supported factory schools in 1843, since all teachers and a majority of the school board would be Anglicans, but they opposed the rate-supported schools urged by Hook since there was no exclusive Church of England control of religious education. In the long run their jealous regard for preserving their own privileges prevented the development of that tax-supported and locally based system of schooling that could educate a country of Anglicans, Roman Catholics, dissenters, and secularists.

In the short run, however, Blomfield and Close were more realistic than their High Church brethren, who abandoned even an ambivalent and expedient view of the state once the state began to promote evangelical and Broad Churchmen to higher ecclesiastical posts. Led by the Archdeacon George Denison, the High Church from 1848 to 1853 fought against accepting any government grants as long as the Committee of Council on Education insisted on the management clause that gave laymen substantial power over small rural schools. They wanted no lay interference in the shepherd's control of his flock, and it was a passion that led them to fierce denunciations of state interference. "The conflict between the Church and the world," said Archdeacon Denison, "is a perpetual conflict." The High Churchmen harbored a deep distrust of government. The Reverend Francis Paget, years earlier, urged strenuous almsgiving for the relief of distress because "Acts of Parliament can not mend it." Some High Churchmen would not even recognize civil marriages, or marriages in any other church. In 1856 the home secretary, Lord Palmerston, received a complaint that the Reverend W. J. E. Bennett (the builder of St. Barnabas) "refuses to recognize any marriage not solemnized by the parish priest." Lord Palmerston had to answer that "there was nothing he could do."[29] In outcries like Paget's and actions like Bennett's, the High Churchmen showed how the paternalism of the Church not only stood in direct opposition to the paternalism of the state, but persisted in pursuing the will-o'-the-wisp of an exclusive monopoly of religious life in England.

When the Church's exclusive rights conflicted with the state's, even the "almost Radical" Hook and the government's friend Blomfield had to oppose state paternalism. Both fought the state over the right to bury the dead. They both continued to crowd their Church's vastly overcrowded graveyards with more corpses than they should hold, even though privately run graveyards were available. They were fighting to save the clergy's burial fees, fees that formed a large part of some clergymen's incomes. Whether it was over burial grounds or workhouse chaplains, rate-supported schools or civil registration of marriages, the vested interests of the Church of England stood in conflict with the growth of a paternal government. That the Church clothed its own self-interest in a religious and moral garb made it all the harder to overcome.

Paternalism in all its varying forms was not of one piece. Its strongest pillar, as Coleridge, Southey, and Chalmers viewed it, or as the duke of Richmond or the Reverend Francis Close viewed it, was the paternalism of property. Its second strongest pillar was the paternalism of the Church. By 1850 both, for all their instances of sacrifice, generosity, and compassion and for all their occasional fine fruits, had failed to meet the avalanche of social abuse and distress brought on by industrialization, urbanization, and an expanding population.

Chapter VII

Captains of Industry

The dreams of the paternalists found expression not only on vast estates presided over by great dukes and in parishes governed by fatherly squires, but also alongside fast-moving streams where the new captains of industry built their textile mills. It was by the Bollin that Samuel Greg built Quarry Bank, by a tributary of the Mersey that Thomas Ashton erected Hyde, and by the Irwell that Henry and Edmund Ashworth established the New Eagley mill. The Ashworths built their commodious and well-ventilated mill of Lancashire stone in a deep and picturesque ravine. Using the same solid glistening white stone, they built on the opposite hill rows of two-story houses each containing four to six rooms and a lavatory. On the opposite side of the ravine from these houses rose Henry Ashworth's estate, The Oaks. It stood at the top of the hill proudly looking over the chimneys, houses, chapel spires, and evergreen-clad hills. The evergreens, like the chimneys, houses, and chapels, were planted there by the Ashworths. Samuel Greg's family house, less elevated than Ashworth's, was no less "near at hand to the cottages" so that the Greg daughters "gave friendly greetings and flowers to the apprentices on their way to church." Thomas Ashton located his estate at Hyde near his men's houses, which he had "built of stone [with] at least four apartments in two stories, with a small back yard and a mews lane . . . improved kitchen grate, with boiler and oven." Greg's houses at Quarry Bank were equally comfortable and well furnished, as were those at Hollymount Mills built by the three Whitehead

171

brothers, cottages of four to six rooms, "none destitute of a clock and a small collection of books." The rent for the Ashworth houses was five pounds a year, a little costlier than the duke of Richmond cottages but much more commodious and well within the average family earnings at Ashworth's mills of 33s 4d a week, earnings far above what an agricultural family would receive from Richmond. The Ashtons, Gregs, Ashworths, and Whiteheads were proud of their two-story stone houses and their good wages, but these formed only a part of their paternalist solicitude. They had an even greater patriarchal pride in their schools, churches, chapels, libraries, playgrounds, reading rooms, news rooms, lecture halls, and baths and washhouses.[1] The unabashed employer of children, Henry Ashworth, had no doubt children could both work and go to school, first to infant schools before employment, then from ages nine to thirteen two hours of school a day after factory work, then after thirteen Sunday and night school. Ninety-eight percent of Ashworth's employees could read, and 45 percent could write. The houses averaged from ten to thirty books in their libraries. His schools taught so much they frightened Lord John Manners and Lord Ashley. Manners after visiting them wrote in his diary that he was "alarmed by all this hot bed intellect." Lord Ashley, after hearing a precocious pupil, told Ashworth it was providential that such "superior intellects" were rare because if not there "would be a difficulty in keeping them in their station."[2]

The lords of the soil feared schooling more than the captains of industry. The former expressed their solicitude toward the laboring classes in the form of seasonal benevolences, clothing and coal clubs, prizes for long service, and clean cottages; the latter expressed their solicitude in the form of reading rooms, lecture halls, libraries, Sunday schools, and temperance societies. Both, of course, supported religious instruction, the one in the parish church alone, the other in both church and chapel—but preferably chapel. The Ashworths were Quakers, the Gregs and Ashton Unitarians, the Whiteheads Methodists. The Ashworths required church attendance of all their workers, though at the denomination of their choice. Henry Ashworth, every bit as autocratic as the duke of Richmond, required more than church attendance of his employees. He required sobriety, industry, respectability, and cleanliness. He posted large rule boards in prominent positions telling of "the virtues of thrift, order, promptitude, and perseverance." He fined the workers at the factory heavily for shoddy work, swearing, loitering, absences, and lateness, but also, realizing the value of positive reinforcement, gave rewards for good work and moral behavior. He personally inspected their houses and if he found them dirty and ill kept, he ousted the tenants. He superintended the morality of the village by creating, as Robert Owen had at New Lanark, special constables and by exercising his office as magistrate to punish the profligate and disorderly. "We exercise a control of superintendence over them," he told the Factory Commission of 1833, "for their moral and social improvement."[3] True paternalism is never without a dictatorial edge, and Henry Ashworth was a true paternalist.

By the 1840s autocracy was a long and deeply rooted tradition for the captains of industry, particularly those in villages and smaller towns. It was Samuel Oldknow's ambition, say the biographers of this early pioneer in textiles, "to control and direct the life of the community." "They seem to have got the notion," said Josiah Wedgwood of his workers after he had moved to a new site, "that they are to do what they please." Both Oldknow and Wedgwood were strict disciplinarians in their mills and potteries and firm governors of their communities because to be both was not just practical, but in fact necessary.

Sidney Pollard, in "The Factory Village of the Industrial Revolution," argues that the rise of a manufacturing paternalism was a function of the growth of the early factory village. Neither Robert Owen of New Lanark nor Samuel Greg of Bollington, Pollard argues, brought to their mills a defined social outlook, but from experience and necessity worked out—as did others in other places—a village-mill paternalism. Where there are cascading streams that can turn the wheels of cotton mills, there are often no houses, laborers, schools, churches, and stores, so if one is to attract labor, one must build houses, schools, churches, and stores. Some of these institutions, moreover, are invaluable in disciplining and training the workers. The best housing thus went to the best behaved. Those who talked of unions and strikes, or drank and were too often late, could be, and were, evicted. Infant and Sunday schools in particular were crucial in the indoctrination of the young in the virtues of promptitude, thrift, sobriety, industry, cleanliness, and respectability. Contemporaries realized how functional was the autocratic management of the mill and village. Andrew Ure in 1835 laid it down, in his *Philosophy of Manfactures,* that "it required a man of Napoleonic nerve and ambition to subdue the refractory tempers of workpeople accustomed to irregular paroxysms of diligence." That such needs led to a

firm and authoritarian paternalism in the factories of the industrial revolution has been elaborated on in the books of two twentieth-century
sociologists, Neil Smelser's *Social Change in the Industrial Revolution*
and Reinhard Bendix's *Work and Authority in Industry: Ideologies of
Management in the Course of Industrialization.*[4]

Autocratic rule was not the only aspect of factory paternalism that
was functional: so were benevolence and friendly intercourse. Henry
Ashworth, with a love of statistics that would delight Mr. Gradgrind,
estimated that "the order and content" of his 1,200 workers was worth
fifty pounds a week. Any friendly intercourse that encouraged such "order and content" was thus profitable, and it thus found many participants, particularly in the intercourse that took place in Sunday schools,
temperance meetings, lecture halls, and chapels. Henry Ashworth in
1844 called together his workers in the lecture hall to discuss the merits
of the Corn Law. They decided, after some suggestive remarks by Ashworth, that that law was the unwise and immoral work of the aristocracy. Samuel Greg, Sr., architect of Quarry Bank, was full of "genial
hospitality" when he met with his workers in the Sunday school and in
the library, while his son, who "established games and gymnastic exer-
cises—quoits, trap and cricket balls and leap frog"—began evening
drawing and singing classes and lessons in geography and natural history
which he himself taught. He invited all to evening parties, "the superior ones" more than others. He also gave the best behaved of the
young "the order of the silver cross."[5]

Archibald Buchanan, a Scottish manufacturer, owner of a factory village in Catrine, was even more friendly. "Being young and athletic, affable and generous, he mixed with the young people in their sports."
Scotland was indeed not without its own Ashworths, Gregs, and Ashtons. Besides Buchanan at Catrine there were James Finlay and James
Smith at Deanston, whose factory counted 200 teetotalers and not one
drunkard, and David Dale of New Lanark fame. Liverpool and Manchester also had their versions of the factory-village paternalist, showing
that great cities were not totally inhospitable to the idea. In Liverpool
the North Shore Mill had excellent schools, a medical program, a library,
and good houses. Once a year there was a boat trip for the Sunday
school. With two steamships chartered by the owners, some six hundred
children, all of "good conduct," sailed forth and enjoyed "sandwiches,
currant loaves, and coffee." Every week one of the three proprietors
(one an Anglican, one a Unitarian, and one a Methodist) read the

church service to three hundred or four hundred of their employees. This would have pleased Mr. Morris of Manchester who believed it so important to lessen the distance between master and servant that he built a library, coffee room, and class room in his mill. He sponsored weekly lectures and industrial training, particularly emphasizing household duties for the girls. Of his 500 hands, 300 were in the temperance society, and he praised highly their "docility and growing desire for instruction."[6]

The assertion that such friendly intercourse and benevolence, with their resulting docility, were functional would have pleased many of these captains of industry. Very few of them were at ease with paternalist rhetoric. There is no evidence that they ever used the term "paternalism." Mostly nonconformists from the north of England or Presbyterians from Scotland, and either self-made men or the offsprings of such, they were strong individualists. They wished their operatives to be the same. W. R. Greg, one of the three Greg brothers, a millowner in Bury and a prolific reviewer in the *Edinburgh* and the *Westminster* reviews, denounced in his writings those feudal principles that demanded deference and servility, while Henry Ashworth insisted that his benevolence arose not from noblesse oblige but from calculated self-interest.[7] He was convinced that there was a harmonious identity of interest that ruled the factory system. Both he and Samuel Greg considered that educated workers produced more cotton and so more profits. No paternalist rhetoric, no florid speeches like those at agricultural meetings accompanied the benevolence and supervision of the captains of industry. They were not, however, without theoretical justifications for their model factory villages, nor without publicists eager to provide such justifications. They found two such publicists in Andrew Ure, professor of chemistry at Glasgow University and W. C. Taylor, a London journalist. Ure in his *Philosophy of Manufactures* and Taylor in his *Notes of a Tour in the Manufacturing Districts of Lancashire* (also published in the *Morning Chronicle*) told all England about the Ashworths, Gregs, Ashtons, and Whiteheads, but neither of them spoke of the duties of property, the need of rank, or the value of deference. Ure, it is true, urged manufacturers to "show parental concern for their children" and implored the masters to set a good example, since "like master like man, is a proverb no less applicable to public works than to private families," but this was as far as he went toward the rhetoric of paternalism. He chose instead Ashworth's individualist argument that treating workers justly is in the self-interest of both workers and employers. "Godliness is great gain," proclaimed this exuberant and uncritical believer in the proposition that the factory system is the laborer's "grand palladium." He saw no servile deference in that grand palladium. He found in manufacturers less "pride" and less "assumption of undue importance" than in landowners. W. C. Taylor believed that a greater equality defined the relations of factory owners with their men than characterized agriculture. Factory workers were, he urged, less deferential than the peasantry. While the agricultural poor lacked independence, Lancashire men "will not stir one inch to do homage to wealth or station." Nowhere does Taylor mention the privilege and duties of property or rank or speak of subordination and condescension; instead he too finds equality, liberty, and an identity of interest defining the relationship of capital and labor. Manufacturing property offered more incentives than did agricultural property for treating the workers fairly. This view of property was a reversal of the position held by E. S. Cayley, the Yorkshire agriculturalist and publicist for landed paternalism. Cayley had argued that very few landowners were harsh on their poor since "their country occupations, the nature of their property are strong inducements to them to live in terms of intimacy and Christian kindness with the tenant and labourers." This was true, he urged, since the landowner realized his welfare depended on tenant and labor. Taylor asserted the opposite, claiming that the manufacturer, because his capital was floating, i.e., tied up in ephemeral machinery, had an immediate incentive to keep his men happy and at work. The landowner, on the other hand, because his capital was fixed, i.e., tied up in imperishable land, could easily evict a tenant, the only result being that the land lay fallow and became more fertile.

Hence the manufacturer is "stringently coerced by circumstances to be very attentive to the health, the intelligence and the morals of the person he employs." Not only did floating property thus require justice, but the factory village itself promoted closer contacts and friendlier intercourse.[8] Taylor's position was also held by *Fraser's Magazine*. In a remarkable outburst of indignation over incendiarism in Suffolk and Norfolk, *Fraser's* said in 1844, "There is no such thing as arcadian happiness." There was none because farmers divided landowner from laborer. *Fraser's*'s reviewer ended by noting that no such middleman divided the millowner from his laborer. The *Eclectic Review* carried this argument another step forward by claiming that "manufacturers in towns, but not landowners in the countryside, had a direct interest in educating and elevating the poor."[9]

W. C. Taylor, in another passage, states that not only is it to the manufacturer's interest that his workers be good workmen but that they also be "good men." To be "good men" was indeed important to the Quaker Ashworths, the Unitarian Gregs and Ashtons, and the Presbyterian Buchanans, Dales, and Finlays. The phrase "good men" suggests an outlook that extended beyond concern with profits. These Bible-reading, Sunday-school-organizing manufacturers were not inspired by mammon alone; they desired as much, if not more, to create godly men, men worthy of their new Jerusalems. In the country valleys of Cheshire, Lancashire, the West Riding, and Scotland, the captains of industry were creating independent, self-reliant, righteous Christians, Christians fit for the new, more equal, Christian commonwealth. "Godliness was gain," no doubt, but these communities were inspired by more noble aims.

Men do not live by self-interest alone. To the functionalism of factory-village paternalism it is necessary to add a second ingredient, an ideological factor: the Puritan and biblical and even secular visions of fashioning a more godly society on earth. Those visions ranged from the millenarianism of the former Methodist, Robert Owen, to the modernist aspiration of Unitarians and Quakers to establish a free, rational, and righteous society based on the ethics of Jesus. Such ideas lay behind the model communities of Gregs, Ashworths, and Ashtons, just as in New England they lay behind the model factories of Lowell, Massachusetts.

Many Englishmen in the 1820s, ranging in the political spectrum from Robert Southey to Jeremy Bentham, looked to New Lanark as a model of manufacturing paternalism. In the 1840s they found that model in Lowell, Massachusetts. Charles Dickens, James Silk Buckingham, and Dr. Scoresby, the vicar of Bradfield, all extolled its virtues in their accounts of America; the *Westminster*, the *Eclectic*, the *Leeds Mercury*, the *Athenaeum*, and the *Mirror* were some of the journals that described its workings in detail; and M.P.s from Lord Ashley to Lord Morpeth sang its praise.[10] None of the writings of Coleridge and Southey, or of any other paternalist, rivaled in the 1840s these accounts of Lowell in popularizing the idea that property had its duties. It is ironical that from the least feudal of countries came that model of paternalism most often praised by the press. No account of any agricultural estate received from the press of the 1840s nearly the attention given to Lowell. The only examples to rival Lowell in the press were the efforts of the Ashworths, Gregs, and Ashton.[11] Few reviews or newspapers wrote accounts of Sir John Boileau or Sir Henry Bunbury

or of the dukes of Bedford and Northumberland, but many wrote of
New Eagley, Hyde, and Quarry Bank. The captains of industry, while
eschewing paternalist rhetoric, expressed in houses, schools, libraries,
baths, lecture halls, gymnasiums, and surgeries the ideals preached by
Burke, Coleridge, and Southey.

Such a fatherly concern was not what Coleridge and Southey had
expected of manufacturers. It did, however, fit the expectations of
Thomas Carlyle and Benjamin Disraeli. Carlyle saw in these captains of
industry England's salvation, while Disraeli saw in them the means of
reviving old feudal ways. Disraeli visited both Ashworth's Turton mills
and John Marshall's majestic temple mill in Leeds. He fused these two
experiences (and perhaps others) to produce Mr. Millbank in *Coningsby* and Mr. Trafford in *Sybil*, two sterling and exemplary captains of
industry. Intellectual developments run in strange ways. The paternalistic factory villages of Lancashire, Scotland, and Massachusetts, whose
intellectual origins lay in part in a democratic and individualistic Puri-
tanism and in part in the functional needs of capitalist discipline did as
much to propagate paternalistic ideas in the 1840s as did the writings
of the Tory romantics. It was a strange partnership and one that shows
that paternalism was the preserve of no single class, intellectual tradition, or religious faith. Not all manufacturers, for example, were
nonconformist. The second-generation Marshall brothers of Leeds had
left their father's Unitarian faith for the Church of England. They built
a colossal factory in the Egyptian style with thirty-four-foot columns,
and on its flat roof grew grass on which sheep occasionally grazed. They
also built various schools. In James Marshall II's speeches, many given
in the mill's large lecture hall and most reported in the *Leeds Mercury,*
and in his many letters to that paper, one finds a fuller acceptance of
paternalist rhetoric than in an Ashworth or a Greg. He is no more re-
luctant than the duke of Richmond to speak of "the duties that attach
to the possession of property, education, and influence," and he looked
to "the aristocracy of the land and the aristocracy of the loom" to treat
their dependents so justly that "there would arise an increase of union
among the people of every station and an enlightened beneficence on the
part of the wealthier classes."[12] Marshall attempted to carry out these
principles in depression-torn Leeds by providing the jobless with allotments, that favorite scheme of the paternalists. But his efforts proved
disappointing. Not only did the other millowners not bother about
allotments, but the Marshall firm could not, in a town the size of Leeds,

carry out its paternalist goals as far as had the Ashworths, Gregs, and Ashtons in their small towns. When the mill day ended in Leeds or Manchester the operatives were swallowed up in a different culture from New Eagley, where Ashworth was able to prohibit all public houses and beer shops, or Hyde where Ashton allowed but one public house. In Leeds or Manchester the benevolent had to turn to a more diffuse philanthropy.

In W. H. Elliot's *The Story of the "Cheeryble" Grants* and in Lord John Manners's account of his visit to these same Manchester calico printers, there is no report that the Grants built houses for their men or even schools or churches. They did help build Presbyterian churches and supported local mechanics' institutes and schools, including Roman Catholic ones. They were praised for liberal support of "ameliorative public movements and educational and charitable institutions." William Grant or his clerk also gave out alms every morning to the poor who gathered before their print works and warehouse. Large cities called for a more general and public benevolence. It was thus the countryside that saw the fullest development of manufacturing paternalism, a fact that James Stuart, a factory inspector and propagandist for paternalism, shrewdly observed. "In the country districts," he wrote, "the owners of the factory pay scrupulous attention to the wants of the population which they have the means of collecting and of which they consider themselves the heads . . . [but] the factory owner in a town knows little or nothing of the people he employs but during the hours of work." Elizabeth Stone, in her novel of 1842, *William Langshawe, Cotton Lord*, discerns the same special nature of isolated and small mills as did James Stuart, but she saw, as Stuart never did, that it could mean tyranny. She writes of millowners "who lived in secluded districts . . . are the sun of a little sphere, the lord paramount," who "had none to restrain them . . . were frequently the only magistrates." "Such plentitude of power," she concludes, "does not soften an arbitrary disposition . . . and unless gifted with great natural goodness [makes them] the tyrannical despot."[13]

If it was easier to be patriarchal in the countryside, so was it easier to be a patriarch if one were wealthy. Model factories were a function of capital as well as environment. "Experience has everywhere shown," wrote W. C. Taylor, "that great capitalists are more equitable and merciful employers than persons of limited fortunes."[14] Men who farmed poor soil or manufactured cotton on a slim margin were more demanding of their men, quicker to dismiss them in bad times, and less interested in building schools and model housing. The ingredients, then, for a successful manufacturing paternalism were a rural site, ample capital, a belief that godliness is gain, and a religious sense of the value of making men good. It was a formula that came together perfectly in Titus Salt, Congregational Sunday-school teacher, man of great capital, canny about gain, and one who consciously moved his firm from overcrowded Bradford to a locality that "was one of the most beautiful and picturesque in the neighborhood of Bradford," three miles from any town and on the banks of the river Aire.

The revival at the grass-roots level of the idea of the paternalism of property reached its apex at Saltaire. It is the paradigmatic case of property doing its duty and the epitome of the model factory village. Its 3,000 operatives worked in a fireproof, well ventilated stone mill as long as St. Paul's and with ceilings fourteen to sixteen feet high. They lived in 850 equally well ventilated stone dwellings that were lined with brick, had three bedrooms and walled-in gardens, and were filled with all the modern appliances. The dwellings cost Titus Salt £106,552. The church cost him £16,000 and the school £7,000, the school being unrivaled, according to the education inspector, for "beauty, size and equipment." There were baths and washhouses, costing another £7,000. The washhouses had very advanced steam-driven machines for washing and drying clothes, which all could use. There were forty-five small almshouses rent free. Married couples living in the almshouses received ten shillings a week and the single persons 7s 6d. The qualification for such an apartment and such an income was "good moral character and incapacity for labour because of age, disease, and infirmity." At the opening of the almshouses Titus Salt said his "sole desire was that [the inhabitants] should be happy." The same desire along with a belief in the value of friendly intercourse led Titus Salt to invite his operatives to a day of festivity at his country estate. Three thousand came by special trains, toured the gardens, roamed the park, found "innocent amusement in running, leaping, dancing," indulged in no intoxicating liquor, and sat down at thirty-two tables to a feast. The following were served: "Beef, 1,380 lbs.; ham, 1,300 lbs.; tongues and pies, 520 lbs.; plum bread, 1,081 lbs.; currant bread, 600 lbs.; butter, 200 lbs.; tea, 50 lbs.; sugar, 700 lbs.; cream, 42 gallons; and a great quantity of celery."[15]

There were not many Saltaires in Britain. There were not even many Ashworths, Gregs, and Ashtons. There were, however, in the United Kingdom, 4,800 cotton and woolen mills, thousands of collieries, and even more thousands of workshops and small manufactures. Leonard Horner, the factory inspector, was well aware of these facts. In 1837 he cautioned his friend the economist Nassau Senior not to lose his sense of proportion. "The [factory] law," he told Senior, "was not passed for such mills as those of Messrs. Gregs and Co. at Bollington, Ashworths at Turton, and Mr. Thomas Ashton at Hyde," but for "the very many millowners whose standard of morality is low, whose feelings are obtuse, whose governing principle is to make money, and who do not care a straw for the children." Horner himself was an apostle of paternalist ideas. He preached them to all the millowners, particularly in his pleas for better factory schools. But the results were disheartening. In 1843 Horner reported that in the eight-by-four-mile area of Oldham and Ashton, containing a population of 105,000 (90,000 of them wage earners) there was "not one public day school for children of the humbler ranks . . . [nor] one medical charity." He doubted if "in any part of the civilized world, out of Great Britain, a parallel case could be met with." Of 117 factory schools he visited in 1842, 101 were "hopeless, a discreditable mockery of education." The same manufacturers, eleven years after the Factory Act of 1833, were still illegally overworking the children "a great deal." Even the model Samuel Greg had been fined twelve times in 1835–1836 for violating the Factory Act, and Henry Ashworth confessed he worked children illegal hours. Robert Saunders, another factory inspector, reported that some manufacturers told him that but for the Factory Act "it would be fearful to contemplate . . . the cruelty that would have been practiced on those who could not protect themselves."[16] These are not flattering statements about factory owners. Yet factory owners were, according to Horner, more paternal than landlords. He was "fully persuaded that as many instances of large pecuniary sacrifices in the establishment of schools and other arrangements for the benefit of their work people may be found among the owners of factories as among any other description of capitalists, whether in trade or agriculture: if I said *more* instances, I do not believe that I should overstate the case." The assertion of "more instances" is a bold one, but others also made it. The Tory *Fraser's* argued its truth as did the radical *Examiner* and *Westminster Review.* The same *Fraser's* article that said arcadian happiness did not exist because farmers divided laborers from landowners asserted that "master manufacturers" are learning that "with the moral and religious improvement of their work people their own success in trade is mixed up." The *Examiner* agreed. Masters of mills are more merciful and kind, it announced in 1844, than the masters of the soil. The year before, in 1843, the *Westminster* contrasted "the silent suffering which is hidden by the rustic cabin, with its thatched roof and its picturesque dilapidations, to the solid comfort and modest plenty which dwells in the square brick cottage of the artisan." What evils the artisan faced, argued W. R. Greg, the author of the *Westminster* article, are due far more to the bad sanitation and overcrowding of the town itself than to the well-lit, well-ventilated, well-paying factories. Greg, the brother of Samuel Greg, and an ex-millowner himself, was arguing ex parte. He had not learned Leonard Horner's sense of proportion. Horner's "more instances" did not mean all instances. "Many millowners," Horner added, "no doubt took no interest whatsoever in the people . . . but this indifference is not confined to the occupiers of factories, for the condition of the largest proportion of the working classes . . . shows that a want of a kind consideration of the employer for the employed is widely spread."[17]

Horner's melancholy conclusion about those in other trades doing even less than factory owners, most of whom did little or nothing, is fully and grimly corroborated by the six volumes of reports submitted to the Royal Commission on the Employment of Women and Children in Mines and Manufactures. These reports, which came out in 1842 and 1843, present a picture of neglect, abuse, oppression, cruelty, and indifference that equals those that revealed the failings of landed paternalism in the parliamentary reports on settlement, game laws, poor-law administration, and women and children in agriculture.

The most scandalous of the exposures were of women and children in the coal mines. Since the press publicized their plight in great detail, the literate public soon knew of five- and six-year-olds opening and shutting trap doors for twelve hours in the total dark, of girls and boys, eight, nine, and ten, dragging coal baskets through seams too narrow for adults, of women nearly naked and men totally naked, of fornication, beatings, accidents, and abusive butties, of little or no time for meals, of long hours for all and night shifts for many. The accounts were painfully graphic and vivid. But less clear was the responsibility of the proprietors, the men on whom rested the duties and privileges of property. Many of these, like Lords Lonsdale, Londonderry, and Francis Egerton, both held a paternalist social outlook and worked children in their mines. Most proprietors, after leasing their mines to contractors, washed their hands of the matter. They begged off the duties of property. Lord Balcarres said he was anxious to exclude women from his mine, but to do so would create a disturbance. Lord Buccleuch, however, did exclude women, and no disturbance followed. Quite the contrary: he "was delighted with the increased morale." The duke of Buccleuch was an exception, more exceptional even than the only one in ten mine owners who had established adequate schools.[18] In the three volumes on labor in the mines, there is not one in fifty mine owners who cared about the housing and education or the moral condition of their employees. The same ratio or even a worse one is found in the later reports to the Commission on the Employment of Women and Children in Mines and Manufactures. Repeated again are poignant scenes of the overworking of the very young, of seven- and eight-year-old "teerers" in print works who, when worked all night, collapsed beneath the work table; of lace works employing nine- and ten-year-old girls fourteen and fifteen hours a day; of young dressmakers and milliners working entire nights to meet rush orders; and of pottery boys aged eight to seventeen vomiting from the poisonous dyes that dirtied their hands as they dipped plates in the coloring.[19]

The inspectors, admittedly, may have selected the grosser cases of abuse, which in turn were selectively summarized in the reports. There were many good features about work in these manufactures, not the least being a generally high family wage and not infrequently warm, dry, and reasonably pleasant places to work. But beyond these advantages there were few amenities. These reports are almost destitute of examples of employers doing anything for the schooling and housing and health of their employees: there are many reports of "the horrible system of huddling cottages together, back to back, in streets without drains—and one privy to 20 or 30 houses." These lieutenants of industry have a record far more dismal than the captains of industry, the Greggs, Ashworths, and Ashtons, more dismal even than the lords of the soil. Thomas Carlyle's belief that "the condition of England question" could be solved by captains of industry was a noble one; and as executed by the more exemplary of them deserves recognition. But what are forty or fifty exemplars to 4,800 factory owners, not to mention thousands of mine owners and tens of thousands of owners of small manufactures and workshops? The parliamentary investigations of the early 1840s should have disabused their careful readers of any trust in property doing its duties very extensively. Carlyle and Disraeli were careful readers of these reports, and yet it was in 1844 and 1845 that Disraeli published *Coningsby* and *Sybil* and 1845 and 1850 that Carlyle published *Past and Present* and *Latter-Day Pamphlets*.

Part Three

The Politics of Paternalism

Chapter VIII

The Idea of a Paternal Government

The phrase "paternal government" enjoyed considerable popularity in the Parliaments and the press of the 1840s. It was used far more often than the phrases "paternal property" or "paternal church," phrases used about as infrequently as the term "paternalism" itself— which was scarcely at all. The paternalist's use of paternal government was indeed paradoxical, since though he looked to property and the church as the protectors of the poor with much more favor than he did to government, it was for government that he reserved the adjective "paternal." It is a paradox that arises from the paternalist's ambivalent view of government. Paternalists could denounce government as furiously as the radicals if it meddled in those spheres reserved for property and the church, just as they could praise government when it suppressed the radicals' seditious writings. These discordant tendencies did not bother the paternalist since they were embedded in a complex concept of government. For Burke government consisted of those many "connections, natural and civil, that regulate and hold together the community of subordination"; for Sewell it was a "state ramified and extended through all ranks"; and for Seeley it was "the old English parish." Coleridge found government at its best in vestries, corporations, and joint-stock companies while Oastler pronounced that the excellence of the English constitution lay in every locality managing its affairs. Yet Burke, Sewell, Seeley, Coleridge, and Oastler were unanimous in demanding a strong monarchy, one that, in the words of Carlyle, "could

187

a little achieve for the people," and one that Disraeli looked to for a resurgent England.

The paternalists' demand for a strong monarchy gives a clue as to why they so often used the adjective paternal for a government that they wished, in most spheres, to be of modest size. In a monarchy where for centuries the government had been His or Her Majesty's Government and where kings and queens had long spoken of the kingdom as a family with the monarch at its head, the use of the term paternal government is not surprising. For most members of Parliament, Queen Victoria's government was a paternal one (to have called it maternal would have been unthinkable in that masculine age). In their political and social outlook, a strong government ruling, defending, and disciplining its subjects formed a parallel to the paternalism of property and the church.

All three strands were dominant in the Parliament and press of the 1840s, and all three played an important role in defining how a paternal government might make up for the failings of property and the deficiencies of the church in grappling with the problems of an urban and industrial society.

But though all three strands of paternalism informed the thinking of most members of Parliament and so defined the legislative responses to urgent social problems, the results were still confusing. Paternalism as a social outlook was even more amorphous than the laissez faire philosophy of the political economists or the self-help ideals of Victorian individualists. Indeed its very amorphousness allowed it at certain times and in certain places to incorporate into itself both laissez faire attitudes and self-help ideals. Its inclusiveness and near indefinability frustrate the analyst and tempt him to dismiss these clusters of varying attitudes as unimportant. But they were important and widespread. They did inform the minds of the M.P.s in Parliament and the editors and writers of the London press.

Very few M.P.s, for example, doubted that property had its duties as well as its rights. On February 27, 1845, for example, Parliament heard once again the usual exhortation on the duties of the landlord: "Let him look after his tenantry . . . [and] his labourers . . . and see that they had sufficient wages, proper and well built cottages, good gardens . . . schools for the children."[1] The speaker of these sentiments was not a Sussex landowner, nor a devotee of Coleridge, neither Tory nor Anglican, but John Bright, manufacturer, dissenter, radical, and a devotee of Adam Smith. His own firm was a model of paternalism and he a captain of industry in the best Carlylean sense. He managed his firm like the duke of Richmond did his estates, and both the duke and the captain of industry were suspicious of the intrusion of a paternal government. Both felt that the rights and duties of property did not always square with the prerogatives of a paternal government. As a cluster of attitudes and ideas paternalism was not only amorphous, but potentially contradictory. Its complexities multiplied with its revival. Many and varied were the property owners who, in debates on Irish distress, Scottish poor laws, enclosures, and ten-hour bills, charged that government interference destroyed the capacity of property to do its duties.

Many M.P.s also believed that the Church of England had its very special mission. It was a belief that involved a certain embarrassment. The Test and Corporation Acts in 1828 and the Reform Act of 1832 made the dissenters a political force, if not in Parliament itself, certainly in many constitutencies where their numbers exercised either a substantial or a crucially marginal effect on elections. Secularism too, ranging from outright atheism to a vaguely Christian modernism, had grown strong. Even more embarrassing was the disagreement within the Church of England about theological and ritual matters and about the proper relation of Church and state. Some, including not a few Tractarians, conceived of a paternal Church as a voluntary one, one quite free of the dictates of the state. Others, of the old school of Hooker and Laud and the new school of Blomfield and Wilberforce, saw the Church as a state Church, one constitutionally established and one that deserved Parliament's exclusive support. Still others, not a few of whom were evangelicals, realized that the Church of England and dissent both had a mission, a mission that state grants to all denominations could aid. Coleridge's ideal of a clerisy very much inspired members of Parliament, but it inspired them in different ways. These different ways, along with the growing strength of secularism and dissent, only complicated the already complicated nature of the politics of paternalism.

A clear idea of the specific aims, functions, and limits of a paternal government might have clarified some of the above complexities, but, unfortunately, there was no such clear idea. M.P.s of all parties used the phrase but agreed neither on its meaning nor on a definite criterion for its application. Some called for government intervention "where it was demanded by the moral and physical condition of the people," and

some "where the object in view is practical right." Others said the interference of government was demanded "by public reason, by public
virtue, by public honour and by the public character," or that the government should interfere "wherever evils are injurious," where "it is
necessary to do that justice which a people had a right to expect from
a paternal government," or where it would bring "the greatest good to
the greatest number."[2]

Diverse and vague as were the criteria for government interference,
there was one criterion that was quintessentially paternalist. It was the
simple call for the protection—as a father would protect a child—of the
weak, helpless, poor, and ill. The preeminent paternalist, Lord Ashley,
put it most directly when he called for the state to "accomplish her
frequent boast and show herself a faithful and pious parent." Many
others varied that cry. John Fielden, the millowner and M.P. for
Oldham, said it was the state's function "to protect the weak from the
strong," Edward Cayley, agriculturist and M.P. for the North Riding,
declared that "legislation should always be for the weak, the strong
could take care of themselves," and Charles Newdegate of North Warwickshire asserted that "the state should assist the helpless." The M.P.
from Dumbartonshire also called for state interference because the state
should "protect the weaker," while Lord Robert Grosvenor of Middle-
sex thought the state should interfere because "we were all members
of one great family."

No abstract yardstick of the greatest happiness but a concrete image
of the helpless, the weak, the poor, and the injured formed the rationale
for government interference. Of all these images of the weak and the
helpless, none was more poignant and affecting than that of the helpless
child. It was the central image in all debates on factories, mines, and
lace- and print-works bills just as it was on education and reformatory
grants. The duke of Richmond invoked it in asking the assistant poor-
law commissioners to visit pauper farms. "It was the duty of the legislature," he said, "to take measures for the protection of . . . children."
Where there were no parents or the parents were cruel or negligent,
the state should step in. In the factory question, said Henry Liddell
from North Durham, "the state should put itself in *loco parentis*."[3]
For the state to act toward orphans *in loco parentis* was long a part of
common law. It was a concept that also covered lunatics and prisoners.
An old common-law doctrine called *parens patriae* (father of the
nation) gave the monarch the power to appear in court as "general

guardian" of charitable trusts and of "infants, idiots, and lunatics."
A parental government intervened, then, not so much to maximize happiness or for reasons of private right or public honor, but where the
weak and helpless of Her Majesty's children needed protection.

Protection, however, is but one of the functions of fathers and
monarchs. There is also moral guidance. There were many bishops or
Christian laymen to invoke this noble duty. The bishop of London was
quite explicit. "That government best answered the purpose of its
institution," he told the House of Lords, "when it came nearest to
paternal rule." When parents neglected those duties, he added, "it was
the sacred duty of the legislature to interfere." The bishop of Gloucester
added to this injunction the specific duty of inculcating morality. "As
Christian legislators," he announced, "it was the most important of their
duties to enforce morality by legislation," a stern requirement but no
sterner than Edward Buxton's claim that it was "the highest duty of the
state to see people were taught religion."[4]

The best of political philosophies has yet to discover a consistent rule
for deciding when a government should intervene and when it should
not. The paternalist's rule was no exception. What children? Children
in cotton mills and mines only or children in tailoring and dressmaking?
Children below eighteen or any subject bereft of reason or who has
been trampled on by the strong? What government? Whitehall? Quarter
sessions? The parish? Or the new poor-law unions? This last issue alone
added some very intractable complexities to the politics of paternalism.
Traditional paternalists valued the small personal sphere of the known
and limited, the sphere of the parish and magistracy, but the failure of
these authorities to cope with pauperism, dirty cities, and manufacturing
labor demanded the impersonal and distant bureaucrat. So even the concept of a paternal government was filled with ambiguities. With M.P.s
not only emphasizing in different ways the duties of property, government, and the church, but also differing in their emphases on a local or
a central government or a voluntary or state church, there was bound to
be some confusion in their debates and votes on paternal legislation.

That confusion was also increased by the ambiguities and complexities
of the legislation itself. How could there be a simple paternalist position
on the 110 clauses of the New Poor Law or even on the Corn Law or the
grant of money to Ireland's Catholic college at Maynooth? To some
paternalists the New Poor Law destroyed parochial bonds and the magistrate's parental protection of the pauper, to others it meant much better

schools for pauper children and a more parental care of lunatics. The
Corn Law protected landed property, the protectors in turn (it was
hoped) of the laborer, but it did not protect the poor from a costlier loaf
of bread. Coleridge was for the Corn Law, Carlyle against it, and both
were paternalists. The Maynooth grant was also ambiguous. To some
the Maynooth grant would train priests to be the teachers and protectors of those Irish peasants who were as much a part of Her Majesty's
family as English laborers, while to others any support of a Catholic
college weakened the Church of England whose special mission it was
to teach and protect all of Her Majesty's subjects.

The members of Parliament were not the only political personages
perplexed by the place of poor relief, corn laws, and Maynooth grants
in a paternal government. The London daily press had also to wrestle
with these ambiguous issues. The politics of paternalism produced quite
as many fervid editorials as eloquent orations. There were few statesmen
who did not find it worthwhile to support, influence, and, if they could,
manage the press. Few statesmen could forget that every weekday in the
year 1845 nine London dailies sold around fifty-five thousand copies of
their newspapers to avid followers of the political scene. Of these nine
newspapers four were not particularly ardent supporters of paternalist
social theories. The *Morning Chronicle,* edited by John Black, the friend
of Bentham, the Mills, and the political economist McCulloch, could
not abide Tory landlords, an exclusive church, or a meddling government,
while the *Sun,* a radical paper put out by a self-made Londoner, Murdo
Young, had little respect for a society based on obedience, inequalities,
special privilege, and deference.[5] The very Whiggish *Globe* and the
licensed victualler's *Morning Advertiser* were not as critical of paternalism as the *Sun* and the *Morning Chronicle,* but the editor of the
Globe, John Wilson, counted himself a utilitarian and friend of Bentham, while the *Morning Advertiser's* columns aimed to please Lon-
doners who visited public houses, not gentlemen and gentlewomen in
their town houses and country estates. The combined circulation of these
four papers came to 23,000.[6]

Though no particular friend of paternalism, the *Morning Advertiser*
did not deny that land had its duties and the clergy their obligations. It
was also not that inimical to a paternal government. "There ought to be
state education," it said, "because it is the duty of a paternal government
to . . . prevent crime."[7] Paternalism's many-sidedness allowed the
truth of certain of its axioms to be held in varying contexts—the *Morn-*

ing Advertiser, like the *Globe*, could thus incorporate some paternalist dictums in its essentially laissez faire outlook. But for a complete dissemination of those paternalist axioms that ranged from a belief in a deferential society to a belief in an exclusive church, one must turn to five other London dailies: the *Morning Herald*, the *Standard*, the *St. James's Chronicle*, the *Morning Post*, and the *vox populi* of the 1840s, the *Times*. Their combined circulation in 1845 came to over 35,000.[8]

In that year Stanley Lees Giffard superintended the first three of these dailies. Giffard was Anglo-Irish, Tory, proudly Anglican, learned in the classics, unstinting in his admiration of Edmund Burke, and a close friend and admirer of Robert Southey. He started the *Standard* in 1828 to fight against Catholic Emancipation. In 1846 he confessed he was at heart a political and religious partisan and a Tory publicist. In 1841 he wrote Sir Robert Peel and offered to devote the columns of his papers to supporting the new Tory administration.[9]

Also at the *Standard* was Alaric Watts. In 1839 Giffard made Watts "principal editor." A romantic, a poet, and once editor of the Tory *Leeds Intelligencer*, he had, in that town, joined Michael Sadler and Richard Oastler to fight for a ten-hour factory act and against the New Poor Law. He also became a friend of Wordsworth, Southey, and Coleridge, winning from the last a warm recommendation as just the person to establish a daily journal in London. Working with Watts after 1845 was Giffard's son Hardinge, the future Lord Chancellor Halsbury. The outlook of these three writers of coruscating leaders was consistently paternalist. In 1848 the *Standard* praised the "subordination of ranks in society" and proclaimed that "Divine Providence has disposed and distributed us into several societies." The *Standard* was held in warm esteem by Lord Ashley, Sir Robert Inglis, and the duke of Newcastle, all intimate friends of and active correspondents with Stanley Lees Giffard. Giffard returned the compliment in the case of Inglis when he had the *Standard* announce in 1845, "rarely do we differ from Inglis."[10]

The *Morning Post* was owned and edited by C. Eastland Michele. He was assisted in the late 1840s by Peter Borthwick. The *Post* enjoyed a good advertising income from those carriage makers and owners of smart shops who knew that copies of the *Post* ended up in the drawing rooms of the fashionable and the clubs of the rich. The paper was sometimes called "the pet of the petticoats." Little is known of Michele besides a letter he wrote in 1840 offering to place the *Post* in Peel's service. Of Peter Borthwick more is known. Indeed he possesses two histories. The *Dictionary of National Biography* states that he was born in Scotland, was trained by a private tutor, graduated from Edinburgh University, attended Cambridge University, and became a barrister. Cyrus Redding tells a different story in his *Recollections*. Redding, a newspaper editor himself, says Borthwick's father was only a porter at a Dalkeith paper mill. The son used a smattering of Latin to become a peripatetic teacher traveling from home to home, in one of which he seduced a servant girl. He did go to Cambridge, but the issuance of a false acceptance there quickly led to his imprisonment. In prison he wrote a theological work that so impressed the evangelicals that they had him released, only to see him attempt a career at the very sinful profession of acting. He failed at that. His real talent was as an orator, a talent he used in defense of slavery in the West Indies, a defense so spirited and successful that it led to a seat in Parliament and an alliance with Young England. He was, concludes Redding "a liar and consummate adventurer, a bold and talented opportunist."[11]

The *Post* had a high esteem for Disraeli and his Young England group, praising its chivalric and humane ideals and inviting its members to contribute articles. For doing so it was severely denounced by the *Standard*. Giffard's *Standard* found Young England "factionists, fops and crazy dotards," and denounced their "drivelling idiocy," as part of "the insanity of the Morning Postites." The *Standard* itself boasted in 1844 of a conservatism that was not "foppish or factional," but one that represented "the really honest and intelligent men of business." It was a Peelite conservatism, one reflecting their admiration of this greatest of statesmen since Chatham, but it was an admiration severely strained by Peel's renewal of the New Poor Law in 1842, Peel's defeat of Ashley's ten-hour amendment to the Factory Act of 1844, and the Maynooth grant of 1845. Finally the alliance broke on the shoals of the repeal of the Corn Law.[12]

Of the 35,000 copies sold daily in 1845 of newspapers that espoused a paternalist social outlook, 22,000 were copies of the *Times*. Though it could not rival the *Post, Herald,* or *Standard* in high Toryism and romantic medievalism, its advocacy of paternalism was just as spirited. John Walter II was a London publisher, a Berkshire squire, and an independent but fiercely anti-Whig M.P. He was an enthusiast for local government, a landowner, a churchman, and a tireless opponent of the New Poor Law. He was, say the editors of the *History of the Times,* "a stalwart supporter of the existing order." His son John Walter III, who took over ownership of the *Times* in 1847, was educated at Oxford where he was influenced by John Henry Newman. The senior Walter in 1841 appointed. J. T. Delane as editor. Delane was also influenced, when at Oxford, by Newman. Delane brought with him to the *Times* and from Oxford Thomas Mozley, Roundell Palmer (later the earl of Selborne), and Frederic Rogers (later Lord Blatchford).[13] All three wrote editorials for the *Times* in the early 1840s and all three were Tories, High Churchmen, and paternalists. Rogers was in 1831 a student at Oriel and a pupil and intimate friend of Newman. From Newman and from John Keble, at whose Sussex parish of Hursley he became a frequent visitor, he learned the social outlook of the Oxford movement. Roundell Palmer learned that outlook earlier in life. His father was the High Church rector of Mixbury in Oxfordshire and a model shepherd of his flock. He taught his son by example and precept the ways of paternalism. At Oxford these ways were reinforced by reading Wordsworth, from whom, he said, "I learned . . . large human sympathies." Thomas Mozley, at Oriel with Newman in the 1820s, rector of Cholderton from 1836 to 1847, editor of the *British Critic* in the 1840s, was the author in that review of impeccably paternalistic articles on the poor.[14]

Three Cambridge men in the 1840s shared with these Oxford Tractarians the writing of the leaders in the *Times*. They were H. A. Woodham, Henry Reeve, and Abraham Hayward. Reeve and Hayward were holdovers from the editorship of Thomas Barnes, the "thunderer," the indignant opponent of the New Poor Law, and the paternal friend of the poor. Both Reeve and Hayward were on the side of Coleridge and Wordsworth and against Ricardo and Bentham. Reeve helped found the *British and Foreign Review,* a journal pronouncedly paternalist. To Reeve, Coleridge was "a great luminary," and he confessed in 1835 to being for "the Catholic and untainted few who cherish . . . the traditions of aristocracy, monarchy, and Christianity." Hayward also admired Coleridge—and Wordsworth and Southey as well, making in his youth a pilgrimage to the Lake District to meet them. Younger than Reeve and Hayward, and from the Cambridge of Kenelm Digby, Maurice's "The Apostles," and Coleridge's ideas, was H. A. Woodham, in the mid-1840s the most unflagging writer of *Times* leaders. Author of a book on heraldry and a book on Tertullian, it is hardly likely that he was antithetical to the Coleridgean outlook of his fellow Cantabrigians, Reeve and Hayward, or to the Tractarian social outlook of

Rogers, Palmer, and Mozley. Delane had as editorial writers men whose social outlook hardly listed toward individualistic egalitarianism, evangelical philanthropy, or Benthamite planning. And to give to the columns of the *Times* the final imprimatur of paternalism, Delane published the many contributions of that exemplary Dorsetshire paternalist, Lord Sidney Godolphin Osborne. The paternalist pedigree of the *Times* was as impeccable as that of the *Standard*, the *Morning Herald*, the *Morning Post*, and the *St. James's Chronicle*.[15]

To those five great dailies with a combined circulation of 35,000 was added in 1847 as an advocate of paternalism, the *Morning Chronicle*. In 1847 William Gladstone, author of *The State in its Relations with the Church*, and Sidney Herbert, soon to publish *Proposals for the Better Application of Cathedral Institutions*, joined with Beresford Hope, author of *Letters on Church Matters* and Lord Lincoln, whose *Speeches . . . To His Tenantry* of 1852 was the exemplification of landed paternalism, to purchase the *Morning Chronicle*. They hired as editor John Douglas Cook, Lord Lincoln's private secretary and recently of the *Times*. Cooke hired as an assistant George Sydney Smythe, a leading Young England M.P., the son of Lord Strangford and the model for the hero of Disraeli's *Coningsby*. Abraham Hayward also helped with articles. With Gladstone, Herbert, Hope, and Lord Lincoln as owners and Smythe and Hayward as editorial writers the London dailies that expressed paternalist ideas now numbered six.[16]

The six dailies mentioned above all supported the idea of a paternal government. Both the *Morning Post* and the *Times* explicitly called for a "paternal government," the *Post* in 1840 in order to promote "cooperation and mutual protection" rather than trusting "to the spirit of hostility of interests called competition," and the *Times* in 1844 in order to mold a society that is not "a mere multitude of rich and poor, everyone making the best bargain for himself."[17] The reasons offered for favoring such a paternal government varied among journalists as they did among M.P.s. There were also many who scarcely gave any theoretical reasons at all. The *Morning Herald* spoke vigorously for the paternalism of property and church and called for church extension and factory acts, but in justifying these policies it never once used the term "paternal government." Instead it said such policies were simply "a matter of pressing humanity." "Is not humanity," it asked elsewhere, "a positive duty?"[18] In the same pragmatic way the *Times* invoked "the welfare of the common people." The *Standard*, edited by the learned

Giffard, however, liked to embellish its demands with theory. It not only claimed that Grotius had proved "it is the duty of the government to see that the property and safety of the people be accomplished," but it also appealed to the axiom of the utilitarians. "The science of politics," said the *Standard* in 1843, "has for its end the means of rendering a nation happy and powerful." Utilitarianism could be learned from Paley as well as from Bentham, or even from Aristotle, Hobbes, Locke, and Priestley. "It is the first duty of every Government," argued the *Morning Post*, "to . . . promote the welfare and happiness of the mass of the people."[19]

More frequently invoked than the principle of the greatest happiness was the need for the government to protect the helpless. The *Times* did so on behalf of sailors in supporting the Merchant Marine Bill of 1850 and the *Herald* on behalf of passengers in supporting the railway legislation in 1842. "Why not leave the sailor to take care of himself?" asked the *Times* and answered, "because he has not common prudence." "It is the imperative duty of the legislature," said the *Morning Herald*, "to omit no enactments for the better security of life and limb."[20] The factory and mines bills provided classic cases calling for a paternal government to protect the helpless. "The case is plainly one calling for legislative interference," said the *Standard* of the factory bill of 1847, and "on this ground, that a helpless class . . . are at the mercy of the men who have every selfish and sordid motive for abusing the power in their hands." A paternal government was above all one that protected the weak and helpless. The *Times, Standard, Post,* and *Herald* all supported Lord Ashley's Mines Act of 1842 and ten-hour amendment to the Factory Act of 1844 as well as John Fielden's Ten Hour Factory Act of 1847. All three of these measures applied only to women, children, and young people. A similar parental protectiveness led the *Times* to support Lord Ashley's Print Works Bill and lunacy bills of 1845 and the *Standard* to support the Print Works Bill and Sir Henry Halford's bill to regulate the rent and fees of hosiery workers. The *Times* could not support the hosiery bill, and the *Standard* said nothing of the lunacy bills. The *Herald* and *Post* said nothing in their columns of the printworks, lunacy, or hosiery bills. Though the *Morning Post* in 1848 claimed that "everyone knows we are advocates of a more careful, considerate and generous government," its specific pleas for particular measures were not very ample. It did, however, as did all these London dailies but the *Times,* support Gladstone's Railway Act of 1844. The act in particular protected the poor from rain, sleet, and cold by outlawing the open cars of the very slow-moving third-class trains.[21]

A paternal government was a directing as well as a protecting one. "Direction and protection are the two great offices," said the *Morning Post* in 1848, "of a rational and well principled government." This belief inspired these papers to urge larger parliamentary grants to the Church of England for the building of churches, endowment of livings, and building and supporting of schools. These paternalist dailies all supported Sir Robert Inglis's Church Extension Bill of 1840, the Factory Education Bill of 1843, and the Minutes of the Committee of Council on Education of 1846, which greatly increased aid to schools.[22]

The London dailies of a paternalist persuasion by no means supported all increases in the power and personnel of the central government. All four had in the 1830s opposed the New Poor Law, denounced measures for a central police, and condemned the establishment of the Committee of Council on Education. In 1848 the *Standard*, the *Post*, the *Herald*, and the *Morning Chronicle* opposed the Public Health Act and in 1847 the Irish Poor Law Act. All but one were silent about or were against Henry Halford's 1847 bill to regulate the rents and fees of hosiery workers, and none supported the 1848 bill doing the same for the frame knitters.[23] The paternalist dailies opposed these measures, which would have strengthened the state, because they were attached to private property, local government, and the Church of England and believed that though legislation could protect the helpless from gross abuses, it could not cure social evils.

Their attachment to private property was deep. "The source of the principle not to invade the property of another," said the *Post* in 1840, "is the religion we profess." The *Standard* in 1845 said the "sacred right . . . and inviolability of property [was] essential to the safety of society." The *Morning Chronicle* agreed. "The public good," it wrote in 1847, "is founded on the rights of property."[24] So beneficent was property, particularly land, that a paternal government should protect its owners as well as the helpless. The *Post, Herald, Standard,* and *Times* all supported the Corn Law, and none of these papers objected to generous loans to English and Irish landowners for those improvements that increased their rents. The *Post, Standard,* and *Herald* also considered parliamentary grants to private railways in Ireland a much better solution to Ireland's wretched condition after the famine than an expanded poor-law relief based on the taxation of land.[25]

These grants to railways did not mean, however, that the railways would be unduly regulated. The *Times* was particularly hostile to the railway bills of 1844 and 1845 that strengthened the powers of the government. The *Standard* in 1845 and the *Post* in 1847 also felt it no business of a paternal government. The *Standard* considered any bill enforcing a maximum fare "foolish" and all railway legislation "a violation of sacred property," while the *Post* found the 1847 bill to expand the duties of the Railway Department "vexatious," "injurious," and "full of needless patronage."[26]

These journals were not unconnected with railway interests. In 1848 Henry Chapman sent Stanley Lees Giffard a clipping from the *Shipping Gazette* that reported how the boom in railway projects made the *Morning Herald* momentarily rich, not only from advertising revenue but from the buying and selling of shares. Chapman also said that the *Times* was jealous and hence had become a Jeremiah about the railway boom, though not about a flagging line in Cornwall. They puffed that line because both the city editor and the business manager (who was J. T. Delane's father) had shares in it. In 1845 the *Morning Post* devoted a twenty-page supplement to railway advertisements. It was an age not overly self-conscious about asserting the rights of private property, an age in which the *Times* could list property along with monarchy and the church as constituting "the heart of the nation."[27]

Property had, according to the wisdom of the age, duties as well as rights, and that wisdom also said that property performed those duties most effectively when untrammeled. The *Times,* therefore, on July 11, 1844, strongly condemned William Cowper's field-gardens bill, a bill that demanded that all future enclosure acts give some allotments, at modest rents, to the neighboring poor. It was not that the *Times* opposed allotments—indeed they championed them when freely given by landlords—but they objected to the bill's creation of field-garden wardens, boards of managers, perpetual leases, and "the whole machinery of regulating rents." Such regulations interfered with what Coleridge had insisted preserved reform and innovation from folly, namely that free agency which belonged to the individual proprietor. For Coleridge and the *Times,* property certainly belonged at "the heart of the nation."

It is surprising that the *Times* did not add local self-government as part of the heart of the nation. It had long and loudly declaimed against centralization. No act of Parliament received such sustained abuse from the *Times* as the New Poor Law. Its worst feature was the destruction of the parish's role in administering relief. In 1849 the *Times* still believed "the parochial system [was] the most perfect scheme ever devised between property, meritorious poverty, and idle indigence." The *Post, Herald, Standard,* and *Chronicle* all agreed. "The principle of local government of local affairs," clamored the *Herald* in 1842, "must be restored." To this end all the paternalist dailies attacked the evil centralization of the New Poor Law, and all befriended parish government. The three most Tory newspapers even stuck by local government in 1848 on the question of public sanitation. On that issue the *Times* alone abandoned local government, but not without great anguish and only because sanitation involved "material concerns where science and uniformity worked." For "moral matters," it added, centralization would never do.

The *Herald* would not even yield on the question of sanitation. "A little dirt and freedom," said the *Herald* in 1848, "may after all be more desirable than no dirt at all and slavery." "There is no necessity," added the *Morning Post* of the Public Health Act, "for commissionerships and elaborate Acts of Parliament." It is "a bad bill," concluded the *Standard,* "because of its uniformity. . . . Have we not heard enough of the effect of centralization in the New Poor Law?" The *Standard* repeatedly praised King Alfred as the founder of local government and so of England's free institutions.[28] The paternalist's idea of a protective and directive government had little place for central bureaucrats. Mere legislation laying down the duties of property would guarantee protection, while the Church would give the direction. "What, after all, we wish to see," said a correspondent to the *Times* in 1838, "is a factory act that will really do justice to all parties and work without certificates and inspectors."[29] The *Time*'s correspondent argued that local magistrates could enforce a clear and unambiguous ten-hour act. The *Standard, Post,* and *Herald* felt town government could do the same with sanitation, and all four papers also called the New Poor Law odious because it denied the local squire and parson, who knew the poor intimately, their sovereign paternal role. These journals applied to day-to-day problems Burke's idea of government as a moral partnership and Coleridge's idea that "the democracy of England resided in the corporation and the vestries, the joint stock companies, etc."

The *Times, Standard, Herald,* and *Post* were all staunch friends of the Church of England. All four in 1839 opposed the establishment of the Committee of Council on Education. It meant more centralization and more uniformity. It meant that state inspectors would rival Anglican parsons in superintending the nation's teachers.[30] In 1843 all four of these dailies supported the factory-education bill that would have created rate-supported schools in manufacturing areas. "There ought to be in every town," said the *Morning Post,* "some effective system of educational superintendence." It should teach that "value of deference, of obedience, of strict and careful attention to duty, . . . of kindly feeling . . . and patient endurance, . . . and humbleness" which arise wherever the catechism is "diligently enforced." The factory schools could provide such an education in the *Post's* view because all the teachers and a majority of the trustees would be Anglicans. The measure would certainly strengthen the Church. So in 1847 would the expansion of state grants to help pay teachers and pupil teachers, since in that year 82 percent of parliamentary grants went to Anglican schools. All of the paternalist London dailies thus championed these grants. The Church of England was to be the centerpiece in the paternal government. "Through the Church alone," said the *Post* in a series entitled "The Monastic and Manufacturing System," "do we look for permanent amelioration." To further that aim the *Post, Standard,* and *Herald* in 1840 unreservedly supported Sir Robert Inglis's bill for parliamentary grants to help build and endow Anglican churches.[31]

In one sense their zeal for these measures meant not a check on but an impetus to the growth of a paternal government because the government helped finance schools and churches. But in a deeper sense it really checked rather than promoted such a growth because their sectarian exclusiveness forced them to oppose any comprehensive measures, whether for church building or education, that would include dissent.

Dissenters in 1840 and 1843 were many and formidable. The 1851 census showed that half of those attending church on a given Sunday were dissenters. Dissent defeated the Church Extension Bill of 1840 and the Factory Education Bill of 1843 on the grounds that the state cannot give exclusive privileges and the taxpayers' money to merely one of many denominations. Dissenters failed to defeat the 1846 minutes, but then many of the Committee of Council grants did go to dissenting schools. The 1846 minutes were not an exclusive measure. But neither were they a comprehensive, effective, rate-supported system of public education, a system England sorely needed. Such a system was anathema to the *Post, Standard,* and *Herald,* so great was their attachment to the Church of England. They thus helped prevent the state from effectively solving the education problem. There was no longer any way for the Church to become the directing arm of a paternal government. Denied that dream, the paternalist presses of London were in no mood to accept boards of education, bureaucratic guidelines, school inspectors, and schools without the catechism and the thirty-nine articles.

The paternalists writing for the *Post, Standard, Herald,* and *Times* were also inhibited from supporting a more active central government by their belief that more departments, inspectors, and laws could not remedy society's more basic ills. Their temperament was not that of planners, innovators, or reformers. They loved the old and abhorred the new. "We hate and dread," said the *Standard,* "the spirit of rash legislation which goes to change every established law." They also dreaded elaborate laws, proliferating bureaucracies, and economic planning, preferring to such mechanisms a reliance on the perseverance of the poor, the protective role of property, and society's identity of interests. The acute economic distress of 1842 certainly could not be cured by a paternal government. "The revival of trade," said the *Morning Herald* in June of 1842, "depends more upon the working classes themselves . . . than upon any measure which the legislature can take for their relief." A month later the *Times* told its readers "no legislation could furnish an immediate remedy."[32] When faced with the deep economic depression of 1842, the *Morning Post* was just as tepid about legislative remedies. "We do not see," it wrote in June of 1842, "that there can be any immediate remedy but in the relief of the poor by an extra-ordinary exertion on the part of the rich." The *Post* a year later argued that no public regulation can "supersede the injunction, 'be ye kind to one another.'" It then added that "the work that government has to do is rather to encourage the poor and the depressed and to uplift the broken hearts from the desolate condition they have been borne by the tide of circumstances." A deep sense of the inevitability of poverty informs this passage, just as it does the *Times*'s claim in 1843, "There is and ever will be a vast body of poor."

The desire of the paternalist dailies to regulate or plan the economy did not go much beyond protecting women and children from long hours and dangerous machinery. None of them supported any significant legislation for remedying the deep depression of 1842. The *Herald* told the workers in 1843, "It is not by a single act of Parliament that the labouring population can be raised." Actually, this laissez faire sentiment of the *Herald* was not that much at variance with its general economic philosophy. In the same year it told its readers "no one now denies . . . the principles of Adam Smith." The *Post* too must have imbibed some of the doctrines of Adam Smith. In 1844 it argued that hard work and thrift, not government aid, would serve the workers best, particularly since "the interests of landowners are ultimately the same as the interests of labourers."[33] The *Post, Herald, Standard, Times,* and *Chronicle* after 1847 believed in the economics of the free market, not in the economics of collectivism. The writings of European socialists throughout the forties and the French Revolution of 1848 frightened them away from any move toward socialism. This fear combined with their hatred of undue legislation (and of the godless ideas of the leading socialist, Robert Owen) led many a paternalist to adopt a laissez faire philosophy. "Nothing can be worse," said the *Post* on May 20, 1848, "than to hold out to all that they may rely upon the institutions of government, independently of their own exertions." A year later the *Morning Chronicle,* now the paper of those stalwart paternalists, Gladstone, Herbert, Lincoln, and Beresford Hope, said, "There is a dangerous similarity of principle between poor laws and communism."[34] The prosperous 1850s relieved the economic crisis of the early 1840s that had encouraged an insistence on a protecting and directing paternal government. In 1844 the *Times* had urged the adoption of a ten-hour limit to factory labor so that "the paternal character of government" not be forgotten. In 1853 the *Times* decided that "socialism we must call every attempt . . . to invoke the interference of the legislature in those contracts which any one man is compelled to make with another."[35] It made the statement in opposition to an act that would have prevented manufacturers from using the device of employing the young and women in two separate shifts in order to work adult men longer than ten hours.

The dislike that the paternalist dailies expressed of commissioners, inspectors, and excessive legislation did not preclude a desire for a strong monarchy and an authoritarian discipline throughout society. The first was a matter of rhetoric and the second of local government, law courts, and the rule of Ireland. The *Morning Post,* easily the most rhetorical and fanciful of the paternalist dailies, insisted that "to secure good government . . . the prerogative of monarchy ought to be superior to the law." The paternalist dailies did not like heretical opinions. The *Morning Herald* in 1840 called for the suppression of socialist publications. Both exalting monarchy and suppressing publications were about as realistic an option in the 1840s as the *Morning Herald*'s Carlylean plea, "The want of England . . . is a master mind." The *Herald,* which believed that "the masses do not reason closely," wanted a strong rule.[36] It was another dream. More realistic was the support given by these dailies for measures that would end beer shops, provide for the whipping of juveniles, make seduction a crime, secure the punishment of prostitutes, and discipline the Irish. The *Post* in particular wanted seduction declared criminal and wanted the Irish "subject to discipline analogous to the military," while the *Standard* favored Sir John Pakington's bill for summary whipping of juveniles since Solomon had made it clear that "for transgressing children the rod is the proper and the only proper instrument of punishment."[37]

In the idea of a paternal government the desire to control morals always loomed larger than the desire to control property. Only in the mid-1840s did the latter desire loom very large. It did so primarily in response to circumstances. The depression of 1838 to 1842 and the melancholy reports of the Commission on Child Labour in Mines and Manufactures, along with the Poor Law Commission's Report on Women and Children in Agriculture had momentarily made it difficult merely to trust in a laissez faire economy and the self-reliance of the individual. The reports of lunacy, education, and poor-law inspectors showed even greater unmet needs. The *Spectator* in 1844 realized clearly how powerful were those unmet needs in generating demands for a more paternal government. In April 13 of that year it published an editorial entitled the "New Faith." After underlining the grievous evils of overworked women and children, the misery of dirty towns, and the fact that the "let alone policies" had failed to end these appalling conditions, it concluded, "So here is a job of work for the advocates of paternal government." The *Spectator,* which the year before had said "the Government ought to be to society in *loco parentis,*" praised the work of Lord Ashley and was elated that his ten-hour amendment passed the Commons in May of 1844. It also praised in October of that year the broad humanity evident in the poems of Milnes, the speeches of Disraeli, and the speeches of John Manners and George Smythe at the Manchester Athenaeum. It hoped to help form a new party that would be inspired by this new faith, one in which liberals such as Charles Buller and Lord Howicke could join with Young England to create a government that would stand *in loco parentis* to those who suffered social grievances.

The idea of a paternal government, like the belief in the paternalism of land and the paternalism of the church, was no preserve of the Tories alone. The *Spectator* was a radical journal. Its Scottish editor Robert Rintoul was a friend of Bentham and the Mills and learned in political economy. His chief editorial writer, Thornton Hunt, was the son of the London radical Leigh Hunt. Yet it was in this journal and not in Tory ones that the idea of a paternal government had its fullest expression. The *Spectator* not only crusaded for ten-hour bills, mining acts, and lunacy measures, but supported poor-law reform, the Public Health Act of 1848, the Irish Poor Law Act of 1847, and plans for state education, all to the shock of parish overseers, town councilors, proud sewer commissioners, ardent churchmen, and Irish landowners.[38]

Rintoul and Hunt of the *Spectator* were liberals and reformers. They saw in much of the above legislation a means of reconstructing society and removing social ills. In their columns the idea of a "reforming state" accompanied the idea of a "paternal government." In supporting the New Poor Law, the Committee of Council on Education, and the Public Health Act, and in calling for many more social reforms, they expressed their belief that poverty, ignorance, and illness could be significantly reduced, other evils remedied, and a new society built. Their aims were quite in contrast to those of a *Morning Post*, which wanted the government mainly to encourage the poor and depressed and to lift up the broken hearts of the desolate. It was a work eminently suited for the clergyman or lady bountiful of the parish.[39] The work of government, said the *Spectator*, was to reform and reconstruct society, to end, not soften, the poor's desolation. It was a work eminently suited for poor-law unions where workhouses deterred men from pauperism and schools trained children to self-reliance and for local boards of health and state rate-supported schools, which would prevent that illness and that ignorance which caused the poor to be desolate. The *Spectator*'s sanguine hope was to combine those liberals and utilitarians who believed in the idea of a reforming government with those Young Englanders who believed in the idea of a paternal government. It was an interesting alliance, and from 1842 to 1845 it lay behind the massive support for Ashley's mines and lunacy acts, Gladstone's regulation of the payment of coal whippers and his Railway Act of 1844, the Print Works Act of 1845, and the momentary triumph of the ten-hour amendment to the Factory Act of 1844. But the repeal of the Corn Law and the Public Health Act of 1848 (as will be seen in chapter nine) destroyed this precarious, fragile, and perhaps ultimately hopeless alliance.

From 1833 to 1854 Parliament established some fourteen new departments of the central government. What influence did the idea of a paternal government have on that growth? A precise answer to that question cannot be given; one can only offer a rough guess. The best guess is that on a few occasions, such as Lord Ashley's two lunacy acts and the Youthful Offenders Act of 1854—reforms that vividly involved the helpless—paternalist ideas did play an active, initiating, and dynamic role, but that on most major reforms they played a negative role. There are four reasons why they did, three of which have been discussed. First, the paternalists' deep attachment to private property, local government, and the church; second, their belief that acts of Parliament could not remove social ills; and third, the fact that advocates of a reforming government, not advocates of a paternal government, saw in innovative poor laws, education schemes, sanitary measures, and railway and merchant marine regulations a means of fashioning a more rational and equitable society.

A fourth reason why the idea of a paternal government played no dynamic and initiating role in the expansion of a strong central government is that economic, social, and bureaucratic forces far more than any set of ideas led to its growth. This is a conclusion brilliantly developed by Oliver MacDonagh in his *A Pattern of Government Growth*. In his analysis of the forces leading to governmental growth, MacDonagh places particular emphasis on the bureaucrats who grappled with the new problems of an industrial society. Given mounting social evils, the reports concerning them written by government agents, and the inadequacy of legislation already passed to meet them, it was understandable that Parliament should create further laws and departments. It is an analysis of the growth of government that is hard to refute. But in that analysis there is a question MacDonagh does not fully elucidate, one that his critic Jenifer Hart raises in her article "Nineteenth Century Social Reform." In that article she says, "Before there can be a problem there must be an attitude to actual conditions. . . . And before one knows what one wants to do about the conditions . . . one must have some principle, or standard." The questions MacDonagh does not ask, or at least fully answer, are: what did the bureaucrats want to do about the conditions? And what "principle, or standard," did they hold?[40]

To a remarkable extent the bureaucrats held the standard of a paternal government, and, in addition, the idea of paternal property and a paternal church. Many of the bureaucrats of the 1840s were more paternalist in their social outlook than they were followers of political economy, utilitarianism, or the voluntarism of dissent. The most dramatic and creative of them, to be sure, such as Edwin Chadwick, Kay-Shuttleworth, Southwood Smith, Joseph Fletcher, E. C. Tufnell, and J. C. Symonds, were possessed of the utilitarian idea of a reforming government, but they administered their departments in partnership with factory, poor-law, prison, and education inspectors of the deepest paternalist convictions. One of the greatest forces within the politics of paternalism that led to a stronger paternal government was not Young England M.P.s or the editorials of the *Post* and *Standard*, but the actual existence of a paternal government and of men in that paternal government who wanted it to grow stronger.

The largest number of these were in the education department, since eleven of the sixteen school inspectors of the 1840s were Anglican clergymen. John Allen, the doyen of school inspectors, attended Cambridge, where he read Plato, Paley, and Coleridge and recorded in his diary, "Virgilium Vide! This day I saw William Wordsworth." After Cambridge he became tutor at King's College, London, where he formed friendships with F. D. Maurice and Thomas Carlyle. He thought Stanley's *Life of Thomas Arnold* the best book of the century, and he knew and admired John Keble. As an inspector he worked tirelessly to expand that moral partnership of state, church, and parish that lay at the heart of the idea of a paternal government. "The let alone doctrines of the political economist are wrong," Allen wrote, "when applied to material doctors (including hospitals) and spiritual doctors (school teachers, clergy) etc."[41] In 1848 the youngest and newest of the inspectors was Longueville Jones, also of Cambridge. His two articles in *Blackwood's* express paternalist attitudes at their purest. As an inspector he worked for the same partnership of church and locality as did Allen and all the other Anglican school inspectors. They would all have agreed with J. P. Norris, who had studied at Rugby under Thomas Arnold, that "we may be deeply thankful that . . . the parental view has ever taken a stronger hold . . . than the civil or political. The *home* is to our nation what the cell is to the plant—the essential element of organization."[42]

The education inspectors were not alone in working to cement a moral partnership between the parson, the squire, and the central government. The assistant poor-law commissioners sought the same alliance. For most of them, being squires or younger sons of the nobility, it came naturally.

When W. H. T. Hawley met with the duke of Richmond it was the meeting of two landowners, and when Edward Twisleton, Colonel Ashe A' Court, and Charles Clements met with a member of the peerage, they felt no strain as they themselves were the sons of peers. Five other poor-law assistants were baronets, and four others are in Burke's *Landed Gentry.*[43] The vestry, the parish overseer, and the local magistrate had managed the old law while the assistant poor-law commissioners, union guardians, magistrates, and union relieving officers administered the new law. Both administrations, Richard Oastler and John Walter II notwithstanding, were but two forms of paternalism. The much abused workhouse, like the dismal and easily forgotten poorhouse of the old law, formed a perfect instrument of paternalism. It combined that mixture of severe discipline and kindly benevolence that was desired in those local spheres where squire and parson thought they could distinguish between the unworthy and worthy poor.

Just as the education inspectors reflected the moral partnership of government and church and the assistant poor-law commissioners the partnership of central and local government and property, so the factory and mining inspectors reflected the moral partnership of government and the captains of industry. Leonard Horner, the doyen of factory inspectors, was enthusiastic about the paternalism of property. He preached it in his reports.[44] So did Robert Saunders, the Tory factory inspector who worked with Dean Hook of Leeds in outlining the Factory Education Bill of 1843, and James Stuart who outdid the other inspectors in detailed accounts of model manufacturers.[45] The mining inspector, Seymour Tremenheere, followed suit. "I have spoken plainly," he reported in 1844, "of the neglect and error of the masters." Equally plain was his hectoring of them to give up the truck system, to cease paying wages in pubs, to end overcrowding in housing, to pay fair wages, to provide good schooling, and to have a "conscientious regard . . . for the comfort and well being of the people."[46]

The prison inspectors and the lunacy commissioners stood to the prisoners and patients they inspected literally *in loco parentis.* Frederic Hill, the liveliest of the prison inspectors, worked hard to create "prisons that have more of a domestic character . . . so important is this family character and so valuable is the tie it creates between the officers and the prisoners." Hill was convinced that such institutions, with fewer bars and punishments and more schooling and friendly intercourse, should be established for juveniles. The Youthful Offenders Act of 1854 resulted from the interplay of bureaucratic forces and the politics of paternalism, and it led to a stronger paternal government. The same *in loco parentis* attitude marked the reports of the lunacy commissioners and led to further reform.[47]

In many of these reports there is a painful discrepancy between ideal and fact. The clergy had not the resources to build and staff schools, few poor-law guardians united to form district schools and district asylums, mill and mine owners did not heed the admonitions of Leonard Horner and Seymour Tremenheere, visiting justices did not build Frederic Hill's "prisons of a more domestic character," and the duke of Richmond and the Sussex patriarchs wanted no expensive county lunatic asylum. There is no doubt Allen, Norris, Horner, Saunders, Tremenheere, and Hill held paternalist ideals and that these ideals informed their reports, but there is also no doubt that these ideals were not being carried out with vigor. The answer to this dilemma was to urge a larger and more efficient central government, one that could play a greater role in the moral partnership. For these utilitarian-minded inspectors a larger and more efficient government would require a centralized, uniform, and rationalized bureaucracy, one that would destroy that moral partnership of Parliament, property, church, and locality which long ago Burke and Coleridge saw as the essence of paternalism. The idea of a paternal government as essentially pluralistic was in conflict with that principle of centralization which was needed to make government truly paternal.

The idea of a paternal government was indeed elusive. As used in parliamentary debates, newspaper editorials, and government reports it could mean different things to different people: a strengthened monarchy for Disraeli and the *Morning Post*, a larger central administration for William Cowper and the *Spectator*, the delegation of more power to local government for Sir Robert Peel and the *Times*, an insistence on the Corn Law for the country squires and the *Standard*, and grants of money and power to the Church of England for the bishops and the *Morning Herald*. Its very diversity made it a popular phrase to employ, particularly since it had behind it a long and respected history and enjoyed a fashionable place in conservative political theory. Many M.P.s would have read in Aristotle how government first arose from the father's role in the family, and many would also have read of the flowering of paternal government in Tudor and Stuart England and of its near universality as a bulwark against revolution in Europe. *Blackwood's* was effusive about and the *Quarterly* admiring of the paternal rule of the emperor of Austria and the czar of Russia. High Churchmen celebrated the paternal kingship of Charles I, while readers of Edmund Burke learned that the paternal government of an *ancien régime* was preferable to the anarchy of a revolutionary one. Rooted in Aristotle, Burke, and English and European history, the idea of a strong paternal government carried great weight in the politics of paternalism.

It was often weightier in rhetoric than in reality; it informed far more speeches than it did acts of Parliament. England was not Europe. The early Victorians wanted no Tudor monarchy, much less a Stuart one. Burke and High Churchmen notwithstanding, country squires wanted no resurgent kingship, captains of industry no conciliar proclamations, and dissent no Stuart church. Many an M.P. and editor, by pleading for a paternal government used a phrase rich in connotations of a firm, protective, personal rule which they did not literally mean. Invoke Austria and Russia as they might, they never meant that English landlords should defer to the servants of the crown, particularly if they were central bureaucrats. For landlords and captains of industry deference was largely for their dependents, not for themselves, and the highest authority in their paternal system was generally not a czar, emperor, or queen, but themselves. Yet at Queen Victoria's court or before Her Majesty's courts of law they could be deferential—and once poor-law commissioners and health inspectors were part of the status quo they would grudgingly defer to the commissioners' and inspectors' orders. Their view of paternal government was never fixed. Just as ambivalence and ambiguity characterized the concept of the paternal state in the writings of Burke and Coleridge and others who sought to construct a theory of paternalism, so did ambivalence and ambiguity characterize the idea of a paternal government as used by M.P.s, journalists, and bureaucrats. One of the clearest statements that can be made about the early Victorians' use of the term paternal government is that it varied according to who used it and in what context and that the user himself was not always sure of its exact meaning.

But not all is ambivalence and ambiguity. Many a Tory squire who used the term in ways quite different from a Whig grandee did use it in ways understandable to his fellow squires, just as did followers of Young England or Peelite ministers. There were distinct varieties of paternalists, and by understanding more fully what characteristics defined those varieties perhaps one can remove some of the ambivalence and ambiguity that obscure that paternalist outlook which was the most popular of social outlooks in the Parliament of the 1840s.

Chapter IX

Varieties of Paternalism

Since paternalism was a cluster of attitudes and ideas that revolved around differing attachments to private property, the Church of England, and various institutions of government, it was bound to produce different varieties among its supporters. Furthermore, since various strands of that outlook could be woven into other social philosophies, the varieties of paternalism in the 1840s became quite bewildering. Even within the House of Commons its diversity was considerable. Many varieties seemed sui generis, like the antique mercantilism of Lord George Bentinck or the parish idolatry of John Walter. These men were eccentric and their views idiosyncratic. For most of his life Lord George thought only of horses and racing. Then Peel's treachery on the Corn Law led him to plunge into the science of economics and to give orations, abounding in statistics, in defense of the Corn Law, Irish railway schemes, and the Navigation Act. John Walter devoted England's greatest newspaper to endless petty and misinformed denunciations of workhouse scandals. But as eccentric as was the paternalism of a Bentinck and a Walter, most M.P.s did fall into certain categories whose prominent characteristics distinguished their paternalism from that of other varieties.

There were in fact five major varieties of paternalist M.P.s: the romantics who looked back to medieval ideals, Peelites out of Oxford who trusted the benevolence of property and the dictums of political economy, churchmen possessed of the ecclesiastical ideal of an active clerisy, country squires wedded to locality and hierarchy, and Whigs with huge estates and an attitude of noblesse oblige. Within each of these varieties in the House of Commons there were those who expressed paternalist sentiments whether in speeches, publications, or model landlordism. The romantics who spoke in debates, published paternalist disquisitions, or practiced its ideals on their estates, numbered only eleven, while fifteen Peelites, thirteen churchmen, twenty-four squires, and seventeen Whigs expressed themselves in one of these three ways. These eighty M.P.s are thus used as prime specimens in the following morphology of the paternalist species. In their variety these M.P.s reveal many of the infinite forms paternalism could take. Among them surely the most colorful, exalted, and bizarre were the romantics.

The Romantics

The romantics were above all young. Seven of them went to Cambridge in the late 1820s and early 1830s. They all came under the sway of Disraeli and were associated with Young England. Alexander Baillie Cochrane, George Sydney Smythe, and Lord John Manners formed, with Disraeli, the hard core of the group, with Augustus Stafford O'Brien, Peter Borthwick, Monckton Milnes, and Henry Hope on its edges. Further out, but ardent admirers of Disraeli, were Quintin Dick and Henry Baillie and the utterly independent David Urquhart. Urquhart's high praise of the feudal ways of medieval England won him the praise of Young England and a place among the romantics.[1] Monckton Milnes shared the same romantic ideals but was excluded from the inner circle because of Smythe's personal hostility to him. Henry Hope was a strong ally. A staunch protectionist and a loyal Disraelian, he was at Cambridge a close friend of Baillie Cochrane and Stafford O'Brien. He worked with Lord John Manners in the founding of the Camden Society for the revival of Gothic architecture. His medievalism included the Tractarian belief that a more catholic Church of England should organize society. He no doubt had also read Kenelm Digby. Digby's influence was pervasive in the Cambridge of the 1830s, and his works, along with Robert Southey's *Colloquies*, exerted a decisive influence on Young England. Smythe called Southey their "founder," while the biographer of Lord John Manners calls Digby's work their "handbook." Coleridge and Wordsworth, of course, also had their impact on early Victorian Cambridge. Wordsworth challenged Byron's ascendancy while Coleridge inspired "The Apostles," a very serious society of earnest Christians founded in the 1820s and including in its membership Julius Hare, F. D. Maurice, John Sterling, Alfred Tennyson, and Monckton Milnes. Milnes admitted that Coleridge's *Church and State* "gave me the only clear idea I ever had of the English constitution."[2]

Milnes, Cochrane, Manners, Smythe, Hope all moved from Cambridge into the London literary world and into the House of Commons. The sons respectively of two wealthy gentry, an admiral, a duke, and a viscount, they employed their inherited privileges of private leisure and public office for the publication of poems and novels and the delivery of parliamentary orations. All were inspired by a romantic worship of the past, a medieval and catholic view of the church, and an aristocratic belief in a hierarchical society. Cochrane's novel *Lucille Belmont* and Smythe's *Angela Pisani* are not unlike Disraeli's earliest romances. They too include paternalist industrialists and landlords, ardent pleas for kindness to the poor, injunctions to give alms, denunciations of utilitarianism, and visions of monasteries and convents. Smythe's literary reputation in that decade came from the publication in 1844 of *Historic Fancies*, a collection of poems and essays that extolled Charles I as the martyred king, James II as the simplest of men and victim of policies not his own, and the French aristocracy, whose nobility was undermined by Louis XIV's centralization of power. It romanticized the martyrdom of aristocratic ladies during the terror in the fashion of Burke's treatment of Marie Antoinette. It called Scott Britain's greatest novelist and regretted the ending of the touching for evil because the practice had involved "the direct communication of the highest and lowest."[3]

The same chivalry and romanticism color the poetry of Lord John Manners and Monckton Milnes. Milnes, in his poem "Alms-Giving," calls for the poor to be patient in their allotted place and chastises the rich for their indifference, a theme he repeated in 1844 in the sterner form of an address to his Pontefract electors. In that speech he defended the Corn Law and urged landowners to regard laborers as fellow Christians and brothers and "to give them employment . . . [and] in sickness and calamity every aid and consolation." Lord John Manners's poetry was even more aristocratic and medieval in sentiment than Milnes's. In "England's Trust" he wrote those lines his critics never allowed him to forget:

> Let wealth and commerce, laws and learning die,
> But leave us still our old Nobility.

Lord John Manners, who called Southey that "great good man" and who was the most idealistic member of Young England, did not really want commerce and learning to die, but only that the nobility be exalted. He also wished to awaken it to "days of feudalism [when] barons . . . were accustomed to sit at the same table . . . with those beneath them." Manners valued the church as highly as the baronage since it alone could "knit together in the sanctifying bonds of Christian joy . . . the high and low, the rich and poor" and wished to revive that monarchy, which would, like the Stuarts, provide a paternal government. The young Cambridge romantics loved the old, the aristocratic, and the spiritual and detested the new, the democratic, and the materialistic. They worshipped Wordsworth and despised Bentham. Augustus Stafford O'Brien so worshipped Wordsworth that he invited the great poet to Lowther Castle to attend a charade in his honor. In that charade O'Brien carried a sword with which he destroyed an altar fitted out with the cherished idols of the nineteenth century: mammon, steam, useful knowledge, and a church turned upside down. All these false idols fell before O'Brien's brave sword.[4] At their collapse the audience turned triumphantly to the great poet himself and applauded. O'Brien had an account of the charade published. There was a dreamlike medieval idealism in the young literati, one that Disraeli himself fostered and indulged in, but one that Milnes later regretted. "When I was young," he said, "I could idealize everything, even Toryism."[5]

Also from Cambridge and also a friend of Young England was Peter Borthwick, later editor of the *Morning Post*. His two histories have already been recounted (in chapter eight). He was, says Reginald Lucas, the biographer of Borthwick's son Lord Glenesk, "in alliance with Young England." Lord John Manners also spoke of Borthwick as "in our little Cabinet." Borthwick joined Young England's onslaught on the New Poor Law. He not only castigated that law but even denounced Henry VIII's confiscation of monasteries that once cared for the poor. He was convinced that the church could relieve the poor much better than a centralized state. Like Manners and Cochrane he looked back at its medieval role with fondness.[6]

One of the most prominent features of the romantic paternalists was their enthusiasm for the past. It was a feature that linked even the irascible Russophobe, David Urquhart, with Young England. "It is to the past we have to look," he writes in his *Wealth and Want* of 1845, "and not the future." Chief of the Urquhart clan, he was the descendant of an ancient family that had been heritable sheriffs of Cromarty since the reign of Edward I. It was a family always loyal to the house of Stuart. With such ancestry it is not surprising that this outspoken Scotsman gave in *Wealth and Want* a spirited defense of villeinage and that he saw in both allotments and ten-hour acts a return to an ancient protectionism. He was too independent and idiosyncratic to work politically with Young England, but his views won their applause. In their *Oxford and Cambridge Review* they praised highly his defense of feudalism and his call for a return to the old ways of the past, and they concluded that his views were very similar to those of Disraeli in *Sybil*.[7]

Peelites and Ecclesiastics

Those Peelites in the House of Commons who expressed paternalist ideas in their speeches and writings were much less given to dreaming of old ways. They were indeed most serious about the present. Monckton Milnes was quick to note that seriousness. In 1838 he wrote, "I go on with the small 'Young Englands' on Sunday evenings, which unfortunately excludes the more severe members—Acland, Gladstone, etc." Gladstone was a luminary who attracted more than Milnes. Smythe and Lord John Manners had such a high esteem of Gladstone's *The State in Its Relations with the Church* that they called themselves "Gladstonites."[8] William Gladstone and Thomas Acland, the "more severe members," were both followers of Sir Robert Peel and men of paternalist convictions, two facts also true of four other young M.P.s who attended Oxford in the late 1820s and early 1830s, Lord Lincoln, Sidney Herbert, Edward Cardwell, and Roundell Palmer. Both Acland and Palmer have left accounts of the Oxford of those stirring times. F. D. Maurice had just arrived from Cambridge and was to form the "Essay Society" on the model of the Cambridge Apostles. By 1829 its members included Gladstone, Egerton, Lincoln, and Acland. The spirited debates of Oxford's Political Union also sharpened the wits of these four men and of their friends Sidney Herbert and Edward Cardwell. For many of these future statesmen Coleridge was the great philosopher. Thomas Acland confessed to reading Coleridge constantly and becoming, as a result, a stronger Tory and a higher churchman. Coleridge, he later recalled, "was the breath of life to [Oxford's] young men." Roundell Palmer agreed. Oxford education, he said, was a mix of Aristotle's *Ethics,* Butler's *Analogies* and *Sermons,* and Coleridge's *Aid to Reflection.* Wordsworth was also widely read. His *Excursion* moved deeply both Acland and Palmer. To read Burke, of course, was still a duty and a pleasure for young Oxonians.

These young men knew each other well and were steeped in Burke, Coleridge, and Wordsworth. It was an Oxford of a seriousness and piety that was about to produce John Henry Newman and the Tractarian movement and to inspire Gladstone to write his *The State in Its Relations with the Church* of 1838 and *Church Principles* of 1840. Both works contain eloquent pleas for those paternalist ideas espoused by Chalmers, Arnold, and Coleridge. Gladstone wanted, above all things, a strong church to remedy and palliate social ills. He wanted a "national clerisy" to supply in every parish "a resident guide and teacher." It was by the church and by the benevolent concern of individuals more than by the compulsory actions of the state that society achieved whatever was beneficial and humanizing. Yet the state had also a role. The government, said Gladstone, stands "in a paternal relation to the people," and its "general duty is to advance the well being of the people by all means, which . . . [it] may not be intrinsically incompetent to employ." The state should work "in close relation of cooperation with the Church of Christ." It was a vision that no doubt impressed a third variety of paternalist M.P. in the Commons, the ecclesiastics.[9]

Of the thirteen M.P.s who spoke most consistently for an enlarged and extended Church of England, six attended Oxford, four Cambridge, and two no university at all; there is no information about the education of the thirteenth. The two without a university education were not, however, disadvantaged. The Birmingham banker, Richard Spooner, went to Rugby and Lord William Cowper to Eton where he began a lifelong friendship with William Gladstone. Lifelong friendships among these young idealists were of great importance. Lord Littleton, to whom Gladstone dedicated *The State in Its Relations with the Church,* attended Cambridge University, where he had developed a friendship with the romantic Lord John Manners. Littleton was a churchman whose paternalism was of the ecclesiastical variety. Charles Adderley who also belonged to that persuasion cemented his friendship with the Peelites Acland and Gladstone by a lifelong membership with them in the exclusive Grillion's Club. Clubs like Grillion's were as important for these serious men as Travellors' and Whites were for the country squires. Grillion's had only forty-five members, but ten of them were Peelite, ecclesiastical, or Whig paternalists. Whigs like Lords Morpeth and Russell joined Peelites like Lords Sandon, Mahon, and Wortley and ecclesiasticals like Inglis and Littleton.[10] These friendships were influential, and often strange and unpredictable.

The strangest of them all was that between the radical William Page Wood and the Tory Walter Farquhar Hook. Their friendship began at Winchester and, as can be seen in W. R. W. Stephens's *Life of Hook*, resulted in a lifelong correspondence, one of the main themes of which was the strengthening of the Church of England. Wood confessed in one of those letters that "our sentiments on most Church matters coincided." Wood supported all of Hook's work in Leeds as well as working himself, from 1834, on the Committee of the Church of England's National Society. He also taught Sunday school in St. John's Parish, Westminster, and founded Anglican schools on his Gloucester estates— where he was also a model squire. "The Church alone," he wrote, "has the means of bringing home religious instruction to the people," a sentiment in keeping with his opening remark to Parliament that he "would never fail to avow his deep attachment to the Church of England."

Wood was a radical and Lord Cowper a Whig. Ecclesiastics came from all parties. Their leading figure was, as were a majority of them, Tory. He was Sir Robert Harry Inglis, indefatigable mover of motions for parliamentary grants for Church extension and an old and trusted friend of Robert Southey. But the Whigs Lord Cowper and Lord Robert Grosvenor were no less ardent advocates of Church extension. Cowper, like Wood, also worked for the National Society in its efforts to build and endow parish schools. As an M.P. he stood for an idea of a church "in which sympathy would permeate all classes." Cowper, the aristocratic Whig and Wood the London merchant who supported the ballot, agreed on the need of a stronger Church as they did in their admiration of their mutual friend Coleridge. Cowper had made a pilgrimage to the Lake District to see Coleridge, Wordsworth, and Scott. One of his favorite pastimes was to walk on the moors "with a pocketful of Coleridge." The radical Wood also gained pleasure from Coleridge. He attended frequently the poet's famous conversations at Highgate.[11]

Coleridge also influenced John Colquhoun, the most ultra-Protestant of the thirteen ecclesiastics. Colquhoun wrote a biography of Coleridge, as he also did of Wordsworth, both abounding in compliments. Colquhoun, once a Whig, became in the late 1830s a Tory. But above all he was a churchman. "He was aware," wrote Disraeli in 1848, "only of the diffusion of the Gospel." Disraeli meant it as a criticism, but it would not have bothered Colquhoun nor M.P.s like Edward Buxton, Lord Robert Grosvenor, and J. P. Plumptre, all evangelicals for whom the spread of the gospel was Christ's most sovereign command. For Plumptre in particular that command was such an all-consuming end that, according to James Grant of the *Morning Advertiser*, "He hardly ever speaks except on religious matters."[12]

A belief in an expanded, more active Church of England was the distinguishing feature of the ecclesiastical paternalists. It quite possessed Charles Adderley, the wealthy land and colliery owner of Warwickshire and Staffordshire. He gave numerous sites and £70,000 to build churches in Warwickshire. Many were part of the model town of Saltley, a town he planned and had built, with streets laid out to prevent slums and schools built to prevent crime. He also wished the gospel preached in New Zealand. Under the powerful influence of John Robert Godley, whom Gladstone called "a king of men," Adderley, Lord Littleton, and Gladstone worked diligently to establish in New Zealand the colony of Canterbury, a colony founded on Church of England and paternalist principles. Littleton and Adderley also worked intimately in Warwickshire and Staffordshire to found schools, establish friendly societies, build parks, and develop reformatories that were schools, not prisons. Adderley called the students of his Saltley Reformatory "my children" and claimed "I work upon their moral faculties through their affection." Adderley, like Littleton and his brother-in-law Forster Mc Geachey, was both intensely religious and decidedly paternalist. Adderley wrote in his *Autobiography* that the greatest of mistakes in life is "the distinguishing between the common objects of earth and matters of religion." He also felt "the principle of submission to authority is always the right side to err upon." It led him to agree with his brother-in-law Mc Geachey's plea to Parliament that "it is the duty of the State to provide spiritual instruction for its subjects through the means of the established Church."[13]

The classification of paternalists as romantics, Peelites, and ecclesiastics has its arbitrary aspects. It places complex people into categories on the basis of a single prominent characteristic. An example of this difficulty is the placing of Lord Ashley among the ecclesiastics when in fact he was Parliament's most complete paternalist, one not only consistently for Church extension, but active in carrying out the duties of property on his own estates and diligent in his work at the Board of Health and on the Lunacy Commission. Called by some a friend of Young England, and yet a Peelite on the issue of the repeal of the Corn Law, he never indulged in the dreamy medievalisms of the former or the severe political economy of the latter. His first and greatest love was always, as it was with his friend Inglis, the Church of England. Classifications usually rest not on a single, but on a most prominent characteristic.[14] With Ashley and twelve other M.P.s that characteristic was their zeal for a more active and stronger Church of England.

The Peelites' most prominent characteristic was their high regard for property, both its rights and its duties. The young Gladstone, whose vision of a clerisy inspired Milnes, Manners, and Smythe in 1838, was at that time a rather pronounced ecclesiastical paternalist. By the mid-1840s public office under Peel had made him a Peelite. By this move he joined not only his Oxford friends Lincoln, Herbert, Cardwell, and Acland, but an older generation of Oxford men, Lords Sandon, Egerton, Mahon, and Wortley. All four were born near the turn of the century, all but Egerton were the sons of peers, and all attended Christ Church, Oxford. Egerton and Sandon became good friends there in 1809. Wortley and Mahon arrived in 1822. Wortley later became Sandon's brother-in-law. All were very wealthy. In 1833 Egerton inherited an annual income of £90,000. All but Wortley won literary renown. Sandon, elected to the Royal Society in 1853, was an accomplished French and Italian scholar. Egerton and Mahon were prolific contributors to the *Quarterly Review*. Mahon also won considerable fame as a historian. They all sat in the unreformed House of Commons, opposed the Reform Act of 1832, and in the 1820s and 1830s won government appointments, Mahon as undersecretary for foreign affairs, Wortley as secretary to the Board of Control, Sandon as a commissioner to inquire into army punishments, and Egerton as William Huskisson's undersecretary.[15] They all enjoyed and exploited the privileges of wealth, title, rank, and good breeding, excellent education, and access to power. They were all paternalists in their social outlook.

Lord Francis Egerton's credentials as a paternalist were as authentic as any model landlord or captain of industry. As an owner in Lancashire of collieries, manufactures, and broad acres, he had the opportunity to play both roles. In his parishes he applied some of his £90,000 to the building of churches, schools, cottages, and libraries. He established "sick, benefit, and superannuation societies," clothing clubs, savings banks, and dispensaries that gave medical care to all. Viscount Sandon was a reforming landlord and promoter of agricultural societies. His father expended much effort and many years to improve the lot of the underpaid clergy. Sandon merged this inherited concern for the underpaid clergy with a general zeal for the Church of England and a humanitarian concern for all suffering. He worked closely with Lord Shaftesbury and was active in the Society for the Prevention of Cruelty to Animals. He also believed property had its duties and told Parliament that in Ireland "the landlords are the only agents through whom the country could be regenerated."[16]

Wortley, whose father, Baron Wharncliffe, possessed collieries and land near Sheffield and ran the quarter sessions of the West Riding with admirable skill and fairness, wrote pamphlets urging the establishment of tribunals of commerce and the granting of government aid to agriculture. More interesting are his private letters to Graham and Peel urging the ten-hour amendment and a more generous administration of the New Poor Law. They are the letters of a compassionate man.

Lord Mahon did not inherit Chevening in Kent and his father's estates in Ireland and Derbyshire until 1855. When he did he visited them all, reassessed rents, and told the tenants he believed in the old adage, "live and let live." He held a great fete at Chevening when his eldest son came of age and assumed, as no previous earl of Stanhope had, a warm and friendly intercourse with his Kentish dependents. In Parliament he pleaded for grants for the education of the poor, since the "higher duty of wealth was that of imparting to others in a lower sphere some portion of the lights which Providence has vouchsafed to the higher."[17]

These four lords were not merely paternalists, but Peelite paternalists. They differed from Disraeli, Cochrane, Smythe, and Manners in the ease, solidity, practicality, depth, and condescension of their outlook. They were fighting no ideological battles. They felt no need to romanticize an outlook that came so naturally to them from their great houses, wealth, secure rank, and access to power.

They were also men of business and public administration, men in their forties. They looked more to Burke and Adam Smith than to Coleridge and Southey, whose *Church and State* and *Colloquies* came out after their social ideas were set. Lord Mahon, who wrote the *History of England from 1713 to 1783* in seven volumes and many historical essays for the *Quarterly*, considered Burke the savior of Europe and Adam Smith comparable to Isaac Newton. Egerton too cites Adam Smith as an authority. Mahon also said Bentham wrote gibberish and the French aristocracy in no way caused the French Revolution. Mahon was every inch a Tory and aristocrat, and yet he greeted Adam Smith as an Isaac Newton. That reception was not an isolated one in the early nineteenth century. Both Egerton and Wortley worked with William Huskisson, the liberal Tory who not only carried out Adam Smith's free-trade ideas but taught them to a generation of future Peelites.[18]

Adam Smith's empirical and practical discussion of economics fitted in with the practical outlook of these elder sons of peers who served in public office when young and later managed large estates. It was also an economic study that the Peelite gentry in the House of Commons liked. Two of those gentry were Montagu Gore and Sir Walter James. Gore was a model agriculturalist in Somersetshire who published a series of pamphlets in favor of allotments, improved dwellings, laborers' friend societies, and free grants of manure. He was a strong paternalist and made many allusions to Burke, Southey, Wordsworth, Alison, and Carlyle. He follows Burke in warning that nothing is so hurtful as the interference of the state and follows St. Paul in warning that "if any would not work, neither shall he eat." But having expressed his regard for self-reliance and the rights of property, he turns to its duties and insists that since the poor cannot build cottages, the landlord must. Sir Walter James, a Peelite M.P. like Gore, in his *Thoughts upon the Theory and Practice of the Poor Laws* follows Gore in accepting Burke's high regard for political economy. "Far be it from me to sneer," he said, "at political economy." He wrote the year before in the *Spectator* a letter entitled "Justice for the Poor." It was a plea for property to be more generous in granting poor relief and for guardians not to bow "to a despotic and hard centralisation." He wanted the guardians to practice moral discrimination in granting outdoor relief, which would go only to the good and deferential poor.[19]

James dedicated the pamphlet to Sir Robert Peel. Some would doubt if such a dedication was appropriate. Was Peel, so lukewarm in supporting parliamentary grants to the Church of England, so zealous for the New Poor Law, and so dogmatically opposed to the ten-hour day, a paternalist at all? Inglis, Oastler, and Ashley doubted it, as did Disraeli, Manners, and Cochrane. If the paternalism of the church and of the state were the only criterion, the critics would be correct. But there was still the paternalism of property, and for such a paternalism Peel was an enthusiast. In 1841 when he was telling the Commons that legislation would do very little for education since it depended on "the exertions of resident clergymen and resident proprietors . . . on those whose moral duty it is to contribute money and time to education of the people," he was writing long letters to the mayor of Tamworth urging the local elite to build new schools. Similarly, when in 1842 he told the Commons that legislation could do little for distress, he sent more letters to the mayor urging the setting up of soup kitchens, the creation of allotments, and the planning of "harmless festivities" for the poor. He sent far longer letters to the mayor of Tamworth on education and distress than he did letters to the home secretary and the president of the Privy Council asking for legislation on such matters. This preference for the local and voluntary exertion of property fitted in with Peel's very Coleridgean belief that the best hope of reforms lies, as he told the Commons, "in social and moral change, rather than a legislative one."

Peel, the squire of Drayton Manor, looked to the paternalism of property for the remedy of social ills far more than did Peel the prime minister look for it in factory acts and education grants. "It is on local exertion," he told the House in discussing education, "that the great reliance must be placed."[20] As the leader of young idealists like Gladstone, Herbert, Lincoln, and Acland, he fashioned a Peelite paternalism, a paternalism characterized by the local and voluntary efforts of property, and by a church working with that property at the local level. The central government might help, but it would be a central government distinguished by efficiency, retrenchment, limited powers, and a laissez faire approach to the economy. It was a paternalism with property writ large and government writ small.

The Oxford to which eleven of the Peelites and six of the ecclesiastics went was an institution of more than one tradition. Some of its teachers followed Burke and blended political economy with a more generous paternalism. Other traditions were not so kind to political economy. The Tractarians disliked its cold selfishness as did those at Oxford impressed with Southey's writings. Two of the latter were Oxford University's M. P. Sir Robert Inglis and the humanitarian Lord Ashley, once of Christ Church. G. F. A. Best in his biography of Ashley speaks of him as "undoubtedly much under Southey's influence." Best then adds the very shrewd comment, "but he could have learnt to look at affairs this way without Southey's tutelage. Plenty of conservative writers besides Southey were . . . making similar analyses."[21] The writings of Peelites, romantics, and ecclesiastical paternalists fully support Best's assertion. They are filled with references to Bacon, Hooker, Butler, Burke, Chalmers, Paley, Alison, Carlyle, Sewell, Digby, and above all Coleridge. But still fifteen of the thirty-nine romantic, ecclesiastical, and Peelite paternalists who sat in the Commons did avow their admiration for Coleridge or Southey. This fact does not mean that these two thinkers defined their social outlook. Much of an Acland's or a Milnes's admiration for Coleridge was for his defense of religion and idealism against skepticism and materialism rather than for his plea for landowners and clergymen to fulfill their duties. Furthermore, the lives of an Acland or a Milnes are far too complex, and far too little is known about them to speak of Coleridge's influence. What can be said is that these M.P.s did admire the ideas of Coleridge and Southey and thus do in some ways represent that outlook. In analyzing their votes and speeches in the Commons one can observe how ideas similar to those of Coleridge worked themselves out in the politics of the 1840s.

The romantic, ecclesiastical, and Peelite paternalists were intellectuals in politics, men of ideas and doctrines, of ideas and doctrines that they had argued over in Cambridge and Oxford common rooms and were still developing in their writings. The same could not be said of most of those paternalists returned by the counties, the country squires.

The Country Squires

Certain letters in the Disraeli papers from the 1840s suggest that the squires from the counties were a quite different variety of paternalist from the Young England devotees of Kenelm Digby. The first of these letters was written by Lord John Manners to Disraeli on October 24, 1844. He told Disraeli, "I take it some of the gentry are not best pleased with our movement." They were not. Neither was Manners later always pleased with the gentry. Though one with them on the Corn Law, he still could not hide his sorrow that Disraeli's support was of the "New-degate and Miles calibre." Newdegate, M.P. for North Warwickshire, he found "a most excellent, mulish, prig of a bigot." Manners liked some of the others a bit better, though still in a condescending way. He found that though Bankes, Jolliffe, Tyrrell, and Henley were part of the ultragentlemen on religion, "they were nevertheless the flowers of the bucolic flock." Another friend of Young England, Henry Baillie, wrote

Disraeli that Bankes of Dorset was the ablest of them except for Sir John Pakington, but then added that Pakington's "abilities were not too great."[22] These letters indicate the intellectual gulf that divided the romantics from the country squires—yet both were paternalists. The squires may not have read Digby, but they didn't need to, since the duties of property and the role of the church were as instinctive a part of rural life for them as they were for the duke of Richmond or the bishop of Chichester.

There were 241 Conservatives who voted against the repeal of the Corn Laws on May 15, 1846. Of these 129 represented counties, not boroughs, and fifty-four represented smaller boroughs. In the following analysis twenty-four of these Conservatives are used as a sample of the paternalism of the country squire, twenty of them in fact representing counties. They were chosen for the sample because they enunciated paternalist ideas in the House of Commons, published such views in pamphlets, or won notice for carrying them out on their estates. These are criteria excluding the silent and including the vocal. The country squires, though weak on publications, were not on talk. They were blunt, outspoken, crusty, and often eccentric. Warwickshire's Newdegate was the wildest of horsemen, Lincoln's Colonel Sibthorp the foe of innovation, whether water closets or railways, while *St. James's Magazine* described Oxfordshire's Joseph Henley as "the Squire of the House of Commons," and a "rough, angular fellow, quaint, dogmatic, self-opinionated." It added that he had "genuine kindliness of heart," and though a "terror to poachers" was ever "the friend of honest labourers" and a "dispenser of rough acts of kindness." He was always the gentleman just as was Sir Richard Vyvyan, M.P. from Helston. To Stanley Lees Giffard, the editor of the *Standard*, Vyvyan was "that noblest model of the high spirited all accomplished English gentleman."[23]

It was the pride of the squires to do acts of kindness. Lincolnshire's Sir John Trollope was, said Mr. Peacock in nominating him at the hustings in 1847, "ever strenuous . . . to ameliorate the condition of the labouring man"; Dorsetshire's George Bankes, "the flower of the bucolic flock," not only would rent no lands unless the farmer promised to pay fair wages but urged all landowners in 1846 to buy and store grain in order to sell it at a just price when the price had later soared upward. Wiltshire's T. H. S. Sotheron at the hustings in 1847 asked that "books, candles and fire" be placed every evening in the parish schoolhouse so "innocent recreation would keep the poor from debauchery"; and Cheshire's John Tollemache built three-bedroom cottages and schools and granted an allotment and a cow to his laborers. Dorsetshire's John Floyer served "the poor, the ignorant, and the insane," by constant activity at the Labourer's Friend Society, the Diocesan Synod, the board of guardians, and the local "lunatic asylum, hospital, school and friendly society." He was, said his biographer, "a country gentleman of the old school" and "first and last a Dorset man." R. A. Christopher was also of the old school and first and last a Lincolnshire man, one convinced that "the only way to promote the welfare of the community" was for the "landowners, land occupiers and labourers to unite" under that "confidence that was reciprocal between friend and friend."[24]

It was their affection for their county that is the key to understanding the country squires. The strongest passion underlying their paternalism was localism, a localism not unrelated to the love of history and of nature. George Bankes wrote local history, and Floyer celebrated with Wordsworth the beauty of nature. Bankes's *Corfe Castle* is the history of his ancestor's landed estate and is full of love of its beauties. He loved Corfe Castle with all the passion with which his friend Floyer loved his little villages of Stafford and Knighton. "In his little villages," says the author of Floyer's obituary, "his heart was always to be found." It is no wonder that the obituary also added, "Wordsworth was his favourite poet."[25]

The bucolic sort were by no means illiterates. Eighteen went to universities, thirteen to Oxford and five to Cambridge. They were not, however, urban sophisticates. Elected in agricultural areas by rural electors who scarcely felt the pressures of urban problems, they saw no need of elaborate legislation and expensive commissioners. Three of them wrote pamphlets protesting the recommendations of the Constabulary Commission, which in 1839 the Whigs proposed, in a modified form, as a bill and the Tories defeated. Cornwall's Richard Vyvyan, Leicestershire's Henry Halford, and Worcestershire's Sir John Pakington all denounced it as despotic. Halford called paid constables "odious and inquisitorial." To Halford stipendiary magistrates were an insult to the great unpaid, and any central commissioner was a tyrannical invasion of the sacrosanct area of country life. These squires, however, were not against all national measures of protection: all supported the Corn Law and the factory acts. But the Corn Law did not bring meddling commissioners into the rural areas, and the factory commissioners only sent their inspectors to those manufacturing areas where, said Halford, the "reciprocal relations" binding rich and poor had broken down. In the countryside, he added, such an intrusion "would weaken existing reciprocal obligations." Furthermore, it would not be a "paternal power" since "its object will not be to prepare for manhood, but to fix irrevocably in infancy, the sole agent . . . of public happiness."[26]

Pakington and Halford were both magistrates, as indeed were most of the squires. And besides being magistrates many were deputy lieutenants, chairmen of the quarter sessions, chairmen of boards of guardians, majors and colonels of the county militia, visitors to prisons or asylums, and trustees of National Society schools. They and their confreres governed their localities. To have elected stipendiary magistrates, protested Halford, would disturb that hierarchy in which it was expected that magistrates be "of higher station." Since they faced no new and alarming problems and their expectations were modest, the magistrates felt they did a good job. For this reason an intense localism marks their paternalism as it does the paternalism of no other variety. To Lincolnshire's R. A. Christopher, centralization was the "greatest evil," for it warred against that government "in which everyone, however humble, bore his part . . . [and] met in boards of guardians and other situations of public trusts those whom it had pleased Providence to place in a better situation." In the country squire's view the paternalism of property was reinforced by the paternalism of the poor-law guardian and the magistracy.[27]

The paternalism of the poor-law guardian and the magistracy added to the squires' outlook a pronounced authoritarianism. The squires, often rough in kindness, were also sternly for obedience. Henley was described as a terror to poachers. So was George Bankes. In a pamphlet on the game laws in 1825, he defended every clause. He wished to sentence all poachers to service on board a man-of-war since nothing else so terrified them.[28] The squires' experiences as landowners who must protect game fused with their experiences both as magistrates who must sentence drunkards and poachers to prison and as poor-law chairmen who must confront the idle and the vagrant. These experiences made them M.P.s who did not shy away from sternness and severity.

The squires were also good friends of the Church of England. They were not enthusiasts for vast extension of the Church into the metropolis as were the ecclesiastical paternalists, but they were deeply attached to the nearby parish church. Three of them, Bankes, Floyer, and Sibthorp, appointed their brothers to the local parsonage. It made for a harmonious, patriarchal, and Erastian community. The *Dorset Chronicle* saw the Floyer brothers, squire and parson, as "church and state personified." Even where no brothers were squire and parson, there was still loyalty to the church. Henry Willoughby, long M.P. for agricultural Evesham, wrote in 1827 in his *Apology of an English Landowner* that it was "of equal importance to every class of society, that there should exist in England a National Church, independent and well endowed," while Henry Halford proudly told the South Leicestershire electors in 1841 that he was a member of the established Church, an institution that "promoted morality and the peace and happiness of mankind."[29] The country squire in Parliament had a firm sense of the exclusive role of the Church of England as established by law. He was undaunted by the fact that dissent and secularism were so powerful in urban England since dissent and secularism were not that powerful in rural Dorset or Somerset. In the rural villages the squire loved the local parish church, which was usually subordinate to his influence. The rector or vicar was the established, recognized, and obeyed ruler of morals and the protector, with the squire, of the helpless. Loyalty to the parish church only furthered the country squire's instinctive, tenacious, and institutionally rooted localism.

The squires considered themselves as part of the "country party." One of that party, Lord Camden, summed up their program in five points for the *Gloucester Journal* of August 1847 as including (1) the maintenance of the Church of England, (2) the cause of the territorial constituency as the foundation of social happiness, (3) the curtailment of the money power, (4) the improvement of the moral and social condition of the working classes, and (5) restrictions on centralization. Camden then concluded that these "principles . . . may be summed up in one word, protection." The protection Camden had in mind would come from laws and grants that strengthened local authorities, not Whitehall departments and inspectors, since the Church, the territorial constitution, and the working classes needed protection not only from money power but from centralization.

Lord Camden's views pointed toward a mercantilist economic theory, but he did not elaborate on them. Country squires were not often very theoretical. The one exception was Edward Stillingfleet Cayley, country squire, M.P., amateur economist, practical farmer, and cricketer (277 not out at Oxford for a record). "He has written more than any other," said the *Farmer's Magazine* of 1844, "on the causes of agricultural distress." It was Cayley's leading argument that excessive machinery, war debts, and bungling legislation, particularly the 1819 return to the gold standard, had transformed England into an "artificial society." He contrasted this, in a speech in the Commons, to "the patriarchical system" in which "old men work on the land and old retainers and pensioners [enjoy] a cheerful old age." He praised Adam Smith and argued for a laissez faire policy toward agriculture because "landlords know their wealth and welfare are entirely dependent on the thriving condition of the farmers and the labourer." This doctrine of the invisible hand or identity of interests, which many a squire called "live and let live" or "leave well enough alone," broke down with the advent of machinery and of legislation restricting the amount of currency. "Labour saved . . . through machinery," Cayley wrote in 1830, "is a livelihood destroyed." Without wages the lower classes could not consume.

This drop in purchasing power, along with the farmers' reduction in income caused by the restriction in currency that resulted from the return to gold meant an inability to consume those goods that an overgrown manufactures based on an overgrown capital had produced. Cayley's economic outlook was a mixture of a hatred of machinery with a dim prescience of Keynesian economics, and it led him to become the leading advocate of protectionism. It was a complete protectionism, ranging from the corn and navigation laws to government regulation of the wages and conditions of labor for handloom weavers and stocking makers. All foreign countries, he wrote, when faced with unemployment, act as fathers do for their sons in their business firms, they employ them. Corn laws, sugar duties, navigation acts, ten-hour acts, and cheaper money would all increase employment. Cayley, like his fellow Yorkshireman Oastler, hated the New Poor Law. Though he called for protective legislation, he wanted it to be self-acting. Legislation should allow local government to protect hosiery workers, and automatic tariffs should protect the price of corn.[30]

Cayley's hatred of manufactures was one of the central passions informing his economic theories. It was a passion that also lay behind one of the most famous—or infamous— of philippics delivered in the Commons in the 1840s, William Busfield Ferrand's denunciation in 1842 of manufacturers for producing fraudulent goods, overworking women and children, and forcing their workers to buy in company stores shoddy goods at high prices. Ferrand's passions ran in the same vein as Oastler's.

As late as 1850 he wrote Disraeli that he had lined up Oastler to organize the manufacturing workers to agitate for a revival of the corn laws. Ferrand was a squire from Bingley and an M.P. from Knaresborough, both in the West Riding of Yorkshire. He was a great believer in landlords granting allotments and entertaining their dependents with festivities. In 1844 he invited Disraeli, Manners, and Smythe to Bingley to help celebrate the success of his allotment scheme and to play some cricket with the people, which they did.[31] In Ferrand's speeches and Cayley's writings there is bitter anger at the excessive growth of manufactures, the power of money, and the teachings of political economy, a bitter anger not present in the squires from the south and west, the Floyers and Bankes and Henleys. Ferrand's and Cayley's Yorkshire was a manufacturing center, containing both old, declining handicraft manufactures and new, burgeoning textile mills. Cayley, chairman of the Common's Handloom Weavers Select Committee, was much moved by the handloom weavers' plight, a plight that showed only too clearly that "labour saved . . . through machinery is a livelihood destroyed." Neither could the earthy and outspoken squire of Bingley, Colonel Ferrand, hide from himself or others the evils of factory labor and truck shops in his neighborhood. The paternalism of these Yorkshire squires had more stridency and less equanimity than that of their southern colleagues. Yorkshire, with its jobless handloom weavers and overworked factory children, forms quite a different world from Bankes's Corfe Castle or Floyer's "little villages so close to his heart."

The Noblesse Oblige of the Whigs

Far different from Ferrand's turbulent West Riding and Floyer's Dorset villages were the palatial country and town houses of the Whigs. It was a world unto itself, wealthy, confident, assured, and enlightened; also often remote and a little haughty, but one seldom unmindful of its obligations to those below them. The Whigs carried with them a relaxed, easy noblesse oblige.

There were some seventeen Whigs in the House of Commons whose speeches, writings, or estate management, or all three, mark them as paternalists. One of them was Sir Francis Baring of the London banking family, later created Lord Northbrook. He had quit London to become a landed gentleman, a new status that led him to write to his son of those duties that would befit his future station, which was to be "that of an English gentleman." He told his son, who was at Oxford, that because "it is of the nature of our government to interfere as little as posssible . . . men of property and leisure must take the lead in the generality of undertakings." He cited as an authority on these duties, not Coleridge or Southey, but the good Whig historian, Bishop Burnet. Burnet's *History of His Own Times* closes with a review of the "sweet duties" of a country gentleman. Baring could have cited himself as a model in the performance of those "sweet duties." "Up to the very last," said the local parson, the Reverend George Sumner, "he was ministering . . . to the ill and suffering. No cottage tenant, whether farmer or cottager, had a better landlord."[32]

The former London banker, Baring, had adopted in a rather self-conscious manner those ideas inherent in landownership. The great Whig families did so with less self-consciousness. One of the greatest of them was Lord Palmerston. His very inheritance made him a paternalist. He had 10,000 acres in Ireland alone, and they challenged his vigorous nature. In 1808 he took his first tour of this estate and ordered cottages, roads, and piers built, the schools repaired and staffed, middlemen abolished, and a Scots farmer brought over to teach agriculture. "Lord Palmerston," said Lady Palmerston's daughter-in-law, "is the best of landlords. He has spent on the [Irish] estate all he gets from it."[33]

Lord Palmerston sat in the Commons because his title was an Irish one. Many of the other Whig "lords" in the Commons enjoyed that title because they were the sons of dukes and earls. Lord John Russell and Lord Harry Vane were the sons of the dukes of Bedford and Cleveland while Lords Morpeth, Milton, Ebrington, Leveson, and Howick were the sons respectively of the earls Carlisle, Fitzwilliam, Fortescue, Granville, and Grey. Fox Maule and Edward Stanley did not enjoy the courtesy title "lord" as they were merely the sons of the barons Panmure and Stanley; but in later life their estate management showed them to be two of the most pronounced of paternalists.

The experience of being the heir, or even the younger son, of a great Whig house was an imposing one. The very size of the house and extent of land could not but give one a sense of authority, one heightened by the deference shown to oneself and more importantly to that stern and remote figure, the paterfamilias. At age ten, Lord John Russell witnessed, on the death of his uncle, his father become the duke of Bedford and owner of 87,500 acres with an income of £141,500. At age fourteen, he attended an agricultural dinner and saw his father toasted and cheered three times, and a few days later he traveled to Dublin to see his father installed as viceroy of all Ireland. Later that year he was in London where he attended plays and met the ministers and generals of the day. Sent to the University of Edinburgh at age seventeen, he lived in the home of Dr. Playfair, studied under the famous Dugald Stewart (at whose home Lord Palmerston lived and studied), and breakfasted with Sir Walter Scott. It was an exceedingly privileged upbringing and one always in the shadow of a great duke who was also a model landlord known for his cottage building and allotments. The young John had even attended sheepshearings with his father.[34]

Lord John Russell's wife came from a similar Whig household. She remembered Minto House in Scotland as one where "the intercourse between the family at the House and the people of Minto village was of an intimate and affectionate nature." Lady Russell later was convinced that "if each proprietor, farmer, and clergyman did his duty there would be no misery," a view not discordant with Lord John's view of the Irish problem. "To sum up shortly the whole matter," he wrote, "we may say, 'property has its duties as well as its rights.' "[35] Many Whig lords held such sentiments though they seldom spoke or wrote of them with the zeal of the romantic paternalists nor with the vigor of the country squires. They were sentiments that were woven into the very institutions of the Whig houses whether through the figure of the paterfamilias or of the lady bountiful. Fox Maule's father, Baron Panmure, was "profuse" in hospitality and "liberal" to his tenants; Lord Howick's father, the Lord Grey of the Reform Act, created at Howick in Northumberland "a happiness that diffused itself through all the family"; and Lord Milton's father, Earl Fitzwilliam, an improving landlord who built good housing for the workers in his iron works and saw to the building of schools and the improvement of the prison, sent his son to his Irish estate for an apprenticeship in paternalism. His letters to Lord Milton warn him about tenants imposing extravagant rents on subtenants and urge him to teach the peasantry to keep cows better since milk along with potatoes is nutritious. Lord Milton, a serious apprentice, wrote back about improving drainage and keeping up the schools.[36] Affectionate intercourse, cottage building, and letters of instruction from the paterfamilias were not the only ways the young absorbed the noblesse oblige of a great Whig house; there was also the benevolence of the lady of the house. Nancy Mitford in *The Ladies of Alderley* gives a glimpse into this world of condescending benevolence when she reprints the letter of Lady Stanley of Alderley Park, Cheshire. In this letter Lady Stanley, the baron's wife, writes, "Louisa and Emmy [her nieces] are enjoying their last day hunting out the poor people and relieving their wants." In 1848 during the cholera scare Lady Stanley's daughter-in-law, the wife of Edward Stanley, M.P., is also busy with the poor "trying what I can do with the people to cleanse their dirt holes." The baron himself was not unmindful of the poor, lowering their rents 10 percent in 1843 but doing so in the form of free manure since such will do "double good." The baron's brother, the local parson and future bishop of Norwich, was indefatigable in promoting schools and visiting the poor. For Edward Stanley and his twin brother William, both Whig M.P.s in the 1840s, Alderley Park was full of parents, grandparents, uncles, and wives, all attentive to the poor.[37]

However natural paternalist ways were to Whig households, there was often one frustration to being an heir to one: not until the father's death did one have an estate to manage. Lord John Russell was prime minister of England before he owned an estate, and it frustrated his wife. "You do not think," she wrote, "how I long for a few acres of our own in order to know and do what little I could do for the poor." It was a frustration others knew, Tory and Whig. Lords Ashley and Morpeth and Fox Maule had to await the death of their fathers before they could become model landlords, which they all did with great zeal. When Lord Morpeth, for example, became earl of Carlisle and lord of Castle Howard in Yorkshire, he immediately entertained 1,000 factory workers on its lovely lawns and gave part of it away as a site for a reformatory. He also inherited Naworth in Cumberland where he was, says his biographer, liked by his neighbors and tenantry, "among whom he moved with native ease and unaffected friendliness of true nobility, always accessible and ready to assist, entering with a keen zest into athletic sport." Heir to 78,500 acres and an income of £49,600, happy at Eton, and earnest at Christ Church, Oxford, he was conditioned naturally to paternalism. In 1830 at his first election he said that the interests of landowners, tenants, and commerce "are not separate and single, but reciprocal and united. . . . It is this sympathy which . . . I wish to see exist and grow among all classes and all ranks." That sympathy Morpeth expanded, unlike the Peelite paternalists, into a strong desire for a paternal government. In 1848 he told the House of Commons, "I claim for British labour and its agents all the assistance and appliances which our fostering care . . . can suggest."[38]

The Whigs had no monopoly on great houses. The romantic pater-nalist Lord John Manners was raised in the duke of Rutland's Gothic Belvoir Castle whose turrets and towers evoked feudal dreams. The Peelite Lords Mahon, Sandon, and Egerton were raised at Chevening, Kent, Sandon House in Staffordshire, and in the three houses of the marquess of Stafford in Shropshire, Staffordshire, and Scotland. Some of these lords' fathers also formed models to imitate and admire. Lord John Manners's constant praise of the duke of Rutland's benevolence, Viscount Sandon's great pride in "the affectionate" conduct of the earl of Harrowby, "as father, husband, master and landlord," and Lord Howick's spirited defense in the Commons of his father, Earl Grey, all reflect the sovereign and impressive role that the paterfamilias played in the great houses of the aristocracy, Whig or Tory.[39] How then did the noblesse oblige of the Whigs differ from the paternalism of the Peelites—or indeed from the paternalism of the romantics, churchmen, and squires?

The Whigs differed from the other four varieties of paternalists on three issues: centralization, religious toleration, and attitudes toward reform and change. The Whigs' love of government commissions set them apart from the country squires; their advocacy of religious tolera-tion, with an accompanying friendliness toward dissent and a drift toward secularism, divided them from the churchmen; their proclivity for innovation set them apart from the romantics with their medieval dreams; and a mixture of all these attitudes separated them from the Peelites.

Their disposition toward reform and specifically toward reform by central commissions is clearly evident in the pamphlets of three Whig M.P.s and paternalists who were not lords, Robert Slaney, Thomas Wyse, and Poulett Scrope. Slaney, a knight and landowner from Shrop-shire was an ardent advocate of government commissions. He was in-deed so frustrated at Peel's failure to create a commission to investigate the sanitation of English towns that he offered to give the government £1,000 of his own money to pay for it. He also wrote five pamphlets advocating social reform between 1819 and 1847. The first two, the *Employment of the Poor* of 1819 and *Rural Expenditure* of 1824, are, like the pamphlets of Montagu Gore and Sir Walter James, filled with paternalist pleas for landowners to reside on their estates, to set good examples, to build cottages, and to be liberal to tenants. By 1847, in *A Plea to Power and Parliament for the Working Classes*, he confesses, as Gore and James never did, that property had not done its duty, that there was thus "a want of a permanent administrative body to watch over the interests of the poor," and that the central government should do much more for the health and education of the people.[40]

Thomas Wyse and Poulett Scrope, like Slaney gentlemen landowners, were at one with him in desiring a central government that regulated factory labor, promoted sanitation, supervised poor laws, and defined landlord and tenant relations. And they were as ardently committed as Slaney to property doing its duties, or indeed as any of the other variety of paternalists. Wyse's 453-page book, *Education Reform*, published in 1836, contains a fuller and more detailed plea for the paternalism of property and the church than anything written by Southey, Coleridge, Sewell, or Carlyle. It is replete with paternalist sentiments. "Each profession, rank, individual," he announces, "has his specific obligations." "The clergy," he observes elsewhere, "have their duty; they also have their rights." He even reflects Coleridge's remarks in *Table Talk*, when he asserts, "Act of Parliament as yet never regenerated a country." The landowner is of course central, and he "must be shown that blessings are not conferred without obligations, and that he is no more permitted to throw off the paternity of his situation than tenants the filial subordination of theirs."[41] Here is as hierarchical, authoritarian, and organic a social world as any paternalist could desire.

Poulett Scrope's numerous pamphlets, though they do not constitute such a full manual of paternalism as Wyse's work, nevertheless urge landowners and magistrates to police vagrants, relieve the starving, "erect decent and comfortable cottages," "stop the multiplication of the poor," and grant allotments. Both Wyse and Scrope were landowners and according to observers model ones. But both, like Slaney, had to admit that both property and the church had failed to do their duties. The church had not been faithful to her stewardship and had not used her talents well, wrote Wyse in 1836, adding that "she has ceased to be the people's church, in becoming too much the church of the aristocracy." He concludes that the government should provide for education since "government has the experience and authority of a parent." Scrope came to the same conclusion about the failure of property. After noting that the extent of pulling down cottages was "disgraceful" and "very near universal," he concludes, the results of "individual or combined benevolence . . . must be wholly inadequate to meet the growing deficiency." Scrope also viewed Peel's reliance on Irish landowners to cope with the Irish famine as useless. Scrope later called for "a paternal government" to solve that problem.[42]

The Whig paternalists, though they favored property performing its duties, simply did not possess the Peelite trust that property would do so. "The landlords of Ireland," said the Peelite Sandon, "are the only agents through whom the country could be regenerated." "The welfare, both moral and physical of the great body of the people," said the Whig Howick in a contrasting note, "I conceive to be the true concern of the government."[43]

Not every Whig was as vigorous in his advocacy of a paternal government as Slaney, Wyse, and Scrope. No species of paternalist is without its own variations. Not all Whig paternalists were alike. Sir Harry Verney, another pamphlet-writing Whig landowner, warned his readers against "an indolent reliance on government." He urged them instead "to consider what is the particular work he can do for himself and others." For the landowners of Buckinghamshire, where he was deputy lieutenant, this meant improving farming, hiring more laborers, and subdividing villages for benevolent and ameliorative work. Verney's distrust of government and trust in individuals was shared by Sir George Grey, the Whig home secretary after 1846. Grey believed that "the social evils of the day were rooted in immorality." Verney and Grey, however, were by no means totally opposed to a paternal government, but only to an excess of it. Grey warmly supported the ten-hour bill and worked hard to pass a bill to help in the erection of public baths.[44]

Both Grey and Verney were evangelicals. Evangelicalism was a religious persuasion that involved different responses to the growth of a centralized government. On some issues, such as the employment of children in factories, and with some men, such as Lord Ashley, it favored centralization, but on other issues, such as Church schools, and with other men, such as Thomas Chalmers, it opposed a stronger central government. In the case of Verney and Grey, the evangelical doctrine that salvation lay in the regeneration and rebirth of the individual led them to look for individual, not collectivist, answers to social ills.

Sir George Grey, though for the ten-hour day in 1847, went no further in urging the regulation of labor in manufacturing. He failed to, in part, because he believed in political economy. Political economy, like evangelicalism, had an ambivalent impact upon paternalist ideas. A belief in political economy was, for example, a part of the paternalism of the Whigs; yet it in no way dampened their demand for more government commissions. Poulett Scrope wrote a book on political economy, Thomas Wyse urged it be taught in all schools, Robert Slaney repeatedly cited "the distinguished author of the *Wealth of Nations*," Lord Morpeth used it at the hustings, Lords Howick and Milton referred to it in urging the repeal of the corn laws, and Lord Palmerston picked it up with ease from Dugald Stewart. Only Lord John Russell cautioned against it, calling political economy "an awful thing."[45] But Russell, also a student of Dugald Stewart, had economic views that were permeated with its teachings. Almost everyone in Parliament in fact was steeped in its rules. Certainly the Peelites were. It is not an ideology that separates Whigs from Peelite paternalists. It did, though, separate Whig and Peelite paternalists from the country squires, romantics, and churchmen, though more in terms of rhetoric than actual behavior. Squires loved property rights and churchmen ecclesiastical rights as fiercely as any Whig. And they were much more rooted in their localities than the Whigs.

The Whigs were not, as were Floyer and Bankes, "Dorset men." Many of their fathers possessed London houses and many of them more than one country house. They also visited the houses of Whig cousins and were often in Europe. They were mobile and so had fewer local roots. Heirs also of a latitudinarian and tolerant Anglicanism, they were not bound to the idea of an exclusivist Church of England. Raised in the historic tradition of Whig reform and progressive thinking—of 1688 and civil and religious liberty—they also saw no need to turn to the medieval past. "Young England," said that paragon of Whig paternalists, the benign Lord Morpeth, "has too much of old England in it." Morpeth's paternalism, and that of the Whigs generally, was one in which the paternalism of property, church, and locality were writ small and the paternalism of government was writ large.

The Anglo-Irish

From 1841 to 1847 more than eight hundred men sat in the House of Commons—for the entire 1840s many more. Among them paternalist attitudes were extremely popular, but in many more forms and combinations than the above five varieties. There were, for example, 105 Irish M.P.s, themselves divided between Catholic repealers and Protestant unionists. There were also a multitude of silent M.P.s, the backbenchers whose sentiments can only be found in election speeches reported in local newspapers. Then there were the eccentrics who fit in no category but were often the most stridently paternalist. Finally, there were those who either held no paternalist attitudes or actively opposed them. These M.P.s formed a miscellany: Irishmen of different religions, eccentrics, silent backbenchers, and critics.

After 1845 about seventy of these M.P.s might have qualified as a sixth variety, one called "Anglo-Irish." Before 1845 these seventy seemed to merge with the silent backbenchers, but then in the spring of that year came the Maynooth Bill and in the autumn the potato famine. These two events ended their silence. From 1845 to 1850 twelve of those seventy Anglo-Irish members spoke and spoke often, and their social message was bluntly paternalist. They never tired of boasting of the landowners' devotion to the poor. They were proud that Thomas Drummond, undersecretary for Ireland in 1835, first used the dictum that property has its duties as well as its rights. That phrase adorned many of their speeches. "A body of men never existed," said Sir Henry Barron, M.P. for Waterford, "who showed themselves more devoted to the poor than the landlords of Ireland."[46] Their high estimate of the landlord's power and benevolence and their jealous regard for his autonomy led the Anglo-Irish paternalists to denounce the Tenant Compensation Bill of 1846 and the Labouring Poor of Ireland Act of 1847, as well as to condemn the Landlord and Tenant Bill of 1848 and the Encumbered Estate Bill and the extra 6d levy on the poor rate of 1849.[47] Measures such as these, according to Sir Joseph Napier, M.P. for Dublin University, destroy those inviolable principles that define the relation of landlord and tenant. For Napier, an evangelical Protestant and dogmatic opponent of state interference with landlords and tenants, the best agreements were voluntary. It was a view shared by the M.P. for the city of Dublin, Sir William Gregory. The Anglo-Irish landowners did not object to a paternal government as long as it encouraged, in Gregory's words, "those who made the best use of the advantages attached to their position." It should also, Gregory added, "endeavour to contract the circle of responsibility into the narrowest limits . . . [since] the narrower the field of action in which everyman was placed, and in which his responsibility rested, the more clearly would that man see his duty."[48] It was a belief identical to that expressed in Coleridge's *Lay Sermons*. It was a belief that also led the Anglo-Irish paternalists to plead for small poor-law districts supervised by proprietors. "You should deal with these pauperized districts," said G. A. Hamilton, M.P. for Dublin University, "as a proprietor." "Let them narrow the responsibility," said Waterford's M.P., Sir H. W. Barron, "and bring home to each landlord [his] duties . . . towards the poor." The smaller the district, argued Henry A. Herbert, M.P. for county Kerry, the greater the local responsibility and the fewer the ejectments.[49]

The Anglo-Irish paternalists, like the English country squires, were strong localists. They looked to property, not to a central authority, for the care of the poor. But the famine reduced the rents needed to carry out that task. And with no indigenously rooted church to fall back on, they had to plead for a more paternal government. Their notion of such a government followed Edmund Burke's idea of government as the moral partnership of those advantageously placed in the social hierarchy and not Jeremy Bentham's idea of government as a centralized bureaucracy. "It was the duty of a paternal Government," said Charles Clements, M.P. from Leitrim, "to have sought out those gentlemen of Ireland in whom they could confidently trust."[50] The help of the English treasury and Irish administration they needed—the famine demanded it—but they did not want large poor-law districts run by Benthamite central commissioners who enforced heavy rates on what they claimed were nearly bankrupt estates. They preferred instead the Burkean moral partnership, one in which Whitehall supplied loans and grants for land drainage, harbors, and fisheries or best of all for Lord George Bentinck's sixteen-million-pound private railway scheme. They also liked treasury grants to relieve those destitute districts with excessive demands for poor-law relief.

That relief, however, should not be too ample, and it should be only in the workhouse. Outdoor relief, said G. A. Hamilton, M.P. for Dublin University, would paralyze industry. Hamilton was very chary of "hasty legislation," for such would end "the spirit of improvement" and would dissuade the Irish cotter from depending on "his own labour and the sweat of his brow for subsistence." The Anglo-Irish paternalists wanted both government money and the autonomy to use it their own way.

These ideas differed little from those of the squires of England, except that the famine forced them to demand a stronger paternal government, while their absenteeism and the fact that their estates were heavily encumbered and heavily rated made their appeals for property to do its duties more edgy, shrill, and even bordering on the hypocritical. The tone differed, but the ideology was the same.

That the ideology was the same is not surprising. Not only were the twelve Anglo-Irish paternalists who spoke often from a solidly agricultural Ireland, they were also part of the same establishment as the English squires. Barron, Napier, Gregory, Lord Claud Hamilton, Herbert, and Clements were hardly social outcasts. Gregory attended Harrow and Hamilton Rugby, and both went to Oxford; Clements and Herbert attended Trinity College, Cambridge, and Barron and Napier Trinity College, Dublin, with Napier later at Gray's Inn, London. In Irish affairs Gregory and Barron were sheriffs of Galway and Waterford, and Herbert and Hamilton deputy lieutenants of Kerry and Dublin. Sir William Gregory's *Autobiography* provides a glimpse into that affluent and powerful world. Raised in London, educated at Harrow and Christ Church, close friend of Disraeli, Smythe, and Manners, a supporter of Lord Ashley's ten-hour amendment, he found Peel's political economy chilly. His kind and generous father died of fever during the famine, a fever acquired during visits to his ill dependents. He thus left Gregory not only an estate earning £7,000 a year but the example of model land-lordship. The *DNB* declares that Gregory measured up to that model, but in his *Autobiography* Gregory admits that his father's excessive kindness, the lure of the turf, and the temptations of the London gaming tables kept him from being an improving landlord.[51]

Not all Anglo-Irish M.P.s had Gregory's or Herbert's English uni-versity education, but of those who did not attend university, four en-tered the army where they rose to the rank of colonel, retired on half-pay to their estates, entered Parliament, and took command of the county militia. In both England and Ireland the army as an education and the militia as an institution were as efficient in teaching deference and authority as public schools and universities. There was a definite estab-lishment in the whole of the United Kingdom, an Anglican and land-owning one, in which the public schools, universities, church, and army were central. The elite of that establishment studied Aristotle, read Burke above all, and probably dipped into either Paley or Coleridge. The outlook of that elite, whether in Ireland, England, or Scotland, was instinctively paternalist.

Paternalism also dominated Parliament. Norman Gash in *Politics in the Age of Peel* has shown how the Reform Act of 1832 caused only modifications of and not a revolution in the aristocratic and deferential electoral system of the old regime. Landed property and rural areas still controlled a large majority of the seats in Parliament. It was a Parlia-ment heavily weighted in favor of land and for that reason heavily weighted in favor of paternalism.

About thirty of the 105 Irish M.P.s were not full-fledged members of that establishment. They were Catholics and repealers, followers of Daniel O'Connell. Among them one can count M.P.s like Henry Grattan, John O'Connell, the great orator's son, and William Smith O'Brien, fierce critic of absenteeism and of landlords who ejected tenants. During the famine these repealers demanded stronger poor laws and firmer government action. Since they were landowners themselves, they did not oppose property performing its duties. But seeing that property did not perform its duties, they urged that the government compel it to do so. "The legislature should compel landlords," said John O'Connell, "to do their duty." He urged the government to set aside the principles of political economy and to help establish manufactures and promote commerce. He praised Lords Devonshire, Londonderry, and Abercorn for doing so, but then confessed such landlords were exceptional. It was in 1847 that he expressed these doubts about landlords doing their duty. The Anglo-Irish condemned him for it. But by 1849 H. A. Herbert, Protestant, landlord, and deputy lieutenant of Kerry had to admit "the Irish proprietors who did their duty were a minority." He admitted this fact "with regret." Well-wishing and generous men saw their most cherished social attitudes falter before the sins of absenteeism and ejectments and break apart on the appalling conditions of the famine.[52]

The Eccentric and the Silent

The Anglo-Irish as a species of paternalists were cousins of the English country squire, their differences arising largely from the tragic environment in which they were placed. The eccentric paternalists conform to no species or cousinhood: each was sui generis. How could one classify Grantley Berkeley, George Hudson, and Henry Drummond? Berkeley was a Whig, a modest landowner, and an M.P. with literary pretensions but limited talents. He lacked the generous noblesse oblige of a Lord Morpeth or a Robert Slaney, but possessed a passion for ensuring the enforcement of the game laws. George Hudson was the son of a farmer and a self-made railway king. Henry Drummond was a London banker who sold his father's Hampshire estates and his hounds as being part of the frivolous world; he then joined the evangelical Irvingites, tried to save Geneva from Socinianism, and preached in Parliament a vigorous mercantilism and paternalism.

Grantley Berkeley, who wrote novels filled with Young England-like scenes of almsgiving at castle gates was also a terror to poachers. An arrogant, hard-riding lover of the hunt and of cockfighting, he bragged of his stern game keeping and landlordism. "As to the labouring population," he wrote, "my rule has ever been, to be severe when . . . in any revolt . . . against the law . . . [but] just, . . . even over liberal when they were well conducted and respected my rights."[53] Berkeley was a lesser aristocrat determined to keep up aristocratic ways, Drummond and Hudson capitalists anxious to ape the aristocracy. With their mercantile wealth they bought country estates—Hudson's many and vast, Drummond's a solitary one in Surrey where he experimented with allotments. Both assumed the garb of a country gentleman, a garb that included a paternalist ideology. But with both men, paternalism had a strong mercantilist overtone. For the Tory M.P. George Hudson the corn and navigation laws were part of an indispensable protectionism, one that not only promoted trade and guaranteed agricultural laborers a living but protected the mansions of the aristocracy. As the greatest of the captains of industry, Hudson was dined and feted in those mansions, and he won from Stanley Lees Giffard's *Standard* the highest praise for his employment of more than 200,000 hands. "Let us hear what man or class of men," challenged the *Standard*, "ever did so much for the population of the country." It was a case of property performing its duties on a monumental scale.[54]

Hudson was a man of action; Drummond, the banker and Irvingite, was a preacher of sermons, and not a few to the Commons. No other M.P. was as ideological, as effusive, and as historical in his paternalism. To Drummond the current school of politics was satanic. It had departed from old Saxon laws, had abolished the Church's revenue for the relief of the poor, and had forgotten "the old system [with] all the people meeting together every Sunday at the parish church." He extolled monarchy, aristocracy, and property and berated all who demanded equality as of unsound mind. A subversion of property was a subversion of society. That any legislation could relieve the poor was as gross a delusion as the claim that misery was not the inevitable lot of most of mankind. Hating abstract thought, he insisted that individual proprietors, not an abstract property, had duties to the poor. The first duty of the proprietor was to defend the rights of property. That property in this sense was also an abstraction he overlooked. There was in his elaborate orations an element of confusion. He often denounced political economy, yet he founded a chair in that science at Oxford, and though he urged that the remedying of social evils be left to landed proprietors, he concluded that Irish proprietors did their duties disgracefully. He was, said Carlyle, "a singular mixture of all things—of the saint, the wit, the philosopher—swimming . . . in an element of dandyism."[55] Carlyle had also called George Hudson "the big swollen gambler." Both Hudson and Drummond were idiosyncratic. Mercantile men turned gentry, they were strident and ill at ease with, but in need of, those paternalist ideas that grew so naturally on Oxfordshire's Joseph Henley and Dorset's George Bankes.

Most of the 658 members of the House of Commons seldom spoke in debate. They were the silent backbenchers, M.P.s like the duke of Richmond's sons, the earl of March and Lord Lennox, and Viscount Downe's son, Lord Dawnay. Ferrand, one of the most garrulous of paternalists, found it a disgrace for Richmond to bring his silent sons into the Commons. "If they could speak in the House," he wrote Disraeli, "all would be well, but . . . they can not say boo to a goose." Lord Dawnay's speech at the hustings in 1841 reveals that Richmond's sons were not the only ones who could not say "boo to a goose." "Ladies and Gentlemen," he said, "I must bring in the Ladies, for I see there are some pretty bonnets. It is a very fine day for the corn. I am a conservative: I have come forward as a candidate . . . at the request of several Gentlemen; it's a very fine day. I hope our cause will be prosperous. I will not detain you longer; it's a very fine day, and I have a great deal of work to do."[56] Dawnay's and Richmond's two sons were Tories, represented rural areas, and voted for the Corn Law, Church extension, and factory acts, all paternalist policies. How many other silent M.P.s held these views is difficult to tell since an examination of their speeches at elections does not reveal much more than Lord Dawnay's. Few candidates at the hustings were explicit about social theories, indicating once again the secondary position that social attitudes took to political loyalties, religious passions, and economic interests.

So various and amorphous were the permutations of paternalist attitudes and their combinations with other outlooks that measuring paternalism's strength in the House of Commons of the 1840s would be like measuring the strength of free-enterprise dogmas in the House of Commons of the 1950s. Such paternalist and free-enterprise ideas are so diffuse and widespread as to become commonplace. They become part of the conventional wisdom and thus are seldom criticized. They die out more by being outdated and overlooked than disproved. There were few instances of M.P.s calling paternalist attitudes wrong or immoral. Lord Macaulay, who in 1828 severely criticized Southey's *Thomas More*, in

1846 denounced a "patriarchal government" as a great pest. But his attack was blunted by his assertion that the doctrine of laissez faire was just as much a pest. Some of the sharpest critics of paternalism were disenchanted former believers. Poulett Scrope, who earlier wrote of the duties of landlords, had by 1847, concluded that such efforts were "local, partial and temporary."[57]

Outright criticism being rare, it fell out that the most effective way to combat paternalism was to be silent about it and clamorous about its alternatives. Such was the method of Charles Villiers, the annual mover of the motion to repeal the Corn Law. Though he came from an aristocratic Whig house, the Clarendons, he received too great a lesson in political economy and became too intimate with Benthamite radicals to stick with a hierarchical, patriarchal view of society. "I do not believe," he said, "that the aristocracy of this country are better than other men; in fact I think they are much the same as other men." Villier's egalitarianism and political economy and his silence about the blessings of property thus disqualify him from being regarded as a Whig paternalist.

Political economy, which could be and was often combined with the "live and let live" attitudes of paternalism could also, if it became an all-embracing ideology, lead away from paternalism. It nearly did so for a Tory as dedicated as Peel's lieutenant, Sir James Graham. There is no example in his speeches and writings, nor even in the three biographies of his life, of any plea that property should do its duties. He never penned a memorandum comparable to that which Peel sent to the mayor of Tamworth. His name is thus not included on the list of the sixteen Peelite paternalists just as Villiers is not on the Whig list. Men like Graham and Villiers, and like Grote, Roebuck, and Molesworth, the Benthamite radicals, looked to alternative ideologies, to political economy, to voluntarism, to self-help, or to a reforming bureaucratic state. The more vigorously an M.P. championed such alternatives, the more did paternalist ideas fade away. But in the early 1840s those ideas were far from fading away. Indeed they were undergoing a revival. Nearly omnipresent as part of the social thinking of many different kinds of thinkers, these ideas played an important role in the politics of the 1840s. That role was not a simple one but rather complex and multifarious and helped to create that intricate mosaic of forces that defined the politics of the 1840s.

Chapter X

A Mosaic of Forces

1844: The Apogee of Paternalism

Paternalism as a literary and political force reached its apogee in the year 1844. It was a year that saw the publication of *The Works of Thomas Arnold*, R. B. Seeley's *Remedies*, William Sewell's *Christian Politics*, Arthur Helps's *Claims of Labour*, George Smythe's *Historic Fancies*, and Benjamin Disraeli's *Coningsby*. *Coningsby*, in particular, with its severe strictures on Peel's new, hard conservatism and its idealization of an old, more organic society, stirred up much discussion, much as Thomas Carlyle's *Past and Present* had the year before with its idealization of Abbot Samson's twelfth-century abbey at Bury St. Edmunds. Talk of monasteries, alms, the harmony of classes, the duties of landlords became the vogue in literary circles.

Paternalist ideas were also the vogue in Parliament. The young and promising William Gladstone, author of *The State in Its Relations with the Church*, had become president of the Board of Trade where he strengthened a paternal government by carrying the Railway Act of 1844, an act that required that third-class trains be covered and that they move at an expeditious rate. It also empowered the government to purchase lines that were badly run or made extravagant profits. Gladstone, who the year before had carried an act for the regulation of the payment of wages to London's coal whippers, was not too diffident in his advocacy of a protecting government. Protection was still a good Tory word, particularly if applied to agriculture. In 1844 Parliament voted to protect the rent rolls of landowners by defeating, 328 to 124, a bill to repeal the Corn Law. Parliament expressed solicitude in 1844 for more than landlords. It also voted in that year to protect investors by an act regulating joint-stock companies and to protect the comfort of passengers in hackney coaches by prohibiting the drivers from smoking on duty. Some in Parliament even tried to encourage landlords to be more protective of laborers by giving them allotments. In 1844 Lord Cowper made his first attempt at passing a field-gardens bill. In 1844 romantic paternalists and country squires also fiercely attacked the New Poor Law for not truly protecting the poor. They forced Sir James Graham, the home secretary, to admit that 85 percent of relief was actually given outside, and not inside, the infamous workhouses, an admission that was a compliment to the obduracy of many a paternalist squire in resisting those ukases from Somerset House that would prohibit outdoor relief.[1]

Of all the triumphs of the paternalists in the glorious year of 1844, none equaled the passage on March 18 of Lord Ashley's amendment to the factory bill, an amendment that required a ten-hour factory day. It passed 179 to 170. Monckton Milnes exclaimed that he "saw banded together on that occasion a large body of men who were more regardful of the interests of the people than of any political consequences."[2] That band of men, of course, included Young England, a group that by 1844 had grown in strength and enthusiasm. Lord John Manners felt that he stood at the dawn of a new era. "There are," he told Disraeli in November, "at least half a dozen Young England newspapers and magazines bursting their shell." In December he wrote Disraeli that Young England was "of greater weight and capacity than its critics thought possible." "Young England," announced *Fraser's* in 1844, "has renovated the whole surface of things, both in politics and literature." "Young England's spirit," said the *Morning Chronicle* in the same year, is "gradually manifesting itself through the press." The medieval dreams, the poetry, the idealism, the chivalry, and the benevolence to the poor won Young England much praise and attention. In August of 1844 the Birmingham Athenic Institute invited Disraeli, Manners, and Smythe to address their members, and in October the same three spoke to the Manchester Athenaeum Soiree. Colonel Ferrand took advantage of their trip north to have them speak at his gigantic and much publicized celebration at Bingley of the success of his allotment schemes. The speeches given on these occasions were immediately published in a pamphlet entitled *Young England*. For that loyal band 1844 was an *annus mirabilis*.[3]

Paternalists of a more religious and serious mood also won praise in 1844, particularly the incomparable Lord Ashley. "He has humanized an age," said the *Morning Herald* in July of that year. The *Spectator*, in its famous editorial in April announcing the New Faith, expressed delight in Ashley's work and in the broad spectrum of opinion in Parliament that supported his ten-hour amendment, a spectrum that included country squires, Whigs moved by noblesse oblige, and romantics inspired by medieval longings. Six Peelites even supported the amendment! Acland, who had read Coleridge at Oxford, Sir Walter James and Montagu Gore, who had written pamphlets on the duties of landlords, and Viscounts Sandon and Mahon and J. S. Wortley, who later were to become free-trade Peelites, defied their leader and voted for the ten-hour amendment. Joining them were seven Whig paternalists, five romantics, six churchmen, and seven country squires from the eighty M.P.s described in chapter nine who wrote, spoke, or practiced paternalist ideals.[4] Two romantics, two Whig paternalists, two country squires, and five Peelites voted against the amendment. That the Peelites numbered so large in opposition was not unrelated to the fact that their leader and England's prime minister was the amendment's most vigorous and outspoken opponent. No churchman let Ashley down. Seventy of the eighty who form our sample sat in Parliament in 1844. Of these, thirty-two voted for the ten-hour amendment, twelve opposed it, and the rest were absent. Perhaps the *Spectator* was not so wrong in speaking of a New Faith arising in 1844, one that advocated a more paternal government.

Forster Mc Geachey was one of that faith. An opponent of the Reform Act and Catholic Emancipation and a partner with Peel and Adderley in building Church of England schools in Staffordshire, he was deeply angered by an England "steeped in suffering . . . the state of the people wretched . . . the rich amassing wealth" and everyone following "the let things alone principle" whether in "preserving game," "preserving profits," or "reckless speculation." He urged greater legislative interference. It was a proposition other Peelite paternalists put forth, though often only in private. John Stuart Wortley, the future second Baron Wharncliffe, told Peel in a confidential letter in 1844 that many millowners were for "a further limitation of the inordinate amount of labour." He also reported that the lower classes hated the New Poor Law. On both counts, he told Peel, the critics had "reasonable grounds." Viscount Sandon also wrote Peel on the day of Ashley's triumph telling him of "a widely extended feeling in favour of a restriction in the hours," a feeling that had "reached quarters which [it] had not reached before."[5] But despite the protests of his friends Sandon, Mc Geachey, and Wortley and of 179 M.P.s, Peel, a paternalist himself within the sphere of Drayton Manor and the town of Tamworth, decided to tolerate no measure that empowered the state to dictate the working hours of adults. He called together his cabinet and put in motion developments that would reverse the 179-to-170 victory for the ten-hour cause. The cabinet met March 25. Gladstone had asked Peel two days earlier, "Are the speeches of John Manners . . . [and] Inglis, not fair indications of the spirit of the party at large in Parliament?" Have not the country members, he added, "not only borne the brunt of League attacks on the issue during the two sessions but borne much with and for the government?" The "much" no doubt included Peel's zeal for the New Poor Law and the free-trade tendencies in his budgets. Gladstone tactfully urged a free vote on the ten-hour issue. He also suggested that Peel accept the duke of Buccleuch's suggestion of a compromise on an eleven-hour factory day, only to be told by Peel that "government interference was wrong in itself." The cabinet yielded. Peel, who confessed his opposition to the regulation of labor, "went much further than the mass of the cabinet" and made the issue a vote of confidence.[6] He thus ensured the reversal of the greatest triumph that the New Faith had yet secured. Adult operatives must not expect protection from a paternal government.

Gladstone dutifully voted on May 13 for Peel's laissez faire views. The author of *The State in Its Relations with the Church*, the admirer of Coleridge, could only record in his notes his disappointment that Peel regarded matters of trade and labor as being as "high a principle" as "cases of spiritual concern and of eternal truth." Lord John Manners and George Smythe had called themselves "Gladstonites," and Milnes found him attractively "serious." He was a person of conviction, brilliance, and eloquence, strong in character and not without charisma. Had paternalist ideas truly counted in his philosophy and politics in 1844, he might have provided the leadership of what Monckton Milnes called that "large body of men . . . regardful of the interests of the people," the same men the *Spectator* called believers in the New Faith. It was, after all, a decade that did witness the breakup of old and the formation of new party alignments. But no such party formed on the issue of a more paternal government. Gladstone did not resign, but voted on May

13 to kill the ten-hour amendment. The Whigs, romantics, and church paternalists remained firm for Ashley, but Peelite votes shifted from six for and five against a ten-hour day to four for and six against. Gore switched his vote, and Acland and Mahon absented themselves. Country squires, who in March were seven for and two against the ten-hour day, were in May ten for and nine against it.[7] These figures on the voting of our sample paternalists among the country squires are small and are therefore not too meaningful compared to the massive change in votes by all M.P.s on this issue between March and May, changes that lowered support for Ashley's motion from 179 to 159 and raised the number opposed to it from 179 to 297. In May, 105 more M.P.s voted than in March. Peel's call for a vote of confidence forced thirty Conservatives to change their votes and forced many absent for the March vote to vote in May against the ten-hour amendment. Peel's decision to make it a vote of confidence was crucial, a fact confirmed by the easy passage of the Ten Hour Act in 1847 after he had left office.

The dramatic reversals of voting in March and May of 1844 show how weak is the operation of social ideals in politics. They are seldom a match for economic interests, party ambitions, or religious passions. Often the expression of social aspirations, they are also at times a means of shaming the political opposition. Even the serious Gladstone unconsciously showed his low respect for social questions. In his memorandum he complained that Peel considered "matters of trade and labour" as of "high principle," a complaint that suggests that Gladstone would never do so. For Gladstone matters of "spiritual concern and eternal truth," not "matters of trade and labour," were of high principle. But such a distinction, his friend Charles Adderley saw, was one of the crucial errors of the age. "There is no greater mistake," Adderley had written, than "distinguishing between the common objects of earth and matters of religion." For Adderley the ten-hour day was an earthly object, but all matters on earth were a matter of "spiritual concern and eternal truth," and so of high principle. Gladstone's abandonment of the operatives on the ten-hour bill showed the limits of his intense piety.

Religious passions themselves, since men held different ones and since they were tied to different institutions, usually overruled the weaker and more evanescent social aspirations that led many to demand a more paternal government. Paternalist ideas in Gladstone's mind, and in the minds of countless other Victorians, offered little rivalry to religious prejudice. Gladstone did finally resign office, not in 1844 on behalf of a ten-hour day, but in 1845 in opposition to a state grant of £25,000 for the education of Catholic priests at Ireland's Maynooth College. The Maynooth grant divided the paternalists. It was a division that, along with their defeat on the ten-hour amendment and their division on the Corn Law of 1846, led to a decided decline in the hopes of those who expected that the revival of England's most traditional and pervasive social outlook would solve its modern problems. Paternalism, in fact, could never be viable as a force encouraging the growth of a paternal government. There were at least four salient reasons for this fact: the fragility of Young England's romantic ideas, the attachment of paternalist M.P.s to property, a tenacious and deeply rooted localism, and the divisiveness of religion.

The Fragility of Young England

The fragility of the visions of Young England and of the social vision of other romantics was momentarily obscured by the ardent enthusiasms of the early 1840s. Early in the decade that small but hopeful group spoke out spiritedly on behalf of the poor in workhouses and children and women in factories and mines. They vied with each other in support of measures to encourage allotments, provide more schools, and return poor-law management to the parishes. They also spoke in defense of that Corn Law that protected the landowners, themselves the protectors of the poor. Until 1846 all eleven of the romantic paternalists in the sample voted to sustain the Corn Law. The nearest they came to unanimity on other issues came when six of them voted for Ashley's ten-hour amendment and only one against it, and when six voted to abolish the Poor Law Commission in 1844 with none voting to retain it.[8] The romantic disciples of Coleridge, Southey, and Digby had a high regard for landed property and locality. Since the repeal of the Corn Law threatened landed property and since the central poor-law bureaucrats threatened locality, the romantics were ardently in favor of a national Corn Law but cold toward a national Poor Law Commission. Stafford O'Brien told the Commons that the Corn Law made government "paternal," while its repeal would make of government "a mere police agent." His reason for this view lay in his high regard for rural parishes, which he called superior to manufacturing parishes because in them landlord and farmer could be held responsible for distress. The Corn Law also protected rent, and rent, said Monckton Milnes, "was a means of supporting the poor."

Young England had a great trust in property. "The community is best served," said Lord John Manners in the House of Commons, "when individual rights and individual duties were properly maintained." Landlords working with farmers and with the clergy and magistrates and poor-law overseers formed what Disraeli, in his defense of the Corn Law, called "your territorial constitution." Such a constitution, based largely on landed property, not only guaranteed local self-government and true English liberties but was the basis for "the revenue of the church, the administration of justice, and the estate of the poor." Such a territorial constitution formed a barrier against the tyranny of centralization and created those attachments that bound together parishioners into an organic community. "In making government strong," said Disraeli, "society might be made weak." This sentiment went to the heart of the paternalism of the romantic M.P.s. Baillie Cochrane echoed it when he told Parliament, "The great object of legislation should be to diffuse through all classes . . . a warm spirit of charity."[9]

There was much that was humane and wise in the vision of these youthful and sanguine literati. Given their own assumptions, theirs was not an inconsistent social theory. One could both attack a centralizing poor law and vote economic favors to landowners if one believed landowners would use larger rents for schools and clothing clubs and their greater local power for the kinder and more intelligent relief of the poor. But if landowners and local power did not behave this way, the theory lost its efficacy. If landlords exploited rather than protected the poor, there was no social reason for the Corn Law. In May of 1846 Cochrane, Milnes, and Smythe may have reflected these doubts when they voted for the repeal of the Corn Law. Very shortly thereafter, Disraeli, in a private memorandum wrote that "the young England myth had evaporated." He then commented on his new role as a spokesman for some 220 protectionists rather than six or eight London literati, "I had become a recognized leader."[10]

Young England, in truth, was as fragile a group as the myths it dabbled in. "I don't pretend to have any principle," Smythe confided privately to Disraeli, a statement supported by Smythe in taking office in 1845 under Peel and abandoning his support of the Corn Law. But people who claim no principles are often only unconscious of them. Though Smythe had called Southey's writings the handbook of Young England, his real heroes, whose virtues he extolled in the *Oxford and Cambridge Review*, were the Whig Earl Grey and the liberal Tory

George Canning. His vote for the repeal of the Corn Law was not his first support of Peelite principles. In 1844 he voted three times against Ashley on factory regulation.[11] There never was much unity among Young England and its allies. In 1844 Lord John Manners denounced a poor-law bill for creating district schools. Education, for Manners, belonged solely to the Church of England. His speech led Milnes to denounce in turn the Church of England for its failures in education, which, he said, should be the business of the state. Milnes, though never a real member of Young England, nevertheless shared both Smythe's laissez faire tendencies and his latitudinarian Anglicanism, and both ended up Liberals. Alexander Baillie Cochrane also went Liberal. Manners, who stayed resolutely Tory, did not always think highly of Cochrane's mind. He was much irked by what he called "the Cimmerian darkness" of Cochrane's "harangues." Milnes was no more pleased with Manners's speeches to the House, seeing in them "an impotent purity that is almost pathetic."[12]

That impotent purity expressed itself in Manners's addiction to ecclesiastical lost causes. He presented bills to establish more national holy days and to reform the law of mortmain. The latter bill, called the Pious Uses and Charities Bill, would allow landowners to bequeath their land to a church, a practice long outlawed by the law of mortmain. It was not an unreasonable reform, but his speeches for it and for more national holy days were so full of talk of almsgiving, monasteries, and church schooling, that the crusty squires, the sharp men of business, and the utilitarian reformers must have viewed them as dreams of "impotent purity." Not even the sturdiest of churchmen, Sir Robert Harry Inglis, supported the Pious Uses Bill. Manners was not the most impressive member of the House. Nor was Monckton Milnes. Disraeli found in Milnes an "insane vanity" and pronounced him "one of the most insignificant members of the House."[13]

All eleven of the romantic paternalists of our group were returned to Parliament in the election of 1847. But, as Disraeli said, the myth had evaporated. The Cambridge University devotees of Digby and Southey now belonged to different parties, were more frequently absent, held more to liberal principles, and often voted differently, though not on the Public Health Act and Henry Halford's Hosiery Bill. None of them supported Halford's efforts in 1848 to protect hosiery workers from exorbitant rents and low payments, and none showed up, on May 18, 1848, to support the Public Health Act. (On May 5 one did support it, Stafford O'Brien.)[14] The Young Englanders now belonged either to the country squires or the Peelites, groups whose members had less fragile visions, though all were wedded to property and many found political economy attractive.

The Pull of Property and the
Attractions of Political Economy

Two of the romantic paternalists emerged after 1846 as leaders of other groups, Stafford O'Brien as a leader of the Irish landowners and Disraeli as a leader of the country squires. This prevented both from becoming advocates of a strong paternal government. Disraeli, an ardent member of the Health of Towns Association before 1846, condemned and voted against the Public Health Act of 1848, while Stafford O'Brien was so attached to the cause of the Irish landowners, of which he was one, that by 1849 he denounced the bill to make the Irish poor law effective and condemned a bill to compensate Irish tenants for the improvements they made on the land they leased. An expanded poor law, said O'Brien, would dry up the landowner's capital. "He could not conceive," he argued, "how Parliament believing in the duty of the rich towards the poor could pass such a bill." Stafford O'Brien, the slayer before Wordsworth at the Lowther Castle charades of the modern idol of mammon, called Parliament's legislative interference to expand the poor law's work during the famine "mischievous." "The only chance of improving the condition of Ireland," he asserted, "was through its landlords."[15] O'Brien reflected the interests of the Irish brigade as Disraeli reflected those of the English squires, and both reflected the interests of landed property. In the debates on Ireland after 1846, they spoke of the duties of property. Indeed in no debate in the 1840s did the doctrine that property had its duties as well as its rights receive more frequent affirmation than in those on the Irish famine. Speech after speech praised the model paternalism of Irish landlords such as Lords Hill, Palmerston, Lansdowne, Londonderry, Waterford, Fitzwilliam, and Sligo, and speech after speech exhorted those who fell short of being model landlords to take better care of their poor. Property, not Irish poor-law boards, must feed the starving. Hence when faced with the stark tragedy of famine, few of the Irish landowners in the Commons or Lords called for a stronger paternal government. The most they did was to vote for Lord George Bentinck's bill to give grants to private companies to build railways in Ireland, another way to aid the poor by aiding property.

Only one Peelite paternalist, Montagu Gore, voted for the grant to Irish railways, while ten voted against it as an unwarranted interference in the economy. The fear of such interference prevented the Peelites from proposing alternative remedies for dealing with the famine. Peel made this fact clear in 1846. He praised the model Irish paternalists and then urged other landowners to build houses and be benevolent, for such reforms "would confer greater benefits in your country than the government or legislature could effect." Sidney Herbert, a landowner in Ireland as well as Wiltshire, and a benevolent and improving one, agreed, as did Lord Lincoln and Edward Cardwell. The Peelite paternalists had a deep attachment to private property. When in 1849 the Irish nationalist Henry Grattan burst forth in indignation against absentee landlords who neither resided on their estates nor cared for the poor, Peel responded by expressing his deep sorrow at such angry outbursts. "I wish to do no violence," he told Grattan, "to the rights of property."[16]

No Peelite ever did, nor did they wish to do violence to the axioms of political economy. Their attachment to both property and political economy laid the basis for a voting pattern that would please the most classical of political economists. Not one Peelite paternalist (in our group) voted for the various bills to protect stocking-frame knitters, lace-mill workers, or tenants in agriculture, and not one voted for loans to Irish landowners, the bill empowering the Railway Commission to review and comment on railway bills, or the bill supporting a government audit of railway companies.[17] Peelite paternalists were, of course, not all alike. They had divided on the ten-hour amendment in 1844 and did so again on the ten-hour bill of 1847. Wortley, Sandon, and Gore had a voting record much less laissez faire than Cardwell, Gladstone, Lincoln, and Herbert, the four most loyal to Peel and to political economy. In 1848 all four voted to repeal the Railway Commission and to end its power to review railway legislation. Lord Lincoln also opposed the Mines Act of 1849, which established an effective mining inspectorate, and Gladstone voted against the 1849 act to mitigate the wretched conditions of merchant seamen. Lincoln said he liked the object of the Mines Act of 1849—to reduce the appalling loss of life from accidents —but as "the representative of the most important mining district in Scotland," he had doubts as to its means. Lord Lincoln knew of the power of constituency. Six times elected county member for South Nottinghamshire, he did not, after his vote to repeal the Corn Law, dare run there again. He ran instead for Falkirk, where he enjoyed the influence exercised by his friend the duke of Hamilton. Winning by only eleven votes he could not again go against the economic interests of his constituency, which in Falkirk were those of the mining lords. Ashley, Acland, and Gladstone, all Peelites, had to give up their constituencies (two county and one market-town borough) and look for more mixed boroughs after their vote for repeal. The economic interests of constituencies counted for much. An overwhelming number of county and small borough representatives voted to keep the Corn Law. Lord John Manners, so very medieval and visionary in his social dreams, was cynical enough to see the part rent rolls played in these matters. He wrote Disraeli in 1849 that the Peel party was at an end and that "many are returning to us." "Party," he concluded, "is merged in property." He did, however, have to confess, "but I can't cover the Bedfordshire Lansdownes by that sentence—to them a Whig government is more than undiminished rent rolls." Manners's letter and Lincoln's votes are remarkably candid confessions that the pull of property proved stronger than those other forces that defined the nature of paternalism.

Supporting this pull were the new and logically attractive doctrines of political economy. Peel, for one, was steeped in them. So was his lieutenant Gladstone. Though early in his career Gladstone had proposed acts regulating railways and coal whippers, he now insisted that free competition was the best regulator of merchant seamen. He also thought free competition the best means to regulate those employed in bakeries, and he opposed a bill to regulate their working conditions. Lord Grosvenor thought him inconsistent. Why, he asked Gladstone, did he want the government to protect coal whippers but not bakers of bread? Gladstone, who at the Board of Trade had learned to apply his subtle and theologically trained Oxford mind to questions of political economy, replied that paying coal whippers in public houses demoralized them and so was a moral, not an economic, question.[18]

Gladstone's reply might not have pleased Lord Grosvenor, but it touched on the Victorians' greater sensitivity to moral evils than to economic exploitation. Stories of naked men in mines and copulating workers in factories were far stronger arguments for governmental interference than mere overwork and low wages. But neither indignation over moral evil nor economic exploitation could offset the pull of property. Lincoln candidly admitted he represented Scottish mine owners as Disraeli admitted privately his loyalty to the mine owner Lord Londonderry. Both voted against the Mines Act of 1849.[19] The country squires, whom Disraeli now led, shared with Peelites like Lincoln and Glad-

stone a high regard for property, particularly landed property, of which
they owned much. The pull of property was more to them by a large
margin than the attraction of political economy. They saw nothing
wrong with corn laws that favored land or with government grants to
Irish railways or with navigation acts protecting English shipping. Their
votes on these issues separated them from the Peelite paternalists. But
they joined Peelites in opposing any attack on landed and commercial
property. Manufacturing property, on the other hand, was to the squires,
as to Coleridge, a different matter. In 1847 eleven of the fifty-eight
M.P.s who supported the hosiery bill were country squires. No Peelite
paternalist, of course, supported this unwarranted violation of economic
laws. Only one squire joined the seventy-seven who defeated it in a thin
House. Seventeen of the squires in the House voted for the ten-hour
Factory Bill of 1847, and not one opposed it. Only two Peelites, Acland,
the fervent admirer of Coleridge, and William MacKinnon, author of a
History of Civilisation, supported it. Six Peelite paternalists opposed it,
along with two Whigs, Baring and Fox Maule, and one romantic, the
cynical Smythe. They were part of but sixty-five M.P.s who stuck by a
policy that was supported by 297 in the 1844 House. None of the ecclesiastical paternalists opposed the ten-hour bill. In 1844 ten squires
from our sample of twenty-five had supported and nine had opposed
Ashley's ten-hour amendment. Now none opposed it.[20] Peel's demand
for a vote of confidence in a Tory ministry in 1844 had had great but
not lasting effect. The theory that the squires voted in 1847 for the ten-
hour act because of their anger over the success of the Anti–Corn Law
League and the betrayal of Peel, is probably exaggerated: the squires
were naturally for regulating manufactures; the artificial and distorting
element came in 1844 with Peel's insistence on loyalty to his ministry.

    Deep in their hearts the country squires did not mind regulating
manufactures. They did, though, object to regulating land. "I oppose,"
said R. A. Christopher in 1849, "all legislative interference between
landlord and tenants." One week after the squires (from our sample)
gave eleven votes for Henry Halford's hosiery bill, they gave eight votes
against and none for Sharman Crawford's bill to guarantee landed
tenants compensation (when their leases ended) for improvements they
had made. Only one of the paternalist squires (in our sample) voted in
1847 for a measure that would require land to do its duty.[21]

    The country squires' attachment to landed property emerged again in
their votes on Irish matters. This fact was particularly evident in their
support of the Irish members' opposition to any poor law requiring

landowners to give more help to the poor. If there must be a poor law, the English and Irish landowners wanted one that made the administrative and rating areas very small, if possible nearly congruent with the landowner's acreage. Stafford O'Brien pleaded in the House for such small areas and used on behalf of his plea the classic argument of paternalism that only in small, circumscribed spheres, where all were intimately and personally known, could benevolence and authority be rightly administered. He persuaded nine of the squires to join seventy-five other M.P.s in support of smaller areas of poor-law administration. None opposed this idea.

The English country squires again joined the Irish landowners in 1849 to protest a poor-law measure that would raise their rates. Ten of them voted against and only two for a measure that would add an extra sixpence on the pound of the Irish poor rate. The extra sixpence per pound was needed for the financing of a £50,000 loan that would immediately relieve some of Ireland's starving peasants. The country squires felt a further sixpence on the pound of landed rentals would threaten property. They resented the fact that it was applied to every electoral division alike no matter what its state of poverty or wealth. They felt it threatened the local landowner's powers. In fact they wanted no legislation. "The government had hurt Ireland," said Dorset's George Bankes in the debate over an additional sixpence charge on the pound of assessed property for the poor rate, "with mischievous legislation."[22] Such legislation as the 1847 Irish Poor Law Bill, which created large administrative units and required relief to all who were destitute, and the 1849 law which imposed a uniform and extra sixpence on the pound of poor-law rates, meant uniformity, centralization, and bureaucracy and struck at those smaller electoral divisions in Ireland that were ruled by local landlords or their agents. It thus struck not only at landed property but at local government.

The Passion for Locality

The squire's attachment to locality was equal to his attachment to property. In the minds of many the two were nearly identical: the property owners were the magistrates and so the rulers of the locality. This local attachment distinguished the country squire paternalist from the Whig and ecclesiastical paternalists and from many, but not all, of the Peelite ones. These differences were rooted both in their social backgrounds and in their constituencies. The social milieu of the Whig and Peelite paternalists was London and the great country houses, and they often represented boroughs under the influence of those houses or the government. The social milieu of the country squire was the squire's park, the local hunt, the agricultural-association dinner, the plowing match, and the petty and quarter sessions. The squires represented the counties or the small boroughs where landlords had great influence, particularly over their dependent leaseholders. These institutions and occasions formed a backdrop different from the Whigs' Bedford House, Holland House, and Stafford House in London, or their Woburn Abbeys, Castle Howards, and Broadlands in the countryside. Stafford House (the Carlton House of today) was particularly preeminent. An invitation to its stately salons was greatly prized by those eminent in science, literature, and politics. The duchess of Sutherland, the sister of Lord Morpeth, presided over the beau monde that assembled there. "She headed," said her biographer, "the philanthropic efforts of the metropolis and willingly joined all schemes for the amelioration of her countrymen."

These varying environments led to differing voting patterns in 1842 and 1847 on the poor law. The staunchest of the squires, Oxfordshire's Henley, Lincoln's Sibthorp, South Leicestershire's Halford, North Durham's Liddell, and North Devon's Buck joined urban radicals like Finsbury's Thomas Wakley and Thomas Duncombe, Oldham's John Fielden and General Johnson, and Rochdale's Sharman Crawford to urge the abolition or the weakening of the Poor Law Commissioners' powers. On the other hand, the Lincolns, Herberts, and Gladstones of the Peelite paternalists joined Whig paternalists like Morpeth, Russell, and Palmerston in defense of that central bureaucracy which, though it meant a stronger government, meant, as Disraeli said, a "weaker society."[23]

The country squires who chose to vote in the rather light divisions on the continuance of the New Poor Law in 1842 and the bill creating the New Poor Law board in 1847 voted in different ways. Only two patterns are discernible in their votes: a hard core of vocal opponents to that centralizing and unconstitutional law, and a group of pragmatic squires who knew the law saved rates and supported the authoritarian and hierarchic structure of rural society. Opponents of the law included Ferrand and Sibthorp, vociferous exponents of the Sadler and Oastler type of paternalism, and Henley, Halford, and Liddell, the crusty, blunt, county type of localists. Those for the New Poor Law in 1842 included men like Sotheron, Tollemache, Pakington, Walsh, and Tyrrell. In 1847 the squires were still divided. But joining Ferrand, Sibthorp, Halford, and Henley as hard-core opponents were Bankes and Floyer, "the Dorsetshire men," and Newdegate, the wild sportsman of Warwickshire. There is no doubt that of the twenty country squires of our sample, men like Bankes and Henley spoke the most vigorously for the rights of their counties and parishes, but they could never persuade the bulk of the country party to end that rate-lowering law. Sir John Pakington still led men like the allotment-developer Tollemache and Wiltshire's Sotheron in support of that law. Even Henley voted in 1847 against Bankes, Ferrand, and Sibthorp on an amendment that would deny the Poor Law Commissioners the right to force on guardians the workhouse test. The mosaic of forces that made up the politics of paternalism was exceedingly intricate and varied. It could vary even within the outlook of the dean of the squires, Joseph Henley. He hated the central commissioners and said in 1848 that "the parochial system" was one from which he "had never been able to see any reason for departing." But he also liked, evidently, the workhouse test, as he upheld the commissioners' right to impose it. The only time the squires acted in unity was in 1847 when they supplied eleven of the fifty-five votes needed to carry Peter Borthwick's amendment ending, for married couples over sixty years old, the Poor Law Commissioners' severe insistence on males and females living in separate quarters. It was a humane amendment from an ex-member of Young England, but not one member of that group or its allies, other than Peter Borthwick himself, bothered to vote for it. One Whig, one Peelite, one churchman from our sample of paternalists helped eleven squires to end this cruel separation.[24]

The New Poor Law presented an ambiguous issue to all paternalists. The law did weaken the prerogatives of locality, but it also defended property from exorbitant rates and systematized the landed classes' control of the poor. The Public Health Act was not so ambiguous—at least to the country squires. In 1848, on two motions, one to postpone the bill indefinitely and the other to reject the clause establishing a central board, eleven of the country squires voted against the bill and none for it. The hard core of localists was again active: Sibthorp, Bankes, Henley, Newdegate, and Floyer, and they were now joined by Walsh and Bennet. Not one squire from our sample of twenty-four supported the act.[25]

Twenty of the twenty-four squires represented rural counties. The Public Health Act was unlikely to touch on their interests, yet their outburst against it was furious: it was despotic, tyrannical, unconstitutional, mere Whig patronage. Not all politics can be resolved into economic self-interest; many political decisions result from previous institutional and cultural conditioning, often an unconscious conditioning. A central board of health would not hurt the country gentleman's income, nor greatly affect the rates he paid, but neither did it seem necessary for solving the problems facing Dorsetshire or Cambridgeshire. It simply brought another intrusion into that local sphere where property, the clergy, and the magistrates performed their duties. The most adamant foe of centralization was the irascible Colonel Sibthorp. He told the House of Commons in 1848 that "he hated commissions, he hated jobs, and he suspected all governments." Sibthorp regarded prison and health inspectors and poor-law and railway commissions as mere disguises for Whig patronage and unconstitutional meddling in local affairs. Dorsetshire's George Bankes, Devonshire's Lewis Buck, and Oxfordshire's Joseph Henley expressed similar feelings. Bankes in 1847 condemned prison inspectors, railway and ecclesiastical commissioners, and poor-law assistants as Whiggish patronage. Buck in 1848 announced that he was "opposed to every kind of commission." And Henley in the same year called the Public Health Act "unconstitutional," "a mass of patronage," and abounding in "novel" and "dangerous" powers.[26] All four of the above would have applauded R. A. Christopher's summation of this matter in 1848: "Centralisation is the great evil!" And all would have agreed with Christopher why it was an evil. It was an evil because it destroyed that feature of the constitution whereby "everyone however humble bore his part . . . and met in boards of guardians . . . those whom it had pleased Providence to place in a better situation than themselves." In 1834 the New Poor Law threatened to incorporate the squire's beloved parishes into the new hateful unions; by 1848 those unions were old and established, and the squires had now become resolved to defend their prerogatives from the encroachments of any new Whiggish commissions, the growth of which they unanimously opposed. In 1848 they voted six for and none against abolishing the Railway Commission, none for and seven against the government providing sites for the Scottish Free Church, and none for and eleven against the Public Health Act.[27]

The paternalist mentality of the country squire was a curious mixture of prejudice, self-interest, local loyalties, and benevolence. They hated the new and the alien, they liked secure rents and low rates, they were jealous of their local prerogatives, and they wanted their own elderly married couples, when in the workhouse, to live together. Colonel

Sibthorp who on the matter of toilets told the House that "he disapproved of the new patent water-closets and much preferred the old system" was deeply bothered that in the present day "change was sought for the sake of change." Change was also usually expensive, and the squires hated rising rates. When Disraeli, bidding for the leadership of the squires, moved for lower expenditures and lower taxes, twenty of the squires from our sample voted for and none against his motion.[28]

Within their localities the squires wished their own class to be sovereign. Seven voted for and two against the Master and Servant Bill of 1844, which would give the magistrates (that is largely themselves, the employers) the right to imprison insubordinate servants. They also voted seven for and one against making all dissenters in their parishes pay church rates, five for and none against capital punishment, four for and none against allowing magistrates to order, without jury trial, the whipping of erring juveniles, four for and none against transporting abroad those who were caught twice stealing dogs, and four for and none against stricter controls of beer shops on Sundays.[29] The number of squires voting in the above six divisions is, of course, not great. The total votes cast by all M.P.s on these minor bills were not large, but the twenty-six-to-three votes on these bills is certainly indicative of an authoritarian outlook, particularly since two of the three antiauthoritarian votes came from Knaresborough's Colonel Ferrand, a man touched with an Oastlerite radicalism, on behalf of the workers. The country squires of pure vintage in fact voted twenty-six for and one against the strong paternal control of dependents.

On these six bills the M.P.s in general voted 519 in favor and 279 opposed. Only the Master and Servant Bill lost, 97 M.P.s voting against it and 54 for it. The Peelite paternalists contributed eighteen votes in favor of these bills and only two votes against them, an expression of authoritarianism the country squires equaled by contributing twenty-six votes in favor of these disciplinary measures and three against. The voting of the churchmen on these six bills was nine for and three against the authoritarian position and the romantics fifteen for and five against. The Whigs of noblesse-oblige persuasion were ten against and eight for the authoritarian positions, seven of the ten votes coming in support of the dissenters' objection to paying church rates, an understandable position as Whigs and dissenters were political allies. These divisions elicited small votes among the M.P.s generally. Though they yield no convincing correlations, they do at least reveal the intricate

patterns and nuances that make up the mosaic of forces behind paternalist politics. They indicate that, though Parliament as a whole voted
less than two to one for these authoritarian measures, the paternalists of
all varieties from our sample voted three to one for them, and if the
Whig paternalists are subtracted, six to one for them.

The squires were the most authoritarian as they were the most dedicated localists, and the correlation is not accidental. The smallest circle
in the social hierarchy of a paternalist society is the family, where the
father enjoys the most local and the most arbitrary of power. The next
circle is the landed estate, and beyond that, or often congruent with it,
the parish—that parish Oxfordshire's Joseph Henley saw no reason to
give up. Beyond that circle came the petty and quarter sessions and
assizes of the magistrates, a circle in which local courts could arrest
Sunday tipplers, vagrants, and blasphemers and order errant juveniles
whipped. A deep attachment to these institutions and to the dominant
classes that controlled them wove itself into a love for the quiet modes of
life and for the bucolic charm of the countryside to form a love of
locality that explains why the old-fashioned paternalism was so hostile
to centralization. It was hostile to it even though the growth of an
industrial and urban society demanded a truly paternal government.

Some of the Peelites realized this fact. Sir Walter James in 1847 told
the House that "the government should follow the course of a truly
paternal one and adopt a wise system of centralisation." It was a
thought repellent to the squires, and even, on occasions, to James's
fellow Peelites, Lincoln, Cardwell, and Sandon, men who usually voted
localist. It was likewise repellent to Peel and Gladstone who, like the
romantics after 1845, seemed strangely absent on these divisions. Centralization was in truth a divisive issue for the Peelite paternalists; so was
religion and for more than Peelites.

The Divisiveness of Religion

The voting record of the thirteen churchmen displays no great coherence
or pattern. Sometimes, to be sure, they did find themselves unanimous,
as on the creation of a bishopric in Manchester, which they all favored.
They, along with various other kinds of paternalists, were also unanimous in 1844 for Ashley's ten-hour amendment, a vote quite in keeping
with their Christian ideals. But on other issues they divided against each
other. They voted five for and three against the Corn Law, three for

and two against creating more bishops, and four for and five against the Maynooth grant. They could more easily unite on factory than on religious issues. Religious issues, in fact, brought a divisive element into the world of paternalism. On the third reading of the Maynooth Bill on May 21, 1845, the issue divided the romantics four for and three against, the churchmen three for and five against, and the squires six for and ten against. The Whig paternalists voted nine for and one against it, and all eleven Peelites supported their leader's measure. Even Gladstone voted for a measure that he had confessed was "in opposition to my own deeply cherished predilections."[30] With such complexities defining a single M.P.'s voting, can the historian ever analyze the influence of social and religious ideas on politics?

Can one even speak of an ecclesiastical paternalism? The answer is yes, but only if it is clear that ecclesiastical ideas varied and that they were weaker than party loyalties. There is no doubt that from the evangelical lords (Ashley, Cowper, and Grosvenor) to the High Churchmen (Inglis and Roundell Palmer) these devout Anglicans believed more deeply in the paternal role of the Church of England than did most M.P.s. But that common piety did not prevent them from dividing on religious issues and yielding to party loyalty on others. Lords Cowper and Grosvenor opposed Plumptre and Inglis on the Corn Law because the former were Whigs and the latter were Tories. Five ecclesiastical paternalists in the House voted to defend the Corn Law in 1846 and only three to repeal it, Ashley being absent because his conscience led him to resign rather than vote for a law that his constituents in Dorsetshire expected him to defend. Ashley's resignation was most exceptional. In the politics of paternalism, party politics, local passions, personal ambition, and economic interests played a far stronger role than sensitivity to social injustice or a sense of equity and fairness. Richard Spooner was a devout and benevolent Christian, quick to defend the poor from the cruel Poor Law Commission, but when confronted by the Public Health Act, a measure that promised so much of benefit to the health of the poor, he could not stifle his hatred of centralization.[31]

Religious loyalty, when tied to established religious institutions, formed a vested interest of its own, one that could even be opposed to the general good. One instance of this was the Church's demand for special privileges in Graham's Factory Education Bill of 1843. The bill called for locally based, rate-supported schools in manufacturing districts. But it tied the public good of such a measure to a vested interest by insisting that all the teachers in these schools and the majority of trustees be of the Church of England. Not even excusing dissenters from Church of England religious instruction could make this Anglican monopoly attractive to those Methodists, Independents, Presbyterians, Baptists, Quakers, Unitarians, Swedenborgians, and freethinkers who quite outnumbered Anglicans in factory towns. Four million signed petitions against the bill, a number so overwhelming Peel withdrew it.[32]

The division between Anglicans and nonconformists was not the only way religion proved divisive in the politics of paternalism. There was even dissension within the Anglicans. Sir Robert Harry Inglis attacked Graham's Factory Education Bill—so favorable to the Church of England—as too secular. High Churchmen and evangelicals could be passionately exclusivist. The evangelicals and squires could also be vehemently anti-Catholic and staunchly Protestant. Such varying passions plagued Disraeli's effort at achieving unity among the protectionists. Such efforts were, said Lord John Manners, disrupted by "this ecclesiastical hubbub," a product of "the Newdegate-Spooner crusade that was being inspired by the Exeter Hall *Herald*."[33]

Religion was too divisive to allow a paternal government to support either an exclusive clerisy in which schools taught but one doctrine, or exchequer grants that helped but one clergy, or a pluralistic clerisy promoting various sectarian schools and churches. The paternalism of the churchmen could no more lay a solid and comprehensive foundation for an effective paternal government than the paternalism of the romantics or the squires.

Whig Commissions

The one variety of paternalism whose social outlook could form the basis of paternal government was the noblesse oblige of the Whig paternalists. These statesmen, many of whom looked down on the world with Olympian benevolence, voted more often than any of the other paternalists in our sample for an effective central government: nine for and one against Maynooth in 1845; eight for and none against a stronger poor law for Ireland in 1849; eight for and none against defending the Railway Commission in 1848; six for and none against and eight for and one against a central poor-law board in 1847; eight for and three against Ashley's 1844 ten-hour amendment; eight for and none against a union rating instead of a parish rating for the support of the poor; and

a resounding twelve for and none against the Public Health Act of
1848.[34] The last vote meant another board and more commissioners and
inspectors. It created, said Sibthorp, more Whig patronage! Sibthorp's
charge was in fact correct; the Whigs loved to establish commissions and
boards. Peelites were not wholly hostile to them, as can be seen in the
Ecclesiastical Commission of 1835, the temporary and investigative
Health of Towns Commission of 1843–1845, and the renewal of the
Poor Law Commission in 1842. But Peel and Lord Lincoln lacked the
boldness to make the Health Commission permanent and supervisory.
Peel was at heart a strong localist. In the early 1840s the Peelites' colleagues were country squires and High Churchmen while the Whigs'
allies were often reformers and dissenters. Allies and colleagues are
powerful in defining policies. The Whigs of the great country and
London houses were keener supporters than the Tories of a paternal
government. This fact was no accident, for the tradition of Shaftesbury,
Fox, and Grey favored change and reform more than the tradition of
Bolingbroke, Castlereagh, and Wellington.

William Aydelotte in his "Voting Patterns in the British House of
Commons in the 1840's" sees no great difference between Whig and
Tory in their votes on social issues. His analysis is careful, quantitative,
and correct, but it is limited to the Parliament that sat from the summer
of 1841 to the summer of 1847. In those years Whigs and Tories did
vote in similar ways on factory bills and poor-law renewals. But the
angry Sibthorp was still right. Most commissions were Whig commissions. Peel's government in the 1840s created no permanent commissions
or boards or inspectorates except a minor commissioner who supervised
the payment of wages to London's coal whippers. Lord Ashley, as a
private member, created an expanded Lunacy Commission and a Mining
Inspectorate, which inspectorate, however, Peel limited to one person.
Ashley had no great faith in Peel's and Graham's administration of social
affairs. "They have," he wrote in his diary in July of 1843, "produced
and carried but few things."

If one widens one's analysis of party action by four years, extending
the period two years before 1841 and two years after 1847, one sees
Whigs establishing the Committee of Council on Education in 1839 and
the General Board of Health in 1848, with all Tories opposing the first
and all protectionists and some Peelites the second. If the perspective is
widened by eighteen years, nine in each direction, one reads of the
Whigs creating the Railway and Poor Law commissions, the Prison,

Factory, Reformatory, and Constabulary inspectorates, and the Merchant Marine Department. They also increased the mining inspectors from one to nine persons and greatly expanded their powers to prevent accidents and improve ventilation and other working conditions.[35] The Whig paternalists constituted the one variety most avowedly in favor of a strong central government.

But were they paternalists—at least paternalists in the older, more traditional sense? In practice, yes. No one can fault the model land-lordism of Palmerston, Morpeth, and Fitzwilliam, nor the rhetoric and ideals in the pamphlets of Slaney, Wyse, Scrope, and Morpeth, early advocates of the duties of property and the mission of the church. But by the 1840s they were having their doubts about the ability of property and the church to meet mounting social evils. The votes of the seventeen Whig paternalists of our group reflect these doubts. Not one of them sided with those romantics, squires, or even Peelites, who, in a series of amendments in 1842 to the Poor Law Renewal Bill, attempted to weaken the central commission and strengthen the local landlord. Their votes for an Irish poor law with large districts in 1847 and in 1849 for a six-pence rate on the pound across the board for Irish poor relief showed they trusted less than did the Peelite Viscount Sandon that Irish landed property would do its duties. Their vote of seven for and none against abolishing ecclesiastical courts, along with their complete opposition to the 1843 pro-Church Factory Education Bill and their failure to produce even one vote for more bishops, also reflects their deepest doubts that the Church of England was the principal vehicle of social and moral reform. None supported the Master and Servant Bill.[36] Instead of voting for more powerful magistrates, more entrenched parishes, more numer-ous bishops, and wealthier and less rated landlords, they voted for more bureaucrats. They did not share Disraeli's fear that the strengthening of government meant the weakening of society, since they had less faith in the ability of that society to cope with the mounting social evils of an industrialized, urbanized, and pauperized England and a famine-stricken Ireland. Such a faith was fast ebbing in the House of Commons, but it still held firm in the House of Lords.

The House of Lords

The greatest landlords in England and the greatest ecclesiastics in the realm sat in the House of Lords. They were the patriarchs of great estates and populous dioceses; in the Lords they served as the hereditary guardians of the welfare of Her Majesty's subjects. Not a few of them were model landlords. As irremovable legislators immune to the vicissitudes of elections, they had an excellent opportunity to fashion a paternal government. They numbered 437, twenty-six of them bishops with an added obligation to look to the moral and spiritual well-being of their pastoral charges. Both lay and ecclesiastical peers had an excellent opportunity to lead in the creation of a truly paternal government.

They did not, however, exploit that opportunity. They had, for one thing, too great a faith in landlords, even when Irish and absentee. Lord Devon, after presiding over a prodigiously comprehensive inquiry into Irish landownership said in 1847, "The landlords of Ireland had . . . in general done their duty," a sentiment echoed by Lord Stanley in 1849, even though there were nearly a million dead of starvation and disease. Lord Stanley then said of Irish landlords, "All of them . . . had a considerable and direct interest in the well-being of the labouring poor." He had confidence in that interest even though he admitted that most of them were absentee. Two years earlier he had declared that property had its duties as well as its rights but had insisted also that "it must be conceded its rights in order to perform its duties," a view Lord Brougham had expressed in a more severe form when he told the Lords that the Irish landlords' "right was a right of perfect obligation and a legal one, whilst their duty was one of imperfect obligation, as moralists call it."[37]

With such proud notions of the "rights" of property it is not to be expected that the lords would welcome the intervention of a meddling bureaucracy. Such meddling, in whatever sphere, whether sanitation, prostitutes, or cockfighting, quite surpassed their basic assumptions and prejudices. "I don't see how it is possible," said the duke of Buccleuch, for the legislature to provide a remedy "for unsanitary housing." The bill to prohibit the use of dogs to pull carts was wrong, said the earl of Malmesbury, because it "laid aside the rights of the proprietors of dogs." The cruelty to animals bill was wrong, said Lord Redesdale, because it would outlaw cockfighting. Prostitution, said the bishop of Exeter, was not a matter for legislation. The mines bill, said Lord Londonderry, was unfair because "some seams of coal required the employment of women." There must be no law against chimney sweeps, said Lord Seagrave, because without them "property in the country would be placed in a state of great danger."[38]

Given such attitudes it is no wonder that the House of Lords not only initiated no single measure to strengthen a paternal government, but succeeded in vetoing bills that would have outlawed the use of young boys as chimney sweeps, guaranteed tenants compensation for improvements, and prohibited the employment of dogs to pull carts. The Lords amended Ashley's mines bill, reducing the age below which children could not be employed from fourteen years to ten years and preserving that system of apprenticeship which many critics found not far removed from slavery. Lord Ashley complained that the Lords had "invalidated the principle of the bill."[39]

The Lords' rhetorical flourishes were not in the 1840s of great importance, and their vetoes of bills on dog carts and allotments did not prevent the passage of the Public Health Act or the repeal of the Corn Law. They certainly did not welcome these advances. Until Wellington and Peel used the influence of the Conservative government to force through the repeal of the Corn Law, no more than six lords had ever voted at one time for its repeal.[40]

Patriarchal attitudes were powerful in the House of Lords, but they led to no move for a more paternal government. In the 1840s the House of Lords took no initiative in the field of social reform. Such initiatives came instead from the House of Commons.

Paternalism as a social outlook was ill suited to be a positive force in Parliament. It was too complex, varied, and tied to different interests; its concept of "paternal government" was too local and personal; its desire for a stronger monarchy was too romantic, its passion for an educating government too weak and too exclusively Anglican, and its desire for a disciplining one, too authoritarian for a liberal age. It was an outlook too attached to old ways to inspire national poor laws, public health acts, and education measures. In a House of Commons that since 1832 had represented manufacturing boroughs and ten-pound householders and in a society of Anti–Corn Law Leagues, mechanics' institutes, athenaeums, and more and more nonconformists, it could hardly form the basis of a majority party. These ideas could not even sustain Ashley's ten-hour amendment to the 1844 factory bill. Gladstone would not even resign to defend the amendment, though he would over a grant to a Catholic college in Ireland.

In Gladstone's political priorities, as in those of most others, paternalist sentiments rated only second, third, or lower. This fact explains the paradox that paternalism could be at once so popular and yet be so weak as a constructive political force. It was a pervasive but shallow sentiment because it was only part, and that a lesser part, of men's outlooks. It formed but one strand of Gladstone's complex views, just as it was only a part of the outlook of the Whig Lord Morpeth, the churchman John Colquhoun, and the squire Joseph Henley. It even proved to be but one strand, and that exaggerated, for those stalwart Young Englanders, George Smythe and Baillie Cochrane. And for Disraeli was it much more than another of his colorful garbs to be worn on apt occasions? To ask such is not so much to doubt Disraeli's sincerity as to point out that paternalist sentiments were within individuals, as within groups, only a part of an intricate and complicated combination of ideas, prejudices, and interests, a combination in which paternalism had to compete with some powerful forces. Above all it had to face the pressures of the M.P.s' constituencies, their own economic interests, and their religious passions. It also had to vie with party loyalties and personal political ambitions. It is not, then, surprising that in such a competition the advocacy of paternalist ideas rated only a second, third, or lower priority.

Social ideals, of whatever kind, seldom form the main passions behind politics—except perhaps negatively. Paternalism in particular did not because as a social philosophy it was itself too mixed and varied. Some viewed it as property performing its duties, some as the church carrying out its mission, and others as the firm rule of local government or the exalted role of monarchy. Within these aspects there were more nuances: for some landed property was superior to manufacturing property, and for others the clergyman was quite superior to the layman as a visitor to the poor. Since paternalism meant different things to different men, it became popular in many different circles. But its diversity and amorphousness also made it even more likely that, in competition with other more explicit interests and opinions, it would not be a first priority. Such a social philosophy is not likely to inspire positive and constructive legislation.

It certainly did not do so in the politics of the 1830s and 1840s. Those two decades saw the origins of a state that took a greater interest in the welfare of its citizens than ever before, but in that evolution paternalism played a minor role.

Conclusion

The many ideas that constituted the paternalist outlook of the early Victorians had a wide and varied history. That outlook was not merely the subject matter of intellectual discussion but was at work on landed estates and in cotton mills, in vestry and county meetings, at Parliament and in the courts, with journalists of all kinds and clergymen of every faith. It inspired the lady bountiful to organize clothing clubs and masters of households to rule their servants firmly. It informed the reports of Her Majesty's factory, poor-law, prison, and education inspectors and influenced the administration of workhouses, prisons, hospitals, and schools of every kind. It was the most universal of social attitudes.

Neither progressive or innovative about social problems nor particularly logical, it owed its universal acceptance to qualities rather the opposite—to its caution, its respect for old ways, its generality and adaptability, its lack of profundity and subtlety, and its plain dictums and homespun truths, dictums and truths as varied as the immemorial customs and entrenched institutions to which they were attached. The paternalist outlook was to the early nineteenth century what the free-enterprise ideology was to the early twentieth century: a powerful ideology, widely held, important in politics, connected with vested interests, socially and economically useful, safely conventional, much esteemed, respectable, but in the face of disturbing challenges, defensive, inept, anachronistic. Both the paternalism of the 1840s and the free-enterprise outlook of the 1930s faced problems they could not solve; yet so in-

269

extricable a part of society were both outlooks that they could not be discarded.

Both social outlooks—outdated in so many ways and yet so useful and prevalent—must be understood in terms of the institutions they reflected and the functions they performed. To understand, for example, how the free-enterprise orthodoxy of the 1930s, with its celebration of self-reliance, harmonious economic laws, and the gold standard persisted during a period of depression, unemployment, currency devaluations, and a turn to government controls and subsidies, one must realize how deeply rooted those ideas were in the leaders of finance, trade, and industry, whether the president of a great city bank or the owner of a neighborhood grocery, or in the members of those allied institutions of newspapers, magazines, chambers of commerce, manufacturing associations, advertising firms, London clubs, private schools, and voluntary charities. Nearly a century of economic prosperity had taught the members of these institutions to talk confidently of wise economic laws and of the poor raising themselves up by self-help.

In much the same way, to understand how the paternalist orthodoxies of the 1840s persisted during a period of rapid industrial and urban growth, economic crises, unemployment, rural pauperism, rising crime, Irish famines, cholera epidemics, drunkenness, and Chartism, one must realize the power of landlords on their estates, magistrates at their petty and quarter sessions, the rural clergy superintending their parishes and schools, the lesser squires and farmers at their vestries and boards of guardians, and all meeting together in agricultural societies and the county militia. And besides these powerful rural institutions there existed model factories, town councils, cathedral chapters, and urban charities, institutions still paternalist when located in small towns, since in smallness lay the key to paternalism.

Only in small spheres defined by personal relations, those in which most persons were known to each other, could human beings be held together by the reciprocal bonds of authority and deference and by clearly defined rights and duties. Burke, Coleridge, and Southey had all insisted on this point, as did Arnold, Sadler, Oastler, Seeley, Sewell, Helps, and the reviewers of the *Quarterly, Blackwood's,* and *Fraser's.* These were the spheres in which property was sovereign, authority and hierarchy secure, and the whole held together organically by personal relations.

The existence of well-defined personal relations formed the cement of paternalism. It was a cement that could not withstand large-scale urbanization, central bureaucracies, and diffuse philanthropy nor the individualism, egalitarianism, and democracy so rudely asserted by the lower-middle and working classes. Only where there were well-defined personal relations could landlords, clergymen, magistrates, and mill-owners exercise a truly fatherly authority and the tenants, laborers, and parishioners show a proper deference. This personal relationship was not intimate. It seldom even involved acquaintanceship. The earl of Chichester did not move in the circles of Charles Thomas and William Gain, both of whom he sentenced to jail, yet he pronounced Thomas "a wicked, bad lad" and Gain "of excellent character." He knew of them, of their circumstances, reputations, and past history, just as Henry Ashworth at his New Eagley mill and the Reverend Charles Jerram in his parish of Witney knew of, or learned of, their operatives and parishioners. These dependents did not dine with Chichester, Ashworth, or Charles Jerram—the very idea was unthinkable—but they knew of them and were in awe of them, an awe that arose from living in a neighborhood where people recognized each other and their respective roles.

These small spheres, these neighborhoods, rested on the rule of property, whether as a source of wealth for landlords, manufacturers, clergymen, and charity trustees, or as the necessary qualification for becoming a lord lieutenant, magistrate, or alderman. The paternalism of church and local government was thus a part of the paternalism of property. Property was crucial. It carried with it many rights though it also, in theory, involved as many duties, the rights and duties together constituting a myriad of quasi-private governments, on estates, in parishes, in towns, all deeply jealous of the intervention of a central government.

Yet the central government also had its role to play, ambiguous, limited, and ill suited to the criterion of smallness as it was. Paternalists did plead for a stronger monarchy, did on occasion denounce the excessive competition and individualism of laissez faire economics, and did join Lord Ashley in demanding factory and mining acts. On the basis of these pleas, denunciations, and demands, later historians have built a tradition of Tory paternalism as a principal source of the welfare state. It is a tradition with no great substance. The plea for a strong monarchy by Coleridge, Southey, Disraeli, and Sewell was largely rhetoric, a rhetoric that no Tory prime minister would have dared put into practice. The frequent denunciations of laissez faire principles arose from a fear of excessive social and political individualism and a distaste for the calculating ethics of the utilitarians more than from a dislike of the workings of a free market. And though many paternalists supported Ashley's mining bill and ten-hour amendment, the former was severely weakened by a Tory House of Lords and the latter defeated by Peel's Tory government. Adequate mining inspection and a ten-hour day had to await Whig governments, as did sanitary reforms and greater efforts to promote education.

That Tory paternalists in the age of Peel created a strong, intervening, protecting central government is a myth. Not until the late 1870s, with Disraeli's measures for sanitary and factory consolidations and for housing, did that tradition gain substance, and then, according to Paul Smith, in *Disraelian Conservatism and Social Reform,* only a modest substance, since these social reforms emerged largely from bureaucratic processes long underway. Disraeli, always politically astute, knew of the value of social reform, particularly since the 1867 Reform Act forced the Conservatives to compete for the votes of the working classes. In Disraeli's sanitary and factory consolidations and housing measure, the Conservative party first expressed in action a belief in the paternalism of a strong central government. It was the beginning of a tradition that Lord Salisbury, Neville Chamberlain, and Harold Macmillan carried on, though again with as much rhetoric as substance.

The tradition also grew strong among intellectuals. From Thomas Carlyle and John Ruskin in the mid-nineteenth century to Alfred Cobban and R. J. White in the mid-twentieth, intellectuals have exaggerated Coleridge's and Southey's calls for government intervention, celebrated too uncritically Disraeli's humanitarian fervor, overlooked Carlyle's confusions and ineffectiveness, and forgotten Lord Ashley's lonely plight in the 1840s as a social reformer. No Conservative government until Disraeli's in the 1870s sponsored legislation that would significantly strengthen the state as the protector of the poor.

That they did not do so is in part because paternalism of the 1840s had no clear, explicit, and unambiguous formula for urban and industrial problems. It was never a neat package. Not only was it ambivalent about what it meant by a paternal government, but it could and did incorporate within itself the tenets of other social outlooks. John Croker of the *Quarterly* could incorporate the entirety of political economy into his paternalism as easily as Lord Ashley and Lord Morpeth could incorporate the idea of an enlarged philanthropy and a reforming government into theirs. Adding even more complexity was the fact that such rival social theories as the Whigs' belief in a laissez faire society, the evangelicals' zeal for philanthropy, and the utilitarians' insistence on a reforming government, could include within themselves elements of paternalism. The Whig Nassau Senior, in the *Edinburgh Review,* a journal second to none in preaching political economy, urged Irish landlords to solve Irish ills by a more paternal care of dependents. The Quaker William Allen, editor and publisher of the *Philanthropist,* ran his community near Brighton on strictly paternalist lines—as did Robert Owen his communities. The utilitarian Edwin Chadwick, unstinting in the espousal of centralization, still wanted local government to be based more on the rights and duties of property than on the democratic doctrine of one man, one vote. Social outlooks in early Victorian England were not as coherent and self-contained as pictured by the polemics of the time or the dramatizations of later historians. They were instead made up of varying combinations of diverse attitudes. The defining element of a person's outlook was not an exclusive doctrine but those particular attitudes that were paramount. If, when confronting social problems, one turned to property, church, and locality to perform their duties within a circumscribed sphere where authority and hierarchy ruled, then one was a paternalist—though being so did not preclude preaching individual self-reliance, urging a "live and let live" economic policy, giving money to urban philanthropies, and supporting factory and mining acts; that is, as long as these last actions did not become paramount. In the 1840s they did become paramount for many of the English governing classes, and to that degree their social outlook became less paternalist. For others property, church, and locality remained paramount, and their social outlook intrepidly paternalist. The difference in these two responses often arose from different opinions as to how effective paternalism was in the 1840s.

Just how effective paternalism was in the 1840s is not an easy question to answer. Its promises and its claims so often exceeded its actual benevolence and efficiency that there is a temptation to dismiss it as rhetoric. To do so, however, would be to overlook the degree to which it was, in fact, functional.

It was certainly functional for the model paternalist, for the duke of Bedford and the earl of Carlisle among peers, Sir John Boileau and Sir Henry Bunbury among squires, Titus Salt and Samuel Greg among millowners, and the reverends Charles Jerram and W. F. Hook among the clergy. These men, and many others just as conscientious and attentive, created in their neighborhoods an ordered and secure social world, a world of steady employment, well-built cottages, coal and clothing clubs, well-administered poor laws, good schools, field gardens, savings societies, and for the operatives of mills, reading rooms and libraries. Many of these institutions, of course, reflected conventional responses of a pedestrian sort, and it would be inaccurate to exaggerate the warmth and benevolence of these worlds, particularly where landlords and mill-owners were often absent and the clergymen too busy. But there were those happy moments that counted, the visit of the duke and duchess of Norfolk to the school with gifts of "hats, bonnets, and frocks," the seasonal benevolences, the roasted ox and free ale at Christmas, the picnic on the earl of Carlisle's estate, the plowing contests with the squire presiding, cricket matches, and even May Day festivities, or in urban environments the Sunday school's annual boat ride with owners of Liverpool's North Shore Mill. A later age may scoff at the condescension that marked these fetes, but to their unsophisticated participants they were just those rituals that, along with steady work and well-built cottages, assured them that they belonged to a community, one in which they would be cared for, if not well, at least adequately, and one in which they felt that they, and others, had an assured place.

Just how many landlords, millowners, and clergymen were as conscientious as Carlisle, Salt, and Jerram is not known. Model paternalists no doubt formed a small minority. But the more research I did into paternalism the larger the minority became, my study of paternalist M.P.s revealing many model landlords overlooked in writing the chapter on "Land and Its Duties." Like the tip of an iceberg, the number of known model paternalists forms but the visible part of a larger mass.

The same metaphor may hold true for the oppressive landlords, the cruel millowners, and the harsh clergymen. They too formed a minority, though from the evidence of royal commissions, select committees, and government inspectors a rather larger minority, a larger tip of a larger iceberg.

In between these two minorities were a vast number of landlords, millowners, and clergymen; landlords of every kind, inefficient, forgetful, absent, but no rack renters or demolishers of cottages; millowners also of varied sorts, some negligent and indifferent, others stern and demanding, but not cruel and exploitive; and clergymen of many kinds, solemn, amiable, lazy, charitable, pedestrian, pompous, but not distinguished by unusual conscientiousness or hard selfishness. These many types, along with sanctimonious magistrates, partially literate poor-law guardians, wooden schoolmasters, insecure shopkeepers, and braggadocian workhouse governors, formed the vast and serried ranks of working paternalists that performed their duties within their allotted sphere with neither saintly benevolence nor villainous oppression, but with varying degrees of perfunctoriness.

Paternalism was indeed well suited to the perfunctory, and in that lay much of its usefulness. Its authoritarianism meant control and order, if not the most perfect of worlds; its insistence on hierarchy assured each a place and an identity, if not equality; and its aspirations for organic unity made many an estate, village, parish, mill, or shop a place somewhat warmer and more personal to live and work in, if not free of suffering and injustice. Paternalism brought an ordered, not an ideal, life to those many small spheres that made up much of English society. Paternalism as a functioning system was no myth. That it was everywhere benevolent is, of course, a myth. But then the essence of paternalism to the early Victorian was not benevolence as much as it was control, guidance, superintendence, and in this respect paternalism throughout the 1840s was, as a mode of social organization, exceedingly functional.

It was also functional in providing an intellectual theory that helped make some sense of a society that was experiencing bewildering changes. The English governing classes not only had to manage estates, parishes, mills, and quarter sessions but develop a basic social theory, however rudimentary, that would, in a decade of economic crises, Chartist riots, Irish famines, and burgeoning cities full of crime and disease, assure one of the rightness of things, particularly old things. Bombarded on every side by endless publications trumpeting natural rights, utilitarian ethics, political economy, anti-corn-law tirades, and French socialism, many needed some theory, if only one that dressed up old dictums and homespun truths in the more elegant dress of medieval ideals, Wordsworthian intuitions, and religious earnestness. The governing classes in reading *Blackwood's, Fraser's,* and the *Quarterly* received those assurances. The reviewers of these journals knew how to satisfy the intellectual aspect of practical men since to a great extent their own ruminations about social philosophy arose from their own intellectual needs to interpret a world turbulent with intellectual and social change. The response of these reviewers to this turbulent world was greatly influenced by reading Burke, Coleridge, Scott, and Southey in their youth and in the 1840s the writings of Arnold, Sewell, Seeley, Sadler, Helps, and Carlyle. In the writings of these theorists and their popularizers a rhetoric of paternalism was evolved that incorporated some of the most powerful intellectual developments of the age: romanticism, religious seriousness, historical scholarship, the cult of the medieval, and other idealistic reactions to the latitudinarianism of the eighteenth century and the mechanistic calculations of nineteenth-century political economy and utilitarianism. The theorists and popularizers of paternalist ideas gave to those ideas a relevance, coherence, and sense of urgency that enabled many practical men of the governing class to meet the doubts within their own minds about the society in which they lived. It also gave them answers for those in their social circles who espoused political economy, radicalism, or the virtues of centralization. Paternalism for the governing classes was functional in two ways, as a useful way of managing estates, parishes, and mills and as a satisfying way of making sense of a society full of intellectual and social changes. Paternalism thus dovetailed two powerful strands of the early Victorian age, the practical need to manage social affairs and the intellectual need for a theory of society. Such a fusion of functions explains why so many early Victorians, ranging from philosophers like Carlyle to politicians like Peel, persisted in advocating paternalism as an answer to all social problems, even for those new ones it was so tragically ill suited to confront.

These new social problems tended to be urban ones. Their newness was often a matter of the degree of their intensity—of a higher crime rate, greater drunkenness, more concentrated prostitution, more congested slums—or they seemed new and more formidable because they fell outside the ministrations of older paternal authorities—belonging to that wilderness of destitution, ignorance, homelessness, and delinquency that marked Whitechapel, St. Giles, and Bethnal Green. But even in rural areas social problems were becoming too formidable for paternalism. Old ways seemed no longer to work. Pauperism increased with the expansion of population, railways brought greater mobility to those in the countryside, seaports, watering places; rural manufactures brought urban problems to rural counties, and most dangerously, brought new expectations, cheaper newspapers, radical ideas, Chartist emissaries. Benign rectors and well-wishing squires could no longer meet these growing pressures. Perhaps they might have, as their forefathers did, simply let them fester, except that new class changes would not allow it.

The growth of self-conscious middle and working classes posed a second and even greater challenge to the viability of paternalism. Many manufacturers and merchants, to be sure, ran their firms on paternalist lines, but in their philosophical societies, athenaeums, chapels, town

councils, and many and varied periodicals, they espoused an individualistic morality, a laissez faire economics, a political egalitarianism, and a
religious voluntarism that fitted ill with the deferential and hierarchic
structure of a paternal society. The urban working classes were an even
greater threat. Trade unionists, Chartists, readers of the radical press,
socialists, all were defiant of authority's demand for deference. But perhaps even more dangerous in the long run were those self-educated
artisans, the frequenters of Methodist chapels, mechanics' institutes,
debating societies, whose upward mobility produced a proud artisan
class, one that would later win the vote, form model unions, and bargain collectively with its masters. Deep class changes and urgent social
problems combined to place an enormous strain on old paternalist ideas.

Mid-century intellectual developments formed a third force making a
locally useful and aesthetically satisfying philosophy of paternalism ill
suited to the pressures of national problems. The romanticism, religious
seriousness, and medievalism of the 1820s, 1830s, and early 1840s had
abated considerably by the late 1840s. Charles Dickens, not Sir Walter
Scott, became the great novelist, evangelicalism grew stale, the Oxford
movement dangerous, and agnosticism more respectable, while the passion for historical scholarship outgrew its tendency to glorify medieval
times. Science, rationalism, empiricism, a belief in progress, all laid the
basis for a new intellectual age.

These ideas were also reflective of that prosperity and ordered life
which dominated Victorian England from 1848 to 1900. This prosperity
and order, more than new social problems, class changes, and intellectual
developments, weakened paternalism since it made a belief in a laissez
faire society a viable social theory. The severe economic depressions of
1839–1842 and 1847 raised doubts about leaving all to the free and
harmonious working of economic laws, just as the dismal conditions of
rural England and the hopeless squalor of urban slums made the preaching of self-reliance as an answer to social problems a mockery. But after
1850 harmonious economic laws did work, and two decades of prosperity made self-help and self-reliance the best way of overcoming—at
least for the more active individual—pauperism and squalor. The ad hoc
growth of a large central administration and the flourishing of philanthropy also took the biting edge off the worst incidents of suffering and
so allowed (a bit paradoxically) the proponents of the laissez faire
society to translate its free-enterprise ideology into a new orthodoxy.

Paternalism had increasingly failed to meet the new problems of an urban and industrial age, to accommodate the new middle and urban classes, to base itself on the intellectual assumptions of science and progress, but until prosperity and order were part of everyday life and until the governing class could be persuaded of the virtues of science, progress, and individualism—until, that is, it could be convinced of a new orthodoxy—it still had to hold firm to an ideology whose intellectual antecedents ran back to medieval times and whose reality lay in its firm connections with those local institutions and customs that had for so long proven functional.

Paternalist M.P.s

The 80 M.P.s listed below spoke often in Parliament on behalf of the paternalist outlook. Many of them also spoke and wrote for that outlook outside Parliament, and many on their estates and as magistrates sought to carry out those ideals. Their speeches, writings, votes, and activities form the basis for the analysis of the politics of paternalism in chapters nine and ten.

Since they differed in quite significant ways they have been grouped into six categories: romantics, Peelites, churchmen, country squires, Whigs, and Anglo-Irish. Selected biographical references have been included for all but two of the eighty paternalists. The many references to the *Dictionary of National Biography* (*DNB*) and to Frederick Boase, *Modern British Biography* (Boase) will supply further information. All eighty of the M.P.s appear, of course, in Charles Dod, *The Parliamentary Companion*.

The Romantics

1. Henry James Baillie (Boase, 4:228).
2. Peter Borthwick (*DNB,* 5:409; Boase, 1:343; Cyrus Redding, *Recollections,* 3:71–74; Reginald Lucas, *Lord Glenesk,* pp. 35–47).
3. Alexander Baillie Cochrane (*Men of the Times,* 1872, p. 231; *DNB,* first supplement, 2:137).
4. Quintin Dick (Boase, 5:98).
5. Benjamin Disraeli (*DNB,* 15:101; Blake, *Disraeli*).

6. Henry Hope (Blake, *Disraeli*, p. 167).
7. Lord John Manners (*DNB*, 36:48; Whibley, *Lord John Manners*).
8. Richard Monckton Milnes (*DNB*, 38:18; T. W. Reid, *R. M. Milnes*; Pope-Hennessy, *Monckton Milnes*).
9. Augustus Stafford O'Brien (Boase, 3:699).
10. George Sydney Smythe (*DNB*, 53:193).
11. David Urquhart (*DNB*, 58:43; Boase, 3:1,068).

The Peelites

1. Sir Thomas Dyke Acland (Acland, *Thomas Acland; DNB*, first supplement, 1:12; Boase, 1:11).
2. Edward Cardwell (Erickson, *E. Cardwell; DNB*, 9:43; Boase, 1:542).
3. Lord Francis Egerton (*DNB*, 17:153; Falk, *Bridgewater Millions*; Beechey, *Two Sermons on Francis Egerton*).
4. Bickham Sweet Escott (Boase, 1:997).
5. William Gladstone (*DNB*, first supplement, 2:280; Boase, 5:418; Magnus, *Gladstone*).
6. Montague Gore (*DNB*, 22:239; Boase, 1:1,184).
7. Sidney Herbert (*DNB*, 26:212).
8. Sir Walter James.
9. Henry Pelham Clinton, earl of Lincoln (*DNB*, 11:98; Boase, 2:116; Martineau, *The Life of Henry Pelham, Fifth Duke of Newcastle*).
10. William Alexander Mackinnon (*DNB*, 35:172; Boase, 2:641).
11. Philip Henry Stanhope, Viscount Mahon (*DNB*, 54:37; Newman, *The Stanhopes of Chevening*).
12. Roundell Palmer (*DNB*, 43:150; Palmer, *Memorials*).
13. Sir Robert Peel (*DNB*, 44:210; Gash, *Mr. Secretary Peel*).
14. Dudley Ryder, Viscount Sandon (*DNB*, 50:42; *Men of the Times, 1872*, p. 462; Ryder, *Ryder Family Papers*).
15. John Stuart-Wortley (*DNB*, 55:113; Wharncliffe Papers).

The Churchmen

1. Charles Bowyer Adderley (*Men of the Times, 1862; DNB*, second supplement, 1:17; Childe-Pemberton, *Life of Lord Norton*).
2. Anthony Ashley Cooper, Lord Ashley (*DNB*, 12:111; Best, *Shaftesbury*).

3. Edward North Buxton (Boase, 1:504).
4. John Campbell Colquhoun (*DNB*, 11:403; Boase, 1:686).
5. William Francis Cowper (*DNB*, first supplement 2:74; Cowper-Temple, *Memorials*).
6. Lord Robert Grosvenor (*DNB*, first supplement, 2:368; Bligh, *Lord Ebury*).
7. Sir Robert Harry Inglis (*DNB*, 29:6; *Christian Observer*, July 1865, pp. 522–527, August 1865, pp. 610–619).
8. Edward John Littleton (*DNB*, 33:369).
9. Forster Alleyne Mc Geachey (Boase, 2:601; *Times*, March 20, 1887).
10. John Pemberton Plumptre (Boase, 6:407; James and Hoare, *Two Sermons Following the Funeral of John P. Plumptre*).
11. Richard Spooner (Boase, 3:691; *Men of the Times*, 1862, p. 720).
12. Lord Dudley Stuart (*DNB*, 55:76).
13. William Page Wood (*DNB*, 62:380; Stephens, *A Memoir of the Right Hon. William Page Wood, Baron Hatherley*).

The Country Squires

1. George Bankes (*DNB*, 3:120; Boase, 1:151; V. Bankes, *A Dorset Heritage*).
2. Philip Bennet (Venn and Venn, *Alumni Cantabrigienses*, 1:229).
3. Lewis William Buck (Boase, 1:460).
4. Edward Stillingfleet Cayley (Boase, 1:577; *Farmer's Magazine*, August 1844, pp. 81–84).
5. Robert Adam Christopher (*Stamford Mercury*, August 13, 1847; Boase, 1:617).
6. William Busfield Ferrand (Boase, 5:288).
7. John Floyer (Boase, 1:1,072; *Dorset Chronicle*, July 14, 1877).
8. Sir Henry Halford (Boase, 1:1,280; J. Foster, *Alumni Oxonienses*, vols. 1–2, p. 586; Foster's *Baronetage*).
9. John Heathcot (M.P. for Tiverton, 1832–1859).
10. Sir William Heathcot (Boase, 1:1,413; Benn, 2:315).
11. Joseph Warner Henley (Boase, 1:1,428; *Men of the Times*, 1872; *St. James's Magazine* 4(1870):771; *DNB*, 25:416).
12. Sir William George Hylton Jolliffe (*Men of the Times*, 1862, p. 429; *DNB*, 30:89).
13. Henry Thomas Liddell (*DNB*, 33:222; Boase, 6:53; Venn and Venn, 3:169).

14. William Miles (Boase, 2:873; *Men of the Times*, 1872, p. 681).
15. Charles Newdigate Newdegate (*DNB*, 40:329; *Bailey's Monthly Magazine of Sports and Pastimes* 47(1887):347).
16. Sir John Somerset Pakington (*DNB*, 43:94; *Men of the Times*, 1872; Turberville, *Worcestershire in the Nineteenth Century*, pp. 293–315).
17. Charles de Laet Sibthorp (*DNB*, 52:188; Boase, 3:566; Foster, vols. 3–4, p. 1,294).
18. Thomas Henry Sutton Sotheron (*DNB*, 18:11).
19. John Tollemache (Boase, 3:982; Tollemache, *The Tollemaches of Helmingham and Ham*).
20. Sir John Trollope (*Stamford Mercury*, August 6, 1847).
21. Sir John Tyssen Tyrrell (Boase, 3:1,062; Venn and Venn, 6:262).
22. Sir Richard Rawlinson Vyvyan (Boase, 3:1,117; *DNB*, 58:399; Bradfield, "Sir Richard Vyvyan and Tory Politics").
23. Sir John Benn Walsh (*DNB*, 59:216).
24. Sir Henry Pollard Willoughby (Boase, 3:1,393; Foster, vols. 3–4, p. 1,578).

The Whigs

1. Sir Francis Thornhill Baring (*DNB*, 3:193; Boase, 2:1,174; Baring, *Journals and Correspondence from 1808–1852*).
2. Hugh Fortescue, Viscount Ebrington (*DNB*, second supplement, 2:41).
3. Sir George Grey (*DNB*, 23:183; Boase, 1:1,241; Creighton, *Sir George Grey*).
4. Henry George Grey, Viscount Howick (*DNB*, first supplement, 2:361; Boase, 5:505; Trevelyan, *Lord Grey and the Reform Bill*).
5. Granville George Leveson-Gower, Lord Leveson (*DNB*, 33:150; Leveson-Gower, *Letters of Harriet Countess Granville*; Fitzmaurice, *The Life of Granville*).
6. Fox Maule (*DNB*, 37:85).
7. William Thomas Spencer Fitzwilliam, Lord Milton (*DNB*, 19:224; Ward, "The Earls Fitzwilliam and the Wentworth Woode-house Estate").
8. George William Frederick Howard, Lord Morpeth (*DNB*, 28:19; Lonsdale, *Worthies of Cumberland*, 3:125–163; Gaskin, *The Vice-regal Speeches . . . of the Late Earl of Carlisle*; Maud, Lady Leconfield, *Three Howard Sisters*).

9. Henry John Temple, Lord Palmerston (*DNB*, 56:16; Jasper Ridley, *Lord Palmerston*).
10. Lord John Russell (*DNB*, 49:454; Boase, 3:343; Prest, *Lord John Russell*; MacCarthy and Russell, *Lady John Russell*).
11. George Julius Poulett Scrope (*DNB*, 51:135; Boase, 3:465; *Men of the Times*, 1872; Scrope, *Memoir of the Life of Lord Sydenham*).
12. Robert A. Slaney (*DNB*, 52:367; Boase, 3:602).
13. Robert Vernon Smith (*DNB*, 52:116; Smith, *Early Writings of Robert Percy Smith*).
14. Edward John Stanley (*DNB*, 54:64; Boase, 3:707; Mitford, *The Ladies of Alderley; Register and Magazine of Biography*, June 1869; *Men of the Times*, 1862, p. 724).
15. Lord Harry George Vane (*Durham Chronicle*, June 25, 1841, August 6, 1847).
16. Sir Harry Verney (*DNB*, 58:263; Boase, 3:1,089; *The Monthly Record of Eminent Men*, September 1890, p. 214).
17. Thomas Wyse (*DNB*, 63:272; Boase, 3:548; Saunders, *Portraits of Reformers*, pp. 94ff.).

The Anglo-Irish

1. Sir Henry Winston Barron (Boase, 1:179).
2. William Smyth Bernard, Viscount Bernard (Boase, 1:257).
3. Charles Skeffington Clements (Boase, 4:686).
4. Edward Michael Conolly.
5. William Henry Gregory (*DNB*, first supplement, 2:355).
6. Lord Claud Hamilton (Boase, 1:1,299).
7. George Alexander Hamilton (*DNB*, 24:158; Boase, 1:1,301).
8. Henry Arthur Herbert (Boase, 1:1,439–1,440).
9. Sir Joseph Napier (*DNB*, 40:65).
10. John Dawson Rawdon (Boase, 3:50).
11. Hugh Morgan Tuite (Boase, 6:715).
12. Sir William Verner (Boase, 3:1,089).

Notes

Introduction

1. Brian Tierney, *Medieval Poor Law*, p. 109.
2. St. Thomas More, *Utopia*, pp. 21–27.
3. Arthur Ferguson, *The Articulate Citizen and the English Renaissance*, pp. xiii, 3–4, 26, 42–43, 135, 137, 148.
4. Sir Thomas Elyot, *The Book Named The Governor*, pp. 1–2.
5. Thomas Starkey, "A Dialogue between Cardinal Pole and Thomas Lupset," 2:cxxix; Ferguson, *Articulate Citizen*, p. 371.
6. William Dunham and Stanley Pargellis, *Complaint and Reform in England, 1436–1714*, pp. 196–198.
7. Elyot, *The Governor*, pp. xiii, 14.
8. Ferguson, *Articulate Citizen*, p. 264.
9. G. R. Elton, *England Under the Tudors*, p. 185.
10. More, *Utopia*, pp. 52–53; J. H. Hexter, "Utopia and Its Historical Milieu," 4:xxiii–cxxxiv.
11. David Willson, *King James VI and I*, p. 131.
12. Hugh Trevor Roper, *Archbishop Laud, 1573–1645*, p. 166.
13. Lord Bolingbroke, *The Works of Lord Bolingbroke*, 4:401; Isaac Kramnick, *Bolingbroke and His Circle*, pp. 92, 215, 221.
14. Bolingbroke, *Works*, 4:61, 152, 165, 166, 548; Kramnick, pp. 65, 69, 73, 76, 104, 206, 220.
15. E. P. Thompson, "Patrician Society, Plebian Culture," pp. 383–397.
16. Ibid., p. 390; Harold Perkin, *The Origins of Modern English Society*, p. 183; Edmund Burke, *The Works of Edmund Burke*, 1:48, 49.
17. Sidney and Beatrice Webb, *English Local Government from the Revolution to the Municipal Corporation Act: The Parish and County*, 1:557, 596.
18. Ivy Pinchbeck and Margaret Hewitt, *Children in English Society*, 1:242–245, 258.
19. Dorothy Marshall, *The English Poor in the Eighteenth Century*, p. 183.
20. Sidney and Beatrice Webb, *English Local Government: English Poor Law History*, pt. one, pp. 149, 155, 197, 281, 424; idem, *Parish and County*, pp. 364, 596.
21. Raymond Williams, *The Country and the City*, pp. 75, 81.
22. Sidney and Beatrice Webb, *Poor Law*, pt. one, pp. 221, 279.

Chapter I

1. William Paley, *The Principles of Moral and Political Philosophy*, 1:126, 239, 249, 230–256. For Paley's popularity see *Lectures on Paley for University Students*; Alexander Bain, *The Moral Philosophy of Paley*; A Member of Cambridge University, *An Epitome of Paley's Principles of Moral and Political Philosophy*; William Smith, *A Discourse on the Ethics of the School of Paley*. There were editions of his complete works in 1834, 1838, and 1845.
2. Edmund Burke, *The Works of Edmund Burke*, 4:213, 245, 252; Charles Parkin, *The Moral Basis of Burke's Political Thought*, pp. 31, 36, 61.
3. Samuel Taylor Coleridge, *Letters, Conversations and Recollections* p. 172; idem, *On The Constitution of the Church and State*, p. 119; Robert Southey, *Sir Thomas More, or Colloquies on the Progress and Prospect of Society*, p. 299.
4. Thomas Chalmers, *The Christian and Civic Economy of Large Towns*. For the individualist strain of his thought, see especially vol. 3. For his paternalist ideas see 1:132, 139, 296, 169–358; 2:98, 126, 132, 150. The best exposition of his ideas is in L. J. Saunders, *Scottish Democracy*, pp. 208–221; Thomas Arnold, *The Miscellaneous Works of Thomas Arnold*, p. 411.
5. Burke, *Works*, 1:213; 4:245, 252; Parkin, *Burke*, p. 36.
6. Coleridge, *Church and State*, p. 55; idem, *Two Lay Sermons*, p. 416; idem, *Specimens of Table Talk*, 2:135.
7. Coleridge, *Lay Sermons*, pp. 224–225, 416, 430; idem, *Letters, Conversations and Recollections*, p. 62.
8. Parkin, *Burke*, p. 30; R. Southey, *Thomas More*, 1:165; T. Arnold, *Works*, pp. 432, 463.
9. R. B. Seeley, *Memoir of the Life and Writings of M. T. Sadler*, p. 448; William Sewell, *Christian Politics*, p. 274.
10. Coleridge, *Table Talk*, 2:227; Chalmers, *Christian and Civic Economy*, 1:132, 139, 296.
11. Thomas Carlyle, *Latter-Day Pamphlets*, p. 56; William Sewell, *Christian Communism*, p. 19; Arthur Helps, *The Claims of Labour*, pp. 12–13, 73.
12. Charles C. Southey, *The Life and Correspondence of Robert Southey*, 6:87; Coleridge, *Lay Sermons*, pp. 359, 393, 416, 419.
13. R. B. Seeley, *The Perils of the Nation*, p. 28; W. Sewell, *Christian Politics*, pp. 278–279.
14. T. Arnold, *Works*, pp. 432–433; Thomas Carlyle, *Chartism*, p. 36; idem, *Latter-Day Pamphlets*, p. 224.
15. Helps, *Claims of Labour*, pp. 9, 34, 35, 48, 58, 63, 64, 68, 75, 92, 94, 97, 118, 129, 140, 151.
16. Carlyle as quoted in ibid., p. 34.
17. R. Southey, *Thomas More*, 2:157; Michael Sadler, *Ireland: Its Evils, and Their Remedies*, pp. 190, 301, 308, 309, 313; Seeley, *Sadler*, pp. 310–317; T. Arnold, *Works*, p. 416; Thomas Carlyle, *Past and Present*, pp. 144–153; Burke, *Works*, 1:46.
18. Paley, *Moral and Political Philosophy*, 1:108–109; John Colmer, *Coleridge, Critic of Society*, p. 57.
19. Cecil Driver, *Tory Radical, The Life of Richard Oastler*, pp. 306, 400.
20. W. Sewell, *Christian Politics*, pp. 222–223, 330.
21. Coleridge, *Table Talk*, 2:53; David Galleo, *Coleridge and the Idea of the Modern State*; Seeley, *Sadler*, p. 448.
22. Driver, *Oastler*, pp. 296–297, 435.
23. Arthur Helps, *Friends in Council*, 1:142; *Quarterly Review*, March 1828, p. 565; July 1828, pp. 60, 62, 64, 77; May 1830, pp. 252–253, 255, 260, 276–277; R. Southey, *Thomas More*, 2:221; idem, *Essays Moral and Political*; Driver, *Oastler*, pp. 296–297, 435.
24. Helps, *Claims of Labour*, pp. 20, 78, 111, 115, 116.

25. R. Southey, *Thomas More*, 1:105; *Quarterly Review*, July 1828, p. 81; Geoffrey Carnall, *Robert Southey and His Works*, p. 205; T. Arnold, *Works*, pp. 125, 414, 420, 493–502.
26. Burke, *Works*, 4:251, 254, 257, 265, 270, 278.
27. Coleridge, *Lay Sermons*, pp. 418, 430; Colmer, *Coleridge*, p. 148.
28. R. Southey, *Thomas More*, 1:165; *Essays*, 1:192, 195; 2:26, 29, 116, 158; W. Sewell, *Christian Politics*, pp. 133, 142, 209.
29. Chalmers, *Christian and Civic Economy*, 1:6–8, 13, 29, 248, 283–284, 295–297; 2:44, 132, 204.
30. Coleridge, *Lay Sermons*, p. 421; idem, *Letters*, 1:27; C. Southey, *Correspondence of R. Southey*, 6:231; R. Southey, *Essays*, 1:149.
31. Burke, *Works*, 4:261.
32. Colmer, *Coleridge*, pp. 44–45; F. M. Todd, *Politics of the Poet, A Study of Wordsworth*, p. 215.
33. Driver, *Oastler*, p. 507; Seeley, *Sadler*, pp. 80, 135, 417; R. Southey, *Thomas More*, 1:134; W. Sewell *Christian Politics*, pp. 165–167, 209; Helps, *Claims of Labour*, pp. 6, 40–45, 58.
34. Burke, *Works*, 4:243.
35. Coleridge, *Lay Sermons*, pp. 415, 417; Colmer, *Coleridge*, pp. 109–110; Seeley, *Sadler*, pp. 45, 339, 604.
36. Burke, *Works*, 7:44; Carnall, *Southey*, p. 149; R. Southey, *Essays*, 1:219; 2:122, 125; idem, *Thomas More*, 1:93; Coleridge, *Table Talk*, 1:201; 2:148, 281–290, 311, 317, 324.
37. W. Sewell, *Christian Politics*, p. 330; Coleridge, *Table Talk*, 2:148; Carlyle, *Latter-Day Pamphlets*, p. 135; idem, *Past and Present*, p. 166.
38. R. Southey, *Thomas More*, 1:105; 2:221; idem, *Essays*, 1:109; 2:23–25; *Quarterly Review*, March 1828, p. 565; July 1828, pp. 60–62, 64, 77; May 1830, pp. 252–253, 255, 260, 276–277; William Wordsworth, *The Poetical Works of William Wordsworth*, 2:416; Sadler, *Ireland*, pp. 187, 193.
39. T. Arnold, *Works*, pp. 220, 462–463, 497–498; Helps, *Claims of Labour*, pp. 77–120.
40. Carlyle, *Latter-Day Pamphlets*, pp. 79, 125, 135, 140–143.
41. Ibid., p. 38; idem, *Past and Present*, pp. 23–33; idem, *Chartism*, pp. 59–68; *Sun*, January 14, 1840.
42. Carnall, *Southey*, pp. 120–130; C. Southey, *Correspondence of R. Southey*, 5:250, 269.
43. *Quarterly Review*, July 1831, p. 448.
44. Augustus Welby Pugin, *Contrasts; or, A Parallel between the Architecture of the Fifteenth and Nineteenth Centuries.*
45. Kenelm Digby, *Broad Stone of Honour*, book 4, *Orlandus*, pp. 82, 90, 92, 93, 94; book 1, *Godefridus*, pp. 86 ff.
46. William Cobbett, *A History of the Protestant Reformation*, 1:142–157, 183–186; 2:14–34.
47. John Wade, *The Extraordinary Black Book*, pp. 20–27, 57.
48. Coleridge, *Church and State*, pp. 43–64; idem, *Table Talk*, 1:199.
49. Chalmers, *Christian and Civic Economy*, 1:8, 29, 169–358.
50. T. Arnold, *Works*, pp. 263, 514–516.
51. W. Sewell, *Christian Politics*, pp. 78, 266–267, 308, 314–318, 363–366, 393; idem, *Christian Communism*, p. 20; Seeley, *Perils*, pp. 217, 224, 307; idem, *Remedies*, p. 130.
52. Frederick Denison Maurice, *The Kingdom of Christ*; C. K. Gloyn, *The Church in the Social Order*, pp. 118–142; N. C. Masterman, *John Malcolm Ludlow*, pp. 62–63, 71, 85, 93, 98–99; *Politics for the People*, July 15, 1848; John Minter Morgan, *Religion and Crime*, pp. 29–30.
53. Elie Halévy, *England in 1815*, p. 428.
54. W. Sewell, *Christian Politics*, pp. 308, 313; Seeley, *Remedies*, p. 165.

55. Coleridge, *Church and State*, pp. 83–86; idem, *Table Talk*, 2:311, 324, 283; T. Arnold, *Works*, pp. 88–94, 263–264, 446–449, 500–502; A. P. Stanley, *Life of Thomas Arnold*, pp. 343, 386.
56. Maurice, *The Kingdom of Christ*, pp. 206, 240, 278, 557–569; idem, *Life of Frederick Denison Maurice*, 1:269, 459; G. F. C. Masterman, *The Life of Frederick Denison Maurice*, pp. 32–33.
57. Chalmers, *Christian and Civic Economy*, 1:169–358; Carlyle, *Latter-Day Pamphlets*, pp. 79, 125, 135, 141–143.
58. Coleridge, *Church and State*, pp. 43–64; idem, *Table Talk*, 1:200–201.
59. W. Sewell, *Christian Politics*, pp. 313, 368.
60. Maurice, *Life of F. D. Maurice*, 1:269, 459, 461; G. F. C. Masterman, *Maurice*, pp. 32–33.
61. Arnold, *Works*, pp. 266–310, 414, 446–449.
62. N. C. Masterman, *J. M. Ludlow*, pp. 71–73, 85; *Politics for the People*, July 8, 1848, pp. 205–210; Terence Kenny, *The Political Thought of John Henry Newman*, p. 172.
63. T. Arnold, *Works*, p. 453; Coleridge, *Lay Sermons*; idem, *The Grounds of Sir Robert Peel's Bill (for the Regulation of Factories) Vindicated*; R. Southey, *Essays*, 2:22.
64. Coleridge, *Letters*, 1:172; R. Southey, *Essays*, 1:178; Helps, *Claims of Labour*, p. viii; T. Arnold, *Works*, p. 459.
65. Bernard Holland, *Memoir of Kenelm Henry Digby*, p. 6; Coleridge, *Letters*, 1:48.
66. Holland, *Memoir*, p. 61.
67. R. Southey, *Thomas More*, 1:134.
68. C. Southey, *Correspondence of R. Southey*, 5:290; Coleridge, *Table Talk*, 2:129; W. Sewell, *Christian Communism*, p. 13; Driver, *Oastler*, p. 432; Cobbett, *Protestant Reformation*, 1:145; Seeley, *Sadler*, p. 33.
69. J. R. Poynter, *Society and Pauperism, English Ideas on Poor Relief, 1795–1834*, pp. 61, 80, 97, 99.
70. Richard Soloway, *Prelates and People*, pp. 76–79.
71. T. S. Grimshawe, *A Memoir of the Rev. Legh Richmond*, pp. 81–93; Rev. Legh Richmond, *Annals of the Poor*; Alfred Blomfield, *A Memoir of Charles James Bloomfield*, pp. 174–183.

Chapter II

1. Richard Altick, *The English Common Reader*, pp. 319, 392–393; Margaret Oliphant, *William Blackwood and His Sons*, 1:97; Miriam M. H. Thrall, *Rebellious Fraser's*, p. 15.
2. George Croly, *A Memoir of Edmund Burke*; *Blackwood's Magazine*, August 1842, p. 220; October 1842, p. 542; January 1843, p. 9; July 1843, p. 66; *Quarterly Review*, September 1846, p. 565; December 1849, pp. 183–184; December 1847, p. 177.
3. Theodore Martin, *Memoir of William Edmondstoune Aytoun*, p. 11; Anna M. Stoddart, *John Stuart Blackie*, p. 18; Myron F. Brightfield, *John Croker*, p. 170; Samuel Warren, *The Intellectual and Moral Development of the Present Age*, p. 32.
4. H. A. Kennedy, *Professor Blackie*, pp. 129, 158; G. S. Merriam, *The Story of William and Lucy Smith*, p. 17; Thomas De Quincey, *Reminiscences of the English Lake Poets*, p. 1.
5. John F. Murray, *The World of London*, 1:131; J. Campbell Smith, *Writings by the Way*, p. 471.
6. Sir Archibald Alison, *Some Account of My Writings, An Autobiography*, 1:187; Oliphant, *Blackwood*, 1:420.

7. Andrew Lang, *The Life and Letters of John Gibson Lockhart*, 2:285; 1:136; *Critic*, July 7, 1860, p. 41; John Croker, *Correspondence and Diaries*, 2:412; *Quarterly Review*, December 1841, pp. 10–11, 79, 387.
8. Katherine Lake, *Memorials of William Charles Lake*, p. 23; Thomas Mozley, *Reminiscences Chiefly of Oriel College and the Oxford Movement*, 2:216–227; James Mozley, *The Letters of James Mozley*, p. 150; R. C. Church, *Essays and Reviews*, p. 343; *Christian Remembrancer*, July 1849, p. 67; T. Thomas Vargish, *Newman, The Contemplation of Mind*, p. 99.
9. *Fraser's Magazine*, May 1857, p. 613; J. K. Laughton, ed., *Memoirs of the Life and Correspondence of Henry Reeve*, 1:36, 44; Charles Whibley, *Lord John Manners and His Friends*, pp. 133, 260.
10. Thrall, *Fraser's*, pp. 11, 26, 30–33, 89, 95–96; *Fraser's Magazine*, February 1840, p. 160; Walter and Esther Houghton, *Wellesley Index to Victorian Periodicals*, 2:309–310.
11. Stoddart, *Blackie*, p. 154.
12. Merriam, *Smith*, pp. 28–29.
13. *Quarterly Review*, March 1842, pp. 10–46; September 1840, p. 447.
14. *Blackwood's Magazine*, April 1830, p. 680.
15. *Blackwood's Magazine*, November 1841, p. 673; March 1849, p. 313; *Quarterly Review*, December 1841, pp. 26–27.
16. *Oxford and Cambridge Review*, August 1845, p. 153; *Fraser's Magazine*, July 1846, p. 93; *Blackwood's Magazine*, May 1845, p. 543; June 1849, p. 715; *Quarterly Review*, September 1841, pp. 341–342. Sewell thought that the "feudal system should be cherished, extended, and strengthened."
17. *Quarterly Review*, September 1840, pp. 469, 501, 447–502; *Fraser's Magazine*, February 1841, pp. 129–130, 133.
18. *Blackwood's Magazine*, March 1849, p. 312; July 1843, pp. 65–66.
19. *British Critic*, 29 (1840):334, 337–338; *Quarterly Review*, September 1840, p. 501.
20. *English Review*, January 1844, pp. 48–104; December 1844, pp. 426–451; May 1845, pp. 179–180; December 1846, pp. 418–431; *British Critic*, 23(1838):174–179, 184–186; 26(1839):359–371; *Christian Remembrancer*, 47(1845):1–28, 453–471; 51(1847):276–291; 53(1849):1–16.
21. *English Review*, January 1844, pp. 71, 86; December 1844, p. 427; *Oxford and Cambridge Review*, July 1845, p. 7; June 1846, p. 458; October 1846, p. 343; November 1846, pp. 492 ff.; *Quarterly Review*, September 1848, p. 359.
22. *Oxford and Cambridge Review*, September 1845, p. 313; August 1845, p. 178.
23. *Fraser's Magazine*, June 1843, pp. 748–749; *Oxford and Cambridge Review*, July 1846, p. 82.
24. *English Review*, December 1844, p. 261; *Quarterly Review*, September 1840, pp. 501–502.
25. *Blackwood's Magazine*, June 1846, pp. 733–734.
26. *English Review*, December 1848, p. 267; *Oxford and Cambridge Review*, January 1846, p. 47; *British and Foreign Review*, January 1840, p. 231; J. C. Smith, *Writings by the Way*, pp. 471–472.
27. Alison, *Autobiography*, 1:24, 35; *Blackwood's Magazine*, November 1841, pp. 659, 672; October 1842, pp. 459–466.
28. *Quarterly Review*, December 1843, pp. 554–555; December 1849, p. 150; *Christian Remembrancer*, October 1848, p. 315.
29. *Blackwood's Magazine*, September 1840, p. 311; May 1843, p. 511; *Fraser's Magazine*, May 1843, p. 511.
30. *British Critic*, 33(1843):249–250, 252, 271.
31. *Fraser's Magazine*, August 1844, p. 251; Samuel Taylor Coleridge, *On The Constitution of the Church and State* and *Two Lay Sermons*, p. 430; *Blackwood's Magazine*, April 1842, p. 520.

32. *Quarterly Review,* April 1835, pp. 485–536; *Blackwood's Magazine,* November 1846, pp. 555–570.
33. *Fraser's Magazine,* April 1841, pp. 377–389; *Blackwood's Magazine,* June 1841, p. 706; November 1846, pp. 555–570; November 1847, p. 642.
34. *British Critic,* 33(1843):254; *Fraser's Magazine,* May 1844, p. 623; *English Review,* December 1844, p. 261; *Quarterly Review,* June 1845, pp. 15–16.
35. *Quarterly Review,* December 1840, pp. 181, 173–182.
36. *Quarterly Review,* September 1846, pp. 377–424; *Fraser's Magazine,* September 1846, pp. 371–372; *Oxford and Cambridge Review,* October 1846, p. 330; *English Review,* September 1846, p. 136.
37. *Blackwood's Magazine,* March 1840, p. 428; May 1848, pp. 540–562; May 1849, pp. 568 ff.
38. *Quarterly Review,* December 1848, pp. 238, 239, 243.
39. *Blackwood's Magazine,* May 1844, p. 649; *Quarterly Review,* December 1846, pp. 245, 252–253, 262; March 1847, pp. 466, 470, 471, 478.
40. *Fraser's Magazine,* February 1843, p. 239; December 1843, pp. 732–739; *Oxford and Cambridge Review,* November 1846, p. 561.
41. *Quarterly Review,* December 1846, pp. 245, 248; September 1849, p. 530.
42. *Fraser's Magazine,* May 1844, pp. 506, 507–515; *Quarterly Review,* June 1844, pp. 234, 257, 224–280; *Blackwood's Magazine,* August 1845, pp. 173–176; November 1845, pp. 637–638, 644.
43. *Blackwood's Magazine,* December 1846, pp. 722, 727; August 1845, pp. 139–140; November 1849, p. 519; *Quarterly Review,* December 1847, pp. 177, 175–203; December 1841, pp. 43–48; June 1841, pp. 92–94; *Oxford and Cambridge Review,* July 1846, pp. 87–89.
44. *Oxford and Cambridge Review,* July 1846, p. 93.
45. *Blackwood's Magazine,* August 1845, pp. 139, 129–140; *Fraser's Magazine,* January 1846, p. 8; April 1848, p. 402; November 1848, p. 557; September 1848, pp. 294–299.
46. *Quarterly Review,* June 1840, pp. 116, 123; March 1843, pp. 436, 449.
47. *Blackwood's Magazine,* October 1842, pp. 646–647, 652; *Quarterly Review,* December 1847, p. 152.
48. *Fraser's Magazine,* September 1847, pp. 371, 366–377; November 1847, pp. 505–515.
49. Alison, *Autobiography,* 1:13.
50. T. T. Carter, *A Memoir of John Armstrong, D.D.,* pp. 6–7, 67.
51. Lang, *Lockhart,* pp. 37, 39, 62, 63, 122.
52. Martin, *Memoir of Edmondstoune Aytoun,* p. 106; *Athenaeum,* May 12, 1883, p. 604; *DNB* (O'Sullivan): p. 1,213; *Blackwood's Magazine,* August 1845, p. 173; November 1845, p. 633; May 1844, p. 638; *Quarterly Review,* March 1847, p. 464.
53. *Quarterly Review,* June 1841, p. 255; Croker, *Correspondence and Diaries,* 2:222, 250.
54. Marion Lochhead, *John Gibson Lockhart,* p. 245; Lang, *Lockhart,* 2:195; Rosaline Masson, *Pollock and Aytoun,* p. 97; Alison, *Autobiography,* 1:131, 559, 602.
55. Lang, *Lockhart,* 2:191, 195; Lochhead, *Lockhart,* pp. 173, 243, 245; Oliphant, *Blackwood,* 2:263.
56. Oliphant, *Blackwood,* 2:268, 346, 355, 367, 369, 381.
57. *Fraser's Magazine,* February 1849, p. 127; *Quarterly Review,* December 1840, p. 180; *Blackwood's Magazine,* July 1844, pp. 3, 7; May 1845, p. 541.
58. T. Mozley, *Oriel College,* 2:172.
59. *Fraser's Magazine,* September 1840, p. 290.
60. *Quarterly Review,* December 1846, p. 170.
61. *Fraser's Magazine,* September 1848, p. 444; February 1844, pp. 210–211.
62. Murray, *The World of London,* 1:85.

Chapter III

1. G. P. R. James, *Charles Tyrrell*, 2:39; Catherine Gore, *Peers and Parvenus*, 1:168; G. P. R. James, *The Gentleman of the Old School*, 1:113, 115.
2. Catherine Gore, *Men of Capital*, 2:56–62; J. F. Murray, *Viceroy*, 1:69, 93–97, 196.
3. William Sewell, *Hawkstone*, 1:79, 90, 94–95, 124, 133; 2:22, 239, 286.
4. Frances Trollope, *Jessie Phillips*, p. 40; idem, *Michael Armstrong, The Factory Boy*, 2:164, 214, 215, 227.
5. Elizabeth Gaskell, *Mary Barton*, pp. 482–483; idem, *North and South*, pp. 164–165, 404–405.
6. Charles Kingsley, *Alton Locke*, pp. 228–229, 286, 345, 360–361; idem, *Yeast*, pp. 88–89, 182, 183, 185; Benjamin Disraeli, *Coningsby*, p. 251; W. Sewell, *Hawkstone*, 2:284.
7. Elizabeth Sewell, *Amy Herbert*, 1:23, 25, 242; 2:54; Charlotte Elizabeth [Tonna], *Helen Fleetwood*, pp. 17, 94, 133, 303.
8. Francis E. Paget, *The Pageant; or, Pleasure and Its Price*, pp. xvi, 7, 8, 39, 61, 78, 190; idem, *The Warden of Berkingholt;* William Gresley, *Clement Walton*, pp. 39, 124, 132, 145, 146, 152, 169, 174, 199; see also his *Church Clavering, Charles Lever*, and *Frank's First Trip to the Continent;* Robert Armitage, *Ernest Singleton*, 1:87, 90, 105, 108, 133, 229; 2:57, 110, 131, 296; 3:35; see also Armitage's *The The Penscellwood Papers*, p. 14; and *Doctor Hookwell*, 2:21, 85, 90, 273; 3:107.
9. Charles Dickens, *Nicholas Nickleby*, p. 424; idem, *A Christmas Carol*, p. 112; idem, *Hard Times.*
10. Dickens, *Nicholas Nickleby*, pp. 341, 354, 359; idem, *A Christmas Carol*, p. 31; idem, *Pickwick Papers*, p. 224.
11. Dickens, *Nicholas Nickleby*, pp. 76, 257–275, 312–314, 359, 444–447; idem, *The Chimes*, pp. 151–154.
12. Douglas Jerrold, *The History of St. Giles and St. James*, pp. 127, 152–153, 211.
13. Charlotte Brontë, *Shirley*, pp. 118, 218, 221, 248, 253, 437; Harriet Martineau, *Deerbrook*, pp. 263, 344, 360–361, 419, 472, 479; Theodore Hook, *Peregrine Bunce*, pp. 12, 26, 29; *Eclectic Review*, December 1849, p. 26.
14. Charles Dickens, *Dombey and Son*, p. 558.

Chapter IV

1. Thomas Horsfield, *The History, Antiquities, and Topography of the County of Sussex*, vols. 1 and 2; F. M. L. Thompson, *English Landed Society in the Nineteenth Century*, pp. 113–117. Thompson notes that in 1883 36 percent of Sussex estates were between 1,000 and 10,000 acres; 9 percent from 1 to 100 acres, 10 percent from 100 to 300, and 16 percent from 300 to 1,000.
2. *Sussex Agricultural Express*, June 15, December 14, 1844; June 13, 1846.
3. Ibid., June 18, 1842; October 28, 1843; June 15, December 7, 14, 1844; January 25, 1845; June 13, 1846.
4. Ibid., December 14, 1844; June 7, 1845; July 23, 1843; April 25, 1840.
5. Ibid., October 9, 1841; June 13, 1846.
6. Ibid., January 2, 1847; Ashurst Turner Gilbert, *A Pastoral Letter*, pp. 8, 13–16; Society for the Propagation of the Gospel in Foreign Parts, *Annual Report*, p. xxiii.
7. Gilbert, *Pastoral Letter*, p. 14; *Sussex Agricultural Express*, December 12, 1840; Julius Hare, *Charges to the Clergy of the Archdeaconry of Lewes*, vol. 1, "1840 Charge," pp. 28, 31–37; "1841 Charge," pp. 14–19, 26–37; "1842 Charge," pp. 27–33, 63–65; vol. 2, "1843 Charge," pp. 14–33, 47, 53–55 supports Arnold's wish for a bishop for each large town.
8. Shane Leslie, *Henry Edward Manning*, pp. 43–51, 69–73; David Newsome, *The Parting of Friends: A Study of The Wilberforces and Henry Manning*, p. 269;

Sussex Agricultural Express, June 15, 1844; James Garbett, *The Secret of the Church's Power,* pp. 11–36.

9. *Sussex Agricultural Express,* October 10, 30, December 5, 1840; April 3, December 18, 1841; January 28, July 1, 1843; January 6, February 10, 1844; June 14, 1845.

10. Ibid., April 11, 1840; September 11, 1841; May 14, 1842; March 1, 1845; October 21, 1843; June 7, 1845.

11. *Parliamentary Papers* (hereafter cited as *P.P.*), 1834, 37:331–333; 38:276; *Sussex Agricultural Express,* October 5, 1845.

12. *Sussex Agricultural Express,* February 8, 1840; January 1, December 30, 1842; July 19, 1845; January 7, 1843; November 1, 1845; February 8, December 5, 1840; February 13, 1841.

13. Ibid., December 26, 1840; January 18, 1841; January 7, 1843; March 14, 1846.

14. Ibid., August 23, 1845; October 14, 1843.

15. Duke of Richmond Papers, Goodwood MSS, boxes 41 and 42; particularly Mary Webb to the duke of Richmond, January 4, 1845; John Nance to Richmond, March 25, 1831; bishop of Chichester to Richmond, October 30, December 17, 1845; *Memoir of Charles Gordon Lennox, Fifth Duke of Richmond,* pp. 68–85; *Sussex Agricultural Express,* December 14, 1844; December 13, 1845; September 7, 1844; November 1, 1845.

16. Poor Law Papers, Ministry of Health Papers, Public Record Office, M.H. 12/13061, J. L. Ellis to Poor Law Commission, January 1847, Thomas Sockett to Chadwick, March 27, 1837; *P.P.,* Select Committee on Poor Laws, 1837, 17:3, 30; Horsfield, *Sussex,* 1:186; *P.P.,* Royal Commission on Poor Laws, 1834, 37:327–331; *Sussex Agricultural Express,* December 11, 1841; September 10, 1843; February 10, 1844; December 19, 1840.

17. *Sussex Agricultural Express,* January 25, 1845; *Memoir of Richmond,* p. 72; Richmond Papers, box 41, Rev. S. Westbrooke to Richmond, 1939; *P.P.,* Reports of Inspectors of Schools, 1845, 35:364–365, 378; 1846, 32:223, 245; 1848, 50:122; 1850, 44:87–133; Poor Law Papers, M.H. 12/12746, William Dukes to Poor Law Commission, May 1, 1838; Richmond Papers, box 42, Sir Charles Burrell to Mr. Dickens, March 25, 1845.

18. Richmond Papers, box 42, Colonel Wyndham to Richmond, February 13, 1845, "must get rid of these people"; *P.P.,* Reports of Inspectors of Schools, 1849, 42: 309; Richmond Papers, box 42, Wyndham to Richmond, November 2, 1845, telling him Sir Charles Burrell "has never given a shilling to the London Society . . . he is more afraid of his pocket than his dignity"; W. M. Powell, *The Sanitary Condition of the City of Chichester;* Poor Law Papers, M.H. 32/39, Hawley to Chadwick, March 7, 1837; *P.P.,* Annual Reports of the Poor Law Commission, 1850, 27:317, 125.

19. For East Sussex Quarter Sessions under the earl of Chichester see *Sussex Agricultural Express,* February 22, December 5, 1840; February 26, May 11, October 22, 1842; February 21, May 25, 1844; April 12, October 4, 1845; February 28, 1846. For the West Sussex Quarter Sessions under Serjeant D'Oyly see the *Express* for January 8, April 9, 1842; April 13, 1844; April 12, 1845. For prisons, *P.P.,* 1840, Reports of Prison Inspectors, 25:376; 1842, 21:198–199; Poor Law Papers, M.H. 12/12750, Rev. J. Read to Commissioners, March 19, 1845; *P.P.,* Royal Commission on the Poor Laws, 1834, 37:327 for Chichester on no relief for indigent.

20. *Sussex Agricultural Express,* August 15, 1846; *P.P.,* Annual Reports of the Poor Law Commission, 1850, 27:317; 1843, 12:153, 164.

21. *P.P.,* Reports of Inspectors of Schools, 1845, 35:375 ff.; 1846, 32:272, 223–269; 1847, 45:61–90; 1848, 50:122 ff.; 1850, 44:66–133; Annual Report of the Poor Law Commission, 1843, 12:167–168, 216; *Sussex Agricultural Express,* April 4, 1840; April 10, 1841.

22. Hare, *Charges to the Clergy,* "1842 Charge," p. 29; *P.P.,* Annual Reports of the Poor Law Commission, 1843, 12:155; Poor Law Papers, M.H. 12/12748, W. Margesson to Poor Law Commission, January 8, 1841; M.H. 12/12855, Clerk to

Poor Law Commission, January 12, 1839 on 10s wages, J. Starr to Poor Law Commission, January 8, 1838, "when weather is bad they sent them back to the vestry for support"; M.H. 12/1285, Gilbert to Poor Law Commission, April 9, 1841, farmers do not hire in winter; *P.P.,* Annual Reports of the Poor Law Commission, 1843; 12:156–157; *Sussex Agricultural Express,* August 23, 1845; February 7, 1846.

23. The best published account of Sussex poor-law unions in action is *P.P.,* Select Committee on Poor Laws, 1837, 17, first and second reports on the earl of Egremont's Petworth and the duke of Richmond's Westhampnett. Some of the best manuscript sources at the Public Record Office are Poor Law Papers, M.H. 12/12748–12750 on the Battle union, where Sir Godfrey and Lady Webster found the chairman a "person of no higher consideration than a parish clerk"; M.H. 12/12832 on Cuckfield where the chairman complained of the turbulent members, March 1840; M.H. 12/12855, 12856 on Eastbourne, where the rector was the champion of the poor and the guardians asked to take in extra children; M.H. 12/12887 on East Grimstead with the earl De La Warr complaining, with others, of overly high parish valuations and where vagrants are whipped.

24. *P.P.,* Annual Reports of the Poor Law Commission, 1848, 33:90 ff. In 1847 real property was rated at £1,343,611 and £144,881 spent on the administration of the poor laws; *P.P.,* Annual Reports of the Poor Law Commission, 1845, 27:353.

25. *Sussex Agricultural Express,* February 10, 1844; September 12, 1840; April 4, 1846; July 25, 1840; July 20, 1844; Richmond Papers, box 42, July 1, 1842, D'Oyly to Richmond.

26. *P.P.,* Reports of Inspectors of Schools, 1849, 42:297–310; Reports of Commissioners in Lunacy, 1850, 23:387.

27. *Sussex Agricultural Express,* May 22, 1847; *Hansard Parliamentary Debates,* 1840, 54:1,037; *Memoir of Richmond,* pp. 94, 142, 143, 164; *Sussex Agricultural Express,* May 16, 1846; March 6, 1847; August 23, 1845; January 31, 1846.

28. Edwin Chadwick Papers, Chadwick to Russell, September 17, 1836; Poor Law Papers, M.H. 12/12746, William Dukes to Poor Law Commission, May 1, 1838; M.H. 37/38, W. H. T. Hawley to Poor Law Commission, November 18, 1834; M.H. 32/39, Hawley to Commission, January 18, 1838, "The Duke of Richmond will introduce me to Colonel Wyndham to help in the reform of Petworth."

29. *Sussex Agricultural Express,* October 18, 1845; *P.P.,* Royal Commission on Poor Laws, 37:327; Reports of Inspectors of Factories, 1845, 25:375; Reports of Inspectors of Schools, 1846, 32:272; Poor Law Papers, M.H. 12/12855, rector of Uckfield to Poor Law Commission, May 22, 1838; M.H. 12/13031, R. H. Baker, to Poor Law Commission, July 15, 1843; M.H. 12/13061 the Reverend Thomas Sockett of Petworth to Poor Law Commission, February 12, 1838.

Chapter V

1. *The Northampton Mercury,* October 26, 1844; *Leeds Intelligencer,* March 30, 1844; *The Western Luminary,* January 19, 1841; *Shrewsbury Chronicle,* November 5, 1841; *Western Times,* January 6, 1844; *Farmer's Magazine,* September 1844, pp. 259–263; December 1844, pp. 529–550.

2. John Mordant, *The Complete Steward,* pp. 377–401; Thomas Gisborne, *An Enquiry into the Duties of Men in the Higher and Middle Classes,* pp. 416–426; Lord Sidney Godolphin Osborne, *The Savings Bank;* idem, *Hints to the Charitable;* idem, *A View of the Low Moral and Physical Condition of the Agricultural Labourers;* G. W. Perry, *The Peasantry of England;* Charles Talbot, Viscount Ingestre, ed., *Meliora or Better Times to Come.*

3. *Northampton Mercury,* August 24, 1844; *Parliamentary Papers* (hereafter cited as *P.P.*), 1843, Select Committee on Allotments, 7:203.

4. Osborne, *Hints,* p. 9.

5. F. M. L. Thompson, *English Landed Society in the Nineteenth Century*, pp. 209–210.

6. David Spring, *The English Landed Estate in the Nineteenth Century*, p. 52; *Journal of the Statistical Society of London*, 1(1839):407; *P.P.*, Reports of Inspectors of Schools, 1852, 40:445; *Salisbury Journal*, August 3, 1844; *Hansard Parliamentary Debates*, 1847, 91:167.

7. John Glyde, *The Moral, Social and Religious Condition of Ipswich*, p. 357; Poor Law Papers, M.H. 32/21, Earle to Lefevre, March 31, 1835; H. T. Ryall, *Portraits of Conservatives*, "Duke of Rutland"; George Douglas Campbell, *Eighth Duke of Argyll (1823–1900) Autobiography and Memoirs*, pp. 129–135, 228, 291–294.

8. Poor Law Papers, M.H. 32/21, Earle to Lefevre, May 31, 1837; *Chambers Edinburgh Journal*, September 24, 1842, p. 286; *Leeds Intelligencer*, November 30, 1844; J. J. Gaskin, *The Viceregal Speeches and Addresses, Lectures and Poems, of the Late Earl of Carlisle*, pp. xvi, lxxxii (Carlisle had "the native ease and unaffected friendliness of true nobility, always accessible and ready to assist, entering with a keen zest into the rural athletic sport"; M.H. 32/27, Gilbert's Diary, January 5, 1839; *Witness*, January 22, 1842; Edwin Hodder, *The Life and Work of the Seventh Earl of Shaftesbury*, 2:367.

9. Sir Arthur Gordon, *The Earl of Aberdeen*, pp. 11–12.

10. John Prebble, *The Highland Clearances*, pp. 291, 295, 301.

11. *Hansard*, 1845, 78:317; *P.P.*, Report of Commissioners of Mines, 1846, 24:396–397; James Grant, *Memoirs of Sir George Sinclair*, p. 313; David Spring, "Agents of the Earls of Durham in the Nineteenth Century," pp. 104–112; idem, *Landed Estates*, p. 52.

12. Owen Chadwick, *Victorian Miniature*, pp. 61, 65; Sir Charles Bunbury, ed., *Memoir and Literary Remains of Lieutenant-General Sir Henry Edward Bunbury*, p. 84; Charles R. Strutt, *The Strutt Family of Terling, 1650–1873*, p. 80.

13. Chadwick, *Victorian Miniature*, pp. 63, 72–74; Bunbury, *Memoirs*, pp. 85, 114, 196–202; Strutt, *The Strutt Family*, pp. 77–78.

14. Chadwick, *Victorian Miniature*, p. 71; Strutt, *The Strutt Family*, pp. 78–79; Bunbury, *Memoirs*, pp. 203–205.

15. John Glyde, *Suffolk in the Nineteenth Century*, pp. 354, 325–355; Hodder, *Shaftesbury*, 2:367.

16. *P.P.*, Annual Reports of Poor Law Commission, 1843, 12:35–40, 73, 88, 92–93, 153, 165, 214–215, 216, 226, 236.

17. Ibid., Select Committee on Allotments, 1847, 11:13–14, 37, 40, 48, 49, 134, 210, 224, 354, 375, 406, 484, 509, 552; *Oxford and Cambridge Review*, July 1845, p. 87; for *Times* citation see H. J. Laski, I. Jennings, and W. A. Robson, eds., *A Century of Municipal Progress*, p. 43.

18. *P.P.*, Select Committee on Poor Laws, 1837, 17:18–20; Annual Reports of Poor Law Commisssion, 1843, 12:21, 29, 44–47, 58, 73, 75, 80, 311.

19. Ibid., Select Committee on Game Laws, 1846, 9:197; 1848, 7:21; 1846, 9:28, 52.

20. Ibid., Select Committee on Allotments, 1843, 7:255; Select Committee on Agricultural Customs, 1848, 7:31–33, 64, 67–70; *Farmer's Magazine*, January 1845, p. 61.

21. *P.P.*, Reports of Inspectors of Schools, 1842, 33:207–208; 1845, 35:4, 101, 102, 147; 1847, 45:211–212; 1852, 40:208.

22. Ibid., Select Committee on Game Laws, 1846, 9:21, 33, 52, 54, 131–148, 179, 258–267.

23. Ibid., Report of the Commissioners in Lunacy, 1847, 33:45, 55, 255; 1850, 23:364–366, 377.

24. Ibid., Reports of Prison Inspectors, 1850, 28:80; 1839, 38:647; 1843, 25:121; 1855, 26:7, 24, 31, 34, 37, 57–60, 77, 85; *Stamford Mercury*, August 22, 1851.

25. *P.P.*, Annual Reports of the Poor Law Commission, 1843, 12:19–39, 65.

26. The other peers were Lords Spencer, King, and Northampton. Poor Law Papers, M.H. 32/21, Earle to Lefevre, July 11, July 22, 1835; May 31, 1837; M.H. 32/39,

Hawley to Nicholls, July 9, 1837; M.H. 32/75; *P.P.*, Select Committee on Poor Laws, 1837, vol. 17, 18th Report, pp. 10–11; Annual Reports of the Poor Law Commisssion, 1838, 38:189–194.

27. Poor Law Papers, M.H. 32/21, Earle to Lefevre, September 11, 1836; Earle to Lefevre, March 31, July 11, 1835; M.H. 32/34, Hall to Nicholls, November 23, 1835; M.H. 32/26, Gilbert to Poor Law Commisssion, June 26, 1836; Gilbert's First Report, 1834; M.H. 32/35, Hall to Chadwick, January 25, 1837.

28. Poor Law Papers, M.H. 32/34, Hall to Nicholls, February 18, 1836; M.H. 32/44, Head to Commissioners, June 1, 1836; M.H. 32/26, Gilbert to Commissioners, January 21, 1836.

29. Anthony Brundage, "The Landed Interest and the New Poor Law," pp. 27–33; for an opposing view see Peter Dunkley, "The Landed Interest and the New Poor Law: A Critical Note," *English Historical Review* (October 1973), pp. 836–841.

30. *P.P.*, Select Committee on Allotments, 1843, 7:204–206, 208, 217, 229, 247, 288, 294, 305–306, 352.

Chapter VI

1. William Howley, archbishop of Canterbury, *A Charge Delivered at His Visitation*, p. 27; Leonard Prestige, *Pusey*, p. 168; Charles James Blomfield, bishop of London, *A Pastoral Letter to the Clergy of the Diocese of London*, p. 7; John Bird Sumner, bishop of Chester, *A Charge*, p. 11; George Kitson Clark, *Churchmen and the Condition of England, 1832–1885*, p. 145.

2. Rev. Hugh Mac Neile, *The Famine: A Rod of God* (1847), p. 30; John Bird Sumner, bishop of Chester, *Christian Charity: Its Obligation and Objects with Reference to the Present State*, p. 22; A. R. Ashwell, *Life of the Right Reverend Samuel Wilberforce*, 1:227–228.

3. Rev. William Gresley, *Practical Sermons*, p. 363; Christian Instruction Society, *A Course of Thirteen Lectures to Socialists and Others*, p. 130; Rev. Arthur Martineau, *What Is My Duty?*, pp. vii, 28, 36.

4. Edward Denison, bishop of Salisbury, *A Charge to the Clergy, 1845*, p. 43; William J. Copleston, *Memoir of Edward Copleston, D.D. Bishop of Llandoff*, p. 246; Rev. Thomas Dale, "The Principle of Christian Stewardship," *Hints on the Culture of Character*, p. 72.

5. Rev. Alexander Watson, ed., *Sermons for Sundays, Festivals and Fasts*, p. 356; Sumner, *A Charge*, p. 22; Rev. Francis Close, *Occasional Sermons*, pp. 338–340; Rev. William Gresley, *Parochial Sermons*, p. 366; Rev. Henry Melvill, *Sermons on Public Occasions*, pp. 47–48; Francis E. Paget, *The Warden of Berkingholt*, p. 64.

6. Rev. T. R. Bentley, "The Christian Law of Forgiveness," in Watson, *Sermons for Sundays, Festivals and Fasts*, p. 325; Rev. Francis Close, *Eighty Sketches of Sermons*, p. 142.

7. Ian Anstruther, *The Scandal of the Andover Workhouse*, p. 16; Diane Mac Clatchey, *Oxfordshire Clergy, 1777–1869*, pp. 98–101; Rev. W. J. Conybeare, *Sermons Preached in the Chapel Royal*, p. 181; and idem, *Essays Ecclesiastical and Social*, p. v.

8. Anstruther, *Andover*, pp. 81–84, 111, 116–117, 123–126; *Parliamentary Papers* (hereafter cited as *P.P.*), Select Committee on Poor Laws, 1837, 17:1 ff.; *Times*, August 11, 25, 1840; October 23, 1843; G. R. W. Baxter, *Book of the Bastiles*, pp. 116, 117, 118, 140, 464. Reports of workhouse horrors in *Book of the Bastiles* are not dependable.

9. J. C. Gill, *Parson Bull of Byerley*, pp. 49–72, 106–117; Baxter, *Bastiles*, p. 276.

10. Georgina Battiscombe, *John Keble*, p. 176; Rev. Robert Armitage, *The Penscellwood Papers*, 2:294; Charles James Blomfield, *1842 Charge*, pp. 63–64; idem, *1846 Charge*, p. 37; Thomas J. Hussey, *The Christian Obligation to the Poor*, pp. 5–6; E. Denison, *1845 Charge*, pp. 33–34.

11. W. R. W. Stephens, *A Memoir of Richard Durnford*, pp. 5–7; James Jerram, ed., *The Memoirs and a Selection from the Letters of the Late Rev. Charles Jerram, M.A.*, pp. 326–352; Lord Sidney Godolphin Osborne, *Hints to the Charitable*, pp. 7–63.
12. Edward Denison, *A Charge to the Clergy of 1842*, pp. 30–32; *1845 Charge*, pp. 26, 44; H. P. Liddon, *Walter Kerr Hamilton, Bishop of Salisbury*, pp. 32–33, 43, 67, 72; R. Arnold, *Our Bishops*, p. 214; Sidney Herbert, *Proposals for the Better Application of Cathedral Institutions*, pp. 22–38.
13. G. F. A. Best, *Temporal Pillars: Queen Anne's Bounty, the Ecclesiastical Commissioners, and the Church of England*, p. 360; idem, "National Education in England, 1800–1870," pp. 163–164; E. Denison, *1845 Charge*, p. 26; Frank Smith, *The Life and Work of Sir James Kay-Shuttleworth*, pp. 147–148.
14. W. R. W. Stephens, *The Life and Letters of Walter Farquhar Hook*, 2:160, 164, 306; C. J. Blomfield, *1846 Charge*, p. 34; Alfred Blomfield, *A Memoir of Charles James Blomfield*, p. 181.
15. Close, *Occasional Sermons*, p. 336; *Cheltenham Examiner*, February 3, 1841; January 31, 1844; *Cheltenham Journal*, June 27, 1842; *Cheltenham Chronicle*, August 14, 18, 1847; Walter F. Hook, *The Duty of English Churchmen*, p. 20; Stephens, *Hook*, 2:87, 306; C. J. Blomfield, *1846 Charge*, p. 42.
16. Kitson Clark, *Churchmen and the Condition of England*, p. 72; P. J. Welch, "Bishop Blomfield," p. 159.
17. Walter F. Hook, *An Inaugural Discourse Preached in the Parish Church at Leeds*, pp. 5–10; idem, *The Duty of English Churchmen*, pp. 7–26; Stephens, *Hook*, 2:159, 165, 319; C. J. Stranks, *Dean Hook*, pp. 58–59.
18. *Cheltenham Examiner*, January 27, February 10, March 10, April 14, October 6, 1841; January 31, February 2, 1844; *Cheltenham Chronicle*, February 9, 16, 23, June 22, August 17, December 21, 1842; April 14, May 19, 26, June 16, 23, September 15, October 6, 20, November 3, 17, 1847; *Cheltenham Journal*, June 27, 1842; Close, *Occasional Sermons*, pp. 220–226; W. E. Adams, *Memoirs of a Social Atom*, 1:11–17, 83–84.
19. Gresley, *Parochial Sermons*, p. 171; John Sanford, *Parochialia*, p. 323; Hussey, *The Christian Obligation to the Poor*; Francis Paget, *Sermons on Duties of Daily Life*, p. 265.
20. F. Bennett, *The Story of W. J. Bennett*, pp. 35–67.
21. John Wade, *The Extraordinary Black Book*, p. 48; Elie Halévy, *History of the English People*, 1:396 ff.; Best, *Temporal Pillars*, pp. 198, 362–367; M. H. Port, *Six Hundred New Churches*, pp. 125–126; K. S. Inglis, *Churches and the Working Classes in Victorian England*, pp. 2, 7, 18 (the churches in London were half empty); C. H. Bromley, *The Church, the Privy Council, and the Working Classes*, pp. 22–23; *P.P.*, Returns of Ecclesiastical Commission, 1851, 42:525–526.
22. *P.P.*, Reports of Inspectors of Schools, 1846, 32:565; 1847, 45:103, 323; 1848, 50: 60, 390–391; Returns of Ecclesiastical Commission, 1851, 42:432–434; Reports of Inspectors of Schools, 1852, 40:84, 344, 346; 1853, 80:456.
23. George Eliot, *Scenes of Clerical Life*, 1:7, 36, 39; 2:14, 21, 22 ("He read nothing at all . . . his mind seems absorbed in the commonest matter"); Anthony Trollope, *The Warden*, pp. 1–25.
24. F. Smith, *Kay-Shuttleworth*, p. 102; Thomas Birks, *Memoir of the Rev. Edward Bickersteth*, (listed in the *British Museum Catalogue* under Edward Bickersteth) 2:9, 133, 164–169; Rev. Isaac Wilberforce, *A Charge*, pp. 8–11.
25. Rev. W. H. B. Proby, *Annals of the Low-Church Party*, p. 353.
26. *Cheltenham Chronicle*, January 5, June 22, 1842; *Cheltenham Examiner*, January 10, 1844; William Charles Henry, "A Biographical Notice of the Late Rev. Richard Dawes, M.A.," pp. 10–14; Richard Dawes, *Remarks Occasioned by the Present Crusade against the Educational Plans of the Committee of Council on Education*, p. 8.

27. J. T. Ward, *The Factory Movement*, pp. 87, 178, 423, 425; *Leeds Mercury*, April 13, 1844; *Leeds Times*, March 16, 1844; C. F. G. Masterman, *The Life of Frederick Denison Maurice*, p. 69.

28. Walter F. Hook, *On the Means of Rendering More Efficient the Education of the People*; Stephens, *Hook*, 1:206–212; Rev. Francis Close, *National Education*; C. J. Blomfield, *1846 Charge*, pp. 44–47.

29. Bromley, *The Church, the Privy Council, and the Working Classses*, p. 23; G. A. Denison, *Notes of My Life*, pp. iii, 147–158; idem, *The Present State of the Management Question*; Home Office Papers, Public Record Office, H.O. 65/5569, Registrar General to Lord Palmerston, April 27, 1856.

Chapter VII

1. W. C. Taylor, *Notes of a Tour in the Manufacturing Districts of Lancashire*, pp. 21–28, 61–66; *Journal of the Statistical Society of London*, (1839): 418–419; Andrew Ure, *Philosophy of Manufactures*, pp. 349–352; William R. Greg, *Enigmas of Life*, pp. x–xiii; *Westminster Review*, September 1840, pp. 390–404, describes fully the Greg mills at Bollington without naming them; *DNB*, 8:530. In the 1840s Henry and Edmund Ashworth, the sons of the founder, ran Turton and New Eagley, Thomas Ashton, Sr. and Jr., ran Hyde (until the father died in 1845). Samuel and R. H. Greg, sons of the founder, ran Bollington and their brother, W. R., the mills at Bury, until they failed. The New Eagley mills were in the village of Bank Top and the Turton mills in the village of Egerton.

2. Rhodes Boyson, *The Ashworth Cotton Enterprise*, pp. 127–132.

3. Ibid., pp. 95, 96, 112, 123, 126, 128.

4. George Unwin, *Samuel Oldknow and the Arkwrights*, pp. 135, 175; Sidney Pollard, "The Factory Village of the Industrial Revolution"; Ure, *Manufactures*, p. 16; Neil Smelser, *Social Change in the Industrial Revolution*; Reinhard Bendix, *Work and Authority in Industry*.

5. Boyson, *Ashworth*, pp. 120, 205; *Westminster Review*, September 1840, pp. 392, 392–398.

6. *Parliamentary Papers* (hereafter cited as *P.P.*), Reports of Inspectors of Factories, 1839, 19:506, 528–531, 533–536; Reports of Prison Inspectors, 1846, 20:574–575; Thomas Beggs, *An Inquiry into the Extent and Causes of Juvenile Depravity*, p. 139.

7. William R. Greg, *Essays on Political and Social Science*, 1:210–213, 354–355, 367–368; Boyson, *Ashworth*, pp. 91, 99, 108, 121.

8. Ure, *Manufactures*, pp. 329, 352, 353, 415, 417; Taylor, *Notes*, pp. 68, 81, 113, 118–121; E. S. Cayley, *Reasons for the Formation of the Agricultural Protection Society*, p. 5.

9. *Fraser's Magazine*, November 1844, pp. 627–628; *Eclectic Review*, September 1843, p. 333.

10. Charles Dickens, *Notes on America*, pp. 78–84; James Silk Buckingham, *The Eastern and Western States of America*, pp. 292–309; William Scoresby, *American Factories and Their Female Operatives*; *Christian Teacher*, 4(1842):2; *Westminster Review*, February 1843, p. 154; *Eclectic Review*, April 1843, p. 384; *Leeds Mercury*, June 21, 1845; October 10, 1846; *Athenaeum*, February 19, 1842, p. 159; *Mirror*, March 19, 1842; *Hansard Parliamentary Debates*, 1846, 83:389–390.

11. Some papers praising Ashworth, Greg, or Ashton are: *Athenaeum*, July 14, 1840, p. 528; *Morning Chronicle*, March 18, 1843; *British Quarterly*, 1(1845):144; *Christian Observer*, 42(1842):699; *Eclectic Review*, September 1842, p. 458; *Journal of the Statistical Society of London*, 1(1839):416; *People's Journal*, March 13, 1847; *Westminster Review*, September 1840, pp. 390–398; *Weekly Chronicle*, September 13, 1840.

12. *Leeds Mercury,* October 23, 1841; March 11, 1843; January 17, 1846; *Leeds Intelligencer,* July 31, 1847; W. G. Rimmer, *Marshall of Leeds, Flax Spinners, 1788–1886,* pp. 120–121, 149, 203–218, 222–223. In the 1840s the four sons of the founder, John Marshall, Sr., ran the enterprise. James Marshall was the most political.

13. *Journal of the Royal Statistical Society,* 1(1838):418; W. H. Elliot, *The Story of the "Cheeryble" Grants,* pp. 123, 125, 175, 184, 200; Charles Whibley, *Lord John Manners and His Friends,* pp. 102–103; Boyson, *Ashworth,* p. 126; *P.P.,* Reports of Inspectors of Factories, 1842, 22:465; Ivan Melada, *The Captain of Industry in English Fiction, 1821–1871,* pp. 115–116.

14. Taylor, *Notes,* p. 117.

15. Rev. Robert Balgarnie, *Sir Titus Salt,* pp. 113–147, 160–163.

16. Nassau Senior, *Letters on the Factory Act,* p. 33; *P.P.,* Reports of Inspectors of Factories, 1843, 27:309, 346–348; 1844, 28:535, 540; 1848, 26:159; J. T. Ward, *The Factory Movement, 1830–1855,* pp. 161, 211.

17. *Fraser's Magazine,* November 1844, p. 625; *Examiner,* May 18, 25, 1844; *Westminster Review,* August 1843, p. 102; *P.P.,* Reports of Inspectors of Factories, 1848, 26:159.

18. *P.P.,* Report of Commissioners of Mines, 1842, 90:23, 33, 41–45, 46, 87, 127, 132, 138, 144–145, 161, 178, 267–270; Royal Commission on Employment of Women, 16:21, 37, 177, 189, 204, 206, 209, 308, 310.

19. Ibid., 1843, Reports from Commissioners Inquiring into Children's Employment, vol. 14, Report A, p. 11; Robert B, pp. 14, 26; Report D, p. 2; vol. 15, Report L, p. 3.

Chapter VIII

1. *Hansard Parliamentary Debates,* 1845, 78:76.

2. Ibid., 1847, 92:942; 1847, 89:1,086; 1842, 62:1,336; 1841, 66:521; 91:1,076.

3. Ibid., 1844, 74:685–686; 1846, 86:400; 1848, 99:86; 1846, 86:471; 1844, 74:944; 1849, 105:823.

4. Ibid., 1847, 92:926; 1842, 65:122; 1848, 98:1,106.

5. Alexander Andrews, *The History of British Journalism,* 2:84–86; H. R. Fox Bourne, *English Newspapers,* 2:12, 94.

6. David Roberts, "Who Ran the Globe?"; *London Journal,* May 10, 1845, p. 168; James Grant, *The Newspaper Press,* 1:283–290, 343; 2:70–72.

7. *Morning Advertiser,* February 9, 1847.

8. The circulation figures are taken from a series of articles in the *London Journal* of 1845. These articles run from March 29 to June 14 and give the following figures: *Globe,* 3,000 circulation, *Morning Chronicle,* 7,000, *Morning Herald,* 6,000, *Morning Post,* 2,000, *Standard,* 2,800. Circulation for the *St. James's Chronicle* is estimated at 2,500 by comparing its stamp sales with those of the *Standard* and *Sun,* in *Parliamentary Papers* (hereafter cited as *P.P.*), 1851, Report from Select Committee on Newspapers, vol. 17, appendix 4, pp. 16–17. These circulation figures should be considered approximations only.

9. Manuscript chapter on "Stanley Lees Giffard—the Complete Independent" in the Halsbury Papers; *Standard,* November 9, 1858; Sir Robert Peel Papers, Add MSS 40, 563, S. L. Giffard to Sir Robert Peel, March 21, 1845; Arthur Aspinall, *Politics and the Press,* pp. 335–337, 440; Alice W. Fox, *The Earl of Halsbury, Lord High Chancellor,* pp. 11–15, 30, 32, 38.

10. Alaric Alfred Watts, *Alaric Watts, A Narrative of His Life,* 1:152, 229–231, 240; 2:309; *Halsbury Papers,* Charles Baldwin to S. L. Giffard, July 27, 1839, Lord George Bentinck to S. L. Giffard; Fox, *Halsbury,* pp. 12–13.

11. Reginald Lucas, *Lord Glenesk and the Morning Post,* pp. 35–47; *DNB,* 2:871; Cyrus Redding, *Fifty Years' Recollections,* 2:71–74; Aspinall, *Politics and the Press,* pp. 441–443; Wilfred Hindle, *The Morning Post 1772–1937,* p. 177.

12. *Standard,* February 27, 1844, March 5, 17, 1845.
13. The Times, *The History of the Times,* 2:7, 46, 47, 119–133; Arthur I. Dasent, *John Thadeus Delane, Editor of the Times,* 1:20, 13–55; Bourne, *English Newspapers,* 2:70–72.
14. George E. Marindin, *Letters of Frederick Lord Blachford,* pp. 6–7, 36–37; Roundell Palmer, *Memorials, Part I: Family and Personal,* 1:58–63, 136, 207, 303; Thomas Mozley, *Reminiscences Chiefly of Oriel College and the Oxford Movement,* 1:4; 2:161–181, 215.
15. J. K. Laughton, ed., *Memoirs of the Life and Correspondence of Henry Reeve,* 1:9–16, 34, 36, 44, 53; Henry Carlisle, *Correspondence of Abraham Hayward,* pp. 9–18, 53–54; *DNB,* 58:204; Boase, *Modern English Biography,* 3:1,484; the Times, *History of the Times,* 2:124–129.
16. Bourne, *English Newspapers,* 2:151; James Grant, *The Saturday Review,* p. 8.
17. *Morning Post,* July 21, 1840; *Times,* March 11, 1844.
18. *Morning Herald,* February 18, 1840; May 5, June 8, 24, 1842; the *Herald* praised Carlyle's *Past and Present* on May 5, 1843 and R. B. Seeley's *Perils of the Nation* on May 6, 1843. On July 26, 1843, it supported legislation regulating the labor of coal whippers because it was "a matter of pressing humanity"; March 22, 1844.
19. *Times,* January 30, 1846; *Standard,* November 4, 1845; April 15, 1843; *Morning Post,* July 21, 1840.
20. *Times,* August 2, 1850; *Morning Herald,* February 11, 1842.
21. *Standard,* March 2, 1842, said Michael Sadler was never mistaken in any instance; August 2, 1842; March 16, 22, 25, 27, July 9, 1844; February 19, April 3, 1845; February 11, 18, 1847; *Morning Post,* June 14, 1842, for mining legislation but very tepidly; March 20, May 13, July 13, 1844; March 10, 1847; on April 19, 1848 it came out "for subdividing . . . neighborhoods that in everyone of them some two or three might have a modified authority over the rest"; *Morning Herald,* June 21, 23, July 16, 1842; March 21, 27, April 10, July 25, 1844; March 6, 1845; *Times,* March 11, 15, 26, April 8, July 10, 1844; June 7, 1845; July 28, 1847.
22. *Morning Post,* April 27, 1848; March 21, June 30, 1840; March 9, 13, 29, 1843; February 9, 1847; *Morning Herald,* February 18, 1840; April 1, 1843; April 22, 1847; *Standard,* May 8, 1840; March 20, 25, April 13, 1843; March 27, April 24, 1847.
23. *Times,* May 2, 10, 17, 26, 1834; August 15, 1838, February 1, March 30, May 21, 1839; *Standard,* May 5, 12, July 25, 1834; May 21, June 5, 1839; *Morning Herald,* June 27, 1840, attacks Education Committee (and is quoted denouncing it in 1839 in the *Standard,* May 21, 1839), May 10, 1848; *Morning Post,* March 10, 1840; February 11, 1848; January 14, 1847.
24. *Morning Post,* April 29, 1840; *Standard,* May 18, 1848; *Morning Chronicle,* March 24, 1848.
25. *Standard,* December 2, 3, 9, 1845; February 11, 13, 17, April 1, 3, 1847; *Morning Post,* July 27, 1842; January 14, 27, 28, February 6, 27, 1847; *Morning Herald,* March 20, May 16, 1840; February 3, 1844; February 18, March 15, 1847.
26. *Times,* July 10, 1844; February 7, 1845; *Standard,* March 22, 24, April 22, 1845; *Morning Post,* June 3, 1847.
27. The Times, *History of the Times,* 2:14, 16, 17; Halsbury Papers, Henry Chapman to Stanley Lees Giffard; *Times,* May 7, 1835.
28. *Times,* June 23, 1849; *Morning Herald,* June 21, 1842; May 10, 1848; *Morning Post,* March 10, 1840; July 22, May 6, 1847; February 11, May 11, 1848; *Standard,* July 20, 1840; February 1, 1841.
29. *Times,* May 18, 1838.
30. Ibid., May 2, July 8, 1839; *Standard,* May 21 (also quotes *Herald* against Committee on Education), 22, 29, 30, June 5, 1839; *Morning Post,* June 11, 1840.
31. *Morning Post,* June 30, 1840; June 23, 28, 1843; April 21, 1847; Anglo-Catholicus, *The Monastic and Manufacturing Systems,* p. 17; April 23, 1847; *Standard,* May 8,

1840; April 24, June 9, March 27, 1847; *Morning Herald,* February 18, July 2, 9, 1840; April 22, 1847.
32. *Morning Herald,* June 28, 1842; March 31, 1843; *Morning Post,* June 14, 1842 (the *Post* wanted regulations preventing "the aggregation of the people into these alarming and unmanageable masses"), June 28, July 27, 1843; *Times,* October, 18, 1843.
33. *Morning Herald,* March 9, May 5, 1843 (the *Herald* noted that "far too much evil is here [Carlyle's *Past and Present*] attributed to our wealth. The wealth of England has done great good"), May 6, 1843; *Morning Post,* May 30, 1844.
34. *Morning Post,* May 20, 1848; *Morning Chronicle,* June 27, 1849.
35. *Times,* March 11, 1844; July 7, 1853.
36. *Morning Post,* July 22, 1844; January 5, 1847; *Morning Herald,* January 30, 1840; February 9, March 31, 1847. They opposed allowing Jews to serve in the legislature.
37. *Morning Post,* March 30, 1847; February 11, 1848; *Standard,* June 3, 1847 (also wanted stripes inflicted on perverse and idle vagrants); *Times,* July 23, 1847.
38. *Spectator,* May 3, 1834, p. 415; May 25, 1839, p. 486; July 30, 1842, p. 734; April 13, 1844, pp. 346–347; February 13, 1847, p. 157; February 20, 1847, p. 181; March 6, 1847, p. 230; April 24, 1847, p. 398; May 13, 1848, p. 467.
39. *Morning Post,* June 28, 1843.
40. Oliver MacDonagh, *A Pattern of Government Growth;* Jenifer Hart, "Nineteenth Century Social Reform," p. 46.
41. David Roberts, *Victorian Origins of the British Welfare State,* pp. 185–202; R. M. Grier, *John Allen,* pp. 31, 55, 67, 102, 103, 246; Anna O. Allen, *John Allen and His Friends,* pp. 6, 34, 93, 107–111.
42. *Archaeologia Cambrensis,* January 1871, pp. 94–95; *Blackwood's Magazine,* May 1848, pp. 540–562; October 1840, pp. 523–534; June 1849, pp. 713–726; *Biograph,* 1881, 6:64–65; J. P. Norris, *The Education of the People,* p. 15.
43. Roberts, *Victorian Origins,* pp. 154–155, 328–329.
44. Katherine Lyell, *Memoir of Leonard Horner,* 2:14, 155; P.P., Reports of Inspectors of Factories, 1839, 19:480–493, 506, 528–536; 1842, 22:464–465; 1843, 27:294. Horner wanted more schools as "evidence to the humbler classes of friendly dispositions and kinder sympathy in those above them; feelings of alienation between employer and employed would be checked and the just influence of property and education would be strengthened"; 1847, 15:444–445.
45. P.P., Reports of Inspectors of Factories, 1839, 19:480–536; 1843, 27:322–327, 356–361; 1845, 25:470; Sir James Graham Papers, Sir James Graham to Gladstone, March 25, 1843; Edward Baines, *Slander Refuted and Duplicity Exposed: In Two Letters to the Rev. W. F. Hook and R. J. Saunders.*
46. H. S. Tremenheere, *Notes on Public Subjects,* p. 107, praises Lowell model paternalist manufactures; Home Office Papers, Public Record Office, H.O. 45/511, Tremenheere report. December 23, 1844; H.O. 45/2365, 1848, report on Shropshire; P.P., Report of Commissioners of Mines, 1846, 24:385–407; 1848, 26:412–414.
47. P.P., Reports of Prison Inspectors, 1844, 29:593, 597; 1845, 23:viii; 1845, 24:131–132, in which Captain Williams the inspector says there will be no decrease in juvenile delinquency until there is "a closer and kindlier intercourse between employer and employed," and until there is an improvement in "the physical and moral conditions of the humbler classes"; 1846, 20:461 ff; 1847, 29:381 ff; 1848, 35:511; Reports of Commissioners in Lunacy, 1849, 22:1–8; 1850, vol. 23.

Chapter IX

1. Brian T. Bradfield, "Sir Richard Vyvyan and Tory Politics"; Benjamin Disraeli Papers, Hughenden MSS, George Smythe to Disraeli, October 1842; Boase, *Modern English Biography,* 4:228; 5:98.

2. *Men of the Times,* 1872, pp. 231, 504; Charles Whibley, *Lord John Manners and His Friends,* 1:53–74, 133, 260; Non-Elector, *Lord John Manners,* p. 2; T. Wemys Reid, *Life, Letters and Friendships of Richard Monckton Milnes,* 1:47–87; James Pope-Hennessy, *Monckton Milnes, The Years of Promise,* pp. 14–76; Beresford Hope, *Essays.*

3. A. B. Cochrane, *Lucille Belmont,* 1:77, 252; 2:20; 3:46, 288; George Sydney Smythe, *Angela Pisani,* 1:146; 2:115, 214, 224, 241; idem, *Historic Fancies,* pp. 11, 15, 22, 59, 67, 91, 95.

4. R. M. Milnes, *Poetry for the People,* p. 49; *Report of the Proceedings for the Establishment of the Yorkshire Protective Society,* pp. 25 ff.; Whibley, *Manners,* p. 43; *Young England, Address Delivered by Lord John Manners,* p. 6; Non-Elector, *Manners,* pp. 39, 52; Augustus Stafford O'Brien, *The History of a Charade on the Immortal Name of Wordsworth.*

5. Pope-Hennessy, *Milnes,* p. 249.

6. Reginald Lucas, *Lord Glenesk and the Morning Post,* p. 40; *Hansard Parliamentary Debates,* 1844, 76:1,341–1,346; 1847, 92:357.

7. *DNB,* 57:43; *Oxford and Cambridge Review,* August 1843, pp. 150–160.

8. Reid, *Milnes,* 1:87, 116, 205 ff.; Whibley, *Manners,* 1:63.

9. A. Acland, *Memoir of Sir Thomas Dyke Acland,* pp. 22, 33, 48–49, 66; Roundell Palmer, *Memorials, Part I: Family and Personal,* pp. 123–145; Lord Stanmore, *Sidney Herbert,* pp. 10–15; John Morley, *Life of Gladstone,* 1:167–172; William Gladstone, *The State in Its Relations with the Church,* pp. 6, 17–18, 83.

10. Whibley, *Manners,* 1:61, 261; William S. Childe-Pemberton, *Life of Lord Norton,* pp. 5, 11–12, 19, 82; P. G. E., *Grillion's Club,* pp. 1, 86.

11. W. R. W. Stephens, *A Memoir of the Right Hon. William Page Wood, Baron Hatherley,* 1:14–15, 17, 51–52, 76–77, 98, 160, 196–197; idem, *The Life and Letters of Walter Farquhar Hook,* 1:232; Georgina Cowper-Temple, *Memorials of William Cowper-Temple,* pp. 9, 17, 28–29, 39, 40.

12. *DNB,* 11:403; John C. Colquhoun, *Scattered Leaves of Biography,* pp. 139–264; idem, *The Constitutional Principles of Parliamentary Reform,* p. 64, Colquhoun says do not give the lower classes the vote but instead "give them education and religion, erect churches for adults, schools for the young, extend relief to their wants, sympathy to their afflictions and through the channels of private charity pour the contribution of private benevolence. These duties . . . will sweeten the intercourse of society"; Disraeli Papers, Disraeli's Observations, n.d. A/X/A/13; James Grant, *The British Senate,* pp. 71–76.

13. Childe-Pemberton, *Lord Norton,* pp. 9, 29, 32–36, 44, 58, 61, 69, 95, 126–130; Rev. Herbert James and Rev. Edward Hoare, *Two Sermons Following the Funeral of John Pemberton Plumptre; DNB,* first supplement, 2:368; *Hansard,* 1844, 75:1,368.

14. *DNB,* 12:111; G. F. A. Best, *Shaftesbury,* p. 83; *Hansard,* 1843, 67:1,465; *Dorset Chronicle,* July 8, 1841; E. V. Bligh, *Lord Ebury as a Church Reformer.*

15. *DNB,* 50:42; Dudley Ryder, first earl of Harrowby, *Ryder Family Papers, Family Reminiscences,* pp. 3–14; *DNB,* 55:113; Alfred Gatty, *Wortley and the Wortleys,* pp. 36–37; Rev. Saint Vincent Beechey, *Two Sermons . . . on Funeral of Francis Egerton, First Earl of Ellesmere;* Bernard Falk, *The Bridgewater Millions;* Aubrey Newman, *The Stanhopes of Chevening,* pp. 299–316.

16. Beechey, *Egerton,* pp. 26, 27, 31, 32, 33, 36, appendix; *DNB,* 17:154; *Hansard,* 1847, 91:339.

17. *DNB,* 54:37; Sir Robert Peel Papers, Add MSS 40, 539, J. S. Wortley to Peel, January 29, 1844; Wharncliffe Papers, J. S. Wortley to Sir James Graham, April 20, 1843; Newman, *The Stanhopes,* pp. 307–312; *Hansard,* 1847, 91:1,198.

18. Lord Mahon, *Historical Essays,* pp. 274, 278–282; idem, *History of England from 1713 to 1783,* 7:335; Lord Francis Egerton, *Speech . . . to the Electors of the Southern Division of Lancashire,* p. 9; idem, *Address Delivered at the 12th*

Annual Meeting of the British Association for the Advancement of Science, p. 6; DNB, 55:113.

19. Sir Walter James, Bart., *Thoughts upon the Theory and Practice of the Poor Laws,* pp. 6–14; Montagu Gore, *On the Dwellings of the Poor,* pp. iv–v; idem, *Allotment of Land,* pp. 5–13; idem, *Letter to the Middle Classes on the Present Disturbed State of the Country,* pp. 3–14; idem, *Thoughts on the Present State of Ireland,* p. 4; DNB, 26:239; also paternalistic in outlook is chapters 5 of volume 2 of William Mackinnon's *History of Civilisation.*

20. *Hansard,* 1841, 57:126; 1843, 67:107–108, 111; 1845, 77:116; 81:376; 1846, 84:781–784; 85:1,106–1,134; Peel Papers, Add MSS 40, 509, Peel to Rev. Dr. Lully, June 1842; Peel to Mr. Willington, mayor of Tamworth; Add MSS 40, 539, Peel to Thomas Bramall, February 3, 1844; Add MSS 40, 536, Peel to mayor of Tamworth; Add MSS 40, 534, Peel to Mr. Savage; Add MSS 40, 500, Peel to mayor of Tamworth, January 14, 1842; Add MSS 40, 545, May 24, 1844 Inglis to Peel, and Peel to Inglis, Peel gives money for monument to Southey.

21. Best, *Shaftesbury,* p. 83.

22. Disraeli Papers, Lord John Manners to Disraeli, October 24, 1844, January 5, 1848, March 20, 1849, December 29, 1847; H. Baillie to Disraeli, November 30, 1848.

23. *Baily's Monthly Magazine of Sports and Pastimes,* 1887, 17:347; DNB, 40:329; *Stamford Mercury,* June 18, 1841, DNB, 52:188; *St. James's Magazine* 4 (1870): 771; Halsbury Papers, "Family History"; *Stamford Mercury,* August 6, 1847.

24. Viola Bankes, *A Dorset Heritage,* pp. 180–185; George Bankes, *Speeches,* pp. 19–34; *Dorset Chronicle,* July 8, 1841; August 5, 1847; *Salisbury Journal,* August 7, 1847; *Dorset Chronicle,* July 14, 1877; *Devizes and Wiltshire Gazette,* August 5, 1847; Major General E. D. H. Tollemache, *The Tollemaches of Helmingham and Ham,* pp. 163–167; *Stamford Mercury,* August 13, 1847.

25. George Bankes, *The Story of Corfe Castle; Dorset County Chronicle,* July 14, 1887.

26. Bradfield, "Sir Richard Vyvyan"; Sir Richard Vyvyan, *A Letter to the Magistrates of Berkshire;* John S. Pakington, *A Charge on the Subject of the County Expenditure;* Henry Halford, *Some Remarks on the Report of the Constabulary Force Commission,* pp. 38, 47–48, 60–61.

27. Halford, *Constabulary,* p. 38; *Hansard,* 1848, 98:1,173; *Stamford Mercury,* August 13, 1847, "The best plan . . . was for the landowner and land occupier and the labourer to unite and let the kindly confidence prevail between them as was reciprocated between friend and friend."

28. *St. James's Magazine* 4(1870):771; George Bankes, *Reconsiderations on Certain Proposed Alterations of the Game Laws.*

29. *Dorset Chronicle,* July 14, 1887; Henry Willoughby, *The Apology of an English Landowner,* p. 8; *Nottingham Journal,* July 16, 1841; *Hansard,* 1848, 98:1,173.

30. *Farmer's Magazine,* August 1844, pp. 81–84; E. S. Cayley, *On Commercial Economy,* pp. 22, 33, 52, 81; idem, *Reasons for the Formation of the Agricultural Protection Society,* pp. 5, 7, 20; idem, *Corn, Trade, Wages and Rent;* idem, *A Letter to H. Handley . . . a Member of the Late Committee on Agricultural Distress.*

31. *Hansard,* 1842, 60:420–431; 62:820–844.

32. Francis Baring, *Journals and Correspondence from 1808–1852,* pp. 191–192; Rev. G. H. Sumner, *Sermon after the Funeral of Francis Baron Northbrook,* p. 13.

33. Mabel Ogilvy, *Lady Palmerston and Her Times,* pp. 35–36; Cowper-Temple, *William Cowper-Temple,* p. 56. "Palmerston has eight schools, an agriculturist to improve the ground and plant and teach the people how to sow . . . and keep their gardens."

34. Spencer Walpole, *The Life of Lord John Russell,* pp. 3–31, 57; John Prest, *Lord John Russell,* pp. 3–16; Rollo Russell, *Early Correspondence of Lord John Russell, 1805–1840,* pp. 11–34.

35. Desmond MacCarthy and Agatha Russell, *Lady John Russell,* pp. 8, 84; John Earl Russell, *Recollections and Suggestions,* p. 184.
36. Sir George Douglas and Sir George Dalhousie Ramsay, eds., *The Panmure Papers,* pp. 9–10, 12, 18, 35; George Trevelyan, *Lord Grey of the Reform Bill,* pp. 89, 103, refers to "the ever increasing preoccupations of a patriarchal state, which made Grey one of the happiest of men"; Lord Edmond Fitzmaurice, *The Life of Granville George Leveson-Gower, Second Earl Granville, 1815–1891,* 1:6–25, remembers a father seldom angry, a father who only once scolded a servant unjustly; he also remembers hunting parties with the duke of Wellington at Wherstead near Ipswich, child balls at Carlton House, and the embassies of The Hague and Paris where his father was ambassador; J. T. Ward, "The Earls Fitzwilliam and the Wentworth Wodehouse Estate in the 19th Century," pp. 19–26; Fitzwilliam Papers, G 44, J. W. Tottie to Earl Fitzwilliam, November 1854; G 65, Earl Fitzwilliam to Lord Milton, July 6, 7, no year; G 60, J. P. Pritchett to Earl Fitzwilliam, letters on Ecclesall jail; G 74, Lord Milton to Earl Fitzwilliam, September 27, October 24, 1845.
37. Nancy Mitford, *The Ladies of Alderley,* pp. xxi–xxv, 23, 49–61, 201–205, 219, 227.
38. MacCarthy and Russell, *Lady John Russell,* p. 84.
39. Ryder, *Ryder Family Papers.*
40. Robert A. Slaney, *State of the Poorer Classes in Great Towns;* idem, *Essay on the Beneficial Directions of Rural Expenditure,* pp. 9–10, 15, 104–105, 113; *Peel Papers,* Add MSS 40, 516, Slaney to Peel, October 1, 1842; R. A. Slaney, *An Essay on the Employment of the Poor;* idem, *A Plea to Power and Parliament for the Working Classes,* pp. 7–16, 39.
41. Thomas Wyse, *Education Reform* pp. 13, 244, 270, 279.
42. George Poulett Scrope, *Suggested Legislation with a View to the Improvement of the Dwellings of the Poor,* pp. 11, 203; idem, *Plea for the Abolition of Slavery in England,* pp. 3, 36, 42; *Hansard,* 1847, 85:1,199, 1,201; 1848, 97:857; Wyse, *Education Reform,* p. 414.
43. *Hansard,* 1844, 74:642.
44. Sir Harry Verney, Bart., *A Letter to the Farmers of Buckinghamshire,* pp. 8–9, 10, 15; idem, *A Letter from Sir Harry Verney,* pp. 10–11; *DNB,* 57:272; David Frederick Smith, "Sir George Grey at the Mid-Victorian Home Office, p. 286; Mandell Creighton, *Memoir of Sir George Grey,* p. 49.
45. D. F. Smith, "Grey," pp. 46, 54, "A believer in the operation of paternalism Sir George resented the extension of central government," pp. 129–133; Scrope, *The Principles of Political Economy;* Wyse, *Education Reform,* pp. 157–159; Slaney, *Rural Expenditure,* pp. 17–19, 37, 163; idem, *Employment of the Poor,* pp. 11, 13, 33, 45–46, 69; *Leeds Mercury,* June 26, 1841; C. B. R. Kent, *The English Radicals,* p. 274.
46. *Hansard,* 1847, 89:221.
47. Ibid., 1846, 87:291, 297–298; 1847, 89:667–668, 711, 726, 731; 1848, 96:686, the Anglo-Irish M.P.s help defeat an investigation into the working of the Irish Poor Law; 97:1,313–1,323; 97:977; 100:104, they oppose bill for giving wastelands to poor; 101:317, 336, 342, 364, attack Irish Education System and want grants to religious schools instead; 103:74–76, 132–135, 216–217, 255.
48. Ibid., 1848, 97:1,315, 1,319; 1847, 89:728.
49. Ibid., 1847, 90:1,362–1,363.
50. Ibid., 1847, 89:743.
51. Lady Gregory, ed., *Sir William Gregory, KCMG, An Autobiography,* pp. 29–32, 36, 38, 81–82, 139–140; *DNB,* first supplement, 2:355.
52. *Hansard,* 1847, 91:181; 1849, 106:838–839.
53. Grantley F. Berkeley, *My Life and Recollections,* 1:245; see also pp. 4, 15, 158, 233; idem, *Anecdotes of the Upper Ten Thousand* 1:241, 251; 2:186–187; *DNB,* 4:356.

54. Richard Lambert, *The Railway King, 1800–1871: A Study of George Hudson.*
55. Henry Drummond, *Speeches in Parliament and Miscellaneous Pamphlets*, pp. 41, 82, 102, 127, 150, 294, 305, 317; *Hansard*, 1848, 98:112–117, 728–729; 99:65–68, 100:909–912; 1849, 103:607–610; 100:208–219; 106:858–859.
56. *Shropshire Mercury*, June 18, 1841; Disraeli Papers, W. B. Ferrand to Benjamin Disraeli, January 3, 1850.
57. *Hansard*, 1846, 86:1,029.

Chapter X

1. *Hansard Parliamentary Debates*, 1844, 76:273, 348, 482–516; 75:1,549.
2. Ibid., 1844, 73:1,263; 74:1,027.
3. Benjamin Disraeli Papers, John Manners to Disraeli, November 4, December 29, 1844; Non-Elector, *Lord John Manners*, pp. 21, 64; *Morning Chronicle*, August 2, 1844; *Young England;* and for more on ferment developing over *Coningsby* in 1844 see the *Morning Post* and the *Morning Herald* of May 16, the *Literary Gazette* of May 18, and *Atlas* of May 25, as well as *John Bull* of June 1 and *Punch* of June 22.
4. *Morning Herald*, July 25, 1844; *Spectator*, April 13, 1844; *Hansard*, 1844, 73:1,263–1,266.
5. *Hansard*, 1844, 73:1,217–1,219. To Mc Geachey "the organization of labour is the grand political problem of the day"; Sir Robert Peel Papers, Add MSS, 40, 539, J. Stuart-Wortley to Peel, January 29, 1844; Add MSS 40, 541, Lord Sandon to Peel, March 18, 1844.
6. Peel Papers, Add MSS, 4777, Gladstone's cabinet memoranda for March 25 and March 30, 1844.
7. *Hansard*, 1844, 74:1,106–1,110.
8. Ibid., 1844, 74:1,106–1,110; 76:384.
9. Ibid., 1846, 83:648; 1849, 102:158; 83:1,460; 1847, 89:914; 1841, 56:382; 1846, 83:1,341–1,347; 1844, 76:331–332; 1841, 56:382.
10. Ibid., 1846, 85:265–269; Disraeli Papers, A/X/A/13, "Observations," p. 32; Robert M. Steward, *The Politics of Protection*, p. 83.
11. Disraeli Papers, A/X/A/13, "Observations," p. 33; *Oxford and Cambridge Review*, August 1845, pp. 195–217; November 1845, pp. 399–410; *Hansard*, 1844, 73:1,263, 1,460; 74:1,106; 76:768–769.
12. Disraeli Papers, Lord John Manners to Disraeli, November 19, 26, 1844. In the November 26 letter Manners complains that "that dog Cochrane is throwing cold water on us"; A/X/A/13 "Observations," p. 32; *Hansard*, 1844, 74:762; 1846, 87:1,254; 1847, 92:718; Lord John Manners, *A Plea for National Holy-Days;* James Pope-Hennessy, *Monckton Milnes, The Years of Promise.*
13. *Hansard*, 1847, 92:718–719; Disraeli Papers, A/X/A/13 "Observations," p. 32.
14. *Hansard*, 1848, 98:802, 1,178; 97:1,113.
15. Ibid., 1847, 89:635, 1,265; 93:1,046–1,047; 1849, 105:1,289, 1,323–1,324.
16. Ibid., 1846, 85:1,128–1,131; 1847, 90:123–126; 1849, 104:878–883.
17. Ibid., 1846, 86:950; 1847, 93:279; 1847, 93:646; 1848, 100:778, 98:1,149, 97:113; 1847, 91:1,130, 146–147.
18. Ibid., 1849, 106:1,343; 107:236–242; 1848, 99:87–89, 97.
19. Ibid., 1849, 106:1,343.
20. Ibid., 1847, 93:279–280; 92:312–313.
21. Ibid., 1849, 103:677; 1847, 90:279–280, 645–666.
22. Ibid., 1847, 91:367, 610; 1849, 104:564, 596.
23. Ibid., 1842, 64:683–684, 694; 1847, 93:887, 898–899, 903–904; Lonsdale, *Worthies of Cumberland*, 3:125.
24. *Hansard*, 1842, 64:683; 1847, 93:887; 1842, 65:340–341, 377; 1847, 93:898–899.
25. Ibid., 1848, 98:741, 1,178.

26. Ibid., 1847, 92:666, 1,173, 1,004–1,006; 1848, 98:738, 722.
27. Ibid., 1848, 100:126, 613; 98:741–743, 1,178–1,179.
28. Ibid., 1849, 105:777; 1848, 98:711; 1849, 103:861.
29. Ibid., 1844, 74:531; 1842, 63:1,637; 1848, 97:591; 1847, 93:5; 1845, 81:383; 1848, 100:1,096.
30. Ibid., 1847, 94:275; 1844, 73:1,263, 1,460; 1846, 85:266; 1847, 94:566–577; 1845, 80:745.
31. Ibid., 1847, 92:368; 93:752, 887, 893, 904, 1,100.
32. Ibid., 1843, 67:1,412–1,472; 68:745; 69:96–97; 70:93, 1,333.
33. Ibid., 1843, 67:1,445; Disraeli Papers, Lord John Manners to Disraeli, November 8, December 16, 1847.
34. *Hansard*, 1845, 80:745–748; 1849, 102:848; 1848, 100:126; 1847, 93:886; 92:1,235; 1844; 73:1,263; 1847, 91:367; 1848, 98:742.
35. W. O. Aydelotte, "Voting Patterns in the British House of Commons in the 1840's"; David Roberts, *Victorian Origins of the British Welfare State*, pp. 35–104; Edwin Hodder, *The Life and Work of the Seventh Earl of Shaftesbury*, 1:478.
36. *Hansard*, 1842, 64:168–171, 257–259, 651–655, 691–693; 1847, 91:610–611; 1849, 104:598–600; 1844, 75:106; 94:567; 74:531.
37. Ibid., 1847, 101:478; 92:116–117; 1849, 102:471; 1846, 84:1,404.
38. Ibid., 1844, 76:1,486; 1843, 68:319–320; 1849, 104:927–928; 1844, 75:877; 1842, 65:106; 1840, 55:433.
39. Ibid., 1840, 55:433; 1843, 68:320; 1842, 65:1,094.
40. Ibid., 1849, 104:101–110.

Bibliography

When two publication dates are given, the first refers to the date of original publication, the second to the edition cited in the notes.

Primary Sources

Manuscript Materials

Edwin Chadwick Papers, University College, London University.
Benjamin Disraeli Papers, Hughenden, Buckinghamshire.
Fitzwilliam Papers, Sheffield Public Library.
Sir James Graham Papers, Netherby, Cumberland.
The earl of Halsbury Papers, in the possession of the heirs of Lord Halsbury.
Home Office Papers, Public Record Office, London.
Sir Robert Peel Papers, British Library, London.
Poor Law Papers, M.H. 12/– and M.H. 32/–, Public Record Office, London.
Duke of Richmond Papers. Goodwood MSS. Sussex County Records Office, Chichester.
Wharncliffe Papers, Sheffield Public Library.

Parliamentary Papers, House of Commons Edition

Annual Reports of the Poor Law Commission: 1837, 31; 1838, 28; 1840, 17; 1843, 21, 12; 1845, 27; 1848, 33; 1849, 42 (Schools); 1850, 27 (Settlement).
Communications of Sheriffs on the Prisons Bill for Scotland: 1839, 38.

Report from the Select Committee on Newspapers: 1851, 17.

Report of the Commissioners Appointed under the Provisions of the Act 5 &
6 Vict. c. 99, to Inquire into the Operation of that Act, and into the State
of the Population of the Mining Districts: 1842, 15; 1846, 24; 1848, 26.

Report of the Commissioners in Lunacy to the Lord Chancellor: 1847, 33;
1848, 35; 1849, 22; 1850, 23.

Reports from Commissioners Inquiring into Children's Employment (Trade
and Manufactures): 1843, 14 and 15.

Reports of Her Majesty's Inspectors of Schools in Minutes of the Committee
of Council on Education: 1842, 33; 1845, 35; 1846, 32; 1847, 45; 1848,
50; 1849, 42; 1850, 44; 1852, 40; 1853, 53.

Reports of Inspectors of Factories to Her Majesty's Principal Secretary of
State for the Home Department: 1839, 19; 1842, 22; 1843, 27; 1844, 28;
1845, 25; 1846, 20; 1847, 15; 1848, 26.

Reports of the Prison Inspectors: 1839, 38; 1840, 25; 1842, 21; 1843, 25;
1844, 29; 1845, 23, 24; 1846, 20, 21; 1847, 29; 1848, 35; 1849, 26;
1850, 28; 1855, 26.

Returns of Ecclesiastical Commission, Archbishoprics and Bishoprics: 1851,
42.

Royal Commission on the Employment of Women and Children, 1842, 15–
17; 1843, 13, 16.

Royal Commission on the State of the Poor Laws: 1834, 37, 38.

Select Committee on Agricultural Customs, 1848, 7.

Select Committee on Allotments of Land, 1843, 7.

Select Committee on Game Laws, 1846, 9.

Select Committee on Prison Discipline, 1850, 17.

Select Committee on Settlement and Poor Removal, 1847, 11.

Select Committee on the Poor Laws, 1837, 17; 1838, 18.

Periodicals and Newspapers

Archaeologia Cambrensis
Athenaeum
Atlas
Baily's Monthly Magazine of Sports and Pastimes
Biograph
Blackwood's Magazine
British and Foreign Review
British Critic
British Quarterly
Chambers Edinburgh Journal
Cheltenham Chronicle

Cheltenham Examiner
Cheltenham Journal
Christian Observer
Christian Remembrancer
Christian Teacher
Critic
Devizes and Wiltshire Gazette
Dorset Chronicle
Eclectic Review
English Review
Examiner
Farmer's Magazine
Fraser's Magazine
Globe
Journal of the Statistical Society of London
Labourer's Friend Magazine
Leeds Intelligencer
Leeds Mercury
Leeds Times
Literary Gazette
London Journal
Men of the Times
Mirror
Morning Advertiser
Morning Chronicle
Morning Herald
Morning Post
Northampton Mercury
Nottingham Journal
Oxford and Cambridge Review
People's Journal
Politics for the People
Punch
Quarterly Review
St. James's Chronicle
St. James's Magazine
Salisbury Journal
Shipping Gazette
Shropshire Mercury
Stamford Mercury
Standard
Sun

Sussex Agricultural Express
Times
Weekly Chronicle
Western Luminary
Western Times
Westminster Review
Witness

Novels and Poems

Armitage, Robert. *Doctor Hookwell*. London, 1842.
———. *Ernest Singleton*. London, 1848.
———. *The Penscellwood Papers*. London, 1846.
Berkeley, Grantley F. *Anecdotes of the Upper Ten Thousand*. London, 1867.
Brontë, Charlotte. *Shirley*. London, 1908.
Cochrane, A. B. *Lucille Belmont*. London, 1849.
Dickens, Charles. *The Chimes*. London, 1844. In *Christmas Books*. New York, 1868.
———. *A Christmas Carol*. London, 1843. New York, 1868.
———. *Dombey and Son*. London, 1846–1848. New York, 1912.
———. *Hard Times*. London, 1854. London, 1858.
———. *Nicholas Nickleby*. London, 1838–1839. London, Chapman & Hall, n.d.
———. *Pickwick Papers*. London, 1837. Boston, Dan Estes, n.d.
Disraeli, Benjamin. *Coningsby*. London, 1844.
———. *Sybil*. London, 1845.
Eliot, George. *Scenes of Clerical Life*. London, 1858. Leipzig, 1859.
Gaskell, Elizabeth. *Mary Barton*. London, 1848. London, n.d.
———. *North and South*. London, 1855. London, 1970.
Gore, Catherine, *Men of Capital*. 3 vols. London, 1846.
———. *Peers and Parvenus*. London, 1846.
Gresley, William. *Charles Lever*. London, 1845.
———. *Church Clavering*. London, 1845.
———. *Clement Walton*. London, 1840.
———. *Frank's First Trip to the Continent*. London, 1845.
Hook, Theodore. *Peregrine Bunce*. London, 1842. London, 1873.
James, G. P. R. *Charles Tyrrell*. New York, 1839.
———. *The Gentleman of the Old School*. New York, 1839.
Jerrold, Douglas. *The History of St. Giles and St. James*. London, 1851.
Kingsley, Charles. *Alton Locke*. London, 1850. London, 1917.
———. *Yeast*. London, 1848. New York, 1858.
Martineau, Harriet. *Deerbrook*. London, 1838. London, 1878.

Milnes, Richard Monckton. *Poetry for the People*. London, 1840.

Murray, J. F. *Viceroy*. London, 1841.

Paget, Francis E. *The Pageant; or, Pleasure and Its Price*. London, 1843.

———. *The Warden of Berkingholt*. London, 1843.

Sewell, Elizabeth. *Amy Herbert*. 2 vols. London, 1846.

Sewell, William. *Hawkstone*. London, 1845. New York, 1848.

Smythe, George Sydney. *Angela Pisani*. 3 vols. London, 1875.

[Tonna], Charlotte Elizabeth. *Helen Fleetwood*. London, 1841. New York, 1858.

Trollope, Anthony. *The Warden*. London, 1855. New York, 1912.

Trollope, Frances. *Jessie Phillips*. London, 1844.

———. *Michael Armstrong, The Factory Boy*. London, 1840.

Wordsworth, William. *The Poetical Works of William Wordsworth*. Edited by E. de Selincourt. London, 1940.

Other Works

Acland, A. *Memoir of Sir Thomas Dyke Acland*. London, 1902.

Adams, W. E. *Memoirs of a Social Atom*. London, 1903.

Alison, Sir Archibald. *Some Account of My Writings, An Autobiography*. London, 1883.

Anglo-Catholicus. *The Monastic and Manufacturing Systems*. London, 1843.

Arnold, Thomas. *The Miscellaneous Works of Thomas Arnold*. Edited by A. P. Stanley. New York, 1845.

Bain, Alexander. *The Moral Philosophy of Paley*. London, 1852.

Baines, Edward. *Slander Refuted and Duplicity Exposed: In Two Letters to the Rev. W. F. Hook and R. J. Saunders*. Leeds, 1843.

Bankes, George. *Reconsideration on Certain Proposed Alterations of the Game Laws*. London, 1825.

———. *Speeches*. Dorchester, 1846.

———. *The Story of Corfe Castle*. London, 1853.

Baring, Francis. *Journals and Correspondence from 1808–1852*. London, 1905.

Baxter, G. R. W. *Book of the Bastiles*. London, 1841.

Beechey, Rev. Saint Vincent. *Two Sermons . . . on Funeral of Francis Egerton, First Earl of Ellesmere*. London, 1857.

Beggs, Thomas. *An Inquiry into the Extent and Causes of Juvenile Depravity*. London, 1849.

Berkeley, Grantley F. *My Life and Recollections*. 4 vols. London, 1865.

Birks, Thomas. *Memoir of the Rev. Edward Bickersteth*. London, 1851.

Blomfield, Alfred. *A Memoir of Charles James Blomfield*. London, 1864.

Blomfield, Charles James. *1842 Charge*. London, 1842.

———. *1846 Charge*. London, 1846.

————. *A Pastoral Letter to the Clergy of the Diocese of London,* London, 1847.

Bolingbroke, Lord. *The Works of Lord Bolingbroke.* 4 vols. Philadelphia, 1841.

Bromley, C. H. *The Church, the Privy Council, and the Working Classes.* London, 1850.

Buckingham, James Silk. *The Eastern and Western States of America.* London, 1842.

Bunbury, Sir Charles, ed. *Memoir and Literary Remains of Lieutenant-General Sir Henry Edward Bunbury.* London, 1868.

Burke, Edmund. *The Works of Edmund Burke.* 9 vols. Boston, 1839.

Campbell, George Douglas. *Eighth Duke of Argyll (1823–1900) Autobiography and Memoirs.* London, 1906.

Carlisle, Henry. *Correspondence of Abraham Hayward.* London, 1886.

Carlyle, Thomas. *Chartism.* London, 1839. London, 1956.

————. *Latter-Day Pamphlets.* London, 1850. London, 1872.

————. *Past and Present.* London, 1843. London, 1897.

Carter, T. T. *A Memoir of John Armstrong, D.D.* London, 1857.

Cayley, E. S. *Corn, Trade, Wages and Rent.* London, 1826.

————. *A Letter to H. Handley . . . a Member of the Late Committee on Agricultural Distress.* York, 1836.

————. *On Commercial Economy.* London, 1830.

————. *Reasons for the Formation of the Agricultural Protection Society.* London, 1844.

Chalmers, Thomas. *The Christian and Civic Economy of Large Towns.* 3 vols. Glasgow, 1821–1826.

Christian Instruction Society. *A Course of Thirteen Lectures to Socialists and Others.* London, 1840.

Church, R. C. *Essays and Reviews.* London, 1854.

Close, Rev. Francis. *Eighty Sketches of Sermons.* London, 1861.

————. *National Education.* London, 1852.

————. *Occasional Sermons.* London, 1844.

Cobbett, William. *A History of the Protestant Reformation.* London, 1829.

Coleridge, Samuel Taylor. *Letters, Conversations and Recollections.* Edited by Thomas Allsop. London, 1836.

————. *On the Constitution of the Church and State.* London, 1829. London, 1839.

————. *Specimens of Table Talk.* London, 1835.

————. *The Grounds of Sir Robert Peel's Bill (for the Regulation of Factories) Vindicated.* London, 1818. London, 1913.

————. *Two Lay Sermons.* London, 1816. London, 1839.

Colquhoun, John C. *The Constitutional Principles of Parliamentary Reform.* London, 1831.

———. *Scattered Leaves of Biography.* London, 1864.

Conybeare, Rev. W. J. *Essays Ecclesiastical and Social.* London, 1855.

———. *Sermons Preached in the Chapel Royal.* London, 1844.

Copleston, William J. *Memoir of Edward Copleston, D.D. Bishop of Llandaff.* London, 1851.

Cowper-Temple, Georgina. *Memorials of William Cowper-Temple.* London, 1890.

Creighton, Mandell. *Memoir of Sir George Grey.* London, 1901.

Croker, John. *Correspondence and Diaries.* Edited by L. J. Jennings. London, 1884.

Croly, George. *A Memoir of Edmund Burke.* Edinburgh, 1840.

Dale, Rev. Thomas. *Hints on the Culture of Character.* London, 1855.

Dawes, Richard. *Remarks Occasioned by the Present Crusade against the Educational Plans of the Committee of Council on Education.* London, 1850.

Denison, Edward. *Charges to the Clergy.* London, 1839, 1842, 1845, 1848.

Denison, G. A. *Notes of My Life.* London, 1878.

———. *The Present State of the Management Question.* London, 1849.

De Quincey, Thomas. *Reminiscences of the English Lake Poets.* London, J. M. Dent, n.d.

Dickens, Charles. *Notes on America.* London, 1842.

Digby, Kenelm. *The Broad Stone of Honour.* London, 1827.

———. *Mores Catholici or Ages of Faith.* 11 vols. London, 1831–1842.

Drummond, Henry. *Speeches in Parliament and Miscellaneous Pamphlets.* London, 1860.

Elyot, Sir Thomas. *The Book Named the Governor.* Originally published 1531. Edited by S. E. Lehmberg. London, 1962.

Egerton, Lord Francis. *Address Delivered at the 12th Annual Meeting of the British Association for the Advancement of Science.* Manchester, 1842.

———. *Speech . . . to the Electors of the Southern Division of Lancashire.* Manchester, 1834.

Garbett, James. *The Secret of the Church's Power.* Lewes, 1844.

Gaskin, J. J. *The Viceregal Speeches and Addresses, Lectures and Poems, of the Late Earl of Carlisle.* London, 1866.

Gilbert, Ashurst Turner. *A Pastoral Letter.* Chichester, 1843.

Gisborne, Thomas. *An Enquiry into the Duties in Men in the Higher and Middle Classes.* London, 1794.

Gladstone, William. *Church Principles.* London, 1840.

———. *The State in Its Relations with the Church.* London, 1838.

Glyde, John. *The Moral, Social and Religious Condition of Ipswich.* London, 1850.

———. *Suffolk in the Nineteenth Century.* London, 1852.

Gore, Montagu. *Allotment of Land.* London, 1831.

———. *Letter to the Middle Classes on the Present Disturbed State of the Country.* London, 1839.

———. *On the Dwellings of the Poor.* London, 1851.

———. *Thoughts on the Present State of Ireland.* London, 1848.

Grant, James. *The British Senate.* London, 1838.

———. *Memoirs of Sir George Sinclair.* London, 1870.

Greg, William R. *Enigmas of Life.* London, 1891.

———. *Essays on Political and Social Science.* London, 1853.

Gregory, Lady Isabella, ed. *Sir William Gregory, KCMG, An Autobiography.* London, 1894.

Gresley, Rev. William. *Parochial Sermons.* London, 1842.

———. *Practical Sermons.* London, 1848.

Grimshawe, T. S. *A Memoir of the Rev. Legh Richmond.* London, 1840.

Halford, Henry. *Some Remarks on the Report of the Constabulary Force Commission.* London, 1840.

Hansard, T. C., ed. *Parliamentary Debates of Great Britain.* 3rd series.

Hare, Julius. *Charges to the Clergy of the Archdeaconry of Lewes.* Cambridge, 1856.

Helps, Arthur. *The Claims of Labour.* London, 1844.

———. *Friends in Council.* London, 1847.

Henry, William Charles. "A Biographical Notice of the Late Rev. Richard Dawes, M.A." *Hereford Times,* March 16, 1847.

Herbert, Sidney. *Proposals for the Better Application of Cathedral Institutions.* London, 1849.

Hook, Walter F. *The Duty of English Churchmen.* London, 1851.

———. *An Inaugural Discourse Preached in the Parish Church at Leeds.* London, 1837.

———. *On the Means of Rendering More Efficient the Education of the People.* London, 1846.

Hope, Beresford. *Essays.* London, 1844.

Horsfield, Thomas. *The History, Antiquities, and Topography of the County of Sussex.* Lewes, 1835.

Howley, William, archbishop of Canterbury. *A Charge Delivered at His Visitation.* London, 1844.

Hussey, Rev. Thomas J. *The Christian Obligation to the Poor of a Sacramental Character.* London, 1844.

James, Rev. Herbert, and Hoare, Rev. Edward. *Two Sermons Following the Funeral of John Pemberton Plumptre.* London, 1864.

James, Sir Walter, Bart. *Thoughts upon the Theory and Practice of the Poor Laws.* London, 1847.

Jerram, James, ed. *The Memoirs and a Selection from the Letters of the Late Rev. Charles Jerram, M.A.* London, 1855.

Lake, Katherine, *Memorials of William Charles Lake.* London, 1901.

Laughton, J. K., ed. *Memoirs of the Life and Correspondence of Henry Reeve.* London, 1898.

Lectures on Paley for University Students. London, 1830.

Lonsdale, Henry. *The Worthies of Cumberland.* London, 1867–1875.

Mackinnon, William. *History of Civilisation.* 2 vols. London, 1846.

Mac Neile, Rev. Hugh. *The Famine: A Rod of God.* Liverpool, 1847.

Mahon, Lord. *Historical Essays.* London, 1849.

———. *History of England from 1713 to 1783.* 7 vols. London, 1854.

Manners, Lord John. *A Plea for National Holy Days.* London, 1843.

Marindin, George E. *Letters of Frederick Lord Blachford.* London, 1896.

Martin, Theodore. *Memoir of William Edmondstoune Aytoun.* London, 1867.

Martineau, Rev. Arthur. *What Is My Duty?* London, 1847.

Maurice, Frederick Denison. *The Kingdom of Christ.* London, 1843.

Melvill, Rev. Henry. *Sermons on Public Occasions.* London, 1846.

A Member of Cambridge University. *An Epitome of Paley's Principles of Moral and Political Philosophy.* London, 1824.

Mordant, John. *The Complete Steward.* London, 1761.

More, St. Thomas. *Utopia.* 1516. In *The Yale Edition of the Works of Saint Thomas More.* New Haven, 1964.

Morgan, John Minter. *Religion and Crime.* London, 1840.

Mozley, James. *The Letters of James Mozley.* London, 1885.

Mozley, Thomas. *Reminiscences Chiefly of Oriel College and the Oxford Movement.* London, 1882. Boston, 1882.

Murray, John F. *The World of London.* London, 1845.

Norris, J. P. *The Education of the People.* Edinburgh, 1869.

O'Brien, Augustus Stafford. *The History of a Charade on the Immortal Name of Wordsworth.* London, 1839.

Osborne, Lord Sidney Godolphin. *Hints to the Charitable.* London, 1838.

———. *The Savings Bank.* London, 1835.

———. *A View of the Low Moral and Physical Condition of the Agricultural Labourer.* London, 1844.

Paget, Francis. *Sermons on Duties of Daily Life.* London, 1844.

Pakington, John S. *A Charge on the Subject of the County Expenditure.* Worcester, 1843.

Paley, William. *The Principles of Moral and Political Philosophy.* London, 1801.

Palmer, Roundell. *Memorials, Part I: Family and Personal.* London, 1896–1898.

Perry, G. W. *The Peasantry of England.* London, 1846.

Powell, W. M. *The Sanitary Condition of the City of Chichester.* Chichester, 1848.

Pugin, Augustus Welby. *Contrasts; or, a Parallel between the Architecture of the Fifteenth and Nineteenth Centuries.* London, 1836.

Redding, Cyrus. *Fifty Years' Recollections.* London, 1858.

Report of the Proceedings for the Establishment of the Yorkshire Protective Society. London, 1844.

Richmond, Rev. Legh. *Annals of the Poor.* London, 1851.

Russell, John, Earl. *Recollections and Suggestions.* London, 1875.

Russell, Rollo. *Early Correspondence of Lord John Russell, 1805–1840.* London, 1913.

Ryall, H. T. *Portraits of Conservatives.* London, 1836.

Ryder, Dudley, first earl of Harrowby. *Ryder Family Papers. Family Reminiscences.* London, 1891.

Sadler, Michael. *Ireland: Its Evils, and Their Remedies.* London, 1829.

Sanford, John. *Parochialia.* London, 1845.

Saunders, John. *Portraits of Eminent Living Reformers.* London, 1840.

Scoresby, William. *American Factories and Their Female Operatives.* London, 1815.

Scrope, George Poulett. *Memoir of the Life of Lord Sydenham.* London, 1843.

———. *Plea for the Abolition of Slavery in England.* London, 1829.

———. *The Principles of Political Economy.* London, 1833.

———. *Suggested Legislation with a View to the Improvement of the Dwellings of the Poor.* London, 1849.

Seeley, R. B. *Memoir of the Life and Writings of M. T. Sadler.* London, 1842.

———. *The Perils of the Nation.* London, 1843.

———. *Remedies Suggested for Some of the Evils which Constitute the Perils of the Nation.* London, 1844.

Senior, Nassau. *Letters on the Factory Act.* London, 1837.

Sewell, William. *Christian Politics.* London, 1844.

———. *Christian Communism.* Oxford, 1848.

Slaney, Robert A. *Essay on the Beneficial Directions of Rural Expenditure.* London, 1824.

———. *An Essay on the Employment of the Poor.* London, 1819.

———. *A Plea to Power and Parliament for the Working Classes.* London, 1847.

———. *State of the Poorer Classes in Great Towns.* London, 1840.

Smith, William. *A Discourse on the Ethics of the School of Paley.* London, 1839.

Smythe, George Sydney. *Historic Fancies.* London, 1844.

Society for the Propagation of the Gospel in Foreign Parts. *Annual Report.* London, 1847.

Southey, Charles C. *The Life and Correspondence of Robert Southey.* 6 vols. London, 1849.

Southey, Robert. *Essays Moral and Political.* 2 vols. 1831.

———. *Sir Thomas More, or Colloquies on the Progress and Prospect of Society.* 2 vols. London, 1829. London, 1831.

Starkey, Thomas. "A Dialogue between Cardinal Pole and Thomas Lupset." In *England in the Reign of King Henry VII,* edited by J. M. Cowper. London, 1878.

Stephens, W. R. W. *A Memoir of Richard Durnford.* London, 1899.

———. *A Memoir of the Right Hon. William Page Wood, Baron Hatherley.* 2 vols. London, 1883.

Sumner, Rev. G. H. *Sermon after the Funeral of Francis Baron Northbrook.* London, 1866.

Sumner, John Bird, bishop of Chester. *A Charge.* London, 1844.

———. *Christian Charity: Its Obligations and Objects with Reference to the Present State.* London, 1841.

Talbot, Charles, Viscount Ingestre, ed. *Meliora or Better Times to Come.* London, 1852.

Taylor, W. C. *Notes of a Tour in the Manufacturing Districts of Lancashire.* London, 1842.

Tremenheere, H. S. *Notes on Public Subjects.* London, 1852.

Ure, Andrew. *Philosophy of Manufactures.* London, 1835.

———. *A Letter to the Farmers of Buckinghamshire.* London, 1844.

Verney, Sir Harry, Bart. *A Letter from Sir Harry Vernet to One of His Constituents on Mrs. Hume's Motions for a Further Parliamentary Reform.* London, 1848.

———. *A Letter to the Farmers of Buckinghamshire.* London, 1844.

Vyvyan, Sir Richard. *A Letter to the Magistrates of Berkshire.* London, 1845.

Wade, John. *The Extraordinary Black Book.* London, 1832.

Warren, Samuel. *The Intellectual and Moral Development of the Present Age.* London, 1853.

Watson, Rev. Alexander, ed. *Sermons for Sundays, Festivals and Fasts.* London, 1846.

Wilberforce, Rev. Isaac. *A Charge.* London, 1843.

Willoughby, Henry. *The Apology of an English Landowner.* London, 1827.

Wyse, Thomas. *Education Reform.* London, 1836.

Young England, Address Delivered by Lord John Manners. London, 1844.

Secondary Sources

Allen, Anna O. *John Allen and His Friends.* London, 1922.

Altick, Richard. *The English Common Reader.* Chicago, 1957.

Andrews, Alexander. *The History of British Journalism.* London, 1859.

Anstruther, Ian. *The Scandal of the Andover Workhouse.* London, 1973.

Arnold, R. *Our Bishops.* London, 1875.

Ashwell, A. R. *Life of the Right Reverend Samuel Wilberforce.* London, 1880.

Aspinall, Arthur. *Politics and the Press.* London, 1949.

Aydelotte, William O. "Voting Patterns in the British House of Commons in the 1840's." *Comparative Studies in Society and History* 5(1963): 134–163.

Bankes, Viola. *A Dorset Heritage.* London, 1953.

Balgarnie, Rev. Robert. *Sir Titus Salt.* London, 1878.

Battiscombe, Georgina. *John Keble.* New York, 1964.

Bendix, Reinhard. *Work and Authority in Industry: Ideologies of Management in the Course of Industrialization.* New York, 1963.

Bennett, Frederick. *The Story of W. J. Bennett.* London, 1909.

Best, G. F. A. "National Education in England, 1800–1870." *Cambridge Historical Journal* 12 (1956):155–173.

———. *Shaftesbury.* London, 1964.

———. *Temporal Pillars, Queen Anne's Bounty, the Ecclesiastical Commissioners, and the Church of England.* London, 1964.

Blake, Robert. *Disraeli.* New York, 1968.

Bligh, E. V. *Lord Ebury as a Church Reformer.* London, 1891.

Bourne, H. R. Fox. *English Newspapers.* 2 vols. London, 1887.

Boysen, Rhodes. *The Ashworth Cotton Enterprise.* Oxford, 1970.

Bradfield, Brian T. "Sir Richard Vyvyan and Tory Politics." Ph.D. dissertation, London University.

Brightfield, Myron F. *John Croker.* Berkeley, Cal., 1940.

Brundage, Anthony. "The Landed Interest and the New Poor Law." *English Historical Review* 87(1972):27–48.

———. *The Making of the New Poor Law.* New Brunswick, N.J., 1978.

Carnall, Geoffrey. *Robert Southey and His Works.* Oxford, 1960.

Chadwick, Owen. *Victorian Miniature.* London, 1960.

Childe-Pemberton, William S. *Life of Lord Norton.* London, 1909.

Colmer, John. *Coleridge, Critic of Society.* Oxford, 1959.

Dasent, Arthur I. *John Thadeus Delane, Editor of the Times.* London, 1908.

Dod, Charles. *The Parliamentary Pocket Companion.* London, 1833–   .

Douglas, Sir George, and Ramsay, Sir George Dalhousie, eds. *The Panmure Papers.* London, 1908.

Driver, Cecil. *Tory Radical, The Life of Richard Oastler.* New York, 1946.

Dunham, William, and Pargellis, Stanley. *Complaint and Reform in England. 1436–1714.* New York, 1938.

Dunkley, Peter. *English Historical Review* 88(1973):836–841.

Elliot, W. H. *The Story of the "Cheeryble" Grants.* London, 1906.

Elton, G. R. *England Under the Tudors.* London, 1960.

Erickson, Arvel, *Edward Cardwell.* Philadelphia, 1959.

Falk, Bernard. *The Bridgewater Millions.* London, 1942.

Ferguson, Arthur. *The Articulate Citizen and the English Renaissance.* Durham. N.C., 1965.

Fitzmaurice, Lord Edmond. *The Life of Granville George Leveson-Gower, Second Earl Granville, 1815–1891.* London, 1905.

Foster, Joseph. *Alumni Oxonienses: The Members of the University of Oxford, 1715–1886.* 4 vols. Oxford, 1887.

Fox, Alice W. *The Earl of Halsbury, Lord High Chancellor.* London, 1929.

Galleo, David. *Coleridge and the Idea of the Modern State.* New Haven, 1966.

Gash, Norman. *Mr. Secretary Peel.* London, 1961.

Gatty, Alfred. *Wortley and the Wortleys.* Sheffield, 1877.

Gill, J. C. *Parson Bull of Byerley.* London, 1963.

Gloyn, C. K. *The Church and the Social Order.* Forest Grove, Oreg., 1942.

Gordon, Sir Arthur. *The Earl of Aberdeen.* London, 1893.

Grant, James. *The Newspaper Press.* London, 1871.

————. *The Saturday Review.* London, 1873.

Grier, R. M. *John Allen.* London, 1889.

Halévy, Elie. *England in 1815.* London, 1960.

————. *History of the English People.* London, 1961.

Hart, Jenifer. "Nineteenth Century Social Reform." *Past and Present.* July 1965, pp. 39–61.

Hexter, J. H. "Utopia and Its Historical Milieu." In *The Yale Edition of the Works of Saint Thomas More.* Vol. 4. New Haven, 1965.

Hindle, Wilfred. *The Morning Post, 1772–1937.* London, 1937.

Hodder, Edwin. *The Life and Work of the Seventh Earl of Shaftesbury.* London, 1886.

Holland, Bernard. *Memoir of Kenelm Henry Digby.* London, 1919.

Houghton, Walter and Esther. *Wellesley Index to Victorian Periodicals.* Toronto, 1972.

Inglis, K. S. *Churches and the Working Classes in Victorian England.* London, 1963.

Kennedy, H. A. *Professor Blackie.* London, 1895.

Kenny, Terence. *The Political Thought of John Henry Newman.* London, 1957.

Kent, C. B. R. *The English Radicals.* London, 1899.

Kitson Clark, George. *Churchmen and the Condition of England, 1832–1885.* London, 1973.

Kramnick, Isaac, *Bolingbroke and His Circle.* Cambridge, Mass. 1968.

Lang, Andrew. *The Life and Letters of John Gibson Lockhart.* London, 1897.
Lambert, Richard. *The Railway King, 1800–1871: A Study of George Hudson.* London, 1894.
Laski, H. J., Jennings, I., and Robson, W. A., eds. *A Century of Municipal Progress.* London, 1935.
Leconfield, Maud, Lady. *Three Howard Sisters.* London, 1955.
Leslie, Shane. *Henry Edward Manning.* London, 1929.
Leveson-Gower, F. *Letters of Harriet Countess Granville.* London, 1894.
Liddon, H. P. *Walter Kerr Hamilton, Bishop of Salisbury.* London, 1890.
Lochhead, Marion. *John Gibson Lockhart.* London, 1954.
Lucas, Reginald. *Lord Glenesk and the Morning Post.* London, 1910.
Lyell, Katherine. *Memoir of Leonard Horner.* London, 1890.
MacCarthy, Desmond, and Russell, Agatha. *Lady John Russell.* London, 1910.
Mac Clatchey, Diane. *Oxfordshire Clergy, 1777–1869.* Oxford, 1960.
MacDonagh, Oliver. *A Pattern of Government Growth.* London, 1961.
Magnus, Philip. *Gladstone.* New York, 1964.
Marshall, Dorothy. *The English Poor in the Eighteenth Century.* London, 1926.
Martineau, John. *The Life of Henry Pelham, Fifth Duke of Newcastle.* London, 1908.
Masson, Rosaline. *Pollock and Aytoun.* London, 1898.
Masterman, C. F. G. *The Life of Frederick Denison Maurice.* London, 1907.
Masterman, N. C. *John Malcolm Ludlow.* Cambridge, 1963.
Maurice, F. D. *Life of Frederick Denison Maurice.* London, 1885.
Melada, Ivan. *The Captain of Industry in English Fiction, 1821–1871.* Albuquerque, 1970.
Merriam, G. S. *The Story of William and Lucy Smith.* London, 1889.
Mitford, Nancy. *The Ladies of Alderley.* London, 1938.
Morley, John. *Life of Gladstone.* London, 1903.
Newman, Aubrey. *The Stanhopes of Chevening.* London, 1969.
Non-Elector. *Lord John Manners.* London, 1872.
Newsome, David. *The Parting of Friends: A Study of the Wilberforces and Henry Manning.* Cambridge, Mass. 1966.
Ogilvy, Mabel. *Lady Palmerston and Her Times.* London, 1922.
Oliphant, Margaret. *William Blackwood and His Sons.* 4 vols. London, 1897.
P. G. E. *Grillion's Club.* London, 1850.
Parkin, Charles. *The Moral Basis of Burke's Political Thought.* Cambridge, 1956.
Perkin, Harold. *The Origins of Modern English Society.* London, 1969.
Pinchbeck, Ivy, and Hewitt, Margaret. *Children in English Society.* 2 vols. London, 1926.

Pollard, Sidney. "The Factory Village of the Industrial Revolution." *The English Historical Review* 79(July 1964):513–531.

Pope-Hennessy, James. *Monckton Milnes, The Years of Promise.* London, 1947.

Port, M. H. *Six Hundred New Churches.* London, 1961.

Poynter, J. R. *Society and Pauperism; English Ideas on Poor Relief, 1795–1834.* London, 1969.

Prebble, John. *The Highland Clearances.* London, 1963.

Prest, John. *Lord John Russell.* London, 1972.

Prestige, Leonard. *Pusey.* London, 1933.

Proby, Rev. W. H. B. *Annals of the Low-Church Party in England down to the Death of Arch Bishop Tait.* 2 vols. London, 1888.

Reid, T. Wemys. *Life, Letters and Friendships of Richard Monckton Milnes.* London, 1890.

Ridley, Jasper. *Lord Palmerston.* London, 1970.

Rimmer, W. G. *Marshall of Leeds, Flax Spinners, 1788–1886.* Cambridge, 1960.

Roberts, David. *Victorian Origins of the British Welfare State.* (New Haven, 1960.

———. "Who Ran the Globe?" *Victorian Periodical Newsletter.* June 1971, pp. 6–11.

Saunders, L. G. *Scottish Democracy.* London, 1950.

Soloway, Richard. *Prelates and People, Ecclesiastical Social Thought in England.* London, 1969.

Smelser, Neil. *Social Change in the Industrial Revolution.* Chicago, 1959.

Smith, David Frederick. "Sir George Grey at the Mid Victorian Home Office." Ph.D. Dissertation, Toronto University, 1972).

Smith, Frank. *The Life and Work of Sir James Kay-Shuttleworth.* London, 1923.

Smith, J. Campbell. *Writings by the Way.* London, 1885.

Smith, Robert V. *Early Writings of Robert Percy Smith.* London, 1850.

Spring, David. "Agents of the Earls of Durham in the Nineteenth Century." *Durham University Journal.* June 1962, pp. 104–112.

———. *The English Landed Estate in the Nineteenth Century.* Baltimore, 1963.

Stanley, A. P. *Life of Thomas Arnold.* London, 1901.

Stanmore, Lord. *Sidney Herbert.* New York, 1906.

Stephens, W. R. W. *The Life and Letters of Walter Farquhar Hook.* 2 vols. London, 1879.

Steward, Robert M. *The Politics of Protection.* Cambridge, 1971.

Stoddart, Anna M. *John Stuart Blackie.* London, 1895.

Stranks, C. J. *Dean Hook.* London, 1954.

Strutt, Charles R. *The Strutt Family of Terling, 1650–1873.* London, 1939.

Thompson, E. P. "Patrician Society, Plebian Culture." *Journal of Social History* 7(Summer, 1974):382–403.

Thompson, F. M. L. *English Landed Society in the Nineteenth Century.* London, 1963.

Thrall, Miriam M. H. *Rebellious Frasers's.* New York, 1934.

Tierney, Brian. *Medieval Poor Law.* Berkeley, Cal., 1959.

The Times. *The History of the Times.* London, 1939.

Todd, F. M. *Politics of the Poet, A Study of Wordsworth.* London, 1957.

Tollemache, Major General E. D. H. *The Tollemaches of Helmingham and Ham.* Ipswich, 1949.

Trevelyan, George. *Lord Grey of the Reform Bill.* London, 1929.

Trevor Roper, Hugh. *Archbishop Laud.* London, 1962.

Turberville, T. C. *Worcestershire in the Nineteenth Century.* London, 1852.

Unwin, George. *Samuel Oldknow and the Arkwrights and the Industrial Revolution at Stockport and Marple.* London, 1924.

Vargish, T. Thomas. *Newman, The Contemplation of Mind.* Oxford, 1970.

Venn, John, and Venn, John Archibald. *Alumni Cantabrigiensis, A Biographical List.* Cambridge, 1922.

Walpole, Spencer. *The Life of Lord John Russell.* London, 1889.

Ward, J. T. "The Earls Fitzwilliam and the Wentworth Wodehouse Estate in the 19th Century." *Yorkshire Bulletin of Economic and Social Research* 11(March, 1960).

———. *The Factory Movement, 1830–1855.* London, 1962.

Watts, Alaric Alfred. *Alaric Watts, A Narrative of His Life.* 2 vols. London, 1884.

Webb, Sidney and Beatrice. *English Local Government: English Poor Law History.* London, 1927–1929.

———. *English Local Government from the Revolution to the Municipal Corporation Act: The Parish and County.* London, 1909.

Welch, P. J. "Bishop Blomfield" Ph.D. dissertation, *London University,* 1952.

Whibley, Charles. *Lord John Manners and His Friends.* 2 vols. London, 1925.

Williams, Raymond. *The Country and the City.* New York, 1973.

Willson, David. *King James VI and I.* New York, 1956.

Index